SELECTED WORKS

Patrick and Beatrice Haggerty
Museum of Art

Marquette University

Commemorating the opening of the Patrick and Beatrice Haggerty Museum of Art,
Marquette University, Milwaukee, Wisconsin, U.S.A., November 11, 1984

Catalogue Published in Association with
PELION PRESS NEW YORK

Library of Congress Catalog Card Number:
84-61315
ISBN: 0-8239-0661-2

PELION
PRESS

Published by Pelion Press, 29 East 21st Street, New
York, New York, 10010, in association with the
Patrick and Beatrice Haggerty Museum of Art,
Marquette University, Milwaukee, Wisconsin,
U.S.A.

Cover Illustrations

Front

St. Francis in Penitence   (59.5)
Francesco Trevisani
Italian (1656–1746)
Oil on canvas, 52 7/8 x 38 7/16 in.
  (134.4 x 97.7 cm)
Gift of Mr. and Mrs. Marc B. Rojtman

Back

Madonna and Child   (63.15)
Goan (early 19th century)
Ivory, 20 1/2 x 4 1/2 x 4 in. (52.1 x 11.4 x 10.2 cm)
Gift of Mr. Norbert Beihoff

Photography by Andrei Lovinescu and University
Staff photographers

Publication of this catalogue was made possible by
the generous support of Mr. Norbert J. Beihoff.

Research and printing of this publication have been
aided by grants from the National Endowment for
the Arts.

Table of Contents

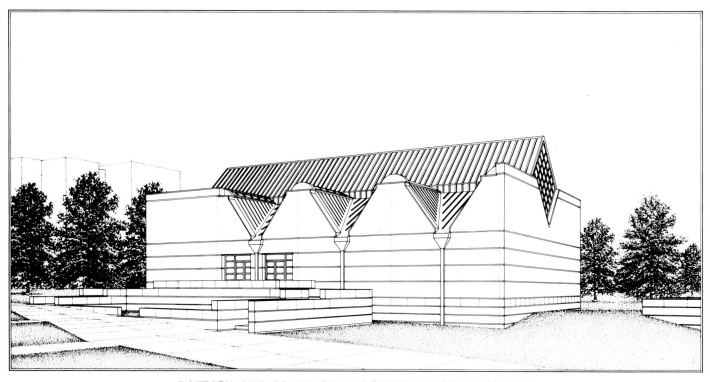

PATRICK AND BEATRICE HAGGERTY MUSEUM OF ART
MARQUETTE UNIVERSITY
Principal Architect   O'Neil Ford, Ford, Powell, Carson, San Antonio, Texas
Associate/Design Architect   David Kahler, Kahler, Slater, Torphy, Engberg, Milwaukee, Wisconsin

This catalogue includes essays on and photographs of the more important works acquired by the Marquette University Committee on the Fine Arts through May, 1984. Additional essays are provided for the Norbert J. Beihoff collection of ivories, the A. J. Conroy collection of miniature paintings, and the Barbara Morgan collection of photographs. A checklist of paintings, works on paper, photographs, sculptures, decorative arts, and non-Western works from the approximately 5,500 items presently in the Collection, with photographs, completes the catalogue.

This catalogue has been in preparation for four years and was initiated in response to a generous gift from Mr. Norbert J. Beihoff. We are deeply appreciative of his support. Matching grants from the National Endowment for the Arts for research and a portion of the printing costs have made possible the completion of the project; we are indebted to the Endowment's Museum Program for its confidence and support.

From the early stages of preparation, Mary L. Ladish, now the museum's Assistant Director, organized the information, with considerable assistance from other staff members and volunteers at Marquette University, and from several prominent scholars, curators, and collectors elsewhere. Robert B. Simon, as Director of the Fine Arts Group of Crosson Dannis, Inc., coordinated preparation of catalogue entries written by himself, John Bandiera, R. Ward Bissell, Curtis L. Carter, Amy Golahny, and J. Douglas Stewart and provided an introductory essay on the collection. Suggestions from the Rev. William E. Dooley, S.J., on format and content have benefited the catalogue throughout. Andrei Lovinescu advised on photography and was the principal photographer.

The following persons provided advice on the catalogue entries and preparation: Nancy Anderson, National Museum of American Art, Washington, D.C.; Dr. Alfred R. Bader, Milwaukee; R. J. Berman, New York; Indira Berndtson, The Frank Lloyd Wright Memorial Foundation, Taliesin West, Scottsdale, Arizona; Robin Bolton-Smith, National Museum of American Art, Washington, D.C.; Suzanne Boorsch, The Metropolitan Museum of Art, New York; Arnauld Brejon de Lavergnée, The Louvre, Paris; Marcus Burke, State University of New York at Purchase; Keith Christiansen, The Metropolitan Museum of Art, New York; the late Anthony M. Clark; Guy Colston, Hood Museum of Art, Dartmouth College, Hanover, New Hampshire; Patrick Coman, The Metropolitan Museum of Art, New York; Joseph Connors, Department of Art History and Archaeology, Columbia University, New York; Malcolm Cormack, Yale Center for British Art, New Haven, Connecticut; Frank DiFederico, University of Maryland, College Park, Maryland; James Draper, The Metropolitan Museum of Art, New York; David Dudley, Upper Midwest Conservation Association, Minneapolis Institute of Arts, Minneapolis; Jacques Foucart, The Louvre, Paris; Barbara Gaehtgens, Göttinten University, West Berlin; Jane Goldsmith, Department of Art History, University of California, Santa Cruz, California; the Rev. Fr. Gregory Gula, Monastery of the Annunciation, Tuxedo Park, New York; Sophie Hanappier, Paris; Julius S. Held, Old Bennington, Vermont; Ulrich Hiesinger, Philadelphia; Rupert Hodge, Witt Library, Courtauld Institute of Art, London; John T. Haletsky, The Lowe Art Museum, The University of Miami, Coral Gables, Florida; Trudy V. Hansen, The Catalog of American Portraits, The National Portrait Gallery, Washington, D.C.; Stanley K. Jernow, Montclair, New Jersey; Frances Kelly, The Minneapolis Institute of Arts, Minneapolis; Ian Kennedy, Christie's, New York; George Keyes, The Minneapolis Institute of Arts, Minneapolis; David Kiel, The Metropolitan Museum of Art, New York; Arthur Liebman, Lake Forest, Illinois; The Metropolitan Museum of Art Print Room staff, New York; J. Patrice Marandel, The Detroit Institute of Arts, Detroit; Raymond Mastroberte, New York; Jennifer Montagu, Warburg Institute, London; Otto Naumann, New York; Patrick Noon, Yale Center for British Art, Yale University, New Haven, Connecticut; Gerald Nordland, Milwaukee Art Museum, Milwaukee; Richard Ormond, National Maritime Museum, London; Janet Parks, Avery Architectural and Fine Arts Library, Columbia University, New York; William Wesley Peters, The Frank Lloyd Wright Memorial Foundation, Taliesin West, Scottsdale, Arizona; Bruce Brooks Pfeiffer, The Frank Lloyd Wright Memorial Foundation, Taliesin West, Scottsdale, Arizona; Elizabeth Prelinger, Museum of Art, Carnegie Institute, Pittsburgh; John Reily, Boston University, Boston; Sophie Riordan, Tuxedo Park, New York; Malcolm Rogers, National Portrait Gallery, London; Roberta K. Tarbell, University of Delaware, Newark, Delaware; Ransom Taylor, Milwaukee; George H. Ulrich, Milwaukee Public Museum, Milwaukee; the late Hermann Voss, Munich; John Wilmerding, National Gallery of Art, Washington, D.C.; Mary Woods, Department of Art History, The Pennsylvania State University, University Park, Pennsylvania; Ian Wordropper, The Art Institute of Chicago, Chicago; Eriz Zafran, Walters Art Gallery, Baltimore; Federico Zeri, Rome, Italy.

Roger Rosen, as President of Pelion Press, brought the publication to completion with unusual care and concern. To all who helped create this catalogue we are deeply grateful.

Curtis L. Carter, Director
Patrick and Beatrice Haggerty
  Museum of Art
Marquette University
Milwaukee, Wisconsin

CURTIS L. CARTER

Building a University Art Collection

University museums in the United States have evolved in various forms as a departmental adjunct intended to exhibit faculty and student art, as a facility for temporary exhibitions, as the locus of a permanent collection, or as a combination of these. At Marquette University the need for an art museum follows naturally the gradual development of the art collection and exhibition program over the past thirty years. Unlike most university museums, this one has emerged without benefit of a well-established art or art history program.

Construction for the Patrick and Beatrice Haggerty Museum of Art was officially launched at groundbreaking ceremonies in April, 1983, against the background of a 100 x 8-foot mural with bold fluorescent orange and black figures and forms designed by Keith Haring, a prominent young graffiti artist from New York, as a part of the construction fence. This installation at the building site had already been preceded, in the fall of 1982, by another, "Ground Covering," a conceptual art piece prepared by Minnesota artist James Kern and the Marquette Students for the Fine Arts for installation on the ground space where the building was later placed. The museum was completed in August, 1984, at a cost of $2.5 million, through the joint efforts of the Marquette University Women's Council funding campaign, after the University Committee on the Fine Arts had demonstrated a need for the facility through a study conducted in 1977. Designed by the late O'Neil Ford of Ford, Powell and Carson, San Antonio, Texas, and associate architect David Kahler of Kahler, Slater, Torphy, Engberg of Milwaukee, the 20,000-square-foot building contains three gallery areas and three storage areas in addition to administrative and technical areas. The museum is equipped with air conditioning and climate controls, fire and smoke detection systems, and an electronic security system. Although the building is relatively modest in size, its unusual architectural forms have already established a commanding presence and a harmonious architectural link with the nearby campus theater and other important buildings on the Marquette campus.

The vertical thrust and angular planes of the interior gallery space, combined with natural skylighting, create a special architectural space, complementing in a strong, rather than a weak or neutral manner, the aesthetic presence of the works of art on display. Purists who believe that a museum space should represent a neutral presence given over entirely to the art on display may not agree with the aesthetic balance represented here. The building nevertheless fulfills the charge given to its designers, that is, to create a work of architecture that meets the functional requirements of a museum while also complementing in its own artistic features the experiences offered by the other works of art on display.

The Fine Art Collection and related programming presently centered in the museum have evolved under the leadership of the University Committee on the Fine Arts established by the Rev. Edward J. O'Donnell, S.J., as a special University President's committee in 1955. The Committee, functioning from 1955 to 1975 under the leadership of John Pick, Professor of English, and from 1975 to 1984 under Curtis L. Carter, Associate Professor of Aesthetics and Philosophy, advanced the Collection to its present state and established an educational program incorporating special exhibitions, visiting scholars, and visiting artists in various media. In addition to the pictorial arts, these programs included dance, music, poetry, performance art, film, and video. Among the highlights of programs in recent years were the exhibitions: "Art and Industry," exploring the aesthetic features that large and small industrial objects share with objects of fine art; "Changes: Art in America 1881/1981," examining the influences of the camera on figurative painting a century apart; and a retrospective of Barbara Morgan photographs, showing dance, photomontage, people, nature, junk, and miscellaneous photo-experiments.

The collections transferred into the Patrick and Beatrice Haggerty Museum of Art in November 1984 contain a substantial body of works not typical of other museums in the region. Highlights include selected master works in several media that would be welcome in any fine collection. A few come to mind immediately: Trevisani's St. Francis in Penitence, ill. front cover and on p. 38; Dalí's widely traveled Madonna of Port Lligat, 1949 version; a collection of sixteenth- and seventeenth-century Old Master prints, including a fourteen-piece set consisting of Christ, St. Paul, and the Twelve Apostles, ref. p. 184; important contemporary prints, including Chagall's Bible series, ill. p. 128, and Rouault's Miserere series, ref., ill. p. 120; Wilhelm Lehmbruck's Geneigter Frauenkopf in bronze; Sèvres porcelain pieces in the Rothschild pattern formerly in the collection of the Duke of Kent; and an important collection of Barbara Morgan photographs.

Until 1984, when an acquisition fund was initiated through gifts in memory of Mrs. Ethel Heller Hyman, the University had relied for acquisitions solely on gifts of art from patrons in the Midwest and throughout the world. From a growing list of over 336 contributors (see p. 237), it is evident that the Marquette University Fine Art Collection represents the generosity of many. A limited number of persons merit special mention here for their continuous or especially noteworthy interest in the Collection's development. Among these the contributions of Mr. (the late) and Mrs. Marc B. Rojtman and the Rojtman Foundation clearly form the nucleus of the European Old Master paintings, which include the Trevisani St. Francis in Penitence (cited earlier); the recently donated Saint Julian of Toledo by the fifteenth-century Girard Master, ill. p. 2; the Lamentation altarpiece by Correa de Vivar, ill. p. 16; and over twenty other paintings

comprising a substantial museum study collection.

Other donors whose contributions over the years have enriched the Collection include the following: Mr. Joseph P. Antonow (sculpture, including the work by Wilhelm Lehmbruck, ill. p. 138, works on paper, and decorative arts); Dr. and Mrs. Alfred Bader (Old Master paintings); an anonymous donor (the A. J. Conroy Collection of Miniature Paintings); Mr. and Mrs. Eckhart G. Grohmann (Old Master paintings); Mr. (the late) and Mrs. Ira Haupt (twentieth-century paintings by Dalí and Villon); Dr. Kenneth Maier (porcelain, other miscellaneous decorative arts, and works on paper); Mr. and Mrs. John Ogden (Barbara Morgan portfolio, decorative arts); the Pinsof family (Asian, African, and works on paper); Mr. Leonard J. Scheller (Rouault Miserere series); Mr. and Mrs. Ray Smith, Jr. (contemporary works on paper, sculpture, and painting); Mr. (the late) and Mrs. Charles Zadok (twentieth-century paintings and decorative arts).

Among recent donors the following have contributed especially important works: Dr. and Mrs. Sidney M. Boxer (Old Master etchings and prints); Brandt, Inc. in memory of Earl William and Eugenia Brandt Quirk (paintings by Bierstadt, ill. p. 58, and Pyne, ref. p. 164; Mr. and Mrs. Marvin L. Fishman (German Expressionist paintings and works on paper ranging from etchings of Piranesi to the Kriegszeit. Künstlerflugblätter series); Mr. (the late) and Mrs. Patrick Haggerty (Chagall Bible series); Lloyd and Douglas Morgan (Barbara Morgan photographs); and an anonymous donor of the Barbara Morgan vintage photographs.

The relative scarcity of the finest works from earlier centuries now available for purchase, and the limited funds that the museum can devote to such purchases, suggest that acquisitions in the immediate future will continue to depend primarily upon the generosity of private collectors and benefactors, with occasional and welcome opportunities for selective acquisitions through purchase or exchange.

Acquiring an art collection in this manner involves a certain randomness of opportunity and choices which, in this instance, has resulted in a collection encompassing a broad range of creative endeavor. Although many of the art works in the collection embody religious themes, the collection includes subject matters from all aspects of human culture and nature. The areas of collecting have included paintings, works on paper, sculpture, and decorative and tribal arts representing the Americas, Africa, Asia, and Europe. The major concentration has been in the areas of European and American paintings and works on paper from the sixteenth into the twentieth century.

Two growing areas of the collection not yet sufficiently developed and researched for a fuller discussion in the present catalogue deserve mention here: a selection of works by Wisconsin artists and a selection of African tribal arts.

The nucleus of the Wisconsin group is a gift of several thousand postcard drawings, a number of paintings, and personal correspondence of the late artist Karl Priebe (1914–1976) given by Mr. Emil Priebe. Other important elements of the Wisconsin group include works by Robert Burkert, John Colt, Edmund Lewandowski, James Watrous, John Wilde, and others. These works have been given by various donors such as Gimbel Brothers; Mr. Frederick D. Gore; Mrs. Dorothy Halmbacher (whose recent gift of thirteen paintings was received subsequent to the preparation of this catalogue); Mr. (the late) and Mrs. Raymond F. Newman, Dr. Richard A. Berk, and others.

The African group is primarily the result of gifts by the Pinsof family and Mr. Avery Z. Eliscu; essentially it consists of human and animal figure sculptures and ceremonial masks. Most appear to be from the nineteenth or early twentieth century, with a few representing an earlier period. The works are from Cameroon, Mali, Nigeria, and the Ivory Coast. Additional research is required before any more definitive statement can be prepared on this part of the Collection.

The broadly ranging nature of the Marquette University Fine Art Collection corresponds to the educational goals of the museum, which include serving a regional population from diverse cultural backgrounds; collaborating with other divisions of the University in educating students along with visitors; and participation with other museums and cultural institutions in common projects. It is fitting that a museum serving a community with diverse cultural backgrounds offers representative art from the various cultures. Similarly, a university program of studies ranging over many cultures and periods of history, philosophy, and literature suggests the need for an art collection capable of providing a broad range of art experiences to augment the studies of students with differing academic interests and needs. A museum with a varied collection likewise has greater capabilities for interacting with other cultural institutions in projects of mutual interest.

Programming in the near future will reflect a strong effort on the part of the museum to explore the relation of visual learning in the arts to other disciplines in the humanities and the sciences. This effort begins with the inaugural symposium, "Word and Image," in which artists and scholars from literature, philosophy, dance, art history, film, and other disciplines join together in a common search. Such projects offer a direction of exploration through which this university museum might find its place as an important source of learning, enjoyment, and inspiration, a place where ideas can be created, discovered, or examined in all media— whether visual or verbal, silent or auditory.

Madonna and Child with Saints and Angels, Jan Provost II, oil on panel

ROBERT B. SIMON

The Marquette University Fine Art Collection

The purpose of a university art collection is an issue often discussed that might best be approached through a series of questions. What can a university museum offer that a large public museum cannot? How comprehensive can or ought its collections be? What is the nature of its audience? What special didactic responsibilities does it have, and to whom? These are questions without firm answers, since a host of special considerations—geographical, educational, financial, temporal—make each situation unique. However, one principle does seem constant in any discussion of the subject: a university museum has a special mission to instruct. Its students are not solely the immediate members of the university community, but also its neighbors, friends, and visitors. Not only does it inform, but it educates—teaching us to teach ourselves.

The basis of an art museum is its permanent collection, and Marquette is fortunate in having one with rich and varied holdings. It is not uniformly a collection of masterpieces, nor can it be said to be historically comprehensive; but it does bring together a notable group of works of art of extraordinary interest and diversity. It is, in short, a superb teaching and learning collection.

The preparation of a catalogue of the Collection has revealed several unusual strengths, particularly in Renaissance and Baroque paintings. The group of Flemish pictures of the sixteenth century is especially important, comprising as it does newly identified works by masters whose works are rarely seen outside their homeland. Ambrosius Francken the Elder's contemplative *Holy Family with Saints John the Baptist and Elizabeth* and Gillis Mostaert's wonderfully bizarre *The Passion of Christ* are noteworthy additions to the relatively small oeuvres of these artists; these are complemented by *The Story of Elijah* attributed to Anthuenis Claeissens and the huge altarpiece of *The Birth of St. John the Baptist* by an anonymous follower of Lambert Lombard.

Italian pictures of the time touch on many of the diverse aspects of Cinquecento painting. Four variations on the Nativity theme illustrate this point dramatically. One work after Sebastiano Mainardi provides us with a direct reflection of a traditional fifteenth-century Florentine altarpiece. A near-contemporary representation, probably by an anonymous North Italian artist, is something of a provincial variation on the same theme. A mid-sixteenth-century Emilian panel reflects the contemporary mannered court styles, while a Veneto-Byzantine work of roughly the same date demonstrates a complete disavowal of all but the most traditional mode of representation.

Two Spanish works of inordinate interest should be noted—the richly decorated figure of *St. Julian of Toledo* by the Girard Master and the *Lamentation* altarpiece by Juan Correa de Vivar, a fascinating and

xi

little-known painter of the sixteenth century.

French seventeenth-century works include the important *Adoration of the Magi* by Claude Vignon; the *Portrait of Françoise Bertaut*, a mysterious work now convincingly attributed to Louis I Elle (called Ferdinand the Elder); a lovely still life by Baudesson; and the curious *Deposition of Christ* from the workshop of Le Brun.

Roman Baroque painting is illustrated by two superb pictures by Francesco Trevisani, the *Mary Magdalen in Penitence* and *St. Francis in Penitence*, and by two quite diverse works by Ghezzi, the charming *Singing Monks* and the austere *Portrait of Cardinal Giuseppe Renato Imperiali*. From Naples come Solimena's *The Christ Child Contemplating His Future Passion* and the *Saint Bruno Refusing the Archbishopric*, attributed to the Circle of Solimena, unusual small-scale works by an artist noted for his grand mural projects, and from North Italy comes a biblical scene by Antonio Carneo.

Seventeenth-century Flemish works include two small panels from the Jan Brueghel-Rubens circle, a *Noli Me Tangere* and a *Mary Magdalene in Penitence*. Schoevardt's festive *Village Festival* and van der Bent's *Wooded Landscape with Figures* are familiar Dutch subjects, in contrast to the more arcane *Discovery of Deuteronomy* attributed to Bramer.

The English school is represented by an odd assortment of portraits by Godfrey Kneller, a follower of Mytens, Joshua Reynolds, and Thomas Lawrence, in addition to two unattributed works, one a most attractive river landscape, from the first half of the nineteenth century. Rudolf Ernst's evocative Arab interior is complemented by other German nineteenth-century pictures—works by Grützner, Schenk, Baumgartner, and others. Landscapes by Diaz de la Peña and Arnold-Marc Gorter and an immense interior by Jozef Israels bring us to this century.

The North American collection is distinguished by a major work by Albert Bierstadt and an enigmatic one by Blakelock, as well as Wilhelm Lamprecht's *Père Marquette and the Indians*, the University's first painting, and Franklin Watkins's *Poison for the King*.

The twentieth-century collection includes two important paintings by Jacques Villon, Salvador Dalí's extraordinary *Madonna of Port Lligat*, and works by Gen-Paul and Berçot. The *Madonna and Child with Angels*, a glazed terra-cotta by a follower of Andrea della Robbia, is the collection's oldest sculpture, whereas Wilhelm Lehmbruck's *Geneigter Frauenkopf* is arguably its most important.

The drawings collection is relatively small but features several unusual items: a religious drawing by Archipenko, two charming watercolors by Boudin, three Lachaise studies, an academic sketch by Lord Leighton, a Vermont watercolor by Paul Sample, and four drawings by Frank Lloyd Wright for the Leesburg (Florida) Floating Gardens.

The more extensive print holdings include Rouault's *Miserere* and Chagall's *Bible* series, as well as individual prints by Dürer. A notable group of Northern Mannerist prints, including works by Goltzius, is a particularly important recent accession.

Special collections provide a more thorough study of particular fields. The Norbert J. Beihoff Collection of Ivories, the A. J. Conroy Collection of Miniature Paintings, and the outstanding group of Barbara Morgan Photographs are briefly discussed below, but space does not here permit a fuller description of these and other collections—particularly those in the decorative arts. It is to be hoped that, with the opening of the museum, and the new life thus brought to these works of art, further work will be undertaken on these challenging and fascinating objects.

Acknowledgments

I would like to express my appreciation to the many individuals whose efforts over the past four years contributed significantly to the publication of this catalogue.

My deepest thanks go to the Reverend William Dooley, S.J., and Barbara Lewczyk for their endless dedication and to Ellen Pedraza, Peggy Clippert, Jennifer Grant, Brian Graf, Carol Mattis, John Braun, Robin Schumacher, Deb Dati, Lisa Rich, Carmen Mittler, Jody Ranbarger, Lucy Rothstein and Caren Rhodes for their many hours of researching and typing.

I also wish to thank Andrei Lovinescu, Dave Foran, Jon Pray, Paul McInerny, Kay Tierney, Dick Eyrise, and Dan Johnson for their contributions to this project.

Mary L. Ladish,
Assistant Director

CATALOGUE ESSAYS

Contributors to the Catalogue:

J.B.	John Bandiera, Emory University, Atlanta
R.W.B.	R. Ward Bissell, University of Michigan, Ann Arbor
C.L.C.	Curtis L. Carter, Marquette University, Milwaukee
A.G.	Amy Golahny, Chatham College, Pittsburgh
R.B.S.	Robert B. Simon, Crosson Dannis Inc., New York
J.D.S.	J. Douglas Stewart, Queens University, Kingston (Ontario)

Notes on the Catalogue Essays

Essays are arranged first by medium, then by century, alphabetically by nationality, and alphabetically by artist.

Dimensions of art works are given in feet and inches and in centimeters. Height precedes width and depth is also given for three-dimensional works. Size is actual for paintings, sculptures, and decorative arts objects, and sheet for works on paper, unless otherwise noted.

The accession number assigned to a work is listed to the right of the title and date.

The three most common references cited are listed in abbreviated form in the essays. They are:

John Pick, *Marquette University Art Collection* (Milwaukee, 1964).

John Pick, *Marquette University Art Collection. Supplement 1964-66* (Milwaukee, 1966).

Curtis L. Carter, *From a Grain of Sand...Marquette University Art Collection Builds*, catalogue of an exhibition at Marquette University (Milwaukee, 1979).

Peasant Family, Jean Baptiste Huet, oil on panel

PAINTINGS

The Nativity of Christ, After Sebastiano Mainardi, oil on canvas

FIFTEENTH CENTURY

SEBASTIANO MAINARDI

Italian (c. 1455–1513)

Sebastiano (or Bastiano) Mainardi was a student and assistant of the great Florentine painter Domenico Ghirlandaio (c. 1448–1494).[1] Very little is known of Mainardi's life, and there are virtually no documented paintings by him. Nonetheless a clear body of work manifestly by one artist has been associated with his name, beginning with the fresco of the *Assumption of the Virgin* (Madonna della Cintola) in the Church of Santa Croce (Florence), which Vasari states was executed by Mainardi from Ghirlandaio's cartoon.[2] Although Vasari's attribution has been questioned (and thus the identification of Mainardi's style),[3] the cohesiveness of the group of works given to the artist[4] makes the association of name and oeuvre convenient if not accurate as well. Mainardi, who came from the towered town of San Gimignano, married the sister (Alessandra Bigordi) of his master Ghirlandaio. He died in 1513.

AFTER SEBASTIANO MAINARDI
The Nativity of Christ   (59.3)

Oil on canvas, transferred from panel, 35 5/8 x 25 3/4 in. (90.5 x 65.5 cm). Unsigned.

Provenance: Collection of Mr. and Mrs. Marc B. Rojtman, Milwaukee; their gift to the University, 1959.

References:
Pick, *Marquette University Art Collection*, 24, as by Jacopo del Sellajo.

Everett Fahy, in a letter (1983), as either an "extensively overpainted original by Mainardi" or "a copy of the Harrach picture."

The Nativity of Christ is closely based on a painting by Mainardi in the Harrach Family Collection at Schloss Rohrau (Austria).[5] That work is one of several variations of a single compositional idea depicting the Virgin kneeling outside a manger in adoration of the Christ Child, who lies before Joseph. The other pictures—of varying shape, medium, and peripheral composition—include a tabernacle fresco at Brozzi (outside of Florence) and panel pictures in Brooklyn,

Cambridge, Dresden, Leipzig, Milan, Providence, and Rome, as well as several formerly on the art market.[6] The Harrach painting is, however, clearly the source for Marquette's *Nativity*, which repeats every detail of the picture with only the most minor alterations. Mainardi did not, as far as is known, produce exact replicas of his own works; generally he introduced variations in the landscape or background when painting popular subjects, as this *Nativity* composition clearly was. Of the two, the Harrach picture is clearly superior in quality, but it is difficult to determine the extent to which the Marquette picture has been compromised by its present condition; at one point the paint surface was somewhat brutally transferred from its original panel support to one of canvas (a process rarely undertaken today), and some distortion and subsequent repainting are evident. It is perhaps prudent to consider the Marquette work "after Mainardi," a replica of the Harrach picture of, at present, indeterminate authorship.

Although the birth of Christ is recorded in the gospels, medieval retellings and expansions of the story form the basis of Renaissance visual representations. In his *Meditations* St. Bonaventure describes Joseph as "seated, downcast," much as one might characterize his presence in the painting.[7] The Infant appears wrapped in Mary's veil (here actually her mantle), resting on the hay that Joseph is described as having laid. The ox and the ass are significant in several ways. Bonaventure states that their breath warmed the Child, who was insufficiently dressed for a cool December night.[8] *The Golden Legend* indicates that the animals recognized Christ's divinity: "Now the ox and ass, miraculously recognizing the Lord, knelt before Him and adored him."[9] And, traditionally, their presence is seen as referring to Isaiah's prophecy, "The ox knoweth his owner, and the ass his master's crib..." (Isaiah 1:3).

In the upper left of the picture the Annunciation to the Shepherds is depicted; an angel appears to the shepherds resting on a ledge, informing them of Christ's birth and the passage to the manger. The arrival of the Magi may be alluded to in the cavalcade seen approaching the bridge in the distance. The significance of the man kneeling before a cave pool (at the left) has not yet been determined.

R. B. S.

Notes:
1. On Mainardi, see Geza de' Francovich, "Sebastiano Mainardi," *Cronache d'arte* IV (May–June 1927):169–193, 256–270; Raimond van Marle, *The Development of the Italian Schools of Painting* (The Hague, 1931), XIII: 186–228; Dominic Ellis Colnaghi, *A Dictionary of Florentine Painters* (London, 1928), 166–167; and, most recently, Everett Fahy, *Some Followers of Domenico Ghirlandaio* (New York–London, 1976), 215–219.
2. Giorgio Vasari, *Le Vite*, Milanesi, ed. (Florence, 1878–1885), III:275.
3. See, for example, Martin Davies, *The Earlier Italian Schools*, National Gallery Catalogues (London, 1961), 326.
4. See, in particular, Fahy, *Some Followers of Domenico Ghirlandaio*, 215–219.
5. Günther Heinz, *Katalog der Graf Harrach'schen Gemäldegalerie* (Vienna, 1960), 44, no. 177; ill. in van Marle, *The Development of the Italian Schools of Painting*, XIII: fig. 128. Dr. Robert Keyszelitz was kind enough to provide information on this picture.
6. Fahy, *Some Followers of Domenico Ghirlandaio*, 215–219.
7. *Meditations on the Life of Christ*, I. Ragusa, trans. (Princeton, 1961), 32f.
8. Ibid., 32–33.
9. Jacobus de Voragine, *The Golden Legend*, G. Ryan and H. Rippberger, trans. (London, 1941), 50.

THE GIRARD MASTER
(Possibly Pedro Girard)

Spanish, Fifteenth Century

The Girard Master is the name given to an anonymous painter active in the Spanish province of Catalonia in the fifteenth century.[1] His major work is a large multi-panel altarpiece, the *Retable of Saint Michael*, in the Museum of Vich. From this and other unsigned paintings attributed to the same author (all of which are located in Catalonia) an artistic personality has been defined, one apparently Valencian in training with an evident debt to Jacomart and Reixach. An otherwise unknown Valencian artist named Pedro Girard, who is documented in Catalonia (he was commissioned to paint a predella in the Cathedral of Vich), has been

Saint Julian of Toledo, Girard Master, oil on panel

2

thought to be this anonymous master. Although what little is known of Girard's life is compatible with the conjectured career of the anonymous artist, the identification is still unproven, and so to reflect the consanguinity of the paintings and the element of doubt regarding the responsible artist the title of "Girard Master" has been coined.

An attractive characteristic of the Girard Master's style is his treatment of ecclesiastical dress. Richly embossed materials, frequently bordered by raised designs of gold lettering, are often worn by his subjects.

Saint Julian of Toledo   (84.7.1)

Oil on panel, 54 x 18 in. (137.2 x 45.7 cm). Unsigned.

Provenance: Collection of the Rojtman Foundation; gift of the Foundation to the University, 1984.

Marquette's *Saint Julian of Toledo*, which is convincingly attributed to the Girard Master, presents the young Saint standing alone holding a book and quill pen. He is dressed in a rich, gold-embroidered dalmatic, the traditional garb of a deacon, which is worn over the long white gown known as an alb. The embroidery, particularly Spanish in design, is edged by a border of raised gold letters—exotic arabesqued characters of apparently only decorative import.[2] The incised lettering is carried out with the Italian *pastiglie* technique (popular in Catalonia as well), which accentuates the raised areas in low light. The head of the Saint is framed by these decorative devices, underscoring his placid, gentle expression.

The halo is the only part of the decorative pattern that is legibly inscribed; it reads, "SANCTI IVLIANVS DIACON" (*sic*) (Saint Julian the Deacon). This title most probably refers to the seventeenth-century Saint Julian who was the leader of the See of Toledo.[3] This Julian was a noted theologian and writer—a fact that would account for the presence of the pen and book held by Marquette's Saint.

Nothing is known of the history of this panel. Although the picture may have been conceived as an independent work of art, it was more probably painted as part of a multipanel altarpiece, now presumably dismembered. Julian would have been accompanied by other saints also standing, all probably flanking a central picture of greater size.

R. B. S.

Notes:
1. See Chandler Rathfon Post, *A History of Spanish Painting* (Cambridge, Mass., 1938), VII, part II.
2. See Donata Devoti, *L'arte del tessuto in Europa* (Milan, 1974) for similar examples. A useful review of ecclesiastical dress is given by George Ferguson, *Signs and Symbols in Christian Art* (New York, 1966), 155–161.
3. See Herbert Thurston and Daniel Attwater, eds., *Butler's Lives of the Saints* (New York, 1956), I:524–525.

SIXTEENTH CENTURY

UNKNOWN ARTIST
Emilian School, Sixteenth Century

Adoration of the Shepherds   (64.14)

Oil on panel, 20 3/8 x 15 1/8 in. (51.8 x 38.4 cm). Unsigned.

Provenance: Geissenberger Gallery, New York (1964); collection of Dr. and Mrs. Joseph E. Halloin; their gift to the University, 1964.

References:
Emil Spaeth, in a letter (1964), as Follower of Raphael, perhaps Giulio Romano.

Pick, *Marquette University Art Collection*, 10, cover ill., as by Giulio Romano.

Burton Fredericksen and Federico Zeri, *Census of Pre-Nineteenth-Century Italian Paintings in North American Public Collections* (Cambridge, Mass., 1972), 216, as Emilian, 16th century.

Arnauld Brejon, verbally (1977), as by Alessandro Allori.

Carter, *Grain of Sand*, 9, no. 1, as attributed to Allori.

Robert Simon, in a letter (1980), as not Allori.

Ian Kennedy, verbally (1981), as not Allori but by another Florentine artist of the studiolo of Francesco I de' Medici.

This lively and colorful panel represents the Adoration of the Shepherds at the birth of Christ. The Virgin appears at the center as Joseph, before her and to the left, together with the shepherds and other attendant figures, surround and venerate the newborn Child. The scene is set outside the darkened manger in a contained foreground area, behind which a hill leads on to a fantastic mountainous landscape.

Luke relates the angel's announcement of the birth of Christ to the shepherds:[1]

> And this shall be a sign unto you; Ye shall find the babe wrapped in swaddling clothes, lying in a manger. And suddenly there was with the angel a multitude of the heavenly host praising God, and saying, Glory to God in the highest, and on earth peace, good will toward men (Luke 2:12-14).

Here, as is traditional, the heavenly host in the form of a glory of angels appears together with the Adoration scene, although temporally it is more properly linked with the subsidiary scene of the Annunciation to the Shepherds (which is depicted on the hill in the right distance). The angels hold aloft a scroll on which is written, "GLORIA IN ECCELSIS DEO," the "Glory to God in the Highest" of Luke and the basis of the "Gloria" that is recited or sung in most masses.[2]

Adoration of the Shepherds, Emilian School, Sixteenth Century, oil on panel

rine of Alexandria, the *Assumption of the Virgin* (both Pinacoteca, Bologna),[7] and the *Assumption with Saints Mary Magdalene and Petronius* (National Trust, Saltram, England) feature similar rounded forms and pudgy, curly-haired children not unlike the one in the Marquette painting. However, the resemblance is not strong enough to sustain an attribution to Sabbatini nor to any of the other artists close to him in style—of whom Orazio Sammacchini, Bernardino India, and Niccolo Roselli might be mentioned.[8]

One elusive figure, whose oeuvre does offer some suggestive analogous passages, is Francesco Menzocchi of Forli (1502-1584). His frescoes at Loreto[9] evidence a style not only indebted to Florentine artists such as Bronzino and Salviati but also reflective of central Italian and Emilian trends. Menzocchi's work at the Villa Imperiale at Pesaro[10] brought him into contact not only with Bronzino, but with Raffaellino del Colle (originally an assistant to Giulio Romano and later a collaborator with Bronzino), elements of whose style, though softened somewhat, may be seen in Marquette's *Adoration of the Shepherds*.

R.B.S.

As is often the case in representations of the scene, the shepherds bring their modest gifts for the Child. Some fruit in a basket is placed in the foreground; behind Mary a lamb is slung over a shepherd's shoulder; other figures hold a sack (presumably of grain), eggs, and fruit. Above all the mood is one of wonder and restrained joy.

Recent proposals have considered the painting a late sixteenth-century Florentine work, either by Alessandro Allori (1535-1607) or by one of his contemporaries.[3] Such attributions would seem to have been suggested by the evident derivation of the Marquette picture from the *Adoration of the Shepherds* (Budapest Museum of Fine Arts) by Agnolo Bronzino, Allori's teacher and the preeminent Florentine painter of the late Cinquecento.[4] That painting, which was in its time much copied and engraved,[5] seems to have been a source not only for the composition of the Marquette *Adoration*, but also for some of its poses, gestures, and devices (for example, the kneeling shepherd with the fruit basket). However, the figure style is not Allori's, nor does it appear to be Florentine; rather it is reminiscent of some Emilian painters of the sixteenth century. Of these Lorenzo Sabbatini (1530-1576) is perhaps the closest, as a comparison with some of his known works would indicate.[6] *The Disputation of St. Cathe-*

Notes:
1. The preceding text is given in the entry on a *Nativity* by an anonymous North Italian painter in the Marquette collection (58.7).
2. In the Vulgate Bible the passage appears as "Gloria in altissimis Deo, et in terra pax hominibus bonae voluntatis." The word "eccelcis" is an Italianate corrupt form of the far more common "excelcis."
3. On Allori see, *inter alia*, Carlo Gamba, "A Proposito di Alessandro Allori e di un suo Ritratto," *Rivista del R. Instituto d'Archeologia e Storia dell'arte* I (1929):265-277; Adolfo Venturi, *Storia dell'arte italiana* (1933), IX-6:75-115; and M. L. Becherucci, "Allessandro Allori," in *Dizionario Biografico degli Italiani* (Rome, 1960), II:506-508. On Allori and his contemporaries active in the studiolo of Francesco I de' Medici, see Luciano Berti, *Il Principe dello Studiolo* (Florence, 1967).
4. Illustrated in Charles McCorquodale, *Bronzino* (London, 1981), fig. 35; for excellent reproductions in color see Vilmos Tátrai, *Cinquecento Paintings of Central Italy* (Budapest, 1983), plates 27-29.
5. Giorgio Ghisi's engraving of 1553 is the best known of the three contemporary prints after the picture. Painted copies or derivations include Bronzino's later altarpiece for Santo Stefano, Pisa (McCorquodale, *Bronzino*, fig. 102) and an altarpiece attributed to Tosini in S. Maria delle Carceri, Prato.
6. For Sabbatini see Diane Degrazia, *Correggio and His Legacy* (Washington, 1984), 330f., with bibliography; and Venturi, *Storia dell'arte italiana*, 460-469.
7. Illustrated in *La Pinacoteca Nazionale di Bologna*, ed. Andrea Emiliani (Bologna, 1967), figs. 159-160.
8. On Sammacchini see Giuseppe Cirolli and Giovanni Godi, "Di Orazio Sammacchini e altri Bolognesi a Parma," *Parma nell'arte* XIV-1 (1982): 7-46; Degrazia, *Correggio and His Legacy*, 334f; and Venturi, *Storia dell'arte italiana*, 695-704. For India's works, see L. Magagnato, *Cinquant'anni di pittura veronese; 1580-1630* (Verona, 1974); cf. India's *Madonna and Child with St. John the Baptist* (Borghese Gallery, Rome); ill. Paola Della Pergola, *Galleria Borghese: I Dipinti* (Rome, 1955), I: fig. 206. On Roselli see Giuliano Frabetti, *L'autunno dei manieristi a Ferrara* (Ferrara, 1978), 35f.
9. See *Restauri nelle Marche*, exhibition catalogue (Urbino, 1973), no. 93, and Floriano Grimaldi, *Loreto; Palazzo Apostolico* (Bologna, 1977), nos. 59-60; cf. as well no. 67.
10. G. Marchini, *La Villa Imperiale di Pesaro* (Milan, 1968) 26f.

ANTHUENIS CLAEISSENS

Flemish (1536–1613)

Anthuenis (or Antoon, Antoine, or Antonius) Claeissens (or Claeis, Claes, or Claeissen) was born in the Flemish town of Bruges in 1536.[1] His father, Pieter, was also a painter, as were Anthuenis's brothers, Gillis and Pieter the Younger. He studied with both his father and Pieter Pourbus and was franchised as a master in 1570. He received the title of official painter of the city of Bruges the same year, a post he held until 1581 (when he was succeeded by his brother Pieter). Anthuenis was three times elected head of the Corporation of Painters in Bruges, where he died on January 18, 1613.

Anthuenis's career has not been generally studied, and his works are often confused with those of his brothers.[2] They are, however, diverse from them in their superior design and draftsmanship and are characterized by a far less provincial style, one that reveals a knowledge of the work of Frans Floris and Jan Massys, in addition to those of his documented masters. Claeissens seems to have preferred allegorical and Old Testament scenes, usually in a large, horizontal format. Among his signed or securely attributed paintings are the *Banquet Scene* and *Mars Crushing Ignorance* (Groeninge Museum, Bruges), *The Infant Moses before Pharoah* (sold Sotheby's, London, July 12, 1978), and *Modesty and Virtue United with Honor* (sold Christie's, London, May 27, 1983).

ATTRIBUTED TO ANTHUENIS CLAEISSENS
The Story of Elijah   (60.3)

Oil on panel, 26 1/2 x 45 in. (67.3 x 114.3 cm). Unsigned.

Provenance: Collection of M. Lempereur, 1783 (?); Mr. and Mrs. Marc B. Rojtman, Milwaukee; their gift to the University, 1960.

References:
Pick, *Marquette University Art Collection,* 11, 14 (ill.), as Frans Floris.

Jacques Foucart, in a letter (1978), as style of Martin de Vos or Frans Floris.

Ian Kennedy, verbally (1981), as by, near, but probably after Floris.

The Story of Elijah has traditionally been attributed to Frans Floris, but despite a similarity in facial types (particularly the woman at center), the attribution cannot be sustained.[3] In composition (but otherwise not in style) the picture resembles the paintings of Jan Massys, which are frequently organized with the protagonists close to the picture plane and subsidiary scenes and fanciful architecture in a parklike setting at the rear.[4] The particular compositional device found in the Marquette picture, that of placing a principal scene in the center foreground with two secondary subjects in the left and right middle ground, is in fact employed in a series of seven paintings representing the deadly sins at the Museo di Capodimonte in Naples.[5] These anonymous pictures seem to be by the same hand as the Marquette *Elijah,* an artist who, it is suggested here, may be identifiable with Anthuenis Claeissens. The attribution is prompted not alone by the similar use of space, figures, and architecture in Claeissens's known work, but also by the closeness in figural and facial types—a kind of harder, broader, less fleshy derivation of Floris's style.[6]

The painting depicts three episodes from the life of the prophet Elijah that take place, in spite of the verdant landscape, during a time of great drought and famine. The scene in the distance at the left shows Elijah being fed by ravens at the brook Cherith (I Kings 17:1–6). At the right Elijah appears seated by the gates of the city of Zarephath, where, according to God's command, he asks a widow for food and water (I Kings 17:9–12). In the center the child of the widow presents Elijah with the cake his mother has baked; the Prophet gestures in response, avowing God's promise that the widow's supply of meal and oil will not fail (I Kings 17:13–16).

Representations of Elijah do appear with increasing frequency in the sixteenth and seventeenth centuries, many commissioned by the Carmelite Order, which considered Elijah to be its founder.[7] Although synoptic depictions of the story, such as the Marquette picture, are rare, many individual depictions of events from the Prophet's life and particularly of the episode of the widow of Zarephath, are known: Relevant examples include Jan Massys's painting in Karlsruhe and Martin de Vos's engraving from the *Theatrum Biblicum* of 1574.[8]

R.B.S.

Notes:
1. The limited literature on Anthuenis Claeissens includes W.H.J. Weale, "Peintres brugeois; V: Antoine Claeissens," *Annales de la Société d'Émulation pour l'étude de l'histoire et des antiquités de la Flandre* LXI (1911),:62-74; Henri Pauwels, *Musée Groeninge; Catalogue* (Bruges, 1963), 92-95; and Max J. Friedländer, *Early Netherlandish Painting* (New York-Washington, 1975), XI:65.
2. Friedländer, *Early Netherlandish Painting,* XI:65, found Anthuenis "by no means easily distinguished from his brother."
3. See Carl van de Velde, *Frans Floris (1519/20-1570): leven en weerken* (Brussels, 1975); Friedländer, *Early Netherlandish Painting,* XIII:34-40; and Dora Zuntz, *Frans Floris* (Strassbourg, 1929).
4. Compare, for example, Jan Massys's *Lot and His Daughters* (versions in the Brussels and Vienna Museums), *Bathsheba Bathing* (Louvre, Paris), or *Susanna and the Elders* (Brussels)—all illustrated in Friedländer, *Early Netherlandish Painting,* figs. 11-14.
5. These have been attributed to Otto van Veen (1556-1629) but are currently considered anonymous.
6. Compare, particularly, *Mars Crushing Ignorance,* signed and dated 1605 at Bruges; see Pauwels, *Musée Groeninge,* no. 65.
7. See Émile Mâle, *Religious Art from the Twelfth to the Eighteenth Century* (New York, 1949), 195f.
8. The Massys is illustrated in Friedländer, *Early Netherlandish Painting,* XIII: fig. 18; the *Theatrum Biblicum* was published in 1674.

The Story of Elijah, Attributed to Anthuenis Claeissens, oil on panel

AMBROSIUS FRANCKEN
THE ELDER

Flemish (1544–1618)

Ambrosius Francken the Elder was born in 1544 in the town of Herenthals.[1] With his brothers Hieronymus and Frans he studied in the workshop of Frans Floris in Antwerp. According to Van Mander,[2] Ambrosius was called to Tournai in 1569 to carry out work for the local bishop, but nothing from this project survives. The following year the artist was in Fontainebleau and perhaps in Italy as well. Ambrosius had returned to Antwerp by 1573, when he entered the Guild of St. Luke. He was made a citizen of the city four years later, shortly before marrying and becoming the dean of the Guild. He seems to have remained there for the rest of his life, marrying again in 1583 (his first wife had died the year before). He died in 1618 and was buried in the St. Andriekerk of Antwerp. Although he

had no children, Ambrosius was the master of his brother's sons Hieronymus (1578–1623) and Hans (1581–1624).

Ambrosius Francken's works have often been confused with those of his brother Hieronymus, whose one surviving religious work is stylistically quite different.[3] The series of altarpieces done by Ambrosius for the Cathedral of Antwerp (now in the Koninklijk Museum voor Schone Kunsten, Antwerp) reveals a lively Italianate style; a fondness for contorted poses, muscular figures, and dramatic (if crowded) compositions; a sureness of line; a liking for interesting faces that suggests a career as a portraitist; and a decorous restraint that begins to disappear in some of the more gruesome martyrdoms. The *Multiplication of the Loaves and Fishes*, which was done for the Bakers' Guild, is dated 1598 and is perhaps the earliest of the Antwerp Cathedral altarpieces that survives.[4] The two scenes from the *Martyrdom of St. George* (actually from St. George's Church rather than the Cathedral, but now also in the museum of Antwerp) most probably date from about 1600.[5] Next follow four scenes from the life of St. Sebastian, wings originally painted for the altar of the Longbowmen's Guild.[6] Two panels from the altar of the Barbers and Surgeons representing Miracles of Saints Cosmas and Damian were painted about 1610, as most probably were the Saint Crispin and Crispinian scenes done for the Shoemakers' Guild and formerly attributed to Hieronymus.[7] Earlier works of more conservative subject matter include the *Triptych of the Holy Sacrament*, *Lamentation*, *Preaching of St. Eloi* (all Antwerp Museum), *Daniel Liberating Suzannah* (Brussels Museum), and *Adoration of the Shepherds* (Art Market, London).[8]

twerp or the woman at the lower left of the *Multiplication of the Loaves and Fishes* (both Antwerp Museum); Elizabeth with the attendant women in the *Lamentation* (Antwerp Museum) and, in costume, the turbaned figures in several of the martyrdom altars; John the Baptist with the figure of the youthful St. Sebastian in the series of scenes from the life of the Saint. More generally, the Marquette *Holy Family* shares with Francken's paintings an active though somewhat contrived composition, incisive drawing, and a rigorous rendering of the human form.

R.B.S.

ATTRIBUTED TO AMBROSIUS FRANCKEN THE ELDER
The Holy Family with Saints John the Baptist And Elizabeth   (61.3)

Oil on canvas, 44 1/8 x 55 in. (112.1 x 139.7 cm). Unsigned.

Provenance: Collection of Baron Delessert, Paris (?); collection of Mr. and Mrs. Marc B. Rojtman; their gift to the University, 1961.

References:
Pick, *Marquette University Art Collection*, 11, 12 (ill.), as by Louis Finson.

J. Patrice Marandel, verbally (1976), as by Finson.

Carter, *Grain of Sand*, 9, no. 6, as by Finson.

Ian Kennedy, verbally (1981), as Antwerp School, possibly Ambrosius or Hieronymus Francken.

In this attractive work the Virgin is seen looking directly at the viewer, her attention momentarily drawn away from her child, who is seated on her lap. Her right hand gently steadies the arm of Christ, who reaches out to touch the hair of the infant John the Baptist. John in turn holds up a small banner inscribed, "ECCE AGNV- DEI,"—"Behold the Lamb of God," John's words about Christ at the Baptism (John 1:36). The reed cross, John the Baptist's customary attribute, is held by his mother, Elizabeth, while Joseph looks down at the scene from a penumbral background.

The *Holy Family's* traditional attribution to the Flemish Caravaggesque painter Louis Finson cannot, for stylistic reasons, any longer be sustained.[9] The recent proposal of Ambrosius Francken, however, does meet with considerable confirmation in the artist's documented work. Analogous figural types appear in several of Francken's altarpieces: the draped Madonna with the mother in *The Preaching of St. Eloi in An-*

The Holy Family with Saints John the Baptist and Elizabeth, Attributed to Ambrosius Francken the Elder, oil on canvas

Notes:
1. The only monographic treatment of Francken is to be found in Juliane Gabriels, *Een Kempisch Schildersgeslacht: De Francken's* (Hoogstraten, 1930); but see also Zoege von Manteuffel's review in *Belvedere* (1934):43-46, and his article in Ulrich Thieme and Felix Becker, *Allgemeine Lexikon der bildenden Künstler von der Antike bis zur Gegenwart* (Leipzig, 1907-1950), 12:337-338. David Freedberg discusses Ambrosius in connection with his martyrdoms done for the Cathedral of Antwerp in an article that is the most reliable on the artist; David Freedberg, "The Representation of Martyrdoms During the Early Counter-Reformation in Antwerp," *The Burlington Magazine* CXVIII (March 1976):128-138.
2. Carel Van Mander, *Het Schilderboeck* (Amsterdam, 1603), ed. Hymans (Paris, 1884-1945), 349.
3. See P.M. Auzas, "L'adoration des bergers, de Hierosme Francken," *Bulletin de la société de l'histoire de l'art Franç* (1966):61-64. See as well P.M. Auzas, *Hierosme Francken dit Franco, peintre du roi Henri III et du roi Henri IV* (Brussels, 1968).
4. Freedberg, "The Representation of Martyrdoms," fig 13. The chronology proposed by Freedberg, 131-132, is followed here.
5. Ibid., fig. 10.
6. *St. Sebastian Exhorting Marcus and Marcellinus, The Miraculous Healing of Zoe, Diocletian Condemning St. Sebastian, St. Sebastian Beaten with Rods.* The main panel of the *Martyrdom of St. Sebastian* is by Michael Coxcie. See Freedberg, "The Representation of Martyrdoms," figs. 6-9, 11.

7

7. Ibid., 131–132, figs, 2–3; the dating is suggested by the pictures' similarity to the monogrammed and dated *Carrying of the Cross* of 1610 (Ghent).
8. Sale Christie's, London, February 24, 1984, lot 75.
9. See Didier Bodart, *Louis Finson* (Brussels, 1970) for a monographic treatment of the artist.

LAMBERT LOMBARD
Flemish (1506–1566)

Lambert Lombard was born in the Belgian city of Liège in either 1505 or 1506.[1] His early training was with a largely unknown artist named Jean Deneuse, although he is thought to have worked with Jan Gossaert, called Mabuse. An architect as well as a painter, Lombard was particularly inspired by archaeological relics uncovered in northern Europe. This antiquarian interest—evidenced in sketchbooks and drawings recording various ancient monuments, reliefs, and sculpture—is reflected as well in the artist's few surviving paintings.

Lombard's compositions are usually clear, if stolidly organized, and legible despite a tendency toward crowding. His figures have a heaviness and independence that makes them appear to be painted statues rather than personages—a quality underscored by the artist's restricted palette and predilection for placing figures in one or two friezelike rows. His figural types are often derived from the classical sources that he admired, although Renaissance reinterpretations of them, particularly from Raphael and his school, seem frequently to have been directly studied.

Lombard visited Italy in 1537–1538, but it is clear that he had already become familiar with both ancient and Italian sources, mostly through prints. His major extant work is the *Altarpiece of St. Denis of Liège*, panels from which survive in the museums of Brussels and Liège, as well as in the church for which it was painted.[2] Lombard founded an influential art academy in his hometown; he had many students, the most notable being Willem Key and Frans Floris. In part because of the number of his followers (many of whom remain unidentified), attributions to Lombard have often been rather capriciously conceived; a scholarly review would no doubt better define the artist's career as well as those of his associates and students.

SCHOOL OF LAMBERT LOMBARD
The Birth of St. John The Baptist   (59.4)

Oil on panel, 47 1/2 x 35 1/2 in. (120.7 x 90.2 cm). Unsigned.

Provenance: Collection of Mr. and Mrs. Marc B. Rojtman, Milwaukee; their gift to the University, 1959.

References:
Pick, *Marquette University Art Collection*, 27, 29 (ill.) as Marten van Heemskerck.

Marquette's *The Birth of St. John the Baptist* has traditionally, if not convincingly, been ascribed to the Flemish Mannerist painter Marten van Heemskerck, but an attribution closer to his compatriot Lambert Lombard seems more plausible. There is no trace of Heemskerck's exuberant and slightly eccentric style in the activity, perhaps more halting than fluid, there represented. The picture does, however, recall Lombard's known paintings in many ways. The figures are similarly statuesque, independently conceived, and, in appearance, represented as if frozen in the course of motion. Facial expressions are limited in the range of emotions depicted, and much of the narrative meaning is communicated through gesture. A scallop-topped panel shape (one employed by Lombard in the Liège altarpiece) is used, as is an interior space with a similar horizon, strong perspective organization, and geometrically pavemented floor. Lombard's *Adoration of the Shepherds* presents other strong analogies, particularly compositional, with the *Birth of St. John*. The *Adoration* is known in many versions, and some of the workshop examples bear an obvious similarity to, and share common weaknesses with, the Marquette picture.[3] These qualities, which suggest an attribution to one of Lombard's students or followers, include a tendency to harsh gradations of light and shadow, flattened facial features, and somewhat disproportionate figures.

The Birth of St. John the Baptist, School of Lambert Lombard, oil on panel

Lombard is often associated with the print medium. Many of his compositions were engraved and survive only in graphic reproduction. Moreover, he made ready use of prints by other artists, both wholly and in part, when creating his own work. *The Adoration of the Shepherds*, for example, is based on an engraving by a follower of Marcantonio Raimondi, which in turn is derived from a tapestry design by Raphael.[4] *The Birth of St. John* is in fact directly based on a print, a sixteenth-century engraving by the Mantuan artist Diana Scultori.[5] That print is nearly identical to the Marquette painting in composition, with only a few disparities of note evident: the scalloped rather than arched (as in the print) top of the design, the addition of putti holding decorative tassels above God the Father, and the introduction of a niche with a candlestick to the left of the door. The reductive handling or malcomprehended rendering of specific details in the painting (the food on the table, drapery folds, floor pattern) suggest that it was based on the print rather than the other way around. The print in turn would seem to be after a lost design by Giulio Romano.[6]

An intriguing analogy can be found in a painting of the *Last Supper* in the Boston Museum of Fine Arts;[7] that work is after a lost design by Lambert Lombard engraved by Giorgio Ghisi.[8] It shares with the Marquette picture not only its genesis from a print source but also much the same handling of forms that differentiated the *Birth of St. John* from the known works of Lombard. Some particularities—the rendering of bowls, the harsh planarity of faces, the deep drapery folds—are notably similar and suggest that the two pictures were painted by the same anonymous follower of Lombard. One clue to this artist's identity may be the addition of the candlestick to the engraved composition. A similar candlestick in a niche in the *Last Supper* is as well the only substantive alteration to Ghisi's engraving. The inclusion in both pictures may be casual but would more probably seem to have some significance—perhaps as a kind of visual monogram, trademark, or signature of the artist.

The birth of St. John the Baptist is related in the first chapter of Luke:

Now Elisabeth's full time came that she should be delivered; and she brought forth a son. And her neighbors and her cousins heard how the Lord had shewed great mercy upon her; and they rejoiced with her (Luke I:57-58).

Although the attendant figures represent the anonymous "neighbors and cousins" mentioned by Luke, there is a tradition that the woman holding the infant is in fact Mary. The *Meditations on the Life of Christ*, long given to St. Bonaventure, describes the scene of John's birth:

When her time had come Elizabeth gave birth to the son whom our Lady lifted from the ground and

diligently cared for as was necessary. The child loved her deeply, as though he understood her, and even when she gave him to his mother he turned his face to the Lady, delighting only in her. She played with him, gaily embracing and kissing him with joy.[9]

The woman in the lower left corner of the painting may thus represent Mary, even though a halo would then be expected, just as one appears behind St. Elizabeth and the Christ Child. Two other aspects of the scene have Marian overtones, although again they do not overtly refer to Mary: the figure embracing Elizabeth and the woman seated with a suckling child. The former is an obvious allusion to the Visitation, the meeting of Elizabeth and Mary when Elizabeth was six months pregnant; the latter may allude to Mary's suggested role as midwife, as mentioned in the popular *Golden Legend* of Jacobus de Voragine:

...The Blessed Virgin dwelt with her kinswoman [Elizabeth] for three months, caring for her in her waiting; and she it was who received the newborn child in her holy hands, and performed in his behalf the duties of midwife.[10]

The leonine dog at the lower right seen standing on a bone would seem to have less theological and liturgical than decorative and humorous purpose.

R.B.S

Notes:
1. On Lombard see *Lambert Lombard et son Temps*, exhibition catalogue (Liège, 1966); J. Yernaux, "Lambert Lombard," *Bulletin de l'Institut Archèologique liègois* LXXII (1957-1958): 267-372; Adolph Goldschmidt, "Lambert Lombard," *Jahrbuch der preussischen Kulturbesitz* XL (1949):206-240; and Max J. Friedländer, *Early Netherlandish Painting* (New York-Washington, 1975), XIII:28-33.
2. See Friedländer, *Early Netherlandish Painting*, XIII:30-31, 82-83, plates 49-51.
3. Church of Saint-Denis, Liège; Aartsbisschoppelijk Museum, Utrecht; Musée des Beaux-Arts, Ghent; Bob Jones College Museum of Art, Greenville (South Carolina); St.-Jean Hospital, Bruges; Mateu Collection, Barcelona; A.A.A. sale, New York, Feb. 21, 1922, lot 50; ex-collection Georges Marlier, Brussels (sold Sotheby's, London, April 7, 1982, lot 143); Wallraf-Richartz Museum, Cologne; Musée Curtius, Liège.
4. See G. Marlier, "Lambert Lombard et les tapisseries de Raphael," *Miscellanea Jozef Duverger* (Ghent, 1969), 247-259. The engraving (Bartsch XV, 75) is reproduced in Goldschmidt, "Lambert Lombard," fig. 22.
5. Bartsch XV, 443, 26. An example is in the Department of Prints at the Metropolitan Museum of Art (49.97.493). See as well Stefania Massari, *Incisori mantovani del '500: Giovan Battista, Diana Scultori e Giorgio Ghisi*, exhibition catalogue (Rome, 1980-1981), 93, no. 148, 253 (ill.), and Gioconda Albricci, "Prints by Diana Scultori," *Print Collector* 3-4, no. 12, (1975):19, no. 9. The print has also been attributed to Étienne Delaune; see A.P.F. Robert-Dumesnil, *Le Peintre-Graveur Français* (Paris, 1865), IX:34.
6. Giorgio Vasari [*Le Vite*, Milanesi, ed. (Florence, 1878-1885), V:550-551] records that Giulio Romano's design was engraved by Sebastiano da Reggio, among other artists. An engraving of

this composition by Sebastiano is said to exist, and Giulio's authorship of the design for Diana Scultori's print has been accepted without question. There are evident connections with Giulio's oeuvre [cf. the anonymous *Birth of the Virgin* after Giulio; Bartsch XVI, 377, 5; ill., *The Illustrated Bartsch*, H. Zerner, ed. (New York, 1979), XXX:282-283], although there is no firm evidence for the attribution. A drawing at Windsor Castle is said to be a copy of Giulio's orginal drawing of the composition [A.E. Popham and Johannes Wilde, *The Italian Drawings of the XV and XVI Centuries...at Windsor Castle* (London, 1949, 236, no. 358].

7. No. 15.290 as Studio of Pieter Coecke von Aelst. Suzanne Boorsch was kind enough to draw this work to my attention and discuss its possible bearing on the Marquette picture.
8. Bartsch XV, 387, 6.
9. *Meditations on the Life of Christ; An Illustrated Manuscript of the Fourteenth Century*, I. Ragusa, trans. (Princeton, 1961), 24-25.
10. *The Golden Legend of Jacobus de Voragine*, G. Ryan and H. Rippberger, trans. (New York, 1969), 323.

GILLIS MOSTAERT

Flemish (1534–1598)

One of the most important Flemish painters of the latter half of the sixteenth century, Gillis Mostaert was born in the town of Hulst, near Antwerp, in 1534.[1] With his elder brother Frans he was a student of Frans Floris and Jan Mandyn in Antwerp, where he received the title of master in 1554. Mostaert's signed or monogrammed works are few, including a *Kermesse* or *Market Scene* (former Rudolfinum, Prague), dated 1579; the *Adoration of the Shepherds* (Dienst door's Rijks versprende Kunstwerken, The Hague) of 1577; and *The Fire* (Louvre, Paris) from 1589. Mostaert's paintings often involve grand panoramic views populated by small figures whose attenuated, flaccid forms distantly reflect contemporary Italian styles (as imported by Floris). The landscape backgrounds that dominate these works are rich and varied with dramatic lighting effects appearing above the diminutive protagonists who, as with Brueghel, often seem incidental to the body of the picture.

The Passion of Christ   (58.9)

Oil on canvas, 43 1/2 x 50 1/2 in. (110.5 x 128.3 cm). Unsigned.

Provenance: Collection of Mr. and Mrs. Marc B. Rojtman, Milwaukee; their gift to the University, 1958.

References:
Pick, *Marquette University Art Collection*, 27, 30 (ill.), as by Gillis Van Valckenborch.

Ian Kennedy, verbally (1981), as by Gillis Mostaert.

This fascinating picture is a synoptic representation of the Passion of Christ, a subject only rarely encountered in Renaissance painting.[2] In it Christ's final days

The Passion of Christ, Gillis Mostaert, oil on canvas

are depicted sequentially, beginning in the lower right corner with his entry into Jerusalem on Palm Sunday. Within the walls of this fantastically architected city the next episode, the Last Supper, appears above and to the left, set within a pedimented house conveniently apertured for our observation. Above and to the right of the house The Agony in the Garden and the Betrayal are depicted in one extended episode: Christ prays on the hill (Gethsemane) as an angel appears to him; by his side sleep Peter, James, and John. On the path below Judas is seen, pointing the way for Jesus's captors, who hold a lantern and a torch to guide their path. To the left and behind the central dome Christ, again inside an open building (this one marked by "official" Roman Corinthian columns), goes before Pontius Pilate. Dangling from a tree at the left is Judas, who has hanged himself. Moving back right into the distance the next episode is represented, the Flagellation.

The progress of the Passion continues with Christ's Carrying the Cross on the road to Calvary. The procession moves out of the city gate and up a winding road to the hill, where the Crucifixion itself is depicted. The Resurrection is portrayed behind and to the right; soldiers sleep beside the empty sepulcher on which an angel sits as Christ rises in a shaft of light. Directly to the right is the *Noli Me Tangere* (Do Not Touch Me) scene, in which Christ appeared to Mary Magdalene. Another appearance is depicted immediately above: Christ's joining two of his Apostles on the road to Emmaus. Finally, in the upper right corner of the painting, the Ascension is portrayed with the Apostles looking up in wonder as Christ rises in a blaze of light.

The attribution to Mostaert, which has only recently been proposed, finds confirmation in several of the artist's known works. *The Passion in the Grand Place of Antwerp* (Antwerp Museum) presents a thematically related subject that can be compared not only for its similarity in compositional organization, but also for its rather particular figure style. So too Mostaert's *Crucifixion* in Copenhagen features, in addition to a similar treatment of the principal subject, a comparable rendering of fantastic architecture and atmospheric phenomena.[3] The restrained, almost monochromatic tonality of the Marquette painting recalls as well Mostaert's painted grisaille frames. A *Crucifixion*, surrounded by Apostles and angels (Museum, Dortmund), *Baptism* (Fondation Custodia, Paris), and, most of all, a *Christ Carrying the Cross*, with scenes from the Passion in the painted border (Art Market, London) further sustain the attribution.[4] The dramatic use of light, panoramic conception of landscape, and relation of figures to natural settings in Marquette's *Passion* find related employment in such works by Mostaert as *The Fire* (Louvre, Paris), *Massacre of the Innocents* (Thyssen Collection, Lugano), *Rest on the Flight into Egypt* (Bank voor Handel en Scheepvaart, Rotterdam), and *Winter Landscape* (Art Market, Frankfurt, 1904).[5]

R.B.S.

Notes:
1. On the artist see Paul Wescher, "Gillis Mostaert," in Ulrich Thieme and Felix Becker, *Allgemeines Lexikon der bildenden Künstler von der Antike bis zur Gegenwart* (Leipzig, 1907–1950), 25:189; Sander Pierron, *Les Mostaert* (Brussels-Paris, 1912); Giorgio T. Faggin, "Gillis Mostaert als Landschapschilder," *Jaarboek: Koninklijk Museum voor Schone Kunsten Antwerpen* (1964), 89–106; Carl van de Velde, "Taferelen met grisaillelijsten van Gillis Mostaert," in *Essays in Northern European Art Presented to Egbert Haverkamp-Begemann on his Sixtieth Birthday,* ed. Anne-Marie Logan (Doornspijk, 1983), 276–282.
2. The earliest and most noted example is Hans Memling's painting now in the Galleria Sabauda in Turin; illustrated in Max J. Friedländer, *Early Netherlandish Painting* (New York-Washington, 1971), VI, part 1, plate 34.
3. *Royal Museum of Fine Arts; Catalogue of Old Foreign Paintings* (Copenhagen, 1951), 208, no. 481 (ill.); cf. Pierron, *Les Mostaert,* 139, 141 (ill.), and Frans Baudouin, "Een Michelangelo-motief bij Gillis Mostaert," in *Miscellanea I.Q. van Regteren Altena* (Amsterdam, 1969), 67f.
4. Van de Velde, "Taferelen met grisaillelijsten van Gillis Mostaert," figs. 2, 4, 1. Other works by Mostaert to be compared include the *Last Supper* (location unknown; ill. ibid., fig. 2); the *Rest on the Flight into Egypt* (Nationalmuseum, Stockholm); *St. John the Baptist Preaching* (Collection Marquess of Lothian, Melbourne Hall; cf. as well another version in the National Museum of Cracow); and an allegorical representation of the Rosary with scenes from the Life of Christ (sold Christie's, London, July 14, 1978, lot 60). A series of twelve panels representing the Passion, monogrammed "GM" and dated 1578, were sold at the Fernand Stuck Estate sale, Palais des Beaux-Arts, Brussels, Dec. 7-8, 1960, lot 89.
5. Illustrated in Faggin, "Gillis Mostaert als Landschapschilder," figs. 3-7.

UNKNOWN ARTIST
German School, Middle Rhine, Sixteenth Century

The Presentation in the Temple   (66.4)

Oil on panel, 12 3/8 x 9 1/2 in. (31/4 x 24.1 cm)
Unsigned.

Provenance: Collection of Dr. and Mrs. Joseph E. Halloin; their gift to the University, 1966.

References:
Pick, *Marquette University Art Collection Supplement,* 8–10 (ill.), as the Niederrhein Master (*sic*).

The Presentation in the Temple, German School, Middle Rhine, Sixteenth Century, oil on panel

The Adoration of the Magi   (66.5)

Oil on panel, 12 5/8 x 9 1/2 in. (32.1 x 24.1 cm)
Unsigned.

Provenance: Collection of Dr. and Mrs. Joseph Halloin; their gift to the University, 1966.

References:
Pick, *Marquette University Art Collection Supplement,* 8–10 (ill.), as the Niederrhein Master (*sic*).

The Adoration of the Magi, German School, Middle Rhine, Sixteenth Century, oil on panel

These two panels are clearly from a large polyptych, an altarpiece made up of several paintings framed in one integral group. The fictive gold tracery that appears in the upper left corner of each of the pictures suggests that the Marquette painting originally appeared on the left-hand side of the altarpiece. Unfortunately, no other elements from this work have been identified, and so the precise location, as well as the origin of the work, can for now only be conjectured.

The paintings are clearly German and have strong stylistic affinities with late fifteenth-century works from the lower and middle Rhine. There is some similarity with the so-called Meister der Mauterndorfer Flügel,[1] but a closer figure may be the anonymous artist known as either the Meister des Lutern or the Meister mit den Affen.[2] This painter is responsible for a large altarpiece of the life of Christ, several panels from which survive in widely dispersed collections.[3] He shares with the author of the Marquette panels a fondness for stocky figures having large foreheads as well as rather severe, harshly delineated features. The *Adoration* and *Presentation* seem to have been painted by an artist close to this apparently middle-Rhenish figure, although their inferior quality and somewhat disparate style would rule out their being by him.

The Presentation in the Temple represents the infant Christ being presented by Mary to the high priest of the temple (Luke 2:23–38). The Hebrew priest is curiously dressed as a traditional Christian bishop; the painted altarpiece in the background, however, seems to depict the Sacrifice of Abraham. *The Adoration of the Magi* is represented traditionally with the three Wise Men presenting their gifts of gold, frankincense, and myrrh to the Christ Child, who is held by Mary. Two of the Magi are visible; only the hand of the third, dark-skinned king appears at the right of the panel—perhaps an indication that the painting has at one time been reduced in size.

R.B.S.

Notes:
1. See A. Stange, *Deutsche Malerie der Gotik* (Munich, 1969), X: fig. 55.
2. Ernst Buchner, cited in Charles L. Kuhn, *A Catalogue of German Paintings...in American Collections* (Cambridge, Mass., 1936), 48; Stange, *Deutsche Malerie der Gotik*, XI:135.
3. These are in the Staatsgalerie, Stuttgart; the Germanisches Museum, Nuremberg; The Dompfarrhaus, Frankfurt; the collections of William Geiger, Philadelphia; an unknown private collection; and recently on the market in London (see Sotheby's sale catalogue of April 8, 1981, lot 94).

FRANCESCO DA PONTE IL GIOVANE (FRANCESCO BASSANO)

Italian (1549–1592)

Called "the Younger" to avoid confusion with his uncle, Francesco was born on January 11, 1549, in the North Italian town of Bassano, the son of the master painter Jacopo da Ponte. By the early 1570s his apprenticeship to his father had evolved into collaboration, and by 1577, the date of the *Circumcision* now in the Museo Civico at Bassano (which although signed by both artists appears to have been executed entirely by the son), Francesco had asserted his own personality. Notwithstanding its basis in Jacopo's art, Francesco's mature manner is distinguishable by the less fluid application of heavy impasto, by the almost phosphorescent glow of colors (above all greens and reds) from their shadowed surroundings, and by a more tortuous drapery style.

Except for certain notable works for religious institutions, such as the exciting Passion cycle once in Sant'Antonio Abbate at Brescia, Francesco Bassano's talents were best suited to easel pictures whose themes, often biblical in source, allowed for a rough-hewn humanity in rustic environments (a genre his father had also practiced). To this group belong many of the so-called nocturnes, the figures therein illuminated by torches and candles, original conceptions

The Exodus of Moses and the Israelites, After Francesco da Ponte the Younger (Francesco Bassano), oil on canvas

which Francesco had devised between 1580 and 1585. Conversely, his training, outlook, and rugged technique did not serve him well for the propagandistic canvases which, beginning in 1580, he produced for the Doge's Palace in Venice. In resisting his natural inclinations in an attempt to adapt his style to the heroic visions of Tintoretto and Veronese and to the pretentious offerings of such painters as the Mannerist Federico Zuccaro, Francesco became self-consciously "arty."

In spite of these experiments and a general lessening of inspiration in his later years, he continued to receive important commissions, among them paintings for S. Luigi de'Francesi (late 1580s) and the Church of the Gesù (1592), both in Rome, and for the abbey of Montecassino (contract signed in October 1591). The last-named project was completed by his brother Leandro; for late in 1591 Francesco, suffering from consumption and, apparently, a persecution complex, threw himself from a window, having already prepared two testaments (1587 and 1589). Eight months later, on July 3, 1592, he died in Venice, and his body was returned to his native town. The workshop, now under the command of Leandro and frequented by the young Gerolamo Bassano, continued to flourish.

AFTER FRANCESCO DA PONTE THE YOUNGER (FRANCESCO BASSANO)
The Exodus of Moses and the Israelites, Eighteenth Century (?) (60.4)

Oil on canvas, 29 x 35 in. (74 x 89 cm). Unsigned.

Provenance: Collection of Lord Yarborough, 1835?; Mr. and Mrs. Marc B. Rojtman, Milwaukee; their gift to the University, 1960.

References:
Pick, *Marquette University Art Collection*, 7, 8 (ill.), as Jacopo Bassano.

Jeri Wind, in a letter (1974), as after Francesco Bassano.

J. Patrice Marandel, verbally (1976), as a damaged and mostly repainted . . . work.

Arnauld Brejon, verbally (1977), as an eighteenth-century copy after Francesco Bassano.

Ian Kennedy, verbally (1981), as a late seventeenth-century Venetian copy after Bassano.

With a sense of sharing appropriate to their mission to the Promised Land, the stalwart Israelite families have gathered with their animals for a humble meal. Their leader, Moses, staff in hand and rays of light crowning his head, walks in the middle distance as if in conversation with his priestly companion. Inasmuch as the Ark of the Convenant is not in evidence, the rays may be taken as identifying attributes rather than as allusions to a specific moment in the journey following Moses's descent from Mount Sinai when "the skin of his face shone because he had been talking to God" (Exodus 34:29). The impact of the color scheme—reds, maroons, yellows, and blues predominating—is compromised by surface soil and deteriorated varnishes.

In a detailed report submitted in 1974, Jeri Wind identified this rustic scene, then assigned to Jacopo Bassano, as a copy after Francesco Bassano's *Pilgrimage of the Israelites* in the Gemäldegalerie at Dresden.[1] Datable to the mid-1570's by virtue of its combination of Francesco's execution and Jacopo's ideas, the Dresden picture is a prime example of its type. Except in quality (see below), its figures, animals, and vessels are duplicated in the Marquette canvas. The landscapes, however, are distinctly different, with the Marquette picture substituting a few spindly trees for the dense foliage that rises at left and right to the top of the Dresden version, and blurring the definition of the background tents. Since the execution of foliage would not have been taxing, and since the result of the changes is to endow the landscape with a bleakness appropriate to the subject, one suspects that the source for the Marquette composition was an autograph variant of the picture in Dresden.

Works of this sort were turned out in quantity by the Bassani, and, it should be noted, a lack of specificity in the literature devoted to them has created unnecessary confusion. Thus the generic title *Israelites in the Desert* might also designate *Moses Striking Water from the Rock*.[2]

Wind's analysis of the qualitative gulf that separates the Dresden and Milwaukee canvases is likewise perceptive. The copyist muddled the spatial relationships, distorted the relative proportions of the figures, sloughed over details, and reduced Francesco Bassano's free and impasto-laden brush to patchiness and angularity. And it is unlikely that the color, even in its pristine state, had the glow of the original. Was, then, the Marquette painting done by a member of the Bassano studio? Unfortunately, its early history is unknown. The claim (memo in the Registrar's files) that the picture was with Lord Yarborough in 1835 has not been verified; it is not mentioned by William Buchanan,[3] nor in the lists of Lord Yarborough's holdings compiled by Gustav Waagen.[4] Conceivably it was one of the works that Waagen had in mind when he wrote: "Other names of good masters appeared to me not to be borne out by the pictures."[5] Furthermore, it has been impossible to judge the quality of the Marquette example against a repetition of the Dresden composition assigned to Francesco Bassano and his workshop in the Fabre Repetto collection at Genoa.[6] In spite of these uncertainties, it seems probable that the present version was produced independently of the Bassano shop, perhaps, as Brejon (report cited) speculates, as late as the eighteenth century.

Still, the *Exodus of Moses and the Israelites* is a lively and inherently interesting picture whose attractiveness would be enhanced by restoration. In view, too, of the issues that it raises, it is an effective study picture that speaks in part to the mission of a university art museum.

R.W.B.

Notes:
1. E. Arslan, *I Bassano* (Milan, 1960), I:186, 216, and II: fig. 210.
2. E.g., Arslan, *I Bassano*, I:225–226; Vienna, Kunsthistorische Sammlung, *Die Gemäldegalerie* (Vienna, 1907), no. 285, 67, and *God Showing to Abraham the Promised Land*, also called the *Departure for Canaan*; e.g., Arslan, *I Bassano*, II: fig. 209.
3. William Buchanan, *Memoirs of Painting*, 2 vols. (London, 1824).
4. Gustav Waagen, *Works of Art and Artists in England* (London, 1838), II: 394–395; *Treasures of Art in Great Britain* (London, 1854), II:86–97; *Galleries and Cabinets of Art in Great Britain* (London, 1857), 64–71, 501–506.
5. Waagen, *Treasures of Art in Great Britain*, 87 n.
6. Arslan, *I Bassano*, I:218, without photograph and bibliography.

UNKNOWN ARTIST
North Italian School (?), Early Sixteenth Century

The Nativity of Christ   (58.7)

Oil on panel, 57 1/8 x 30 3/4 in. (145.1 x 78.1 cm). Unsigned.

Provenance: Collection Duke of Devonshire (?); Lord Northwick (?);[1] Mr. and Mrs. Marc B. Rojtman, Milwaukee; their gift to the University, 1958.

References:
Pick, *Marquette University Art Collection*, 11, 13 (ill.), as by Pier Francesco Fiorentino.

Burton Fredericksen and Federico Zeri, *Census of Pre-Nineteenth-Century Italian Paintings in North American Public Collections* (Cambridge, Mass., 1972), 234, as North Italian, sixteenth century.

J. Patrice Marandel, verbally (1976), as North Italian or South German.

Ian Kennedy, verbally (1981), as possibly Neapolitan School, early sixteenth century.

Keith Christiansen, verbally (1983), as possibly Genoese, early sixteenth century.

This large painting of the Nativity is set out-of-doors beneath the arches of Roman ruins.[2] The Virgin kneels in adoration of the Christ Child, who lies on a cloth atop Joseph's sack. Joseph gestures in awe at the (here rather diminutive) Child, whose miraculous birth he has just witnessed. In the middle distance appear the traditional ox and donkey, while in the background the Annunciation to the Shepherds is represented—an event described by Luke:

> And there were in the same country shepherds abiding in the field, keeping watch over their flock by night. And, lo, the angel of the Lord came upon them, and the glory of the Lord shone round about them: and they were sore afraid. And the angel said unto them, Fear not: for behold, I bring you good tidings of great joy, which shall be to all people. For unto you is born this day in the city of David a Saviour, which is Christ the Lord (Luke 2:8–11).

The Marquette *Nativity* was no doubt painted as a church altarpiece, but the identity and even the nationality of the responsible artist have so far proved elusive. The composition is a fairly conventional variation of fifteenth-century Italian types, but the figure style, which seems generally consistent with a somewhat later date, cannot be firmly associated with any particular artist or region. This apparent chronological discrepancy suggests that the artist was active in the early sixteenth century, but in a provincial (at least in an artistic sense) area.

The proposals that the painting may be either Genoese or Neapolitan signal the picture's affinity

real), *Adoration of the Shepherds* (Cathedral, Valencia), the destroyed retable from the church of Gandia, and the *Adoration* altarpiece in Barcelona (Despujol Collection).[5] Although an attribution to this artist cannot be justified, these idiosyncrasies and general traits may point to the identity of the Marquette artist among the lesser-known artists in Paolo's circle.[6]

R.B.S.

Notes:
1. The reverse of the panel is inscribed in a late nineteenth-century hand, "from the Devonshire Collection and Lord Northwick's." However, the picture is not identifiable in catalogues and descriptions of those collections—including the noted Lord Northwick sale at Thirlestane House, Cheltenham (Phillips, 26f. July, 1859, and April 10, 1860); see George Redford, *Art Sales* (London, 1888), I:155-157.
2. On the Nativity subject see Marquette's painting after Sebastiano Mainardi (59.4).
3. Compare, for example, the *Adoration of the Kings* (Glasgow Art Gallery) by the Neapolitan artist termed by Zeri the Master of the Glasgow Adoration, for which see Federico Zeri, "Two Early Cinquecento Problems in South Italy," *Burlington Magazine* XCVI (May 1954):147-150.
4. On Paolo da San Leocadio, see Chandler Rathfon Post, *A History of Spanish Painting* (Cambridge, Mass., 1953), XI:8f.; Adele Condorelli, "Paolo da San Leocadio," *Commentari* XIV (1963):134-150, 246-253; and J. M. Doñate Sebastía, *Los Retablos de Pablo de Santo Leocadio en Vallarreal de los Infantes* (Castellón de la Plana, 1958).
5. Illustrated in Post, *A History of Spanish Painting*, figs. 3, 4, 5, 6, 7; Condorelli, "Paolo da San Leocadio," 12-14, 18-22.
6. Interesting analogies may as well be seen in the works of the Portuguese painter Vasco Fernandes (c. 1480-1543); cf. his *Creation of the Animals and Pentecost* (exh. *Arts of Portugal*) (London, 1955/6), nos. 150, 153.

The Nativity of Christ, North Italian School (?), Early Sixteenth Century, oil on panel

with Spanish, and particularly Valencian, paintings of the time.[3] However, here too no convincing attribution has been forthcoming. The works of Paolo da San Leocadio, an Emilian painter active in Valencia from the 1470s, do provide an interesting parallel and seem stylistically related to the Marquette picture.[4] One might note the smooth, planar handling of figural forms; broad folds of drapery; stiff and awkward gesturing; and quaint but simplistic architectural backgrounds in such works of Paolo's as the *Dormition of Sta. Clara* (Diocesan Museum, Valencia), *Bulls Bringing the Body of St. James to Queen Lupa* (Church of Santiago, Villa-

JUAN CORREA DE VIVAR

Spanish (act. 1539-1562)

Juan Correa de Vivar was one of the most prominent painters in sixteenth-century Castile, yet so little is known about him that until recently there had even been some question about his true name.[1] Documents place the artist in Toledo at various times between 1539 and 1552. He is recorded as having executed a retable for the church at Mondéjar in Guadalajara in 1556 and is noted again in Toledo in 1561.

Two principal cycles form the basis of our knowledge of the artist's work: a group of paintings from the Hieronymite monastery of Guisando and a series once in the Cistercian monastery of San Martín de Valdeiglesias. Both of these entered the collections of the Museo del Prado in Madrid but are now dispersed among that institution and other provincial museums in Spain.

Correa's style is characterized by broad, cleanly defined forms; simple, legible compositional organiza-

15

tion; and a rich tonality perhaps derived from contemporary Italian painters. He would seem to have been a student, or at least a strong admirer, of Juan de Borgoña, whose works are stylistically close to his.[2] Both are associated with the *foco toledano*, a group of artists active in mid-sixteenth-century Toledo who drew inspiration from both Flemish and Italian sources.

The Lamentation of Mary over the Body of Christ with Angels Holding the Symbols of the Passion, Juan Correa de Vivar, oil on panel

The Lamentation of Mary over the Body of Christ with Angels Holding the Symbols of the Passion (58.5)

Oil on panel, 56 1/2 x 47 in (143.5 x 119.2 cm). Unsigned.

Provenance: Collection of Mr. and Mrs. Marc B. Rojtman; their gift to the University, 1958.

References:
Chandler Rathfon Post, *A History of Spanish Painting* (Cambridge, Mass., 1947), IX, 1:331, fig. 108, as stylistically between Juan de Borgoña and Juan Correa de Vivar, but closer to the latter.

W. Th. Kloek, in a letter (1979), as in the circle of Pieter Coecke van Aelst.

Ian Kennedy, verbally (1981), as Spanish, early sixteenth century.

This imposing work, which surely served as an altarpiece, represents Mary grieving over the prostrate body of Christ. He lies on a shroud in the foreground, having recently been removed from the cross (seen in the middle background), which is flanked by those still holding the two thieves. The open sepulcher can be seen at the extreme right, and in the distance at left the city of Jerusalem, rather fantastically rendered, appears. Angels hover overhead carrying the *Arma Christi*, the symbols of the Passion.[3] In addition to the crown of thorns and the nails of the Crucifixion, which lie here at Christ's feet, these include the column of the flagellation and the calipers that removed the nails (at the left) and the lance, rod with sponge, hammer, whip, and bucket for the vinegar (on the right).

The scene is reminiscent of Northern representations of the Lamentation, although stronger analogies are to be found with the Antwerp Mannerists than with Pieter Coecke van Aelst, to whom the present picture has been traditionally ascribed.[4] The attribution to Correa de Vivar, in any case, seems relatively assured given the strikingly similar treatments of the subject and of individual figures in the San Martín de Valdeiglesias cycle. Correa's *Lamentation* (Prado, Madrid) is a more fully populated composition, but one that presents clear analogies both in the picture as a whole and in individual aspects (such as Christ's countenance and posture).

The strongest bonds to Correa's work, however, are to be found in two representations of the Crucifixion, both thought to be chronologically later than the monastic cycles.[5] One of these remains *in situ*, in the Chapel of Sta. Catalina of the Church of San Salvador in Toledo; the other is now in the cathedral of Włocławek in Poland.[6] In these the combination of Flemish and Italianate sources—in composition, iconography, color, landscape treatment, and physical type—recalls that of the Marquette *Lamentation*. The figure of the crucified Christ and that of the grieving Mary in both the Crucifixion scenes are particularly close to their counterparts in the *Lamentation*. Other comparable details—for example, the fantastic architecture seen in the distance and the dramatic rendering of the darkened midday sky—underscore the stylistic association, which suggests that the three altarpieces are roughly contemporary works, probably from the 1550s, by Correa de Vivar.[7] As such, the Marquette *Lamentation* is an important addition to this artist's infrequently encountered corpus.[8]

R. B. S.

Notes:
1. He has been mistakenly called Diego; see Post, *History of Spanish Painting*, IX, 1, 302f. In addition to Post see on Correa de Vivar, José M. Gomez-Minor, "Juan Correa de Vivar; algunos Datos Documentales sobre su vida y su obra," *Archivio Españo! de Arte* XXXIX, no. 156 (1966): 291–303.
2. On Juan de Borgoña, see D. Angulo Iñiguez, *Juan de Borgoña* (Madrid, 1954).

3. On the *Arma Christi*, see Gertrud Schiller, *Iconography of Christian Art* (Greenwich, Conn., 1972), II:164f.
4. Cf., for example, the *Lamentation* by the Master of the Antwerp Adoration (Art Market, Vienna); ill. Max J. Friedländer, *Early Netherlandish Painting* (New York-Washington, 1975), XI: no. 48, plate 51 (reversed), and *Apollo*, CXIX (March 1984):17 (advt.). Cf. as well Juan de Borgoña *Lamentation* in the parish church at Illescas. Although the Marquette painting is, strictly speaking, a Lamentation rather than a Pietà (in which Christ lies across Mary's lap), it would seem likely that the artist had knowledge of, and was to some degree responding to, Michelangelo's famed marble *Pietà* (Vatican) of 1497.
5. See Anna Dobrzycka, "Juan Correa de Vivar z Wloctawskiej Katedry," *Studia Muzealne* VIII (1970): 18–27.
6. The Toledo *Crucifixion* was first anonymously attributed to Correa in 1901 [*Boletín de la Sociedad Española de Excursiones IX* (1901):173]. August Mayer [*Geschichte der Spanischen Malerei* (Leipzig, 1922), 165] concurred, noting the Italianate qualities. Post (Post, *History of Spanish Painting*, 314, fig 96), however, hesitated, suggesting the work as either by Correa or Francisco de Comontes. With the publication of the *Crucifixion* in Wloc-
lawek, it now seems evident that these three works are from the same hand.
7. The Christ type appears as well in Correa's *Crowning of Thorns* (Prado, Madrid) from the Valdeiglesias cycle.
8. For a *Lamentation* attributed to Correa, but not by him, see Julius S. Held, *Museo de Arte de Ponce: Catalogue I: Paintings of the European and American Schools* (Ponce, 1965), 41–42.

Adoration of the Magi, Veneto-Byzantine School, Sixteenth Century, tempera on panel

UNKNOWN ARTIST

Veneto-Byzantine School, Sixteenth Century

The Adoration of the Magi   (84.7.2)

Tempera on panel, 29 x 40 in. (73.7 x 101.6 cm). Unsigned.

Provenance: Collection of the Rojtman Foundation; gift of the Foundation to the University, 1984.

This brilliantly colored panel is a superb example of late Italianate Byzantine painting. It is traditional in composition but atypically Western in the rendering of forms, space, light, and scale. This strange amalgam suggests that the picture might have been painted by one of the "madonneri," painters in the Byzantine style (predominantly of Madonnas) active in Venice throughout the Renaissance. Very few of these artists are known by name and of these, hardly any information survives. It is not known, for example, in what century lived Andrea Rico da Candia, whose signed *Madonna and Child* in the Uffizi Gallery (Florence) bears some stylistic affinity with the Marquette *Adoration.*[1]

The composition of the painting seems derived if not copied from some earlier source. The general format is reminiscent of Lorenzo Monaco's *Adoration of the Magi* (Uffizi, Florence) of c. 1420, while the landscape background with its buildings, mountains, and lake scene recalls Venetian paintings of the late fifteenth century.[2] The author of the Marquette *Adoration,* working in a clearly *retardataire* if not anachronistic style for an evidently conservative audience, may still

have based his composition on a more modern, though still unidentified, source. A roughly contemporary painting by one of the "madonneri," a *Man of Sorrows* in the Musée d'Art et d'Histoire of Geneva, is a "Byzantinized" copy of a picture by Giovanni Bellini of about 1495.[3].

The Adoration of the Magi, the three Wise Men, is briefly told in the second chapter of the Gospel of Matthew (2:9-12). The Wise Men followed the miraculous star to Jerusalem, from where they were directed to Bethlehem by Herod.

> When they had heard the king, they departed; and, lo, the star, which they saw in the east, went before them, till it came and stood over where the young child was. When they saw the star, they rejoiced with exceeding great joy.
> And when they were come into the house, they saw the young child with Mary his mother, and fell down, and worshipped him: and when they had opened their treasures, they presented unto him gifts; gold, and frankincense, and myrrh.

The Wise Men are usually represented as kings, an association derived from a passage in Psalm 72:

> The kings of Tarshish and of the isles shall bring presents: the kings of Sheba and Seba shall offer gifts. Yea, all kings shall fall down before him: all nations shall serve him (Psalm 72:10–11).

17

As in most representations of the Adoration of the Magi the kings are shown to be of three distinct ages—elderly, middle-aged, and youthful. They appear twice in the painting: in the foreground, where they present their gifts to Christ, and in the right middle ground, where they are seen on horseback. The latter representation depicts their journey to Bethlehem as they point to and follow the star that appears directly over Christ's head. They hold their gifts and are accompanied by camels and exotically capped servants, the same figures that appear in the center holding the horses of the Magi.

An ox and a donkey appear behind the Virgin, as they often do in Nativity scenes;[4] Joseph sits in the lower left corner. One aspect of the composition that is iconographically at variance with traditional icon painting is the setting of the manger in a cave. This motif appears in the apocryphal Infancy Gospel and was popular throughout the Middle Ages and Renaissance.[5]   R. B. S.

Notes:
1. *Gli Uffizi; Catalogo Generale* (Florence, 1979), no. P75 (ill.).
2. Gertrud Schiller, *Iconography of Christian Art*, J. Seligman, trans. (Greenwich, 1971), I: plate 293. Compare, for example, Carpaccio's *Nativity* of 1508 in the Gulbenkian Museum of Lisbon [ill. Bernard Berenson, *Italian Pictures of the Renaissance: Venetian School* (London, 1968), I: plate 431].
3. See Mauro Natale, *Peintures Italiennes du XIVᵉ au XVIIIᵉ Siècle; Musée d'Art et d'Histoire* (Geneva, 1979), 15, no. 14, plate 11.
4. Compare the *Nativity* after Sebastiano Mainardi in the Marquette collection (acc. no. 59.3).
5. *The Evangelium of Pseudo-Matthew* or *The First Gospel of the Infancy of Christ*; see *The Lost Books of the Bible* (New York, 1926), 38–39.

SEVENTEENTH CENTURY

UNKNOWN ARTIST

Byzantine School, Seventeenth Century

Scenes from the Life of St. Elias (The Prophet Elijah)   (84.7.3)

Tempera and oil on panel, 50 x 38 in. (127 x 96.5 cm). Inscribed in Greek in the upper center: "Holy Prophet Elias."

Provenance: Collection of the Rojtman Foundation; gift of the Foundation to the University, 1984.

This unusually large icon represents St. Elias, or, as he is more commonly known from his Old Testament name, Elijah. He dominates the central scene, which depicts him seated in a cave as ravens bring him sustenance. Above and below, six events from the Saint's life are represented in subsidiary fields.

Elias is the most important of the Old Testament saints in the theology of the Eastern Orthodox Church.[1] Both as a type or precursor of Christ and as a holy figure in his own right, Elias has been the subject of devotion and, in the visual form of icons, veneration.

The story of Elijah is recounted in the first and second books of Kings.[2] A great drought was prophesied to the wicked King Ahab by Elijah, whom God commanded to hide by the brook Cherith. There "... the ravens brought him bread and flesh in the morning, and bread and flesh in the evening; and he drank of the brook" (I Kings 17:6). This is the subject of the principal field as ravens, traditionally the most rapacious of birds, are seen depositing food in a little basket that conveniently hangs at the entrance to Elijah's cave. The flowing brook at the lower right, out of which a bird drinks, is banked by luxuriant trees that stand in contrast with the arid and barren landscape depicted in the left background. Elijah holds a scroll on which his words are inscribed in Greek: "... I have been very jealous for the Lord God of hosts: because the children of Israel have forsaken thy covenant, thrown down thine altars, and slain thy prophets with the sword" (I Kings 19:14).

The icon of Elijah was a popular image throughout the Orthodox Church, in part because of its illustration of God's implicit control of natural phenomena—here, most obviously, the ravenous birds and the flowing brook.[3] Marquette's painting, although particularly

Scenes from the Life of St. Elias (The Prophet Elijah), Byzantine School, Seventeenth Century, tempera and oil on panel

large for an icon, is traditional in composition. Elijah is seated *a vate* in the traditional pose of the inspired prophet or poet.[4] Although Elijah is depicted contemplating the miracle of his nourishment, his placement in a cave alludes as well to God's calling of the Prophet as he dwelled in a cave on Mount Horeb—the occasion for Elijah's words inscribed on the scroll in the painting (I Kings 19:9-14).

The six panels depict subsequent events in the life of the Prophet.[5] At the top left the seated Elijah asks for food from the widow of Zarephath (I Kings 17:9-16).[6] The second scene shows Elijah curing through his prayer the sick child of the widow (I Kings 17:17-24). The third depicts the fiery acceptance of Elijah's sacrifice (I Kings 18:22-39). At the bottom left an angel succors the sleeping Prophet (I Kings 19:4-8). In the center Elijah, accompanied by his disciple Elisha, divides the waters of the Jordan with his mantle (II Kings 2:7-8). The last panel shows the ascent of the Prophet in his chariot of fire as Elisha receives his mantle below (II Kings 2:11-13).

By its size the Marquette *Elias* would seem to have been an altarpiece—presumably, considering the inscriptions, within a Greek Orthodox church. Its precise origin, however, is difficult to determine in light of the wide diffusion, in time as well as place, of traditional icon painting. However, the introduction of rational perspective in the landscapes and the naturalistic treatment of the birds, trees, and subsidiary figures throughout—qualities foreign to the strict Byzantine style—suggest a source at least slightly familiar with Western artistic conventions. A date for the painting in the seventeenth century seems most plausible because of these relatively modern variations and the evident age of the panel.

R. B. S.

Notes:
1. I am grateful to Brother Gregory of the Monastery of the Annunciation, Tuxedo Park, N.Y., for discussing the iconography and theology of Elias with me.
2. In the Third and Fourth books in those editions of the Bible that count the two books of Samuel among the books of Kings.
3. See Leonid Ouspensky and Vladimir Lossky, *The Meaning of Icons* (Boston, 1969), 142-145.
4. A fascinating Renaissance interpretation of Elijah's iconic posture is to be found in Giovanni Girolamo Savoldo's *Elijah Fed by the Raven* in the National Gallery of Art, Washington (no. 1397); this work preserves the Byzantine composition while presenting the Prophet in the current sixteenth-century idiom. See Fern Rusk Shapley, *Catalogue of the Italian Paintings; National Gallery of Art* (Washington, 1979), I:418-419; II: plate 299.
5. A Greek iconographer's manual published by Didron as the "Byzantine Guide to Painting" contains the essential details of these scenes; see Adolphe Napoleon Didron, *Christian Iconography; The History of Christian Art in the Middle Ages*, E.J. Millington, trans. (New York, 1886), II:28-82.
6. Compare the sixteenth-century Flemish depiction of the scene in Marquette's *Story of Elijah*, attributed to Anthuenis Claeissens (acc. no. 60.3).

JOHANNES VAN DER BENT

Dutch (c. 1650-1690)

According to Houbraken, van der Bent studied painting with Philips Wouwerman and Adriaen van de Velde; he remained unmarried and lived in a house among some peculiar men or foreigners ("vreemde menschen").[1] By unknown means, perhaps through inheritance, van der Bent came into the possession of a small fortune, which, living as he did, brought him nothing but trouble. Suspicious of his associates and nervous in his dwelling, he died of consumption at about the age of forty.

Wooded Landscape with Figures, Johannes van der Bent, oil on canvas

Wooded Landscape with Figures (63.19)

Oil on canvas, 23 1/2 x 32 1/8 in. (59.7 x 81.6 cm). Unsigned.

Provenance: Collection of Mrs. George Raab; her gift to the University, 1963.
References:
Pick, *Marquette University Art Collection*, (1964), 27.

Unsigned, this Italianate landscape has been traditionally attributed to van der Bent.[2] Depictions of travelers and shepherds in wooded landscapes were painted fairly often by this artist. Typical of his work are the horizon broken with a prominently placed tree and the dynamic sky.[3]

A. G.

Notes:
1. Arnold Houbraken, *De Groote Schouburgh der Nederlantsche Konstschilders en Schilderessen*, The Hague (1718-1722), 3:288-290. See further E. W. Moes in Ulrich Thieme and Felix Becker, *Allgemeines Lexikon der bildenden Künstler von der Antike bis zur Gegenwart* (Leipzig, 1907-1950), 3:352; and Walther Bernt, *The Netherlandish Painters of the Seventeenth Century* (London, 1970), 1:9 and plates 79 and 80.

2. Probably correct, this attribution has been supported by J. Patrice Marandel and Otto Naumann (notes, files).
3. Compare to the *Italian Mountain Landscape with Waterfall, Sheep and Cattle*, in Budapest, Museum of Fine Arts, ill. in Bernt, *Netherlandish Painters*, plate 79.

LEONARD BRAMER

Dutch (1595-1674)

Often placed among the artists of the Rembrandt circle, Bramer may be more properly considered a somewhat independent painter having a certain affinity in style and subject matter to Rembrandt, but with an artistic formation and style independent of him. In 1614 Bramer traveled to Italy, stopping in France on the way; only in 1628 did he return north and settle in Delft, where he entered the Guild of St. Luke the following year and was elected its governor five times between 1654 and 1665. His stay in Rome was decisive for the development of his style. There his admiration for Elsheimer's meticulous, small-scale narratives apparently inspired Bramer to paint similar works. Moreover, his contact with Gerrit van Honthorst seems reflected in Bramer's dark interiors animated with flickering luminous strokes.[1]

Famous in the seventeenth century for his wall paintings in various Dutch palaces and public buildings, Bramer was keenly interested in architectural decoration. However, few of his wall paintings have survived, and this aspect of his work may be studied in his drawings.[2] Today Bramer is best known for his drawn illustrations to various literary works, and for his paintings, which frequently depict biblical and literary subjects in small scale, with highly contrasting lights and darks. These paintings, often on copper, were especially admired by the Dutch biographer Houbraken, who praised both their invention and spirited style.[3]

Discovery of Deuteronomy, Attributed to Leonard Bramer, oil on panel

20

ATTRIBUTED TO LEONARD BRAMER
Discovery of Deuteronomy (81.36)

Oil on panel, 14 1/2 x 19 1/2 in. (36.8 x 49.5 cm). Inscribed on base of throne: "2 REGUM 22/CAP VERS 8/IOSIAS."

Provenance: Collection of Count Alexis Bobrinsky; Sotheby, May 21, 1971, no. 67; Mr. and Mrs. Eckhart G. Grohmann; their gift to the University, 1981.

References:
Alfred Bader, *The Bible Through Dutch Eyes*, catalogue of an exhibition at the Milwaukee Art Museum (Milwaukee, 1976), 122, no. 56 (ill.), as Bramer.

Jane Goldsmith, verbally, (1983), as appearing to be a copy after Bramer.

Julius S. Held, in a letter (1983), as appearing to be a copy after Bramer.

George Keyes, verbally (1984), as in the style of Bramer.

For this image of an obscure subject, Bramer appears to have been directly inspired by the biblical text.[4] Without the inscription, which labels the painting as the presentation of the book of Deuteronomy to King Josiah, the episode represented would be difficult indeed to identify. In any case, this rarely illustrated scene has its source in the Second Book of Kings, Chapter 22, verses 8-11, where it is related how, during repairs to the temple in Jerusalem, workmen discovered the scroll of Deuteronomy, and how Hilkiah, the high priest, told Shaphan, his secretary, that he has found the book of the law in the temple; Hilkiah gave the book to Shaphan, who read it before the King.

In Bramer's composition, Josiah wears a crown and wields a scepter as attributes of his kingship; his throne, too, signifies his office. His concentration is focused upon the kneeling figure before the throne; this figure turns the page of a folio volume resting upon a lectern. The high hat may identify him as a priest or one who fulfills a priestly role. A regally dressed figure stands to the right, and four others kneel at the left. The sparsely furnished setting is nonetheless clearly palatial.

While sophisticated in conception and strongly reminiscent of Bramer's lively pictorial style, the Marquette picture seems somewhat atypical of the artist's documented works, generally characterized by stronger draftsmanship and thicker highlights. These qualities might suggest an attribution of the *Discovery of Deuteronomy* to an associate or a student of Bramer's, one perhaps working from a design by the master.[5] Such a suggestion, however, must remain tentative; further research, it is hoped, will clarify Bramer's artistic career and the position of this painting within it. Another version of this rarely depicted subject, one closer to Bramer's usual style, was in the Janssen collection of Brussels in 1923;[6] that work, however, presents notable compositional variations from the Marquette picture.

Bramer's predilection for unusual subjects parallels that of the group of artists called the Pre-Rembrandtists. Foremost among these is Pieter Lastman (c. 1583–1633), one of the teachers of Rembrandt.[7] Frequently inspired by textual sources, as well as by pictorial tradition, Lastman and the other Pre-Rembrandtists painted narrative history pictures with a rigorously literal approach. Bramer, while not actually belonging socially or stylistically to this group, nonetheless shares its serious consideration of the written word; he often seems to have been more inspired by textual sources than by pictorial precedent. The *Discovery of Deuteronomy* may well have been prompted by Bramer's keen reading of the biblical text.

A. G.

Notes:

1. The basic monograph about Bramer is still H. Wichmann, *Leonaert Bramer* (Leipzig, 1923). See further Susan Donohue Kuretsky, in *Gods, Saints and Heroes: Dutch Painting in the Age of Rembrandt*, catalogue of an exhibition at the National Gallery of Art (Washington, 1980), 258, and Jane ten Brink Goldsmith, "From Prose to Pictures: Leonaert Bramer's Illustrations for the 'Aeneid' and Vondel's Translation of Vergil," *Art History* (1984), 7:21–37.
2. For example, see *Musicians on a Balcony*, Philadelphia Museum of Art, illustrated in Arthur Wheelock, Jr., *Vermeer* (New York, 1981), 16, fig. 8.
3. Arnold Houbraken, *De Groote Schouburgh der Nederlantsche Konstschilders en Schilderessen* (The Hague, 1718), I:164.
4. Alfred Bader, *The Bible Through Dutch Eyes*, catalogue of an exhibition at the Milwaukee Art Museum (Milwaukee, 1976), 122, emphasized the work's relationship to the biblical narrative.
5. Jane Goldsmith (communication 1983) and Julius S. Held (correspondence 1983) concur that the panel appears to be a copy after Bramer.
6. W. Martin, *Catalogue de la collection de peintures du Baron Janssen à Bruxelles* (Brussels and Paris, 1923), 10, cat. no. 7, *Scène biblique*; this painting was mentioned as *Herod and the Scribes* by Wichmann, *Bramer*, cat. no. 95.
7. For the Pre-Rembrandtist artists, see Astrid Tümpel and Christian Tümpel, *The Pre-Rembrandtists*, catalogue of an exhibition at the E. B. Crocker Art Gallery (Sacramento, 1974); for the conception of iconography and narrative in the work of these artists, see especially 127–147.

DANIEL MYTENS

Dutch (c. 1590–1647)

Daniel Mytens was Dutch, born in Delft, but he is almost always considered a British artist.[1] The year of his birth is not known, but his entry into the painters' guild of The Hague in 1610 suggests that he was born around 1590. By 1618 he was in London, where he received the patronage of the Earl of Arundel. Mytens was subsequently granted royal commissions, his first payment for work for the Crown coming in 1620; in 1624 James I awarded him £25 and an annual life pension of £50 for his "good service." The following year he received the title of official painter to Charles I. Mytens was well patronized in England until about 1634, when he returned to Holland; he died in 1647.

Portrait of a Man, possibly Edward, 2nd Viscount Conway, Follower of Daniel Mytens, oil on canvas

FOLLOWER OF DANIEL MYTENS
Portrait of a Man, possibly Edward, 2nd Viscount Conway (60.7)

Oil on canvas, 26 1/16 x 22 1/4 in. (66.2 x 56.5 cm). Inscribed upper right quadrant: "AEta: Sua:41/1656"[?].

Provenance: Collection of Mr. I. A. Dinerstein, Milwaukee; his gift to the University, 1960.

References:
Pick, *Marquette University Art Collection*, 20, 21 (ill.), as Daniel Mytens, a portrait of Edward, Earl of Conway.

Ian Kennedy, verbally (1981), as School of Mytens.

Malcolm Rogers, in a letter (1984), as British, mid-1630s, possibly a portrait of Edward, 2nd Viscount Conway.

This portrait of a man has traditionally been ascribed to Daniel Mytens. However, the presence of an inscription with the date 1656 (nine years after the artist's demise) seems to cast doubt on the accuracy of the attribution. The inscription is, however, only imperfectly preserved and may have been altered during an old restoration; the style of the dress and collar suggests a date in the mid-1630s, and a date of 1636 may thus be proposed. In any case the portrait would not seem to be by Mytens himself, but rather by a close follower.

The subject is elegantly attired in an embroidered dress topped with an ornate lace collar. He is seen through a fictive oval frame, painted in perspective to create an illusion of distance between the subject and viewer. His hair and beard are stylish but well manicured, even though the artist has taken pains to record an errant lock of hair. In format and style the portrait is very typical of its time, but with an individuality conveyed by the quiet self-assurance and intriguing half-smile of the subject.

The subject had been thought to represent Edward, Earl of Conway; however, his dates (c. 1623–1683) unsettle that assertion. More probably it is his father, Edward, 2nd Viscount Conway (1594–1655), who is portrayed. There is some similarity to the elder Viscount Conway's known portrait types, and the proposed date of 1636 would accord well with the inscription (which states that the subject was forty-one years of age when the portrait was painted.).[2]

R. B. S.

Notes:
1. On Mytens, see C. H. Collins Baker, *Lely and the Stuart Portrait Painters* (London, 1912).
2. M. Rogers (see references).

UNKNOWN ARTIST

Dutch, Seventeenth Century

St. Jerome   (64.33)

Oil on panel, 9 1/4 x 8 1/8 in. (23.5 x 20.6 cm). Unsigned.

Provenance: Collection of Mrs. William P. Hayes; her gift to the University, 1964.

This diminutive panel shows St. Jerome as he appears to hearken to a voice emanating from the upper left and as he writes with quill pen upon a large sheet propped against a tablet. His desk—a stone slab—is strewn with inkpot, skull, crucifix, and stone. Thus, he is here represented as both penitent, bared to the waist and with stone nearby, and scholar, engaged in writing.

In Renaissance and Baroque art, Jerome was most frequently depicted as either a penitent, a scholar in his study, or a Church Doctor in cardinal's robes. Dür-

er's well-known engraving *St. Jerome in His Study* of 1514 (see checklist entry p. 00) established an oft-imitated standard for representing the Saint as a learned hermit surrounded by the attributes of the office of cardinal. Although Jerome was never made a cardinal, since the office had not yet been established, he is often represented as one since he held an appointment under Pope Damasus I.[1] Images of St. Jerome were immensely popular during the Renaissance and Baroque periods, serving in part as emblems of two aspects of civilized life: piety and scholarship.

Jerome (c. 340–420) apparently received his sainthood not merely because of his own sanctity but in recognition of service rendered to the Church. After many travels, from his native Dalmatia to Italy and throughout the Mediterranean, Jerome adopted the life of a hermit. Ambitious to become a scholar of the Scriptures, he journeyed to Palestine. There, "with only the scorpions and wild beasts for company," he studied Hebrew. Eventually he settled in a monastery in Bethlehem, where he translated the Old and New Testaments from Hebrew into Latin. The value of Jerome's translation cannot be overestimated, for it became the authorized text from which all other versions were made.

Although this panel of St. Jerome as penitent and scholar entered the Marquette collection as by Adriaen van der Werff, such an attribution seems unlikely.[2] The Saint's angular and foreshortened figure is foreign

St. Jerome, Dutch, Seventeenth Century, oil on panel

to van der Werff's elegantly classical forms and may be compared to depictions of the Saint by various Dutch painters. Similar compositions of St. Jerome by Dutch artists include representations by Willem Key (Munich, Alte Pinakothek), attributed to Hendrick Bloemaert (Oslo, National Gallery of Art), and by E. van der Maes (Rotterdam, Museum Boymans-van Beuningen). The sensitively rendered aging body of the Saint and the sharp contrast between the illuminated and the darkened portions of the panel seem to indicate an attribution to an artist who was familiar with the achievements of the Dutch Caravaggisti, yet active some years later.

A. G.

Notes:
1. For a discussion of the representation of St. Jerome, see James Hall, *Dictionary of Subjects and Symbols in Art* (New York, 1974), 168–169.
2. This traditional attribution to Adriaen van der Werff has been questioned by Julius S. Held in a letter (1983) and Barbara Gaehtgens in a letter (1984).

PHILIPS WOUWERMAN

Dutch (1619–1668)

During a working career of little more than thirty years, Philips Wouwerman produced well over one thousand paintings, while simultaneously supplying figures for landscapists Jan Wijnants, Jacob van Ruisdael, and Cornelis Decker. Obviously an artist of great facility (but surprisingly patient, unimpetuous), Wouwerman, like so many of his contemporaries in Dutch art, was also a specialist. Except for a very limited number of landscapes in which the human activity is religious, mythological, or historical in import, and a handful of portraits, Philips's efforts were devoted to small panels and canvases depicting genre scenes set within the natural world: peasants, soldiers, and the higher classes, engaged in such activities as working, fighting, hunting, relaxing, attending fairs, traveling (and suffering the attacks of bandits), training horses, and the like—and all as if actually observed.

The biography of this prolific master is disappointingly problematic. He was born at Haarlem, in the Northern Netherlands, on May 24, 1619, to be followed by his brothers Pieter (1623–1682) and Jan (1629–1666), who likewise became painters. While it may be supposed that Philips received his initial training from his father, Paulus Joosten Wouwerman, there is no decisive documentation to support the traditional claims that he then studied under the famous Haarlem portraitist Frans Hals and subsequently with Pieter Cornelisz Verbeeck, a specialist in the representation of

horses. His student years may have been behind him when in 1638 he turned up in Hamburg with the artist Evert Decker, and surely by 1640 when, back home, he met with the authorities of the painters' guild (for which he served as commissary in 1645). Nothing else is known of his travels; it has been conjectured, on the basis of certain activities and motifs within his pictures, that Wouwerman journeyed to the borders of Holland and visited France and Italy.

Since pictures by Wouwerman that bear dates or are datable by other unimpeachable evidence are also extremely rare, an exact chronology of his development cannot be charted. His early manner, inspired in part by the art of Pieter van Laer and the *Bamboccianti* (see the catalogue entry that follows), tends to emphasize a limited number of figures, generally common folk, in a relatively restricted space and enveloped in a brownish tonality suggestive of evening. As the number of figures was multiplied and hence the compositions became more complex, the landscapes increased in breadth and recession. Along the way the tonality lightened and the paintings assumed that attractive coloration (rich local colors for the figures, lush green foliage, blues for the distances and skies) for which Wouwerman is known. With greater artistic sophistication went a particular taste for episodes involving the well-to-do. Always Wouwerman had a sharp eye for lively incident and for the look and feel of nature, its light, its atmosphere, its vitality.

Philips Wouwerman was buried in Haarlem on May 23, 1668, leaving behind a number of students and imitators, some of whom carried elements of the master's style into the eighteenth century. And, of course, he left the legacy of his enormous output, much to the enrichment of collections and museums throughout the world.

Dutch Cavalry before a Sutler's Tent, Philips Wouwerman, oil on canvas

Dutch Cavalry
before a Sutler's Tent,
c. 1640-1650 (71.4)

Oil on canvas, 10 3/4 x 13 7/8 in. (27.3 x 35.4 cm).
Unsigned.

Provenance: Collection of Mrs. Jetta Muntain Smith, Milwaukee; her
gift to the University, 1971, in memory of her son, Aurel Muntain.

References:
J. Patrice Marandel, verbally (1976), as one of the *Bamboccianti*,
or French.

Toward evening, perhaps, the last light of the sun setting ablaze the rump of a white horse, a small group of
cavalry has descended upon a field canteen. More precisely, the locale is a sutler's tent (from the Dutch *soe-
telaar*, originally "one who does dirty work"),
recognizable by its flags and garland-bedecked pole
and by some of the services that the sutler traditionally provided (drink and female companionship for the
men, water and/or feed for the horses). While being in
fact conventionally staged (see below), the scene
appears as if objectively recorded, struck at in a
moment, its details and atmosphere convincingly true.
No concessions are made to notions of military hero-
ism, to an ideal of physical beauty, nor to decorative-
ness. The technique is equally direct: Colors, predominantly those of the earth, are rather ruggedly
applied, sometimes as shorthand notations.

It was with good reason, then, that Patrice Marandel
(report cited) was reminded of the *Bamboccianti*, those
Rome-based followers of the Dutch painter Pieter van
Laer (1592/1595-1642), dubbed *Il Bamboccio* because
of his ill-favored appearance. A native of Haarlem, van
Laer arrived in Rome about 1626, initiating there the
so-called neo-realist movement that was to involve the
Italian Michelangelo Cerquozzi and such members of
the Northern community as Jan Miel, Michiel Sweerts,
and Johannes Lingelbach. In fact, recent scholarship
proposes to assign to Lingelbach's years in Rome (c.
1644-1650) several paintings whose attributions to
van Laer had appeared secure, most notably the famous *Ciambellaro* in the Palazzo Corsini at Rome.[1] Certainly the *Ciambelle Seller* may be taken as typical of
van Laer's warmly human approach if not specifically
his brush: common folk engaged in common activities
honestly presented.

The Marquette picture, although less nuanced with
regard to personality and the magic of light, shares
with van Laer several basic elements. Conspicuously
absent from the canvas, however, are those fragments
of the ancient past and other characteristic features of
the Italian scene, city or *campagna*, that so often
appear in the paintings of *Il Bamboccio* and the *Bamboccianti* strictly speaking. Conspicuously present are
motifs that have come to be indelibly associated with
the Haarlem master Philips Wouwerman. In his cata-

logue of Wouwerman's oeuvre, J. Hofstede de Groot
lists (and in many cases describes) more than one
hundred works whose imagery is that of cavalry
before a sutler's tent or booth.[2] In them are found
repeatedly, and at times almost identically, the elements of the Marquette picture: the flags and garland;
the strongly lighted white horse; the trumpeter sound-
ing a call, seen from the back and mounted on a diago-
nally placed steed; the beer drinker; the embracing
couple; the dogs; the plumed hats. Only two among
the numerous extant works by Wouwerman of this
type need be cited here:

(1) *Army Camp*, Amsterdam, Rijksmuseum, oil
on panel, .36 x .42 m.[3]
(2) *Army Camp*, The Hague, Mauritshuis, oil on
canvas, .70 x 1.00 m., and thus unusually
large for Wouwerman's activity in this genre.[4]

It should also be emphasized that although panel was
the support preferred by Wouwerman, at least fifteen
of the above-mentioned works are on canvas of equally
small scale.

Nonetheless, an attribution to Philips Wouwerman
of the Marquette example must recognize that the
quintessential Wouwerman is invariably less intimate
and more sophisticated. The landscape settings are
more expansive, showing wide sweeps of sky, deep
spatial recession, and a fuller range of atmospheric
effects. Color is richer and more varied, the light
clearer, the execution more careful yet fluid. Of the
paintings given to Wouwerman and familiar to the
writer, only one (known by way of the Stoedtner
photograph) truly parallels the close-up character and
the rugged directness of the present picture: the
Peasant Leading A Gray Horse in Front of a Cavalier,
located by Hofstede de Groot in the museum at Stuttgart.[5] Yet the claim for Wouwerman's authorship of
this unpretentious work is relatively recent, and the
panel does not figure in the *Katalog der Staatsgalerie
Stuttgart: Alte Meister* (Stuttgart, 1962).

Thus the necessarily tentative conclusion to this
study: the *Dutch Cavalry before a Sutler's Tent* is an
early work by Philips Wouwerman, datable not after
1650, under the influence of the straightforward works
of Pieter van Laer. Van Laer, whose importance for
Wouwerman has been underlined by Briganti,[6]
returned to Holland from Italy about 1638. After a stop
in Amsterdam, he settled in Haarlem, where Philips
surely came into contact with him and where he died in
1642. A full resolution of the question may require specialized research into the studio of Wouwerman during
the master's early years, and therefore into such
apparently shadowy figures as Koort Withalt, Jacob
Warnars, and Nicolaes Ficke.

R. W. B.

24

Notes:
1. Among the pioneering studies see G. Hoogewerff, "Pieter van Laer en zijn vrienden," Oud-Holland XLIX (1932): pt. I, 1-17; pt. II, 205-220; and L (1933): pt. III, 103-117; pt. IV, 250-262; G. Briganti, "Pieter van Laer e Michelangelo Cerquozzi," Proporzioni III (1950):185-198 and plates CCII-CCXXXIII; idem, I Bambocci-anti: pittori della vita popolare nel seicento, exhibition catalogue (Rome, 1950). For the subsequent reevaluations, see T. Kren, "Jan Lingelbach in Rome," The J. Paul Getty Museum Journal X (1982):45-62 with extensive bibliography, including doctoral dissertations by A. Janeck, Untersuchen über den holländischen Maler Pieter van Laer genannt Bamboccio (Würzburg, 1968), and C. Burger-Wegener, Johannes Lingelbach, 1622-1672 (Berlin, 1976).
2. J. Hofstede de Groot, A Catalogue Raisonné of the Works of the Most Eminent Dutch Painters of the Seventeenth Century, trans. and ed. by E. G. Hawke (London, 1909), II:529-551.
3. Ibid., cat. no. 843, 529-530; All the Paintings of the Rijksmuseum in Amsterdam: A Completely Illustrated Catalogue (Amsterdam and Maarssen, 1976), cat. A 484, 616 and ill.
4. Hofstede de Groot, Catalogue Raisonné of Dutch Painters, cat. no. 853, 533; Mauritshuis: Illustrated General Catalogue (The Hague, 1977), cat. 220, 262 and ill.
5. Oil on panel, .23 x .29 m.; Hofstede de Groot, Catalogue Raisonné of Dutch Painters, cat. no. 187, 315, where it is called "genuine but unimportant."
6. Briganti, I Bamboccianti, 14.

PETER PAUL RUBENS

Flemish (1577-1640)

Classically educated and apprenticed to the Antwerp painter Otto van Veen, Rubens went to Italy and, briefly, to Spain between 1600 and 1608. Upon his return to Antwerp, he quickly became recognized as that city's leading artist. He received commissions from the leading monarchs and aristocrats of Europe and was ennobled by Charles I of England and Philip IV of Spain. For the archduchess Isabella, Regent of the Spanish Netherlands, Rubens served as diplomat and confidential adviser. Perhaps no other artist had such a pervasive role in both the art and politics of his time, and few were so well versed in classical history and literature and ancient and contemporary art as Rubens.[1]

CIRCLE OF PETER PAUL RUBENS

FLEMISH

Noli Me Tangere   (59.2)

Oil on panel, 18 x 27 3/16 in. (45.7 x 69.1 cm). Unsigned.

Provenance: Collection of Mr. and Mrs. Marc B. Rojtman; their gift to the University, 1959.

References:
Pick, Marquette University Art Collection, 9, as Jan Brueghel and Hendrik van Balen.

Arnauld Brejon, verbally (1977), as Jan Brueghel and Hendrik van Balen.

Ian Kennedy, verbally (1961), as probably Franz Wouters.

Otto Naumann, in a letter (1982), as an imitator of Rubens, possibly Jan Boeckhorst or Theodor van Thulden.

The contrast between delicate landscape and robust figures in this small panel suggests that two painters may have collaborated here. The figures appear stylistically close to those artists who studied with Rubens, most notably Jan van den Hoecke (1611-1651).[1] The Magdalene and Christ may be compared with the figures in van den Hoecke's Hercules between Virtue and Vice (Florence, Palazzo Pitti).[2] Other artists who have been proposed for the figures in the Noli Me Tangere include Franz Wouters, Hendrik van Balen, Jan Boeckhorst, and Theodor van Thulden (see References, above); only the last seems a plausible alternative to Jan van den Hoecke, who appears the most likely painter of the figures in this panel.

The landscape approaches the style of Jan Brueghel the Elder (1568-1625), who was frequently responsible for the landscape and floral background of paintings with figures by other artists.[3] Although the flowers and landscape in the Noli Me Tangere resemble the general style of those in Brueghel's work, the similarities are not sufficiently strong to warrant a secure attribution to him or his immediate workshop, which includes his son, Jan Brueghel the Younger (1601-1678).

In this panel, the subdued sunlit sky and shaded trees provide a graceful foil for the foreground figures. The combination of dainty flowers in the style of Brueghel and sturdy figures in the style of Rubens was a popular one, made so by the collaboration of the two Antwerp artists, Jan Brueghel the Elder and Rubens, during the second decade of the seventeenth century. Perhaps their most renowned joint efforts are the Garden of Paradise (The Hague, Mauritshuis) and Archelous's Banquet (New York, Metropolitan Museum of Art). In both, Brueghel provided a lush, meticulously rendered setting for Rubens's powerfully proportioned figures. Such a juxtaposition of delicate naturalia and physically strong figures is present in the Marquette Noli Me Tangere, which would have been painted in imitation of the collaborative works by Rubens and Brueghel.

The episode of Christ's appearance to Mary Magdalene after his resurrection and before his ascension has retained its traditional Latin title: Noli me tangere (Do not touch me).[4] The Magdalene, at first believing Christ to be the gardener, only recognizes his true identity after he has called her by name. Expressed in the encounter between Christ and the Magdalene are initial doubts, a need for reassurance, and finally, reaffirmation of faith on her part and divine comfort and admonition on his part. The painter of these figures has used gesture and gaze to convey the Magdalene's complicated feelings and Christ's gentle benediction.

A. G.

25

Notes:

1. For accounts of the life and work of Jan van den Hoecke, see Ulrich Thieme and Felix Becker, *Allgemeines Lexikon der bildenden Künstler von der Antike bis zur Gegenwart* (Leipzig, 1907–1950), 17:182–183, and Didier Bodart, *Rubens e la pittura fiamminga del Seicento*, catalogue of an exhibition at the Palazzo Pitti (Florence, 1977), 146ff.
2. Bodart, *Rubens*, 150, cat. no. 50.
3. For a survey of Brueghel's life and work, see Gertraude Winkelmann-Rhein, *The Paintings and Drawings of Jan "Flower" Brueghel* (New York, 1968); see further K. Ertz, *Jan Brueghel der Ältere* (Cologne, 1979). For an example of Brueghel's collaboration with Hendrik van Balen in a painting of Christ appearing to the Magdalene, see *Le siècle de Rubens dans les collections publiques françaises*, catalogue of an exhibition at the Grand Palais (Paris, 1977), 50, cat. no. 17: *Le Christ jardinier* (Paris, Musée des Arts Décoratifs).
4. Mark 16:9; John 20:11–17.

Village Festival, Mathys Schoevaerdts, oil on canvas

MATHYS SCHOEVAERDTS
Flemish (c. 1665–after 1694)

A Fleming who specialized in landscapes with numerous figures, Schoevaerdts's oeuvre is not fully defined.[1] Primarily a painter, he made a small number of etchings of genre scenes.[2] He studied with Adriaen Frans Boudewyns and contributed figures to paintings by that master and by Jacques d'Arthois. Between 1692 and 1694 he is documented as a member of the painters' guild in Brussels; little is know of him after that date.

Village Festival (64.16)

Oil on canvas, 18 x 22 7/8 in. (45.7 x 58.1 cm). Unsigned.

Provenance: Collection of Mr. and Mrs. Richard B. Flagg; their gift to the University, 1964.

References:
Pick, *Marquette University Art Collection Supplement*, 11, 12 (ill.), as Schoevaerdts.

Jacques Foucart, on a photograph (c. 1978), as Schoevaerdts or Pieter Bout.

A picture that combines harvesting of grapes and wheat with merrymaking, this work may well have been intended to represent autumn in a series of the four seasons. Thematically, it may be compared to other pictures of the seasons by Schoevaerdts.[3] Typical of this artist's paintings are the feathered brushstrokes in the foliage and the lively figures.

Noli Me Tangere, Circle of Peter Paul Rubens, oil on panel

26

In the sixteenth century Pieter Brueghel the Elder made fashionable scenes of village merrymaking and harvests. Such merrymaking pictures proliferated in the seventeenth century, partly because of the popularity of similar works by David Teniers the Younger and his workshop. Schoevaerdts's *Village Festival*, although restrained in comparison to Bruegel's village feasts, nonetheless belongs to the tradition of open-air revelry established by Bruegel.

A. G.

Notes:
1. See Walther Bernt, *The Netherlandish Painters of the Seventeenth Century* (London, 1970), 3:105 and plates 1049 and 1050; Ulrich Thieme and Felix Becker, *Allgemeines Lexikon der bildenden Künstler von der Antike bis zur Gegenwart* (Leipzig, 1907–1950), 30:239; R. H. Wilenski, *Flemish Painters 1430–1830* (New York, 1960), 1:647 and 2: plates 798 and 816; and Didier Bodart, *Rubens e la pittura fiamminga del Seicento*, catalogue of an exhibition at the Palazzo Pitti (Florence, 1977), 339–340.
2. A von Wurzbach, *Niederländisches Künstler-Lexikon* (Vienna, 1910), 2:580.
3. See *Etudes sur les peintres des écoles hollandais, flamande, et néerlandaise qu'on trouve dans la Collection Semenov et les autres collections publiques et privées de St. Petersbourgh* (St. Petersburg, 1906), 267, addenda to clxxxvii, note 2, for discussion of two paintings by Schoevaerdts of summer and autumn, in the Kosloff collection; for another representation of summer, this one signed by Schoevaerdts, see that sold at the Palais des Beaux-Arts, Brussels, March 16, 1954, lot 157. One painting that may be stylistically compared with the Marquette canvas is *The Procession of the Fat Ox in Front of the Swan Inn*, ill. in Wilenski, *Flemish Painters*, 2: plate 798.

UNKNOWN ARTIST
Flemish

Mary Magdalene in Penitence, c. 1630   (61.5)

Oil on panel, 14 1/2 x 22 in. (36.8 x 55.9 cm). Unsigned.

Provenance: Collection of Mr. and Mrs. Marc B. Rojtman; their gift to the University, 1961.

References:
Pick, *Marquette University Art Collection*, 9 (ill.), as Jan Brueghel and Hendrik van Balen.

Ian Kennedy, verbally (1981), as Jan Brueghel the Younger and Pieter van Avont.

Although this picture contains a consistently delicate brushwork in both landscape and figural elements, it nonetheless may have been a collaborative effort of two artists. The landscape, foliage, and flowers appear to be by a follower of Jan Brueghel the Elder (1568–1625), who often contributed such elements to pictures with figures painted by others.[1] The foremost follower of Brueghel was his son, Jan Brueghel the

Younger (1601–1678), who inherited the family workshop following his father's death; he may well have taken on those projects left unfinished at the elder Brueghel's death, and of these some may have been collaborations with other artists. However, the landscape and flowers are painted more thinly than is usual in pictures that are securely attributed to the younger Brueghel.[2]

The figures may be by an artist close to Hendrick de Clerck (c. 1570–1630).[3] The Magdalene's features have a particular affinity to certain heads by de Clerck, and may be compared to those in his *Entombment of Christ* (Cambrai, Musée Municipal).[4] Other artists who have been proposed as authors of the figures in the Marquette panel include Pieter van Avont[5] and Hendrik van Balen;[6] however, for stylistic reasons, de Clerck seems a more likely possibility than either of these two artists. Small, finely wrought panels such as the *Magdalene in Penitence* would have been painted without commissions and intended for collectors' cabinets, where, in spite of their religious imagery, they would hang near pictures of genre, mythological, or portrait subjects.

Images of the Magdalene in penitence, popular since the Middle Ages, became more so after the Counter-Reformation.[7] According to medieval French legend, the Magdalene made a pilgrimage to Provence and lived there many years as a hermit; from this legend, the cave setting became associated with the repentant Magdalene. Such pictures often depict the Saint partially clad, with hair arranged provocatively upon her shoulders and with eyes lifted toward a vision of heavenly angels. While ostensibly serving as devotional aids to the devout, these pictures allude to the Magdalene's existence as a prostitute before her conversion to a faithful follower of Christ. The painter of the Marquette figures has imbued his Magdalene with attributes of both sides of her character: Even as she repents, she displays her sensuous breasts and hair.

A. G.

Mary Magdalen in Penitence, Flemish, Sevententh Century, oil on panel

Notes:
1. For a survey of the life and work of Jan Brueghel the Elder, see Gertraude Winkelmann-Rhein, *The Paintings and Drawings of Jan "Flower" Brueghel* (New York, 1968).
2. For comparison, see the *Madonna and Child in a Floral Garland* (private collection), in James A. Welu, *The Collector's Cabinet: Flemish Paintings from New England Private Collections,* catalogue of an exhibition at the Worcester Art Museum (Worcester, 1983), 12, cat. no. 1.
3. For Hendrick de Clerck, see Ulrich Thieme and Felix Becker, *Allgemeines Lexikon der bildenden Künstler von der Antike bis zur Gegenwart* (Leipzig, 1907-1950), 7:85-86.
4. Published in *Le siècle de Rubens dans les collections publiques françaises,* catalogue of an exhibition at the Grand Palais (Paris, 1977), 55, cat. no. 20.
5. For Pieter van Avont (1568-1625), who did collaborate with Jan Brueghel the Elder, see I. Jost, "Hendrik van Balen der Ältere," *1430-1830* (New York, 1960), I: plate 605, signed by both van Avont and Brueghel.
6. For Hendrik van Balen (1575-1632), who also collaborated with Brueghel the Elder, see I. Jost, "Hendrik van Balen der Ältere," *Nederlands Kunsthistorisch Jaarboek* (1963), 14:83-123. See further the *Madonna and Child in a Floral Garland,* published by Welu, *The Collector's Cabinet,* for an example of cooperation between van Balen and Brueghel the Younger.
7. See James Hall, *Dictionary of Subjects and Symbols in Art* (New York, 1974), 202.

Still Life with Flowers, Attributed to Nicolas Baudesson, oil on panel

NICOLAS BAUDESSON

French (1611-1680)

Born at Troyes in 1611, the son of a carpenter and sculptor, Nicolas Baudesson must be considered one of the more important French flower painters of the seventeenth century. Unfortunately, his life and career are rather difficult to document. It is known that he worked in Rome from the 1630s until 1666. In France he was admitted to the Royal Academy in 1671. In 1673 he exhibited four paintings, including his *Morceau de Réception,* and was named a counselor of the Academy. He was also represented at Versailles, though he was less favored than Jean-Baptiste Monnoyer in the dispensing of official patronage. (It is possible that Baudesson's friendship with Pierre Mignard earned him the hostility of the *Premier Peintre* (Charles Le Brun.) The fact that Mariette engraved his works in the 1740s indicates that he was held in high esteem well into the eighteenth century. Baudesson's reputation has suffered largely because of confusion about the nature and scale of his oeuvre. The fact that he did not sign his works adds to the already difficult task of attributing flower paintings to him. As a result, Baudesson's works have been assigned to other painters, among them Monnoyer, Fontenay, Mario di Fiori (Nuzzi), and his own son François. Baudesson died in Paris in 1680. As more works are attributed to him, and as more is known about the chronology of his career, he will no doubt rise to greater prominence.[1]

ATTRIBUTED TO NICOLAS BAUDESSON
Still Life with Flowers (66.11)

Oil on panel, 24 3/4 x 33 in. (62.9 x 83.8 cm). Inscribed at a later date, l.r.: "J. B. Monnoyer."

Provenance: Collection of Miss Paula Uihlein; her gift to the University, 1966.

References:

Pick, *Marquette University Art Collection,* 7 (ill.), as Monnoyer.

Carter, *Grain of Sand,* 8 (ill.), 9, no. 12, as Monnoyer.

Ian Kennedy, verbally (1981), as not Monnoyer, possibly Belin de Fontenay or Baudesson.

This flower piece has been attributed to Jean-Baptiste Monnoyer (1636?-1699), but it is most unlikely that it is by his hand. It has been determined that the signature is not original and was probably put on well after the painting was completed. (That is not unusual, since Monnoyer was the most renowned seventeenth-century flower painter. His signature would certainly make a painting more valuable and salable.) Equally significant is the fact that the Marquette painting cannot be accepted as a Monnoyer from the standpoint of style and execution. Monnoyer's elegant works are typified by an overabundance of densely compacted flowers, all scrupulously drawn. His flower pictures are also composed in the manner of Baroque history paintings with great diagonals and swirls of movement. None of this grandiloquence can be seen in the Marquette work, which is simple and intimate. It is in fact much more acceptable as a work by Nicolas Baudesson.[2]

Baudesson typically adopts a point of view that is

very close to the motif. As a result, his bouquet occupies more of the area of the picture than would be the case in a picture by Monnoyer. He also places his flowers in baskets or vases of glass, metal, or terra-cotta set on very simple and unornamented tables and sideboards of wood and stone. This once again is in contrast to Monnoyer, who uses props such as curtains, decorated silver vases, molded cornices, and similar devices in his works. Another distinguishing feature of Baudesson's art is the apparent influence of the chiaroscuro effects of Italian painting in general and of the Italian flower painter Nuzzi in particular. He typically sets strong reds and blues against dark backgrounds, and this is certainly the case in the Marquette work. His painting technique, moreover, is marked by a rather loose execution (although there are passages that appear flat and metallic) with areas that appear almost blurred. This blurring of detail is also quite evident in the Marquette painting.

Flower paintings of this type cannot be viewed as mere decoration, though they were, and still are, wondrously decorative. Works by Baudesson and other contemporaries such as Jacques Linard (1600–1645) convey a feeling of intimacy and quiet meditation on nature altered and arranged according to man's aesthetic and intellectual designs. Baudesson, unlike many painters of the Dutch, Flemish, and to a lesser extent French schools, did not employ symbolic elements in his pictures. The charm of his works derives largely from the intensity of his observation and the painterly skill evident in his harmonious compositions, which exhibit balanced forms and color areas and sympathetic reflections. The result, as illustrated in this picture, is understated and engaging works that are representative of the sensitivity and technical prowess of the French Baroque flower painters.

J. B.

Notes:
1. Peter Mitchell, *European Flower Painting* (London, 1973), 42–43.
2. Cf. ibid., 43, fig. 49; Michel Faré, *La Nature Morte en France* (Geneva, 1962), II: fig. 225 and colorplate VI.

LOUIS I ELLE, called FERDINAND THE ELDER

French (1612–1689)

Louis I Elle Ferdinand, or Ferdinand the Elder, was the most prominent member of the Elle family of portrait painters, active at the French court in the seventeenth century. The apparently ordinary works of his father, Ferdinand Elle (c. 1580–1649), are preserved only through reproductive engravings, and little survives as well by Louis's brother Pierre Elle (1609–1665). His son Louis Elle Ferdinand (1648–1717), also a portrait painter, was known as Ferdinand the Younger.

Although nearly forgotten today, Louis Elle Ferdinand (the Elder) was highly esteemed in his time. He was active at the court of Louis XIV and was, to judge from the illustrious ladies he is known to have painted, at home among the elegant salons of the day: Portraits are recorded of Mme. de Grignan, Mme. de Sévigné, Mme. de LaFayette, M. de Monthausier, and Ninon de Lenclos. Mariette called him "one of the most skillful portrait painters to have appeared in France,"[1] and his talents were acknowledged by his election as one of the first twelve members of the Academy in 1648.[2] He received the title of professor in 1659 and exhibited at the Salon in 1673.[3] He died in December 1689.

Portrait of Françoise Bertaut, 1664   (79.3)

Oil on canvas, 70 3/16 x 35 7/8 in. (178.3 x 91.1 cm). Signed center left (on the base of the column): "Fait par Ferdinand L[?]...E[?]...1664"; and signed on the verso: "Fait par Ferdinand Léné 1664 / Madame Mauteville."

Provenance: Collection of John Clifford Dinnies, New Orleans; gift in 1879 to his daughter, Marie Louise Grünewald; thence by descent to the donor, great-granddaughter of the previous; anonymous gift to the University, 1979.

References:
Grandpa [John Clifford] Dinnies, "The Unveiling of the Painting," printed broadsheet (Schönberg, Miss., 1879), as a portrait of Princess Louise Marie, daughter of Louis XV, c. 1770.

S. J. Gudlaugsson, in a letter (1960), as Flemish, c. 1670, but with some resemblance to the works of Nicholaes Rosendael.

Pierre Bautier, in a letter (1961), as Flemish, seventeenth century.

Carter, *Grain of Sand*, 8 (ill.), 9, no. 11, as attributed to Ferdinand Léné.

Marion Hirschler, in a letter (1979), as Follower of Elle, possibly Louis I Elle.

Arnauld Brejon, verbally (1980), as circle of Henri and Charles Beaubrun.

John Bandiera, provisional catalogue entry (1981), as probably the only known work by Ferdinand Léné.

Sophie Hanappier, in a letter (1983), as attributed to Louis I Elle, and as a portrait of Françoise Bertaut, wife of Nicolas Langlois.

The authorship and subject of this large and imposing picture have long proven elusive. Traditionally called a portrait of Louise Marie, daughter of Louis XV, the painting was thought to represent the princess in 1770, the date of her entry into the Carmelite convent of St. Denis. An attribution to Jean Marc Nattier, court painter to Louis XV, was, despite the artist's death in 1766, suggested as well. That the picture is of the seventeenth, rather than eighteenth, century has been evident to most modern critics, whose tentative

Portrait of Françoise Bertaut, Louis I Elle, oil on canvas

ers encountered are *l'aisné* and *laisné*), the normal term for "the elder." (The distinction between the elder and younger Ferdinands was made in the artists' lifetimes; engraved portraits are, for example, subscribed "Ferdinand père," and "V.E.," for *Vetus Elle.*) The attribution to the elder Louis Elle is substantiated by a comparison of the Marquette picture with known works by the artist—both paintings and, because of the rarity of these, graphic reproductions. These include the engraved portraits of Madame Cornuel[4] and Marie de Rohan,[5] as well as the extant painted portraits of Françoise de Sévigné[6] and the unknown ladies in the Musée de Bordeaux[7] and ex. -A. Marie collection.[8]

The inscription on the verso of the canvas gives the subject only as "Madame de Mauteville," but now, thanks to Hanappier's research, the specific identity of the sitter is known; it is Françoise Bertaut, who in 1639 married Nicolas Langlois, Lord of Motteville (she is known to have written the name as "Mauteville"). This "Madame de Mauteville" was a friend and confidante of Anne of Austria and lived at court from 1643 until the Queen's death in 1666. Then she retired to the Convent of the Visitation at Chaillot (where she had been a secular tertiary, a lay member of the order) and there remained until her death in 1689. Two engravings of a slightly younger Françoise Bertaut survive;[9] they clearly portray the same person depicted in the Marquette portrait.

The portrait represents the subject standing in a rich, silken dress beside a column. On a table at her side stands a small crucifix. Adjacent is the book she has just put down (her thumb marks her place), which is inscribed along the fore-edge, "SAINT GERAUME."

The diaphanous veil denotes modesty and renunciation of the world and, perhaps, indicates as well the widowhood of the subject. Held in her left hand, but at some point overpainted, is a skull, the most familiar symbol of mortality, here functioning both as a memento mori and as an indication of the seriousness of the subject's devotions. The formal pose, austere composition, and muted tonality—more expected in a religious than in a secular commission—underscore this pious presentation. But more than that they suggest that the subject has chosen to represent herself in the role of a saintly predecessor, of whom the most likely is the fourth-century Roman saint Paula.

Paula, a wealthy Roman matron widowed at an early age, became associated with St. Jerome and soon adopted a devout, ascetic existence. She left Rome, together with her daughter St. Eustochia, and followed Jerome to Antioch, where she established a hospice, monastery, and convent. She served for many years as an assistant to Jerome, who described and praised her life in one of his noted letters.[10] The presence of the crucifix (associated with Jerome), the evident widowhood of the subject, and the volume inscribed "SAINT GERAUME" all suggest an allegorical identification of the subject with St. Paula.[11] In this regard what little

attributions have proposed a variety of Flemish and French painters of the 1600s. Restoration of the picture in 1979 revealed the inscription and fragmentary signature of a Ferdinand Léné, an artist completely unknown and unrecorded, while the cleaned state of the picture suggested a new attribution to Louis I Elle. Hanappier has plausibly suggested that the word "Léné" does not refer to the artist's surname but is rather a variant spelling of the sobriquet "*l'ainé*" (oth-

we know of Françoise Bertaut's life proves of some interest.

Like Paula, Françoise was a wealthy widow, and she similarly sought respite in a religious community— first as a secular, later, perhaps, as a regular tertiary in the Convent of the Visitation of Chaillot (Paris). The dress that she wears in the picture is of a type associated with the Carmelite order,[12] but whether the exposed sandaled foot of the subject refers specifically to the Discalced (Barefooted) Carmelites or simply recalls the association with the Roman St. Paula cannot be said. In any case, the Marquette picture is not only an impressive example of an interesting and rare artist, but an enduring representation of a noblewoman and her religious conviction.

R. B. S.

Notes:
1. P. J. Mariette, Abecedario . . . (Paris, 1853-1862), II:224.
2. Georges Wildenstein, "Les Ferdinand Elle," Gazette des Beaux-Arts, 6 per., L (Oct. 1957):225-236, discusses and reviews the works of the Elle family.
3. Ibid., 232.
4. Engraved by B. Fessard; ill. ibid., fig. 5.
5. Engraved by Balechou.
6. Château de Bussy-Rabutin; see Revue de l'Art LXIII, no. 341 (Jan. 1933):7.
7. Inv. 7.068.
8. A. Marie sale, Rouen, Nov. 3-4, 1975.
9. Both, uncovered by Hanappier, are in the Bibliothèque Nationale, Paris. One, engraved by I. Gillberg, is subscribed, "Françoise-. . . Bertault/ Dame de . . . Motteuille/ Morte en 1689 . . . Agée de 75 ans" (no. N2 s.v. Motteville). The second, of a later date, is inscribed as after a portrait by Mignard (Anonymous, vol. 10, no. NE63).
10. The letter is no. 108 of Jerome's Letters; published in J. P. Migne, ed., Patrologia Latina (Paris, v. d.), XXII: cc. 878-906. On St. Paula see Herbert Thurston and Daniel Attwater, eds., Butler's Lives of the Saints (New York, 1956), I;171-172.
11. Cf. the compositionally similar Portrait of a Widow by Jacopo Chimenti da Empoli in the Art Institute of Chicago (1960.1).
12. Hirschler notes its similarity to the dress of the Virgin in the anonymous Vision of St. Theresa in the Parochial Church of Lissenwege; ill. Cécile Emond, L'iconographie Carmélitaine dans les anciens Pays-Bas méridionaux (Brussels, 1961), II:131, fig. 66.

CLAUDE VIGNON

French (1593-1670)

Claude Vignon, the "unseizable" and "disconcerting" French painter, the man who "spent as much time on his horse as at his easel" (all in the words of Brejon and Cuzin), was baptized in Tours on May 19, 1593. His father, Guillaume, royal silversmith and valet de chambre to Kings Henry III and Henry IV, apprenticed the young Claude to a Parisian atelier. Thus Vignon was trained in the tradition of French Late Mannerism and, it has reasonably been supposed, specifically by such practitioners of this mode as Georges Lalle-

mand and Jacob Bunel. An independent master upon his reception into the Corporation of Painters at Paris in 1616, Vignon then moved to Rome.

His arrival in the Eternal City can be set at least as early as 1617, when he signed and dated the Martyrdom of St. Matthew, now in the Musée d'Arras, an ambitious canvas that serves well as an introduction to Vignon's complex artistic inclinations and inimitable personality. On the one hand, the Martyrdom of St. Matthew reveals the impact of the great Caravaggio's interpretation of the theme in the French national church of San Luigi de'Francesi. From Caravaggio, Vignon adapted the poses of the three figures (Saint, executioner, angel) and the powerful contrasts of light and shadow, and appropriated such characteristically Caravaggesque motifs as the dirty feet and perspiration-soaked headband. Yet Caravaggesque borrowings do not necessarily a Caravaggio make. Instead of the Italian master's drama of expectancy, Vignon portrays the brutal stabbing and fails to appreciate Caravaggio's gift for emphasis and subordination. The forms are crowded together without breathing room, and the still life and angel's wings—rendered with graphic precision —threaten to upstage the participants, who are themselves crude, non-Italian types. And within it all there emerges a taste for the painterly, for rich pigments ruggedly applied, and for shot-colors.

Already with the Martyrdom of St. Matthew, then, much of the quintessential Vignon is in evidence: the horror vacui, "graphic complications," fanciful coloration, and exaggerations of his French Mannerist beginnings; a pungent realism, a love of the particular of Flemish and even more of Dutch stamp; a Caravaggesque veneer; and a feeling for the special properties of oil pigments. In more basic terms, this painting reveals Claude's capacity to assimilate any number of influences (the situation has been drastically simplified here) and his propensity for the effect-seeking (including the bizarre and a dazzling display of virtuosity).

All of these elements are found in abundance during these Roman years, when Vignon was patronized by such important collectors as Cardinal Ludovisi, the Marchese Vincenzo Giustiniani, and Cardinal Francesco Maria del Monte. He took a trip (or trips) to Venice, where be became enamored of Venetian colorism and pageant (see the canvases of the Adoration of the Magi—Dayton Museum of Art and St. Gervais, Paris—discussed in the catalogue entry that follows). The artist continued to indulge his appetite for travel. He was married in Paris on January 21, 1623, but in the spring of that year he was again in Rome (to which he returned in 1630 and 1659-1661). Between 1624 and 1628 Vignon twice (?) visited Spain. His work as a painter never ceased to hold surprises. Thus in 1624, probably back in Paris, Vignon executed the Esther before Ahasuerus in the Louvre (again, see below), a precious jewel of a picture in which French Mannerist features return in force. Simultaneously he practiced what might be called a monumental manner, often under the influence of Rubens, sometimes looking to the *Caravaggeschi*.

Vignon became a prominent member of the French Academy (he was also a book illustrator and an agent-dealer) within a few years of its formation in 1648. His late period embraces the years between 1643 and his death in Paris on May 10, 1670. Ever the "chameleon" (Ivanoff), Claude Vignon painted such works as the *Circumcision of Christ* (1651; art market, New York, as of 1963) and the *Christ Washing the Feet of the Apostles* (1653; Musée des Beaux-Arts, Nantes), in which the extravagant and petite manner of the *Esther* is combined with a truly magical illumination—fitting finales to the career of this spirited and imaginative master.

Adoration of the Magi,
c. 1625–1630 (60.5)

Oil on canvas, 36 x 46 in. (91.4 x 116.8 cm). Unsigned.

Provenance: Collection of Procter Esyne Clifton, Bristol, England (according to a label on the reverse of the frame); Mr. and Mrs. Marc B. Rojtman, Milwaukee; their gift to the University, 1960.

References:
Pick, *Marquette University Art Collection*, 27 (ill.), 30, as school of Veronese.

Fredericksen and Zeri, *Census* (1972), p. 227, as either Italian or French, seventeenth century.

J. Patrice Marandel, verbally (1976), as perhaps Vignon.

Arnauld Brejon, verbally (1977), as Vignon, without question.

Carter, *Grain of Sand*, 9, no. 16, as Vignon.

La peinture française du XVII ͤ siècle dans les collections américaines, exhibition catalogue (Paris, 1982), 374, no. 8 and ill., as studio of Vignon.

Ian Kennedy, verbally (1981), as very close to Vignon.

At once director, choreographer, set designer, and costumer, Claude Vignon offers here a wonderful pageant for our edification and delight. Ensconced between architectural remains symbolic of the now-superseded Old Dispensation, the Holy Family—the vigilant St. Joseph in blue and mustard-colored garments, the Madonna in her traditional red dress and blue mantle steadying the Christ Child—receives the adoration and gifts of the Eastern Wise Men. We, imagined as worshippers in the entourage, are directed to the object of our devotion by the meditative Melchior, dressed in a gold-brocaded green robe lined in red. The aged Caspar, equally resplendent in his golden drapery embroidered with blue designs, cradles the Child's right arm, while behind him Balthasar, the young black Magus in

gray-blue and red, seeks recognition, his entreaty seconded by a page. Deep in a recess at the extreme right, another man seems to contemplate the significance of the gathering; an afterthought, perhaps, but in function an extension of the painter. The seriousness is tempered by light moments (the peering dog and the recalcitrant camel) and by the sheer gorgeousness of the ensemble. The richly colored robes alive with highlights, the jewel-bedecked turbans, the precious vessels, and the polished marbles create a world of gemlike splendor and exoticism to which even the most stoic must succumb.

Vignon and his patrons recognized that the subject of the Adoration of the Magi was ideally suited to his temperament and talents. At least nine extant paintings of the theme (including the present canvas), ranging over a period of more than thirty years, have been confidently assigned to the master.[1] Furthermore, three interpretations of the theme are listed in the 1643 inventory of Vignon's workshop, eight in the accounting made upon the artist's death in 1670, and seven (all but one for religious institutions) in other sources.[2] Even if one acknowledges likely duplications in these lists and the possibility that the Marquette version is one of the documented but "lost or unidentified" pictures, the extent of Claude's infatuation with this iconography is remarkable and revealing.

The series (and this demonstration of both authorship of the Marquette canvas and its place within the artist's career) begins with the *Adoration of the Magi* in the Dayton Art Institute, Dayton, Ohio, datable about 1619 on the basis of the related engraving by Vignon executed in Rome in that year.[3] Although bracketed by some of Vignon's adaptations of the Caravaggesque style, the Dayton *Adoration* bears an entirely different cultural stamp.[4] In place of Caravaggio's earthy, morally grave humanity shown close up as if of a piece with actual existence, Vignon presents an imaginary world of uncommon enchantment and opulence. While this taste for spectacle and for expressive color and painterly handling may have been cultivated during a stay in Venice, it is the tradition in which Vignon was initially trained, with its roots in the sixteenth-century Italian *maniera*, that seems best to explain the extravagance and the figure types of the canvas.[5] Thus, for example, the black Magus in his bizarre plumed headdress has rightly called to mind Lallemand and Callot, and the tiny-headed Madonna of elegant profile as well as the kneeling king have been likened to Emilian art in the mold of Correggio.[6]

In 1624 Vignon signed and dated the *Adoration of the Magi* today in St. Gervais at Paris.[7] With this brilliantly colored picture he made a definitive commitment to an operatic staging of the theme and rehearsed certain motifs (the eccentric black king, the placement of the full-length St. Joseph forward of the Virgin, and of the elder's turban and offering in the immediate foreground) that had been introduced in the Dayton version. But now the Italian experience asserts itself more forcefully—in the more compact composition, the greater amplitude of form, and the tremendous confidence in the manipulation of succulent pigments. Paolo Veronese, the Bassani, and, from Vignon's own time, Domenicho Fetti (with his poetic vision and abundant technique) are recalled.

Then, during the same year, 1624, with predictable unpredictability, Vignon created the *Esther before Ahasuerus* in the Louvre.[8] Approximately half the size of the aforementioned *Adorations*, in effect it seems even smaller. Elegant, elongated figures, move gracefully within an extensive space and before a breathtaking set that fades into the distance. In short, Vignon reaffirms his beginnings and—if, as one suspects, the picture was done after the artist's return to France—his allegiance. Here indeed is the aesthetic of Georges Lallemand, of the engravings of the *Adoration of the Magi* and the *Finding of Moses*.[9]

In the *Esther before Ahasuerus* there appears in fully developed form what would thereafter be one of Vignon's trademarks: the electric highlights on the robes, luminous filaments that endow the whole with a vibrating energy.[10] Thus at the middle of the 1620s Vignon was practicing simultaneously a monumental and a precious manner. The *Adoration of the Magi* at Marquette represents, or so this study proposes, a magnificent blending of these two modes. The size of the canvas is roughly that of the *Esther* and of the Newhouse *Adoration*. The shimmering draperies are passed in review, the old king is delicate and doll-like, and the character, pose, and position within the work of the standing Magus were based directly upon this figure in Lallemand's *Adoration of the Magi* (see above). Yet the Madonna is a twin to the Virgin in the Parisian example. And the overall impression of the Marquette work is not one of petiteness.

In effecting this synthesis Vignon appears to have looked once again to Paolo Veronese, and in fact to a specific image conceived by the Venetian master. Vignon's interpretation shares numerous features with Veronese's *Adoration of the Magi* in the National Gallery at London: the shiny and brocaded materials; the general richness and animation; the grouping of the old Magus, Madonna and Child, and St. Joseph; and even the particulars of dog, truncated column, and figure looking down from an elevated position on the architecture.[11] These relationships cannot be easily dismissed as coincidences, because the groom disciplining the camel in the left middleground of the Marquette *Adoration* was lifted from Veronese's painting. During his Italian years Vignon could have studied this altarpiece, then in San Silvestro at Venice. He may have renewed his acquaintance with Paolo's interpretation shortly before he executed the Marquette picture.

This latter suggestion is prompted by the circumstances of Vignon's trip (or trips) to Spain. He is thought to have gone to Spain about 1624 and was surely in that country sometime between 1625 and 1628. In the Prado at Madrid there is today a reduced copy, possibly by Paolo Farinato (1524-1606), of Veronese's San Silvestro canvas.[12] Was this copy in Spain by the late 1620s and did Vignon see it? Against the uncertainty arising from these as yet unanswered questions can be set the observation that the French painter was surely always on the alert for other artists' renditions of a subject dear to his heart. As Brejon and Cuzin imply,[13] one of these may well have been Angelo Nardi's recently completed *Adoration of the Magi*, signed and dated 1620, in the Iglesia de las Bernardas at Alcalá de Henares, twenty miles east of Madrid.[14] Common sources in Veronese and the Bassani seem insufficient to explain the strikingly similar glitter of jewels and brocades, the dazzling highlighting of drapery.

This reconstruction of how and when the picture came into being (no earlier than 1624, the year of the St. Gervais *Adoration* and the Louvre *Esther*, and during or shortly after a stay by Vignon in Spain) is more logical than was Claude Vignon's career, and should therefore be considered somewhat speculative. At all events, the Marquette *Adoration of the Magi* is an example of the art of Vignon at a most certain moment, to be savored for its pictorial beauty and for the genial sentiments it conveys.

R. W. B.

Notes:

1. In addition to the examples documented and discussed below, see W. Fischer, "Claude Vignon (1593-1670)," *Nederlands kunsthistorisch Jaarboek* XIV (1963):168, fig. 48, 173-174, cat. no. 1, 175; cat. no. 8, 176; 145-146 and fig. 32, cat. no. 15, 176; 172-173, cat. no. 35, 178; Arnauld Brejon de Lavergnée and Jean-Pierre Cuzin, *Valentin et les caravagesques français*, exhibition catalogue (Paris, 1974), 196, with ill.

2. B. de Montgolfier, "Deaux tableaux de Claude Vignon," *Gazette des Beaux-Arts* CIII (1961):327, 330, nn. 26-27; Fischer, "Claude Vignon," cat. no. 3, 182.

3. Oil on canvas, 1.98 x 1.39 m.; Brejon and Cuzin, *Valentin et les caravagesques français*, cat. no. 60, 194-196, with ill., full bibliography, and the suggestion that the engraving and its preparatory drawing were done subsequent to the painting.

4. For example, see the *Martyrdom of St. Matthew*, Arras, Musée, 1617, and the *David with the Head of Goliath*, New York, Suida-Manning Collection, c. 1620-1622; ibid., cat. no. 58, 188-191 with ill., and cat. no. 61, 196-198 with ill.

5. Ibid., 187, 196.

6. Ibid., 196; N. Ivanoff, "Claude Vignon e l'Italia," *Critica d'arte* XI, nos. 65-66 (1964):43.

7. Oil on canvas, 1.65 x 2.62 m.; Montgolfier, "Deux tableaux de Claude Vignon," 322-327 and figs. 6-11; Ivanoff, "Claude Vignon et l'Italia," 46-47 and fig. 57; Rosenberg, "A Vignon for Minneapolis," *The Minneapolis Institute of Arts Bulletin* LVII (1968):11, 16, n. 14.

8. Oil on canvas, .80 x 1.19 m.; Fischer, "Claude Vignon," XIII (1962): 132, fig. 17, 134ff.; C. Sterling, "Un précurseur français de Rembrandt: Claude Vignon," *Gazette des Beaux-Arts* LXXVI (1934):123-136 with ills.

9. Fischer, "Claude Vignon," 136-137, 138 and fig. 19, 139, fig. 20; Sterling, "Claude Vignon," 133, 135, fig. 9. Equally luxuriant and fanciful is the *Adoration of the Magi* with the Newhouse Galleries at New York in 1975 (oil on canvas, .83 x .99 m.; *Burlington Magazine* CXVII (Jan., 1975):xv), close in time to the *Esther*.

10. See also the related version at Bob Jones University in Greenville, South Carolina; Fischer, "Claude Vignon," 139–141 and figs. 21–22.
11. 1573; T. Pignatti, *Veronese* (Venice, 1976), I: cat. no. 180, 136–137, and II: fig. 463.
12. Ibid., I:136.
13. Brejon and Cuzin, *Valentin et les caravagesques français*, 187.
14. D. Angulo Iñiguez and A. E. Pérez Sánchez, *Historia de la pintura española: escuela madrileña del primer tercio del siglo XVII* (Madrid, 1969), cat. nos. 1–6, 282, 276, and plate 208.

ANTONIO CARNEO

Italian (1637–1692)

Virtually nothing is known of the first thirty years of Antonio Carneo's life. He was born in 1637 in the town of Concordia Sagittaria in Friuli, but no record of him has been found prior to his coming under the protection and patronage of Count Giambattista Caiselli in 1667. His artistic education can only be conjectured on the basis of his mature works, which are characterized by a vivid, richly chromatic style that bespeaks a variety of sources and concerns. Many names have been suggested as contributing to that style: Tintoretto, Veronese, and Pordenone—all sixteenth-century Venetian painters whose work was accessible to the young Carneo; Padovanino, Palma Giovane, Strozzi, Domenico Fetti, and Jan Liss—of a slightly later generation; and, perhaps most important of his own time, Pietro della Vecchia. Elements from such disparate artists as Maffei, Rubens, Luca Giordano, and Eberhard Keil (Monsù Bernardo) have been discerned as well. All of these supposed sources might suggest that Carneo was merely derivative, if eclectic. Rather they indicate the difficulty critics have had in accounting for the artist's exuberant, self-assured, though slightly eccentric, paintings.[1]

For twenty years Carneo lived under the patronage of Count Caiselli in Udine, where he received many commissions, both public and private. In 1687 he retired—in misery, it is said—to the village of Portogruaro, where he died five years later. His entire career was spent in Friuli, a fact which, according to his earliest biographer, Guarienti, accounts for there being so little documentation of the artist.[2]

Carneo's works range from portraits—such as several done of members of the Caiselli family (Udine, Private Collection)—to large altarpieces, the most noted being the *Charity of St. Thomas* in the parish church of Besnate (Varese).[3] Most often, however, he painted mid-sized pictures for domestic environments, both secular and religious in subject. Lanzi rather prosaically described him as "ingenious, innovative in composition, bold in drawing, happy in coloring (especially skin-tones), expressive in all varieties of emotions," while De Renaldis found the artist "strong and natural in expression, frank in drawing, although not always exact."[4] With a more modern eye Rizzi frankly but evocatively characterizes Carneo as

cantankerous and non-conventional; of a complex temperament, abundant in experience, and guided by a sensibility in perpetual evolution; morbidly curious of all forms in nature; bubbling with ideas, constantly changing his mind, and often incomprehensible in his spontaneous brushwork; gifted with an inexhaustible, but erratic and disconcerting, pictorial language—this is Antonio Carneo, a "difficult" painter.[5]

Abimelech Restores Sarah to Abraham, Attributed to Antonio Carneo, oil on canvas

ATTRIBUTED TO ANTONIO CARNEO
Abimelech Restores Sarah to Abraham (81.23)

Oil on canvas, 49 5/8 x 46 in. (126.1 x 116.8 cm) (sight). Unsigned.

Provenance: Starhemberg Collection, Schloss Purbach, near Wels (Austria); sold to Franz Sobek, Vienna; collection of Mr. and Mrs. Eckhart G. Grohmann, Milwaukee; their gift to the University, 1981.

References:
Robert Eigenberger, on verso of a photograph (1964), as by Andrea Celesti, giving Starhemberg provenance.

This painting has previously been called *Abraham and Sarah before Pharaoh* and was thought to represent the moment when Pharaoh, having kept Sarah in his house believing her to be Abraham's sister, restored her to her husband (Genesis 12:11-20). However, there is reason to believe that the subject is actually the return of Sarah from King Abimelech. The two events are similar in most aspects. Abraham and Sarah are traveling in a strange land (Egypt or Gerar); fearing that if they were known to be married his attractive wife might be abducted and he murdered, Abraham insists that Sarah pretend to be his sister. Sarah does so but is nonetheless taken by the local ruler (whether Pharaoh or Abimelech) and held until God makes known her identity to her captor. She is then given back to Abraham. The Marquette work might well represent either event, but one previously overlooked detail in the painting makes it clear that it is the Abimelech rather than the Pharaoh tale portrayed. That is the gesture of the crowned figure's pointing to a plate filled with coins (at the lower left)—an action alluded to in the biblical text (Genesis 20:14-16):

> And Abimelech took sheep, and oxen, and men-servants, and womenservants, and gave them unto Abraham, and restored him Sarah his wife. And Abimelech said, Behold my land is before thee: dwell where it pleaseth thee. And unto Sarah he said, Behold, I have given thy brother a thousand pieces of silver: behold, he is to thee a covering of the eyes, unto all that are with thee, and with all other: thus she was reproved.

The giving of the thousand pieces of silver is one of three related moments in the story that are compressed by the artist into the single instant of the picture. The return of Sarah, the principal subject, is of course another and is graphically indicated by Abraham's taking his wife's right hand as she tenderly places her left on his shoulder. The third moment (actually the first chronologically) accounts for Abimelech's questioning expression and the gesture of his left hand pointing to himself. This refers to the passage immediately preceding Sarah's restoration (Genesis 20:9-10):

> Then Abimelech called Abraham, and said unto him, What hast thou done to us? and what have I offended thee, that thou hast brought on me and on my kingdom a great sin? thou hast done deeds unto me that ought not to be done. And Abimelech said unto Abraham, What sawest thou, that thou hast done this thing?

A black servant boy holds the tray of coins at the lower left, and two figures attendant on the King complete the composition. With the somewhat arbitrary placement of architectural details (particularly the diagonal cornice at the right), an x-shaped structure seems to inform the painting with the principal axis running from the top left to the bottom right, underscoring the dramatic interplay of Abimelech and Abraham.

Perhaps because of its Austrian provenance, this picture was thought to be by Andrea Celesti (1637-1712), a Venetian artist who was active in Austria and Germany.[6] Although there is some similarity to Celesti in composition and, to a degree, in subject matter, the Marquette work is quite at variance with Celesti's known painting style, not to mention his unique, unmistakable physiognomic types.[7] The attribution to Carneo, which is proposed here for the first time, can, however, be supported by several analogies from the artist's secure works. Of these, one of the most striking is the parallel between Abraham and the figure of Solomon in Carneo's painting of *Solomon before the Idol* in the collection of Count Westerholt: Not only are these figures physiognomically close, but their similar bending posture and compositional function emphasize the bond.[8] Of quite similar type as well is the bearded elder occupying the lower right-hand corner of the nearly square composition once in the Calligaris collection at Terzo di Aquilea.[9] Other figures have their counterparts in Carneo's oeuvre—for example, Sarah with the St. Anne of the *Education of the Virgin* in Udine.[10] Perhaps more telling are the broader analogies in composition (almost inevitably based on crossed diagonals), figural poses (often with awkward passages—for example, twisting necks), and drapery folds (coarsely but effectively rendered) that are evident in works such as Carneo's *The Expulsion of Hagar* (Trieste),[11] *Banquet of Thetis* (Udine),[12] or the evocative *Woman with a Distaff and Girl with Wheat* (Rome).[13]

R. B. S.

Notes:
1. On Carneo, see Aldo Rizzi, *Antonio Carneo* (Udine. 1960); idem, *Mostra del Bombelli e del Carneo*, exhibition catalogue (Udine, 1964); and Carlo Donzelli and Giuseppe Maria Pilo, *I Pittori del Seicento Veneto* (Florence, 1967), 107-110, with bibliography.
2. P. Guarienti, in Antonio Orlandi, *Supplemento all'Abecedario pittorico* (Florence, 1776), I:119.
3. Ill. Donzelli and Pilo, *I Pittori del Seicento Veneto*, plate 115.
4. Luigi Lanzi, *Storia pittorica dell'Italia* (Bassano, 1789, but cited here from Milan, 1823 edition), III:186-187; G. DeRenaldis, *Della pittura friulana* (Udine, 1789), 113.
5. Rizzi, *Mostra del Bombelli e del Carneo*, LXIV.
6. On Celesti, see A. M. Mucchi and C. Della Croce, *Il Pittore Andrea Celesti* (Milan, 1954). Celesti's principal work in Austria is at Stift Sankt Florian, near Linz.
7. For example, compare Celesti's *Death of a King* (Coll. Princes of Thurn and Taxis, Castello Nuovo, Duino); ill. *La Pittura del Seicento Venezia*, exhibition catalogue (Venice, 1959), no. 214.
8. Schweb Hall; ill. Aldo Rizzi, *Storia dell'Arte in Friuli: Il Seicento* (Udine, 1969), fig. 146.
9. Ill. ibid., fig. 154.
10. San Cristoforo, Udine; ill. ibid., fig. 163.
11. Museo di Storia e Arte, S.1045; ill. Rizzi, *Mostra del Bombelli e del Carneo*, no. 41.
12. Private Collection; ill. ibid., no. 81.
13. Coll. Conte Jacopino del Torso; ill. Donzelli and Pilo, *I Pittori del Seicento Veneto*, fig. 114.

ROMAN MASTER
Bust-Length Portrait of a Cardinal,
c. 1600-1625   (75.17)

Oil on canvas, 23 1/8 x 18 in. (58.7 x 46 cm). Unsigned.

Provenance: Collection of Mr. and Mrs. Raymond F. Newman, Milwaukee; their gift to the University, 1975.

References:
J. Patrice Marandel, verbally (1976), as after Gaulli (?).

Arnauld Brejon, verbally (1977), as in the style of Domenichino.

Carter, *Grain of Sand*, 9, no. 20, as unknown Italian artist.

Recognizable as a cardinal by virtue of his red *biretta* and *mozzetta*, but without other identifying attributes, this austere churchman must remain anonymous pending discovery of a documented likeness of him.

This investigation can be confined, however, to the Roman milieu between approximately 1600 and 1625. In general, the painting rejects the psychological challenges and stylistic conceits of Mannerist portraiture while not displaying the flair of the developed Baroque. More specifically, both in interpretation (objective, honest, without decorative trappings) and in style (the strongly lighted form projecting in considerable relief from a dark background), this image belongs within that tradition of Roman portraiture of the last decade of the sixteenth century and the first decades of the seventeenth century of which the following pictures are representative:

(1) Scipione Pulzone, *Portrait of a Cardinal*, Rome, Galleria Nazionale, 1590s.[1]
(2) Domenichino, so-called *Self-Portrait*, Florence, Uffizi, oil on canvas, .71 x .57 m., c. 1610.[2]
(3) Nicolò Renieri (Nicolas Régnier), attributed to, *Portrait of a Young Man with a Sword*, Detroit Institute of Arts, oil on canvas, .73 x .622 m., c. 1615-1620.[3]

Significantly, Zeri viewed Pulzone's portrait in London as anticipating Domenichino,[4] while the latter's *Self-Portrait* was invoked by Pierre Rosenberg in connection with the "Renieri" *Young Man with a Sword*.[5]

Yet even as such comparisons establish the art historical context of the Marquette canvas, they also underscore its shortcomings. Being rather emotionally neutral and somewhat hard and dry in handling, the picture must be assigned to an early Baroque painter of the second rank, perhaps one working from an existing portrait of the Cardinal.

R. W. B.

Notes:
1. Photo GFN Rome, E32034; cited by E. Vaudo, *Scipione Pulzone da Gaeta, pittore* (Gaeta, 1976), 43. Another, slightly varied, version is in the National Gallery at London (oil on tin-plated copper, .943 x .718 m) ibid., 42-44 and plate 52; F. Zeri, *Pittura e Controriforma: l'arte senza tempo di Scipione da Gaeta* (Turin, 1957), 81-82 and fig. 89; London, National Gallery, *Illustrated General Catalogue* (London, 1973), 586, no. 1048.
2. E. Borea, *Domenichino* (Milan, 1965), 190-191 and plate G opposite 128. A connection of the Marquette portrait to Domenichino has been suggested by Arnauld Brejon (report cited).
3. E. P. Richardson, "Renieri, Saraceni, and the Meaning of Caravaggio's Influence," *Art Quarterly* V (1942):232, 235-236 (ill.).
4. Zeri, *Pittura e Controriforma*, 81.
5. Pierre Rosenberg, in a letter dated July 12, 1963, Registrar's Files, Detroit Institute of Arts.

Bust-Length Portrait of a Cardinal, Roman Master, Seventeenth Century, oil on canvas

FRANCESCO TREVISANI

Italian (1656-1746)

Decades before his death on July 30, 1746, Francesco Trevisani had already established himself as one of the most sought-after and progressive painters in Rome and as a master of international reputation. For more than forty years, beginning in the late 1690s, he had been under the direct protection of Cardinal Pietro Ottoboni (d. 1691), the city's foremost patron. Working in oil on canvas and copper, from small to monumental scale, and equally adept with religious, historical, and mythological themes and portraiture, he counted among his clients not only the princes, Popes, and prelates of Italy but also Lothar Franz von Schönborn (Arch-Chancellor of the Holy Roman Empire), the courts of St. Petersburg and Bavaria, and notables in France, Spain, Portugal, and Italy.

Even a cursory review of Trevisani's achievement should explain this esteem. The artist was trained in northern Italy, first in Capo d'Istria (or Capodistria), where he was born on April 9, 1656, and where he received instruction in drawing from his architect father, Antonio Trevisani; and then at Venice, where Francesco studied and worked with Giuseppe Heintz and Antonio Zanchi. The former specialized in city views populated by scores of tiny, spirited figures; the latter practiced that dark, dramatic manner, a Caravaggism passed through such masters as Luca Giordano and Giambattista Langetti, that then dominated Venetian painting.

Trevisani probably took the required pilgrimage to Rome as early as 1678, although he is not documented there until 1682, at which time (and for the next ten years) he was employed by Cardinal Flavio I Chigi. While searching for a personal style, he executed some genre paintings (now considered lost) presumably in the manner of Heintz, and religious works that drew variously upon Zanchi and upon the Roman-Bolognese traditions to which he was now exposed. In 1697 Trevisani was admitted to the Accademia di San Luca. The main impetus for this honor may have been provided by the success of the canvases and frescoes (his only exercise in this medium) that he had completed in 1696 for the Crucifixion Chapel in San Silvestro in Capite. Some of these superb paintings display the realistic types, earthy coloring, and tenebrist light of Caravaggesque origin that the artist had restudied, now at its source. But in others Francesco introduced elements that were to set the future course of his art: cool, pastel colors; a softer, warmer light; and, especially in the lunette of the *Agony in the Garden*, a new delicacy of sentiment, lyrical more than dramatic, moving but not threatening. Here, writes Frank DiFederico, Trevisani "disassociates his art from the charged emotionalism and epic grandeur characteristic of the seventeenth century."

Since in their own ways artists such as Ludovico Gimignani and Giuseppe Chiari, also participants in the decorative program at San Silvestro, were taking comparable paths, Trevisani was clearly responding to a general change in Roman taste. This inevitably raises the issue of the role played by the Accademia degli Arcadi, founded in 1690 and established at the Villa Ruspoli. The mission of this academy, to characterize it in overly broad terms, was to purge contemporary literature of Baroque conceits, of bad taste as it was said, through a return to classical forms and hence to a clearer, more rational, more didactic expression. Trevisani was inducted into the Accademia degli Arcadi

in 1712 and was, in DiFederico's view, unquestionably influenced by its aims. An opposing position has been stated by Francis Dowley, who correctly notes that the Accademia had not formulated a policy for the visual arts (in part because the classicizing manner of Carlo Maratti and his school was already in place) and that Trevisani's paintings neither availed themselves of antique models nor rejected the kind of sensuality that would have displeased the Arcadians. Perhaps rather than postulating causal relationships one should speak of a spirit of moderation in the intellectual air of which both Trevisani and the Arcadians partook. For Trevisani it had its most noticeable effect (especially in composition) on the classicizing canvases of 1713-1715 for the Cathedral at Narni, after which Trevisani's art generally showed a more measured quality than it had previously. Still, one must not forget that even in his late years, as in the magnificent cartoons of 1732-1743 for mosaics in St. Peter's, Francesco Trevisani was perfectly capable of paintings whose robustness and drama continue to evoke the seventeenth century.

Considered in toto, however, Trevisani's art after the turn of the new century is best characterized by the term *barochetto*: lighter in tonality than the Baroque, more subtle in modeling, intentionally less grand and emotionally demanding, more elegant; yet, at the same time, often energetic, rarely slight or merely frivolous. It was for others—and Francesco's influence spread beyond Italy to France, Germany, and England—to develop elements of his style into a fully Rococo idiom.

St. Francis in Penitence, c. 1695-1700 (59.5)

Oil on canvas, 52 7/8 x 38 7/16 in. (134.4 x 97.7 cm). Unsigned.

Provenance: Collection of Mr. and Mrs. Marc B. Rojtman, Milwaukee; their gift to the University, 1959.

References:
Pick, *Marquette University Art Collection*, 24-25 (ill.).

Fredericksen and Zeri, *Census* (1972), p. 205, as Trevisani.

Anthony Clark, in a letter (1976), as Trevisani.

J. Patrice Marandel, verbally (1976), as Trevisani.

Arnauld Brejon, verbally (1977), as Trevisani.

Arnauld Brejon and Pierre Rosenberg, "Francesco Trevisani et la France," *Antologia di belle arti*, nos. 7-8, (Dec. 1978):276, n. 86.

Carter, *Grain of Sand*, 9, no. 15, as Trevisani.

Ian Kennedy, verbally (1981), as Trevisani.

Frank DiFederico, in a letter (1982), as Trevisani.

Isolated in his rocky retreat, St. Francis fixes his entire being on the crucifix before him. The stigmata by which he received the gift of God's love are visible in his hands, and a tear compounded of remorse for his

St. Francis in Penitence, Francesco Trevisani, oil on canvas

sins and sorrow at the thought of Christ's suffering streams down his cheek. A crude stone altar serves as a resting place for a large book propped up by a disturbingly animated skull and for two root vegetables, further signs of the humbleness of Francis's life and in their slender, pointed shapes evocative of the nails of the Crucifixion.

Depictions of such states of feeling have a way of overstepping the boundary between the moving and the maudlin; Francesco Trevisani's interpretation is notable for its honesty and psychological insight. All of St. Francis's actions, down to the charged fingers of his outstretched hand, seem truly motivated from within, and the spiritual life of the artist's patron saint is communicated with considerable pictorial force. The solid, monumental figure dominates the picture space. The light—that which glows behind the cave and on the horizon and that which enters obliquely from the upper left to saturate the book, inspire the crucifix, vitalize Francis's flesh and robes, and cast grave shadows—is rich in range and dramatic authority. And detail is incisive, from the patched habit to the crystalline tear and the still-life objects.

While in sentiment the canvas points toward an eighteenth-century sensitivity, it remains essentially grounded in the Baroque. Especially relevant in this regard is a St. Francis in Penitence in the Galleria Capitolina at Rome, variously attributed to Annibale Carracci and to a follower of Ludovico Carracci.[1] Except that in the horizontally oriented Capitoline picture the Saint's left arm is also extended (and the emotion therefore more externalized), the two works are so strikingly similar in composition, setting, and still-life elements as to recommend the early Baroque painting—or another version of it—as Trevisani's direct source. Francesco's attraction to Bolognese classicism is noted by his biographers Nicola Pio (1724) and Lione Pascoli (1736), both of whom cite the Carracci.[2] In the case of the Crucified Christ for the Cathedral at Besançon, this attraction led Trevisani virtually to copy one of Guido Reni's already famous compositions.[3] The Besançon canvas is documented to 1699 and, with the addition of the Magdalen, was repeated contemporaneously by Trevisani in a picture now in the Pinacoteca at Lucca.[4] Additionally, the realism and bold lighting of the Marquette St. Francis bring to mind Trevisani's indoctrination as well into the Caraveggesque tradition as manifested, for example, in paintings of 1695-1696 for San Silvestro in Capite.[5] And the pose and type of St. Francis seem variations not only upon the Carracci signaled above but upon the figure identified as St. Bernard in Trevisani's own Holy Trinity with Saints, finished in 1684 for the church at La Cetina at Cetinale.[6]

A dating of the present canvas to approximately 1695-1700 finds confirmation in the stylistic and expressive differences between it and ostensibly similar works by the master. His St. Mary Magdalen in Penitence of c. 1706 in the Schloss Weissenstein at Pommersfelden parallels the St. Francis as an iconographic type and in its intensity of concentration.[7] Yet, allowances made for the dictates of gender, the Pommersfelden painting is decidedly less aggressive, displaying as it does a more idealized physiognomy and a softness of handling. A reduced crispness of descriptive realism and a sentimental sweetness also characterize the monogrammed St. Francis exhibited by the Heim Gallery of London in 1971; for all that, Francis's facial features and the kind and placement of the crucifix are repeated with little change from the Marquette canvas.[8]

The latter seems even further removed from Trevisani's other interpretations of the Saint known to the writer: the St. Francis Receiving the Stigmata (1719) in the Stimmate di San Francesco at Rome, with its supernatural elements (although similar in physical type); the St. Francis in Ecstasy (1729) in Santa Maria in Aracoeli at Rome; and the St. Francis with a Violin-Playing Angel (1630's) in the Gemäldegalerie at Dresden endowed, as the preceding, with Rococo prettiness and languor.[9] The distance is likewise great between the alert Saint of the Marquette picture and the entranced St. Francis (?) of Trevisani's canvas monogrammed and dated 1730 and offered as a St. Jerome by Christie's of London in 1978.[10] For these reasons, the writer is unable to follow DiFederico's proposal (letter cited) that the Marquette painting, which he considers autograph, dates from the 1720s or 1730s.

The special qualities of the present St. Francis in Penitence are reaffirmed in the light of an almost identical composition bought by Peretti from Sotheby's at London in 1973.[11] The photograph of this canvas (Witt Library, Courtauld Institute, London), the auction house's designation of it as by F. Trevisani (i.e., "in our opinion a work of the period of the artist which may be wholly or in part his work"), and the extremely low sale price (190 pounds) together suggest that it is a copy after the Marquette original. Whether it and a St. Francis called "identical" to the Milwaukee canvas and located by Frank DiFederico (letter, citing a photo in the Witt Library) in the David Peel collection at London are one and the same remains to be determined.

So also does the provenance of the Marquette version. Already by 1710 two vertical paintings of the theme by Trevisani belonged to the French "Commissaire ordinaire de l'artillerie" Jacques Béraud.[12] Trevisani's enormous popularity in France—Louis XIV, for example, owned twenty-five pictures by him in 1706—owed much to the offices of his major patron, Cardinal Pietro Ottoboni, who was legate to Avignon from 1689 to 1692 and, after 1709, "Protecteur des Affaires de France" at Rome.[13] It is tempting to suppose that during the 1690s Cardinal Ottoboni had secured a French client for the stunning painting here extolled.

St. Mary Magdelen in Penitence, c. 1710–1715 (59.6)

Oil on canvas, 39 x 30 in. (99 x 76.2 cm). Unsigned.

Provenance: Collection of Mr. and Mrs. Marc B. Rojtman, Milwaukee; their gift to the University, 1959.

References:

Pick, *Marquette University Art Collection*, 7, as Pompeo Batoni.

Fredericksen and Zeri, *Census* (1972), p. 205, as Trevisani.

Anthony Clark, in a letter (1976), as Trevisani.

Arnauld Brejon, verbally (1977), as Trevisani.

Arnauld Brejon and Pierre Rosenberg, "Francesco Trevisani et la France," *Antologia de belle arti*, nos. 7–8 (Dec. 1978):276, n. 86, as Trevisani.

Carter, *Grain of Sand*, 2 (ill.), 9, no. 14, as Trevisani.

Ian Kennedy, verbally (1981), as Trevisani.

Frank DiFederico, in a letter (1982), as student of Trevisani or later hand.

The golden-haired, rosy-cheeked Magdalen, her beauty unblemished by the rigors of penance, sits in seclusion, cut off by a natural wall from the wider world glimpsed at the left. Partially clad in a bluish mantle and with her clasped hands resting on the death's-head and enfolding a crucifix, she is lost in a state of reverie, virtually oblivious now even to the objects of her con-

St. Mary Magdalen in Penitence, Francesco Trevisani, oil on canvas

templation. Beginning with sixteenth-century Venetian painting, to which this compositional type is ultimately indebted, the theme of the penitent Magdalen found favor for reasons in addition to, and sometimes other than, its didactic function; as religious iconography that nonetheless acceded to a display of feminine charms, it was irresistible to artists and patrons alike. Francesco Trevisani was among those attracted by the subject. The Marquette canvas is one of several depictions of penitent female saints that came from his brush, of which the following may be singled out as most relevant in the present context:

(1) *St. Mary Magdalen in Penitence,* Pommersfelden, Schloss Weissenstein, oil on canvas, .70 x .54 m., probably 1706.[14]
(2) *St. Mary of Egypt in Penitence,* Pommersfelden, Schloss Weissenstein, oil on canvas, .88 x .72 m., dated 1708.[15]
(3) *St. Mary Magdalen in Penitence,* Penicuik House, collection of Sir John Clerk, Midlothian, Scotland, oil on canvas, .99 x .76 m., second decade.[16]

All three of these paintings share with the Marquette picture common formal solutions (half-length figures sheltered between stone prayer desks and rocky outcroppings from which foliage struggles to grow) and common attributes (books; skulls, the teeth described with clinical accuracy; and, for the Magdalens, wavy blond locks shimmering with highlights). However, sensible differences between them in interpretation and handling allow one to establish with considerable accuracy the place of the Marquette example within this progression. The monumental presence and the expression, mouth open, eyes upturned, of the Pommersfelden *Magdalen* recall certain penitents of Guido Reni and his followers[17] and the Bolognese-inspired *St. Francis* by Trevisani from the previous decade (see previous catalogue entry). With the *St. Mary of Egypt,* dated 1708, this outward display of passion is exchanged for a savory trance, quietistic in its implications;[18] and the exposure of one breast, the right hand clutching the other breast, and the melting quality of the flesh introduce a mildly erotic note. Dreaminess and tempered sensuality also characterize the Marquette *Mary Magdalen,* but now all manifestations of grief are omitted in favor of a more poetic statement free of any psychological complications. Before long the Magdalen will smile gently, as does the comely girl in the example at Penicuik House.[19]

Stylistic considerations likewise situate the Marquette *Magdalen* between the second of the Pommersfelden canvases and the picture in Scotland. The brushwork is underplayed throughout, the flesh somewhat marmoreal. Only the most understated diagonals relieve the basic planarity of the composition. In short, both in sentiment and style the *Magdalen* exhibits a restraint and lucidity that may legitimately be called classicizing and that unite the painting to such contemporary pictures by Trevisani as those for the Cathedral at Narni (1713-1715) and the *Madonna Reading with the Sleeping Christ Child* (c. 1715) in the Palazzo Corsini at Rome.[20]

At this point, Frank DiFederico's recently expressed doubts concerning the authorship of the Marquette *Magdalen* must be acknowledged. He writes (letter cited): "The Magdalene is fairly close to the picture in the collection of Sir John Clerk, Penicuik. But the face of the figure bothers me a good deal. Somehow it is too soft and too pretty. My final judgment, based on the photograph, is that the picture is by a student and could even be late 18th- or early 19th-century." Prof. DiFederico's opinions in these matters are not lightly to be dismissed, and the highly polished flesh does indeed give one pause. It should be pointed out, however, that the surface of the canvas appears to have been subjected to a too forceful cleaning in the past. And one can question whether the Magdalen as an ideal of youthful female beauty is distinguishable from other women depicted by the master, and in particular from the Virgin who, before a strikingly similar setting, contemplates the instruments of the Passion in Trevisani's canvas in the Palazzo Corsini.[21]

Finally, while theories regarding possible affinities between Francesco Trevisani's works and tenets of the Accademia degli Arcadi must be cautiously drawn, it may not be a coincidence that the Marquette *St. Mary Magdalen in Penitence*, surely a picture of consummate taste, apparently belongs to the period during which the artist joined that prestigious group.

R. W. B.

Notes:
1. P. Cooney and G. Malafarina, *L'opera completa di Annibale Carracci* (Milan, 1976), 131, no. 209 with ill.; D. Posner, *Annibale Carracci* (London, 1971), II:11.
2. See F. DiFederico, *Francesco Trevisani, Eighteenth-Century Painter in Rome* (Washington, D.C., 1977), 85 and 87 respectively.
3. Brejon and Rosenberg, "Francesco Trevisani et la France," 266, fig. 2, 269, 274, n. 36.
4. Ibid., 269; M. Chiarini, "I quadri della collezione del Principe Ferdinando di Toscana," *Paragone* XXVI, no. 305 (July 1975):83 and plate 56.
5. DiFederico, *Francesco Trevisani*, 10ff., 42-44, and especially plates 10-11.
6. Ibid., cat. no. 1, 39 and plate 1.
7. Ibid., cat. no. 39, 49 and plate 31.
8. *Faces and Figures of the Baroque*, catalogue of an exhibition at the Heim Gallery (London, 1971), cat. no. 19, 8 and fig. 8.
9. DiFederico, *Francesco Trevisani*, cat. no. 74, 59 and plate 61; cat. no. 86, 64 and plate 71; cat. no. 87, 64 and plate 72, respectively.
10. Dec. 1, lot 138, with ill.
11. 1.32 x .965 m.; *Catalogue of Old Master Paintings*, April 18, 1973, lot 42, without provenance.
12. M. Rambaud, *Documents du minutier central concernant l'histoire de l'art (1700-1750)* (Paris, 1971), II:800.
13. Brejon and Rosenberg, "Francesco Trevisani et la France," 265.
14. DiFederico, *Francesco Trevisani*, cat. no. 39, 49 and plate 31; A. Griseri, "Francesco Trevisani in Arcadia," *Paragone* XIII, no. 153 (1962):33-34.
15. DiFederico, *Francesco Trevisani*, cat. no. 40, 49-50 and plate 32.
16. Ibid., cat. no. 57, 54; Griseri, "Francesco Trevisani in Arcadia," 34 and plate 41.
17. Cf. ibid., 34.
18. Cf. F. Dowley, review of DiFederico's *Francesco Trevisani* in *Art Bulletin* LXI, no. 1 (1979):150.
19. To all indications, Trevisani's versions of *St. Mary Magdalen in Penitence* in a Florentine private collection and in the J. Paul Getty Museum at Malibu postdate the Penicuik work and thus are outside the present argument. See, respectively: Griseri, "Francesco Trevisani in Arcadia," 29, 33, and plate 40; B. Fredericksen, *Catalogue of the Paintings in the J. Paul Getty Museum* (Malibu, Calif., 1972), cat. no. 67, 57 and fig. 67.
20. DiFederico, *Francesco Trevisani*, 17-18, cat. nos. 64-67, 55-57, and plates 52-55; cat. no. 71, 58-59 and plate 59.
21. C. 1715-1720; ibid., cat. no. 72, 59 and plate 60.

EIGHTEENTH CENTURY

SIR GODFREY KNELLER

English (1646-1723)

Born in Lübeck in 1646, Kneller studied first with Ferdinand Bol and Rembrandt in Amsterdam. In 1672 he traveled to Rome, where he was in contact with Carlo Maratta; and to Venice, where he painted with Sebastiano Bombelli. He returned to Germany in 1675 but in 1676 went to England, where he remained for the rest of his life, aside from brief trips to France in 1684 and to Flanders in 1697. In his early years he painted subject pictures and portraits, but then specialized in the latter. He succeeded Lely as the most fashionable English court portraitist, was knighted by William III, and was given a baronetcy by George I, thus becoming the most honored British painter until Frederic Lord Leighton. His influence shaped British portraiture until the age of Reynolds.

Self-Portrait with (?) James Huckle, c. 1705 (61.14)

Oil on canvas, 22 x 22 in. (55.9 x 55.9 cm). Unsigned.

Provenance: Collection of Mr. I. A. Dinerstein; his gift to the University, 1961.

References:
On the back of the canvas is a label fragment that reads (in print): "...erida/...alle/SHERI.../AUCTIO.../LONG BE.../" and (in handwriting): "$\frac{10}{T}$".

Pick, *Marquette University Art Collection*, 16, 18 (ill.), as Kneller.

J. Douglas Stewart, *Sir Godfrey Kneller and the English Baroque Portrait* (Topsfield, Mass., 1983), cat. no. 18A, 90, plate 119A.

When the picture was given to the University, although it was recognized as a painting by Kneller, the sitters were unknown. The figure on the left can be identified as the artist himself, from his features, and because he wears the sword and gold chain that were presented to him by King William III in 1692 and 1699. These items appear also in another small-scale self-portrait, painted about 1706–1711, now in the National Portrait Gallery, London.[1] As the artist seems a little younger in the Marquette painting, it may date from around 1705.

The identity of the young man at the right is uncertain. James Huckle, Kneller's son-in-law, is the likeliest candidate for an intimate, "family" picture of this type. Unfortunately, no portrait of him is known, and little of his life. He must have married Kneller's daughter Catherine by 1708, the date of birth of their child, Godfrey, who later took his grandfather's name and was known as Godfrey Huckle Kneller. James Huckle died in 1710.[2]

Apart from this picture, and the National Portrait Gallery self-portrait, Kneller painted several other intimate small-scale "proto-Rococo" works in the first decade of the eighteenth century, which anticipate to a degree the conversation pieces of Hogarth in the 1730s.[3]

The composition of the Marquette picture derives from van Dyck's *Earl of Newport and Lord George Boring* (Petworth).[4]

J. D. S.

Notes:
1. See J. Douglas Stewart, *Sir Godfrey Kneller* (London, 1971), no. 3.
2. This information on Kneller's family derives from Chancery suits brought against Lady Kneller after the artist's death. The full documentation appears in J. Douglas Stewart, *Sir Godfrey Kneller and the English Baroque Portrait* (Topsfield, Mass., 1983). Previously Kneller's daughter was thought to have been called Agnes, and the birth of her son to have been in 1710. (See Stewart, *Sir Godfrey Kneller*, nos. 6 and 7.)
3. Ibid., nos. 69 and 70.
4. See E. Larsen, *L'Opera Completa di Van Dyck* (Milan, 1980), 2: no. 861.

SIR JOSHUA REYNOLDS

English (1723–1792)

Joshua Reynolds was born in Plympton, Devonshire. He showed a precocious talent for painting, and his father, the Reverend Samuel Reynolds, apprenticed him in 1740 to the portraitist Thomas Hudson. After three years in Hudson's London studio, Reynolds embarked in 1743 on an independent career, working alternately in Devonshire and London. The influence of Hudson on Reynolds's art was quite marked at this early stage. A great turning point in his career came in 1749, when he was invited by Augustus Keppel to accompany him to Algiers and Minorca. Reynolds used this trip as an opportunity to reach Italy, and he arrived there in 1750. His travels in Italy took him to Rome, then to Florence, Parma, Bologna, and Venice. This experience opened his eyes to the Old Masters of Italian art, and he sketched their works avidly. He soon became imbued with the idea of elevating the British school to the level of the Grand Manner painting he had encountered in Italy.

After a brief stopover in Paris, Reynolds settled in London in 1753, where he was to practice for the remainder of his life. The late 1750s and the 1760s were extremely productive years for Reynolds. He had hundreds of sitters, whom he frequently represented in antique costume or as figures from classical mythology. With these "Heroic" and allegorical works Reynolds established a new portrait type—works intended to be instructional pieces and to be publicly exhibited. The works from Reynolds's mature career are idealizing to varying degrees. Some, such as his *Georgina Countess Spencer and Her Daughter*, are extraordinarily intimate, sensitive, and sympathetic. Regardless of their degree of idealization, Reynolds's works are consistently executed with great suavity and technical virtuosity.

It was this great skill, along with his command of Old Master traditions and his penchant for didacticism, that made Reynolds the natural choice as first President of the Royal Academy after its founding in 1768. In this capacity he delivered his famous annual

Self Portrait with (?) James Huckle, Sir Godfrey Kneller, oil on canvas

Discourses, lectures that constitute the fundamental statement of art theory of the period. Reynolds carried on his academic manner of painting throughout the 1770s. It was not until after 1781, when he visited the Low Countries and came into contact with Dutch Baroque painting, that his academicism gave way to a greater ease and naturalism. In 1782 he had a paralytic stroke, but he continued to paint until 1789, when he lost the sight of one eye. He died in 1792.

Portrait of an Officer in a Red Jacket, Attributed to Sir Joshua Reynolds, oil on canvas

ATTRIBUTED TO SIR JOSHUA REYNOLDS
Portrait of an Officer in a Red Jacket (61.13)

Oil on canvas, 30 x 25 in. (76.2 x 63.5 cm). Unsigned.

Provenance: Collection of Mr. I. A. Dinerstein, Milwaukee; his gift to the University, 1961.

References:
Pick, *Marquette University Art Collection*, 21 (ill.), 22, as Reynolds.

On the stretcher a label (now lost) read: "_____ _____ Colnaghi & Company" and "Pall Mall East London."

This work clearly dates from the early ears of Reynolds's independent career. The very stiff and formal bearing of the half-length figure, which recalls the manner of Reynolds's teacher, Thomas Hudson, is characteristic of his work up to about 1755. After that date the sitters are portrayed in a more relaxed and much more elegant manner. This formality is accentuated by the standard hand-in-vest pose used in several works (e.g. *Hon. Augustus Keppel*, 1749; and *Simon 1st Earl Harcourt*, 1755[1]) from this period. There are also marked physiognomical similarities linking this work to others done by Reynolds c. 1748–1755 (e.g. *Richard 2nd Lord Edgcumbe*, c. 1748; and *George Lord Anson*, 1755[2]). At this early stage in his career, Reynolds treated his subjects in a somewhat formulaic manner, with full-rounded face, slightly protruding lower lip, long wide nose, high forehead, stiffly drawn eyebrows, and narrow, almond-shaped eyes. All of the above features, as well as the hand-in-vest pose, can be seen in Reynolds's *Sir George Colbrooke* of 1755, the work closest in style and spirit to the Marquette painting.[3] That portrait, like Marquette's, displays the three-quarter view favored by Reynolds at the time, and the manner of dress of the figure is also very similar. The short curled periwig and the gold-brocaded jacket (seen also in the *Captain Robert Orme*, 1756, National Gallery, London) make a date of c. 1755 practically certain.[4]

Reynolds typically portrays his sitters as being proud but not overbearing; as alert and intelligent; and, despite their stiff bearing, as human and approachable. All of these qualities apply to the Marquette work. The precise identity of the sitter is not known, but one possibility is that it is Captain the Honorable John Hamilton (1713/14–1755), whom Reynolds is known to have painted at least twice.[5] The 1753 portrait of Hamilton bears a strong resemblance to the Marquette painting, which may have been executed after the sitter's death. In any event, the unpretentious nature of this work suggests that this is a middle-class person and a man of achievement. It is a good example of Reynolds's work before he began to concentrate on elegant and fashionable portraits of the upper class.

J. B.

Notes:
1. Ellis K. Waterhouse, *Reynolds* (London, 1941), plates 13 and 20.
2. Ibid., plates 4 and 22.
3. Ibid., plate 26.
4. For the dress compare as well Reynolds's *Portrait of Henry Van Sittart*, sold Sotheby Parke Bernet, New York, Jan. 8, 1981, lot 99.
5. Waterhouse, *Reynolds*, plate 8.

AFTER CHARLES LE BRUN

French (?), Eighteenth Century

Deposition of Christ (76.60)

Oil on canvas, 19 1/8 x 11 5/8 in. (48.6 x 29.5 cm). Inscribed at a later date l.r.: "Marcos Liberi."

Provenance: Collection of Dr. John M. Gules, Milwaukee; his gift to the University, 1976.

References:
J. Patrice Marandel, verbally (1976), as signature not autograph; attribution must be verified.

Ian Kennedy, verbally (1981), as Italian.

Jennifer Montagu, in a letter (1983), as after Le Brun."

The task of lowering Christ from the Cross has fallen to four men. Two of them, the partially nude figure on the ladder who supports the lifeless body on his back, and the man holding a rope with a noosed end that cuts into the Savior's flesh (an indignity better reserved for the thieves, whose now-empty crosses are glimpsed at left and right), are apparently regulars at such executions. They are assisted by Nicodemus above, in a maroon shirt, and St. John the Evangelist below, wearing a salmon robe that provides the dominant color note. St. John embraces Christ's legs, which are enveloped by a section of the shroud; this action may be likened to that of the priest, his hands covered with the humeral veil, as he displays to the faithful the monstrance housing the Host. Among the four mourners, whose expressions range from shock to deep inner sadness, are the Virgin in her red mantle and blue garments and a figure hooded in a brownish mantle with orange highlights.

This small canvas was attributed with misgivings to a Marco Liberi on the basis of a "signature" that appears at the lower right: Marcos Liberi. Aside from the strange combination of a given name ending in "s" with an Italian surname, the letters seem too distinct for the apparent age of the picture and may have been painted over varnishes applied after the picture was completed. Is this later inscription a misspelled record of a venerable attribution? The Venetian master Marco Liberi (born 1640 or 1644), son and imitator of Pietro Liberi (1605-1687), is known today by way of a tiny oeuvre dominated by erotic mythologies. Neither these paintings nor the fully Baroque religious canvases of Pietro are in the least reflected in the character of the Marquette picture.[1]

In fact, as Dr. Robert B. Simon has discovered, this work depends almost exclusively upon two distinct interpretations of the theme by the French master Charles Le Brun (1619-1690), artistic dictator under Louis XIV. The first of Le Brun's conceptions, datable to the mid-1640s, that is, during or immediately following his study trip (1642-1646) to Rome, is recorded in an engraving marked *LeBrun pinxit* by François de Poilly,[2] and in three extant painted versions:

(1) Prague, National Gallery, oil on canvas, 78 x 60 cm.[3]
(2) London, Victoria and Albert Museum, oil on canvas, 78.7 x 63.5 cm.[4]
(3) Saint-Germain en Laye, Musée de Ville, oil on canvas, 81 x 64 cm.[5]

Of these canvases Montagu has written: "All three were clearly directed by the same artist [Le Brun], and quite possibly produced by the same hand. Whether this was in fact the hand of LeBrun is much less certain, and it remains probable that all are workshop replicas of the same lost original."[6] The question of the autograph nature of the above examples need not be at issue here, for Le Brun's responsibility for the design is

Deposition of Christ, After Charles Le Brun, oil on canvas

attested by Poilly's print, and it is this design that the author of the Marquette *Deposition* in large part appropriated. Specifically, he took over directly the entire composition of Christ and the four men involved with lowering His body, the hooded figure, and most of the woman against the stone at the lower right. There are, however, a number of omissions, most notably the scowling horseman at the left, the crucified Good Thief above him, and, at the right, the rising group of the fainting Virgin and two female mourners.

The void thus created at the lower left was filled by a seated woman, head in hands, and, above and behind her, the standing Madonna. At the same time, the legs of the figure by the stone, no longer supporting the recumbent Virgin, had to be redesigned. In effecting these additions and alterations, the artist of the Marquette canvas drew upon another and later *Descent from the Cross* by Charles Le Brun, that commissioned about 1679 for the Carmelites of Lyon and today in the Musée des Beaux-Arts at Rennes, oil on canvas, 5.45 x 3.27 m.[7] But now the borrowings were subjected to transpositions and reversals for which not the Rennes original but rather Benoit I Audran's (1661-1721) engraving, showing Le Brun's huge altarpiece in reverse, seems to have served.[8]

The Marquette *Deposition* is therefore another indication of the extreme popularity of Le Brun's conceptions—a fourth picture of the early version was sold out of Cardinal Fesch's collection in 1845,[9] and a number of paintings inspired by the Rennes canvas or by Audran's engraving after it are known.[10] When, then, might it have been executed? Its quality—very competent but not up to Le Brun's standards—and its character as a pastiche of pictures separated in time by more than three decades exclude the master's authorship. It is even doubtful that Le Brun would have sanctioned the issuance of such a composite from his workshop, the more so as its expression is rather removed from those of the still unmistakably Baroque models: Without the complex figure groupings and insistent diagonals of Le Brun's inventions, the Marquette canvas is considerably less dynamic. With its overlapping parallel planes, symmetrical balancing of masses, and use of a triangular scheme to embrace all the forms and render the picture a contained whole, it exhibits a strongly classicizing structure. The answer as to whether the Renaissance-like simplicity of this attractive and art-historically fascinating canvas is due to the artist's awareness of his limitations, or reflects a late eighteenth-century or early Neo-Classical taste, may have to await a solution to the "Marcos Liberi" puzzle.

R. W. B.

Notes:
1. See S. de Kunert, "Notizie e documenti su Pietro Liberi," *Rivista d'arte* XIII (1931):539-575; R. Pallucchini, *La pittura veneziana del seicento* (Milan, 1981), I:196-206 and passim, and II: figs. 614-652.

2. J. Montagu, "The 'Descent from the Cross' by Charles LeBrun," *Victoria and Albert Museum Bulletin* IV, no. 4 (Oct. 1968):130, fig. 2.
3. J. Thuillier in *Charles LeBrun 1619-1690: peintre et dessinateur*, catalogue of an exhibition at Versailles (1963), 28 (ill.) and cat. no. 12, 29; Montagu, "Descent from the Cross," 129, 130, fig. 3, and 131, n. 2.
4. Ibid., 128-131 (ill.).
5. Ibid., 129, 130, 131, incl. n. 3.
6. Ibid., 131.
7. Thuillier, *Charles LeBrun*, 120 (ill.) and cat. no. 41, 121; Montagu, "Descent from the Cross," 129.
8. Montagu, "Descent from the Cross," 131, fig. 4; Thuillier, *Charles LeBrun*, 121.
9. Montagu, "Descent from the Cross," 129 and 131, n. 4 with bibliography.
10. Thuillier, *Charles LeBrun*, 121.

BRITISH SCHOOL

Last Quarter of the Eighteenth/First Quarter of the Nineteenth Century

Moses Breaking the Tablets (79.13)

Oil on canvas, 50 1/4 x 40 1/2 in. (127.6 x 102.9 cm). Inscribed indistinctly, l.l.c.: "B...n..." [Bone?, Bunce?].

Provenance: British Provincial auction, 1950s; Art Market, Michigan;[1] collection of Mr. and Mrs. Eckhart G. Grohmann, Milwaukee; their gift to the University, 1979.

References:
John Wilmerding, verbally (1981), as possibly workshop of Benjamin West.

Allen Staley, in a letter (1982), as not by West.

Dorinda Evans, in a letter (1982), as by an English or American follower of West, c. 1800.

This large canvas represents the descent of Moses from Mt. Sinai after he has received the Commandments. He is accompanied by Joshua and stands over the camp of the Israelites, who are singing and dancing in praise of the Golden Calf, the idol created by Aaron in Moses's absence.

And Moses turned, and went down from the mount, and the two tables of the testimony were in his hand: the tables were written on both their sides; on the one side and on the other were they written. And the tables were the work of God, and the writing was the writing of God, graven upon the tables. And when Joshua heard the noise of the people as they shouted, he said unto Moses, There is a noise of war in the camp. And he said, It is not the voice of them that shout for mastery, neither is it the voice of them that cry for being overcome: but the noise of them that sing do I hear. And it came to pass, as soon as he came nigh unto the camp, that he saw the calf, and the dancing: and Moses' anger waxed hot, and he cast the tables out of his hands, and brake them beneath the mount (Exodus 32:15-19).

The painting of large history pictures—of religious, literary, and historical subjects—underwent a tremendous revival in late eighteenth-century England.

Moses Breaking the Tablets, British School, Late Eighteenth-Early-Nineteenth Century, oil on canvas

With such notable projects as Boydell's Shakespeare Gallery and Fuseli's Milton Gallery, numerous paintings by a variety of artists were created and brought to public attention.[2] Representations of scriptural stories, in the past usually limited to engraved book illustrations, were now painted on the grand scale as well, although not in the formalized setting of, for example, the Shakespeare and Milton series.

Benjamin West (1783-1820), to whom the *Moses* was erroneously attributed, met with notable success painting such religious compositions, but in a cooler, more Neo-Classical style.[3] The Marquette *Moses* would seem to be by a British follower of West and perhaps one associated with the other literary series. One possible author would be Henry Tresham (1751-1814), an Irish artist active in Rome and London.[4] His paintings are predominantly of biblical, classical, or literary subjects, and his painting style, which

has been characterized as "flimsy and mannered,"[5] is quite reminiscent of Marquette's canvas.

R. B. S.

Notes:
1. Information provided by Dr. Alfred Bader.
2. See A. E. Santaniello, introduction to *The Boydell Shakespeare Prints* (New York, 1979), and Peter Tomory, *The Life and Art of Henry Fuseli* (New York-Washington, 1972), 34-40.
3. See John Dillenberger, *Benjamin West: the Context of His Life's Work* (San Antonio, Texas, 1977). The attribution to West was evidently inspired by an optimistic reading of the signature on the painting as "B. West"; the generally abraded state of the picture surface, however, makes any reading conjectural. Moreover, the placement of the fragmentary lettering some distance from the corner of the canvas suggests that an inscription, rather than a signature, might have been intended.
4. Ellis Waterhouse, *The Dictionary of British 18th Century Painters in Oils and Crayons* (Woodbridge, 1981), 373; Walter G. Strickland, *A Dictionary of Irish Artists* (Dublin, 1913), 453-457; and Nancy L. Pressly, *The Fuseli Circle in Rome: Early Romantic Art of the 1770's* (New Haven, 1979), 101-106.
5. Waterhouse, *Dictionary of British 18th Century Painters*, 373. Cf. Tresham's *The Earl of Warwick's Vow Previous to the Battle of Towton* (Manchester City Art Gallery), exhibited at the Royal Academy in 1797; ill. *Concise Catalogue of British Paintings: Manchester City Art Gallery* (Manchester, 1976), I:189.

PIER LEONE GHEZZI

Italian (1674-1755)

Pier Leone (or Pierleone) Ghezzi cut an impressive figure in Rome during the first half of the eighteenth century. Draftsman, painter in oil and fresco, engraver, and restorer, as well as anatomist, antiquarian, and musician, he was a familiar personality on the artistic scene. His connections to the center of power were likewise close, since he was called to portray Popes and the highest prelates, invited to vacation with the Governor of Rome, Cardinal Alessandro Falconieri, and appointed Pittore della Camera Apostolica, in which capacity over the course of almost forty years (1708-1747) he cared for the papal painting collections and supervised the production of mosaics, tapestries, and festival decorations. Convinced of his own important place in these circles, he kept a diary that has served as an important resource for research on his life.

Ghezzi's beginnings were propitious. He was born in Rome on June 28, 1674, the son of the painter Giuseppe Ghezzi, who was shortly to serve as Secretary and chief theoretician to the artists' Accademia di San Luca. The success of Giuseppe's program for Pier Leone's training, which included producing drawings after his father's paintings, received official recognition as early as 1695, when the younger Ghezzi was awarded first prize in an Academy competition. The first decade of the new century saw Pier Leone's induction into that institution (1705) and his creation of engraved illustrations for books by Pope Clement XI. With his father's connections and his own wide-ranging interests and wit, and fancying himself a sensitive and cultured person (as can be seen already in the *Self-Portrait* of 1702 in the Uffizi at Florence), Ghezzi became one of Roman society's most welcome members.

But Ghezzi made his living through art. His paintings, ranging in scale from small easel pictures to altarpieces and frescoes, and in type from genre and portraits to religious, mythological, and allegorical themes, have never been systematically studied. One's sense is that as a painter Ghezzi was more versatile than innovative, capable of working in several manners and with varying degrees of commitment to expressive depth and craftsmanship. The frescoes in the Villa Falconieri at Frascati (1723–1727) and in the Castello Falconieri at Torre in Pietra (1712–1732) are notable for their audacious trompe l'oeil effects and for their animation and humor. A penetrating observation also informs Ghezzi's genre scenes and even the religious canvases, which can move from the robustly brushed and bombastic to the carefully executed and charming.

Pier Leone's fame has always rested above all on his caricature drawings. Done in pen and ink (at first combined with wash), they chronicle the look, manners, and personalities of a wide spectrum of Rome's residents and visitors. The early caricatures (some with the dates 1697 and 1702) are more spontaneously executed and amusing. As plaudits continued to come Ghezzi's way and as (or so it seems) his intellectual and social pretensions became even more confirmed after the death of his father in 1721, the drawings lapsed into convention and stiffness, the latter the result of a rejection of modeling and an insistent use of parallel strokes in the manner of printmakers. As a body the drawings provide a vivid feeling of the age. It is an age viewed rather objectively, with limited exaggeration when one considers what Bernini and Mola had done, and hardly moralizing or satirical in relation to what Hogarth was then doing and Daumier was to do. By the time Ghezzi died in 1755, having produced thousands of these caricatures, he knew that he was assured the acclamations of posterity, with its connoisseurs and its historians of Roman art and culture.

The Singing Monks (Matins), Pier Leone Ghezzi, oil on canvas

The Singing Monks (Matins)
c. 1715-1730   (60.2)

Oil on canvas, 32 1/2 x 18 3/4 in. (82.6 x 47.6 cm). Unsigned.

Provenance: Collection of Sir Charles Eastlake; Sir Robert Witt; J. Leger and Son, London, 1957; Mr. and Mrs. Marc B. Rojtman, Milwaukee; their gift to the University, 1960.

References:
Hermann Voss, letter of expertise, July 14, 1952, as "characteristic work of P. Ghezzi."

"Notable Works of Art Now on the Market," advertising supplement to the *Burlington Magazine* XCIX (December, 1957): plate XX and corresponding discussion, as Ghezzi.

Pick, *Marquette University Art Collection*, 15-16, (ill.), as Ghezzi.

Federico Zeri, in a letter (1968), questioning Ghezzi.

Anthony Clark, in a letter (1976), as Ghezzi.

J. Patrice Marandel, verbally (1976), as eighteenth century, but questionable attribution to Ghezzi.

Arnauld Brejon, verbally (1977), as Ghezzi.

Ian Kennedy, verbally (1981), as definitely Ghezzi.

Twenty tonsured Franciscans, some wearing white robes over their brown habits and one dressed in a gold-brocaded chasuble, have assembled as two groups in a monks' choir for chanting the Divine Office. Beside them stands a secular figure, no doubt a benefactor of the order, in a light blue coat of eighteenth-century fashion. The occasion may be the canonical hour of Lauds (formerly called Matins). The rising sun—often viewed as symbolic of Christ's Resurrection—burns away the clouds of night and floods the interior with an early morning freshness as the men sing, perhaps in antiphony, the psalms of praise.[1]

The attribution of the canvas to Pier Leone Ghezzi, first proposed by Hermann Voss in 1954, has been accepted by several scholars (see above). Those features that most recommend Ghezzi's authorship and render the picture altogether convincing might be subsumed under a single heading: perceptiveness. As demonstrated by the unending stream of drawn caricatures, Pier Leone's eye embraced reality from its broadest aspects to its nuances, and his pen recorded what he perceived with unvarnished directness. The liberties he took were inherent in his subjects, and he backed away from fantasy in both representation and interpretation. The *Monks' Choir,* too, is simultaneously typical and particularized. The earnestness with which the hymns are offered is to be found among any such gathering of devout monastics. The men run the gamut from young to old, from ascetic to obese, and in this sense may even be considered stock types. Yet each figure is studied as to physiognomy and feeling. The mouths, the eyes (one pair peering through pince-nez), and the sets of the heads are variously those of tenors, baritones, and bassos, of the phlegmatic and the beatific. Could it also be that the monk at the foot of the stairs is tapping the rhythm while he at the center raises a hand to stifle a yawn? None of this is especially profound or moving, of course, and surely there is no intent to satirize or teach a moral lesson. And that in itself points to Ghezzi.

The artist's perceptiveness extends to the environment. The locale is viewed down to the bell and the curtain pulls, and the light is wonderfully true as it shines off bald plates and the large lectern, saturates the white garments, bathes the pavement, works its way into the deepest recesses, and suggests the time of day.

Pier Leone Ghezzi appears to be at work in the Marquette picture in other ways as well. The figure of the benefactor is particularly diminutive. This man was probably the artist's patron and was flattered to be the object of the most famous caricaturist in Rome. Ghezzi lived up to his reputation by exaggerating the short stature of the one individual in the painting who was not meant to remain anonymous. Also relevant to the genesis of the work may be the artist's own musical interests as a violinist and as host to weekly concerts in his home.[2]

It is in fact the range of types within the vast repository of caricature drawings that most consistently points to Ghezzi as the author of the *Monks' Choir.*[3] Such pen and ink studies as the group portrait of *Baron Stosch and a Gathering of Roman Antiquarians*[4] and the *Cellar of a Monastery* are cases in point.[5]

Pier Leone's paintings, on the other hand, are somewhat less suggestive of his responsibility for the Marquette picture. Most relevant by virtue of its diminutive figures, unpretentiousness, and spirited handling is the fresco of the *Arrival of Pope Benedict XIII* for the Castello Falconieri at Torre in Pietra.[6] As for works by Ghezzi in oil on canvas that might reasonably be introduced in this context, the best that can be said is that the following small paintings do not contravene the foregoing arguments: (1) *A Woman Giving Alms to a Beggar,* Cambridge, Mass., Fogg Art Museum, oil on canvas, .74 x .61 m.[7], and (2) *Paolo di Matteis at His Easel,* U.S.A., private collection, oil on canvas, .395 x .292 m., signed and dated 1727,[8] published by Clark who, as noted, believed the *Monks' Choir* to be an autograph Ghezzi. The Fogg picture of anonymous humanity has an objectivity and sobriety that compare favorably with the Marquette example, while the *Paolo di Matteis,* being of a specific individual in an informal situation, is a painted caricature.

The spontaneity, lack of affectation, and assured brushwork that distinguish the *Monks' Choir* would seem most in accord with the middle years of Pier Leone Ghezzi's career, and thus a date of c. 1715-1730 is here assigned to this part of Roman life.

Portrait of Cardinal Giuseppe Renato Imperiali, Attributed to Pier Leone Ghezzi, oil on canvas

ATTRIBUTED TO
PIER LEONE GHEZZI
Portrait of Cardinal
Giuseppe Renato Imperiali,
c. 1710-1715   (73.17)

Oil on canvas, 51 1/4 x 38 1/2 in. (130.2 x 97.8 cm). Unsigned.

Provenance: Gift of Schroeder Hotels, Inc., to the University, 1973.

References:
J. Patrice Marandel, verbally (1976), as possibly an artist around Batoni, Mengs, or Anton von Maron.

Arnauld Brejon, verbally (1977), as Pier Leone Ghezzi.

Ian Kennedy, verbally (1981), as probably Francesco Trevisani.

Frank DiFederico, in a letter (1982), as close to Trevisani.

Separated from its historical matrix, this painting was relegated to an anonymity totally unbefitting its strength as a visual image and a characterization. The identity of the individual portrayed may now be restored and the canvas placed within the Roman artistic mileau of the first part of the eighteenth century.

It has always been obvious that the man who confronts us here, dressed in a red *mozzetta* and white lace surplice, was an important member of the Catholic cardinalate. Against an olive-colored curtain and a vaulted library, he is depicted close up, his right hand, the arm of the carved chair, and the edge of the equally ornamental reading desk crowding the picture plane. The head and hands, boldly modeled in light and shadow, assert themselves with considerable force, and the textures of skin, hair, cloth, and wood are persuasively true. But the Cardinal exists above all as a personality: temperate but not ascetic; reserved but not solemn, his lips formed into a slight smile; able simultaneously to acknowledge the observer and to process the thoughts running through his mind, the alertness of which is communicated by the keen eyes, the somewhat unkempt hair, and the streak of light that on the right sets off the head from the background.

This dignified presence is Cardinal Giuseppe Renato Imperiali (1651-1737), identifiable beyond question on the basis of a bust-length portrait engraving published in 1751 by M. Guarnacci and inscribed:

JOSEPH RENATVS S. R. E. PRIOR PRESBYTERORVM
CARDINALIS IMPERIALIS IANVENSIS
CREATVS DIE XIII FEBRVARII MDCXC
Obÿt die 15. Januarÿ 1737[9]

Drawn and engraved by Gaspare Massi, this portrait was no doubt based on an earlier painted likeness of the Cardinal, a painting, moreover, which may have been adapted with variations in the drapery from the Marquette canvas. The upper right corner of the print bears the eagle of the Imperiali coat of arms, the same eagle that perches on the back of the Cardinal's chair in the Marquette picture.

Imperiali's stature within the Catholic hierarchy was highly distinguished.[10] Giuseppe Renato was born on April 26, 1651, the son of a Genoese nobleman, Michele Imperiali, Prince of Francavilla and Marchese d'Oria in the heel of Italy. Under the guidance of his great-uncle, Cardinal Lorenzo Imperiali, he was educated at Rome in the Collegio Hungarico e Germanico, received the Cross of the Knights of Jerusalem, and entered the priesthood. Having served as Clerk of the Camera Apostolica for Clement X (Pope, 1670-1676), he was promoted by Innocent XI (Pope, 1676-1689) to the post of Treasurer General with the charge of collecting and administering all revenues from the Church patrimony. An album of presentation drawings, some adorned with the Imperiali eagle and dating from 1688 to 1735 (discovered and discussed by Gambardella), documents Imperiali's involvement with the construction of ecclesiastical edifices and public works in several cities under papal control.

On February 13, 1690, Giuseppe Renato was elevated to the cardinalate by Pope Alessandro VIII and designated legate to Ferrara. Upon returning to Rome in 1696 he received the appointment of Cardinal Prefect of the Sacra Congregazione del Buon Governo, a powerful judicial body. Other prestigious and sensitive assignments were entrusted to him, including that of heading the papal delegation that met in Milan in November 1711 to recognize Charles, newly proclaimed Hapsburg Emperor and contender for the Spanish throne. Unfortunately, the Cardinal's perceived sympathy with Austrian politics worked against him when in the conclaves of 1724 and 1730 his candidacy for the papacy was opposed by France and especially Spain.

The sources confirm what the foregoing brief account and the impressive painting in Milwaukee have already suggested: Cardinal Giuseppe Renato Imperiali was a man of great intellectual gifts, of rigorous moral standards, and of total dedication to and competence in his work. Demanding the same qualities of those with whom he surrounded himself, he was at once an enlightened force and a moderating influence in a situation hardly immune from conflict and from unscrupulous, self-serving schemes.

What now of the row of books, eagle-topped cartouches marking the various sections, that are featured in the Marquette portrait? On the upper floor of his Roman palazzo Cardinal Imperiali amassed an extraordinarily rich private library. Consisting of three rooms disposed—the painting indicates—in an H-shaped configuration, the Biblioteca Imperiali was frequented by major scholars from Italy and beyond. In 1711 Giusto Fontanini issued a catalogue of these vast holdings under the title *Bibliothecae Josephi Renatis Imperialis Sanctae Romanae Ecclesiae Diaconi Cardinalis Sancti Giorgi Catalogus Secundum Auctorum Cognomia*, Romae, MDCCXI. (The Catalogue, of preface i–v and 738 pages, measures approximately 33.5 x 24.5 x 6 cm). After Imperiali's death on January 15, 1737, the library was divided between Cardinal Spinelli and the Castello Imperiali at Francavilla Fontana, in which town, in the Biblioteca Comunale, a fraction of Giuseppe Renato's collection may still be found.

The commissioning of this large, formal, carefully crafted portrait must have been prompted by special circumstances. It is here theorized that the work was executed in consequence of two major events in the Cardinal's life during the year 1711: the publication of the grand *Catalogus* (perhaps the very volume, its real size diminished by foreshortening, bookmarked by Imperiali's left index finger) and the mission to Milan as major representative of Clement XII: The prominence of the library in the Marquette picture and the fact that the Cardinal called upon Cristiano Reder to paint a huge canvas "representing His Excellency [Imperiali] when he made his magnificent entrance into Milan as legate *a latere* to the ruling Emperor" favor this proposal.[11] Furthermore, in 1711 Cardinal Imperiali was sixty years old, an age consistent with his appearance—thin, grayed and receding hair—in the portrait.

Both of the artists—Francesco Trevisani and Pier Leone Ghezzi—to whom the picture has been assigned on stylistic grounds were working in Rome at this time, and arguments can indeed be advanced in support of either attribution. Among Trevisani's portraits known to the writer, that of *Cardinal Pietro Ottoboni* in the Bowes Museum at Barnard Castle, England, most closely parallels the *Cardinal Imperialis*.[12] Variously dated c. 1689 and c. 1700–1705, Trevisani's picture—in which the family emblem of the two-headed eagle, wings extended, crowns the chair—is notable for its sense of personality, forcefulness of form, and precise rendering of garments and accessories. The painting has that aggressive presence which is the dominant quality of the Marquette picture. In addition, the compositional structure, including the architectural perspective at the right, of Francesco's portrait presumed to be of the *Abate Carlo Colonna*, signed and dated 1691, is comparable.[13] And Pascoli reports that Trevisani executed a portrait of Cardinal Imperiali, a work listed by DiFederico (p. 78) as "Unlocated."[14]

Notwithstanding, Trevisani's responsibility for the Marquette portrait is problematic. Its solid manner is somewhat removed from the fluidity and Rococo elegance of Francesco's later portraits and, if by him, would seem better placed during the 1690s than around 1711, the date recommended by the biography and apparent age of Cardinal Imperiali. Recently Frank DiFederico (letter cited), introducing as well the *Ottoboni* and *Colonna* portraits, has written: "The attribution to Trevisani...I find very credible on all levels, except for the strongly realistic handling of the head and the elongation of the figure."

It is this trenchant realism that brings to mind Pier Leone Ghezzi, although consideration of his authorship is complicated by the artist's mercurial nature, the uncertainty of his chronology as a painter, and the paucity of scholarship devoted to his activity as a portraitist. Thus the signed *Portrait of Clement XI* in a private collection at Rome, datable c. 1711–1712, has a brutal frankness and impulsive technique that are not compatible with the Marquette canvas.[15] Anthony Clark, commenting on Ghezzi the portrait painter, speaks of a "daring and obvious sense of style" and of a "slap-dash virtuosity."[16] Yet the *Portrait of Benedetto Falconcini, Bishop of Arezzo*, acquired as a Ghezzi by the Worcester Art Museum in 1978 and dated c. 1704, is anything but slapdash.[17] In fact, it meets the *Portrait of Cardinal Imperiali* at a number of points. Falconcini is seated obliquely on a chair, close to the picture plane, his legs shown only to below the knees. He is backed by a curtain that is drawn to reveal on the right a bookcase filled with books (although here the view of the library is a restricted one). As in the Marquette work, the forms are modeled by a palpable light that enters from the left.[18] Clearly Ghezzi could blend formality with a direct recording of facts and a measured honesty of characterization.

Additional supporting evidence is provided by the lunette of *Benedict XIII Blessing*, which Ghezzi frescoed in 1725 on the end wall of the great hall in the Castello Falconieri at Torre in Pietra.[19] Here twenty-eight distinct personalities flank the Pope in an elaborate trompe l'oeil balcony scene. The fourth man from the left, gesturing as if to doff his *biretta*, has been identified as none other than Cardinal Giuseppe Renato Imperiali.[20] Therefore, as Arnauld Brejon (oral report cited) has surmised, the Marquette painting may well have come from the brush of Pier Leone Ghezzi, favorite of the prominent in eighteenth-century Rome.

R. W. B.

Notes:

1. See G. E. Schidel in the *New Catholic Encyclopedia* (Washington, D.C., 1967), VIII:531-532, and J. Pascher, ibid., IX:463-464.
2. M. Loret, "Pier Leone Ghezzi," *Capitolium* XI (June 1935):297. Also on Ghezzi's life-style see L. Pascoli, *Vite de'pittori, scultori, et architetti moderni* (Rome, 1736), II:205-207.
3. The reader is directed to: H. Bouchot, "L'ambassade de France à Rome en 1747: portraits-charges par Pier-Leone Ghezzi," *L'Art* I, 3rd ser. (1901):197-217; F. Hermanin, "Un volume di disegni di Pier Leone Ghezzi," *Bollettino d'arte* I (1907):17-24; Loret, "Pier Leone Ghezzi," 297; D. Bodart, "Disegni giovanili inediti di P. L. Ghezzi nella Biblioteca Vaticana," *Palatino* XI, No. 2 (April-June 1967):141-154; idem, "Pier Leone Ghezzi, the draftsman," *Print Collector* VII, no. 31 (March-April 1976):12-31; M. Benisovich, "Ghezzi and the French Artists in Rome," *Apollo* LXXV (May 1967):340-347.
4. Vienna, Albertina; A. Stix and L. Fröhlich-Bum, *Beschreibender Katalog der Handzeichnungen in der graphischen Sammlung Albertina* (Vienna, 1932), III: cat. no. 892, 85, plate 190, fig. 892.
5. Rome, E. Galluppi collection; Bodart, "Disegni giovanili inediti di P. L. Ghezzi," 20, 23, fig. 16.
6. 1725; A. Busiri Vici, "Ritratti inediti di Benedetto XIII," *Studi romani* V, no. 3 (May-June 1957):305 and plate LII, fig. 1; A. LoBianco, "Pierleone Ghezzi a Torre in Pietra," *Storia dell'arte*, no. 29 (1977): 62 and, for a related fresco, fig. 7.
7. Listed in the *Fogg Art Museum: Acquisitions 1968* (Cambridge, 1969), 122 (ill.), 144, as by an unknown eighteenth-century Roman artist, the picture has been given to Pier Leone Ghezzi by Anthony Clark in *Painting in Italy in the Eighteenth Century: Rococo to Romanticism*, exhibition catalogue (Chicago, 1970), 194.
8. Clark, *Painting in Italy in the Eighteenth Century*, cat. no. 81, 194-195 with ill.
9. M. Guarnacci, *Vitae et res Gestae Pontificorum Romanorum e S. R. E.*, Rome, I; reproduced by A. Busiri Vici, "Ritratti inediti di Benedetto XIII," plate LIV, fig. 3, and as the frontispiece to A. Gambardella, *Architettura e committenza nello stato pontifico tra barocco e rococo. Un amministratore illuminato: Giuseppe Renato Imperiali* (Naples, 1979).
10. Gambardella's study, previous note, supported by a full bibliography, is here taken as the most recent and accessible account of his life and achievements.
11. Pascoli, *Vite de'pittore, scultori, ed architetti moderni*, II:355.
12. F. DiFederico, *Francesco Trevisani, Eighteenth-Century Painter in Rome* (Washington, D.C., 1977), 21-22, cat. P5, 73, and plate 100; E. Waterhouse, "Some Old Masters other than Spanish in the Bowes Museum," *Burlington Magazine* XCV (1953):121, fig. 4 and 123.
13. Ibid., cat. P3, 72 and plate 98.
14. Manuscript life of Trevisani, 1736, transcribed in ibid., 91.
15. F. Negri Arnoldi, "Il ritratto di Clemente XI di Pierleone Ghezzi e una medaglia dell'Amerani," *Paragone* XXI, no. 239 (1970):63ff. and plates 61-62a.
16. Anthony Clark, "Pierleone Ghezzi's Portraits," *Paragone* XIV, no. 165 (Sept. 1963):16-17; reprinted with annotations by E. P. Bowron in A. Clark, *Studies in Roman Eighteenth-Century Painting* (Washington, D.C., 1981).
17. "La chronique des art," in *Gazette des Beaux-Arts* CXXI (1979):38, no. 188 (ill.).
18. As also in the *Portrait of Cardinal Alessandro Albani* sold as a Ghezzi by Sotheby's of Florence on May 24, 1963; *Burlington Magazine* CXV (April 1973):x.
19. Vici, "Ritratti inediti di Benedetto XIII," 304-308, and plates L-LIII.
20. Ibid.

FRANCESCO SOLIMENA

Italian (1657-1747)

In Book III of his *El Museo pictórico* of 1715, the Spanish artist-writer Antonio Palomino praised Francesco Solimena as the greatest painter then working in Europe. With Luca Giordano having died in 1705 and Carlo Maratti in 1713, Francesco Trevisani restricting himself to works in oil, and Giambattista Tiepolo just beginning to make his mark, Palomino's judgment had much to recommend it. Even in the decades that followed, this conception of the dominance of Solimena, whose talents extended to poetry, music, and architecture, was often to be sustained, not the least because of the brilliant achievements of such students as Sebastiano Conca, Corrado Giaquinto, and Francesco de Mura.

Francesco Solimena was baptized at Canale di Serina, in southern Italy, on October 11, 1657. His father, the painter Angelo Solimena, saw to his first education in the town of Nocera, and the two men were later to collaborate on some commissions. But Francesco's real instruction began in 1674, when he arrived in Naples, from which city he worked for the remainder of his life. It might be said, as a gross generalization, that during the years of his formation Solimena was especially attracted by two essentially different manners: the early pictures of Luca Giordano, products of Neapolitan Caravaggism, and the grand, light-filled productions of the Bolognese painter Giovanni Lanfranco, who had resided in Naples from 1633 to 1647.

Both of these interests were to have implications for the directions that Solimena's art was to take. His paintings of 1689-1690 in the sacristy of San Paolo Maggiore at Naples epitomize his first mature phase. Under the impact now of the contemporary works of Luca Giordano, these frescoes dazzle by their airiness

51

and luminosity, their highly complex and energetic composition, and their vigorous brushwork. Yet before long Solimena was to abjure much of what he had done. During the 1690s, apparently feeling that he had carried this fiery manner to its ultimate conclusion and in the process had lost touch with reality, Francesco turned back to the Caravaggesque tradition, and in particular to the art of Mattia Preti. Individual forms take on a greater nobility and, being struck by a powerful spotlighting, a greater sense of sheer physical presence (see, for example, the *Dream of St. Joseph* and the *Flight into Egypt* in Santa Maria Donnalbina at Naples).

The last-mentioned canvases were painted about 1699. And in 1700 Solimena made his first (and perhaps only) trip to Rome, where, however, he remained for but a month. The Roman experience, during which he confronted the classicizing pictures of Carlo Maratti and those of such early Bolognese classicists as Domenichino and Annibale Carracci, and a realization that the Preti-inspired tenebrism of the previous decade had degenerated into formula, were decisive. Furthermore, Solimena had ties to the Arcadian movement (see the biography of Francesco Trevisani) with its reaction against Baroque "excess" in literature. Striving for a greater dignity of form and expression, he now emphasized the sculpturesque and compositional clarity. At times, however, this classicizing of the Baroque was pushed to the point of academicism. Thus once again Francesco Solimena, not averse to self-cricitism, renewed himself with, for example, the dramatic chiaroscuro of the St. Martin scenes for the Certosa di San Martino at Naples (c. 1732–1733) and, at the end of his long and prolific career, the astonishingly free *Allegories* now in the Pinacoteca di Capodimonte.

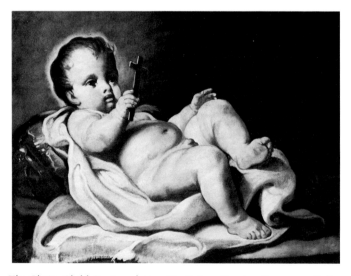

The Christ Child Contemplating His Future Passion, Francesco Solimena, oil on canvas

The Christ Child Contemplating His Future Passion, c. 1720–1730 (61.4)

Oil on canvas, 19 3/4 x 25 7/8 in. (50 x 65.7 cm). Unsigned.

Provenance: Collection of the Earl of Derby; Mr. and Mrs. Marc B. Rojtman; their gift to the University, 1961.

References:
Pick, *Marquette University Art Collection,* 24 (ill.), as Solimena.

J. Patrice Marandel, verbally (1976), as perhaps Solimena.

Arnauld Brejon, verbally (1977), as Solimena.

His head encircled by a golden radiance symbolic of his divinity and of that illumination by which he already perceives his future suffering for mankind, the Christ Child contemplates the small cross in his right hand. In this context the encradling white blanket may allude to the shroud of the Passion.

The attribution to Solimena of this private devotional image is sustainable. With his small but heavy-lipped mouth compressed between chubby cheeks, the right leg bent and the left drawn up and twisted so as to reveal the sole of the foot, the infant is of a type first developed by Solimena early in his career and used interchangeably for putti-angels and the Christ Child. Parallel examples are found in the frescoes for the Chapel of St. Anne in the Chiesa del Gesù Nuovo (1677) and for Sta. Maria Donnaregina (1681–1684) and in the altarpiece of the *Madonna and Child with SS. Peter, Paul, and Angels* (1684) for San Nicola alla Carità, all in Naples.[1] Furthermore, Luca Giordano's *Sleeping Christ Child* (c. 1660) in the Pinacoteca Vaticana may be taken as a Neapolitan precedent for Solimena's equally small-scale depiction of the isolated, reclining Child.[2]

In style, however, the Marquette picture has neither the luminosity and painterly fire of Solimena's Giordanesque productions from the 1680s nor the powerful, sometimes vehement tenebrism especially evidenced by his works of the 1690s. Rather, in the present canvas an ostensibly dynamic play of light is schematized, above all in the bulbous drapery, into a strict chiaroscuro patterning that in part disguises the facileness of the brushwork. These stylistic particulars, which bring to mind the *Mater Dolorosa* in the Gemäldegalerie at Dresden and the *St. Michael* in a private collection at Rome,[3] assigned to the years 1723 and 1725, respectively, coupled with the general insistence upon the sculpturesque, appear to mark *The Christ Child Contemplating His Future Passion* as a product of Solimena's activity during the 1720s. Final justification for both the attribution and the dating here proposed is offered by the chubby, ruddy, solidly modeled Child in Solimena's mature *Madonna and Child* in the Abadía at Monserrat.[4]

St. Bruno Refusing the Archbishopric, Circle of Francesco Solimena, oil on canvas

CIRCLE OF FRANCESCO SOLIMENA
St. Bruno Refusing
the Archbishopric,
c. 1725–1750 (73.16)

Oil on canvas, 18 3/8 x 14 1/8 in. (46.5 x 36 cm). Unsigned.

Provenance: Collection of Cavaliere Giuseppe Niccolò (?), Rome; Campanile Galleries, Gian L. Campanile, Chicago; Dr. and Mrs. John E. Cordes, Milwaukee; their gift to the University, 1973.

References:
J. Patrice Marandel, verbally (1976), as circle of Solimena or De Mura.

Arnauld Brejon, verbally (1977), as circle of Solimena.

Ian Kennedy, verbally (1981), as Trevisani.

Frank DiFederico, in a letter (1982), as eighteenth-century Italian.

St. Bruno (c. 1030–1110), founder of the Carthusian Order whose white habit he wears, calls the attention of Christ (his presence working through the crucifix) to a mitre and crozier held by a somewhat perplexed child-angel. The painting therefore recounts that episode in the Saint's life to which above all Michel-Ange Slodtz's marble group of 1740–1744 in St. Peter's at Rome bears such memorable testimony: Bruno, in an act of scorn for all worldly glory, refusing the Archbishopric of Reggio Calabria in favor of a life of monastic simplicity and prayer.[5] The iconography of St. Bruno is here completed by the traditional meditational device of the death's-head and by the analogy of the crucifix to a living branch, an allusion to Bruno's having established monasteries (that is, having planted the Cross) in the woods near Grenoble, France, and later at La Torre in Calabria.[6]

This small canvas entered the Marquette collection with an attribution to the Spanish Baroque master Francisco Zurbarán (1598–1664), famed for his depiction of dazzling white garments (as in the series of monks for the Merced Calzada in Seville). It was subsequently argued that the painting (hitherto identified simply as a *Bishop Saint in Adoration of Christ*) was to be assigned rather to an eighteenth-century Neapolitan artist in the circle of Solimena (see the preceding biography and catalogue entry). A comparison of the *St. Bruno* to Solimena's altarpiece of 1710 now in the Cathedral at Aversa, *St. Bonaventure Receiving the Banner of the Holy Sepulcher from the Madonna,* can alone demonstrate the correctness of this recent designation.[7] The robes of St. Bruno appropriate the drapery style that Solimena had developed during the 1690s and that continues in the Aversa altar (broad, intensely lighted planes against deep pockets of ponderous dark, the natural fall of cloth and a sense for expressive patterning brought into a striking union). St. Bruno represents the bishop's emblems to the Divine in much the same way as St. Bonaventure; his glance directed toward the upper right and his hand gesturing toward the lower left recommends the kneeling devotee to the enthroned Madonna. Admittedly this mode of communication across and into space had long been an artistic convention, and thus in itself would not mark the Aversa composition as the source for the Marquette example. Yet the putto-angel, legs kicking, drapery trailing behind, at the summit of Solimena's picture, the bunched cherubim heads, and the seated angel below holding a cardinal's hat and acknowledging the worshipper, are also paralleled in the *St. Bruno.* Furthermore, the fame of the Aversa canvas was such that it engendered "numerous replicas and studio copies;"[8] accessibility to Solimena's conception would hardly have been restricted.

Notwithstanding these relationships, the two canvases reveal contrasting expressive intentions, and for this the differences in scale and theme cannot be held primarily accountable. Everything about Solimena's work speaks of grandeur and power. The *St. Bruno*

53

strives for a delicacy of sentiment and handling and, through them, to charm as much as to stir. This transposition of Solimenesque ideas into a less dramatic key, this manifestation of a more purely Rococo mentality, suggests a date in the second quarter of the eighteenth century. Were the canvas to be cleaned and relieved of old in-paintings, which no doubt compromise its quality, a specific attribution might be possible, perhaps even (as Marandel speculated) to an artist in the train of Solimena's former pupil Francesco De Mura.[9]

R. W. B.

Notes:
1. F. Bologna, *Francesco Solimena* (Naples, 1958), 180, 259–260, and fig. 15; 181, 262, and figs. 46–47; 181, 263, and figs. 64–65, respectively.
2. Oil on canvas, .60 x .72 m.; O. Ferrari and G. Scavizzi, *Luca Giordano* (Naples, 1966), II:49 and III: fig. 606.
3. Bologna, *Francesco Solimena*, 251 and fig. 157, and 273 and fig. 169.
4. .66 x .57 m.; J. Urrea Fernández, *La pintura italiana del siglo XVIII en España* (Valladolid, 1977), 362 and plate CXXVII, fig. 2.
5. F. Souchal, *Les Slodtz, sculpteurs et décorateurs du roi (1685-1764)* (Paris, 1967), cat. no. 159, 670–671 and plate 35.
6. See L. Réau, *Iconographie de l'art chrétien* (Paris, 1958), III, pt. 1: 249–252.
7. N. Spinosa in *The Golden Age of Naples: Art and Civilization under the Bourbons 1734-1805*, catalogue of an exhibition at the Detroit Institute of Arts (Detroit, 1981), cat. no. 43, 140–142, with ill.
8. Ibid., 142.
9. Cf. De Mura's *Bishop Saint* and *St. Mary Magdalen before the Crucifix*, both in the Misericordia at Naples; R. Causa, *L'opere d'arte nel Pio Monte della Misericordia a Napoli* (Naples, 1970), 113, no. 118, and fig. 40, and 114, no. 121 and colorplate XLI, respectively.

MIGUEL CABRERA

Mexican (1695–1768)

During a documented working career of three decades, Miguel Cabrera established himself as the most esteemed painter in Mexico: appointed *Pintor de cámara* to the Archbishop Manuel Rubio y Salinas; chosen in 1751 to produce a copy of the *Virgen de Guadalupe* for presentation to none other than the Pope; elected president-for-life of a private painting academy founded in 1753; and, upon his death in 1768, honored by burial at the foot of the painters' altar in Santa Inés. The master who in 1719 had come from his birthplace at Oaxaca to Mexico City, had studied there under Juan Rodríguez Juárez or Juan Correa, and whose dated works begin in 1740, was inundated with commissions for religious themes and portraits.

The artistic results of this fame, to which Cabrera's great entrepreneurial talents contributed, were very uneven. The demand for his works, which range in scale from altarpieces and other major church decorations to small copper panels, and from single pictures

to cycles, could only be met by a combination of compromises: employment of a large number of assistants who churned out paintings under his name; dependence upon the paintings and prints of other for compositional and figural ideas, hence conventionalism and—except in his portraits and depictions of donors—little direct confrontation of reality; a limited palette, dominated by the primaries of red and blue; repetition and superficiality; and susceptibility to unscrupulous copyists. Along the way, Miguel substituted decorative flourishes and tempered sentiments for what remained of Baroque passion that invested the best works of his predecessors (e.g., José Ibarra).

Possessed of obvious facility if not inventiveness, Cabrera clearly satisfied contemporary tastes, and one may wonder whether these tastes or his own personality or lack of proper academic training account for the seeming naiveté of so many of his pictures. In any case, there are paintings by Cabrera's hand—as distinct from workshop productions—which by virtue of their more considered handling and poetic moods rise above the bulk of his output to please the eye and raise the spirit.

The Holy Family during the Journey into Egypt, Attributed to Miguel Cabrera, oil on copper

ATTRIBUTED TO MIGUEL CABRERA
The Holy Family during the Journey into Egypt, mid-eighteenth century (72.20)

Oil on copper, 26 1/8 x 19 3/4 in. (66.4 x 50.2 cm). Unsigned.

Provenance: Collection of Dr. and Mrs. Alfred Bader, Milwaukee; their gift to the University, 1972.

References:
Anthony M. Clark, in a letter (1972), to Alfred Bader, as Spanish, perhaps 1740-1760.

Ian Kennedy, verbally (1981), as definitely Miguel Cabrera.

> And when they were departed, behold, the angel of the Lord appeared to Joseph in a dream, saying, rise, and take the young child and his mother, and flee into Egypt; and be thou there until I bring thee word: for Herod will seek the young child to destroy him. When he arose, he took the young child and his mother by night, and departed into Egypt; and was there until the death of Herod: That it might be fulfilled which was spoken of the Lord by the prophet, saying, Out of Egypt have I called my son.

Not content with this brief biblical account (Matthew 2:13-15) of the Holy Family's journey into Egypt, successive writers of the apocryphal Infancy Gospels wove marvelous tales of angelic visitations and miracles experienced en route.[1] With disregard for the unities of time, the artist of the present picture telescoped several of these legends into an image that is at once a *Flight into Egypt* and a *Rest on the Flight:* the guiding angel, looking appropriately celestial in his star-studded garment; the miracles of the bending palm tree that shaded and nourished the Virgin, and the water that sprang from its roots; and, at the far left, the fall of the pagan idols. Then, as if to forestall any conceivable misreading, the painter introduced the flowering rod of Joseph, which logically belongs to Joseph's prenuptial rites, and the fruit in the Child's hand, which identifies him as the New Adam who was to die to save mankind from original sin.[2]

As a compositional type, the Marquette painting finds close parallels in Spanish art. Thus, for example, all of its major elements, including the right-to-left passage, the same dramatis personae in the same relative positions, and even (except for the arms) an identically posed angel, clearly recall José Moreno's *Flight into Egypt* of 1662 in the Minneapolis Institute of Arts[3] and, to a somewhat lesser extent, Moreno's *Flight into Egypt* of 1668 (?) in the Museo del Prado.[4]

Yet a comparison of the Marquette painting to such Spanish Baroque prototypes also underlines two of the former's most salient aspects: its eighteenth-century sensibility and its provincialism. The would-be elegant, doll-like figures, the delicacy of execution, the avoidance of dynamic movements and bold chiaroscuro contrasts, and above all the dreamy sentimentalism mark the Marquette example as a product of "Rococo" mentality. Poetic and visual enchantment, a lovely fantasy-land undisturbed by worldly cares, count more than do drama and didacticism. And in adapting previous works of art to his own ends, the painter unwittingly introduced amusing incongruities, among them the simultaneous appearances of forward progress and pause, the somewhat misdirected glances, and the precarious balance of Joseph's staff.

Ian Kennedy, after Anthony Clark's attribution (letter cited) of the *Flight into Egypt* to a Spanish artist of the period 1740-1760, has recently (report cited) assigned the picture to the Mexican master Miguel Cabrera.[5] Kennedy's opinion is persuasive. As noted, the tone is that of the eighteenth century, with the addition of an amiable naiveté and less-than-correct draftsmanship that do not speak of a highly sophisticated ambience. (In these respects, as in the detailed decoration of the angel's garment, the Marquette copper panel is heir to such works as Juan de Pareja's version of the subject, signed and dated 1658, in the John and Mable Ringling Museum of Art at Sarasota, Florida.)[6] As a pastiche of various pictorial sources and thematic moments, the Marquette painting is consistent with Cabrera's practice of drawing heavily and not necessarily discriminatively upon works of art, especially prints, issuing from Europe. The following two works by Cabrera might be taken as representative of his manner: *Christ as the Good Shepherd* in the Museo de Arte Religioso at Mexico City,[7] and *The Precious Blood of Christ* in the church at Tepotzotlán.[8] Both the former painting and the *Flight into Egypt* are characterized by bucolic moods, fertile landscapes, and an overall preciousness, and Christ's jauntily angled shepherd's hat is in effect comparable to the bonnet worn by the Madonna. In *The Precious Blood of Christ* the physiognomies of the Virgin, St. Joseph, and the cherubim are strikingly similar to those of their counterparts in the Marquette work. And the three pictures share such marks of Cabrera's signature as large heads, tiny hands (which when they emanate from drapery appear curiously detached), and seemingly arbitrary shifts in gaze. Finally, notwithstanding the production-line reputation of Cabrera's studio, the small and lovingly executed *Flight into Egypt* may be adjudged a mature creation, datable about 1750-1760, of the master's own brush.

R. W. B.

Notes:
1. See Louis Réau, *Iconographie de l'art chrétien* (Paris, 1957), II, pt. 2: 273ff.
2. Ibid., 170-171.
3. See Edward Sullivan in *Painting in Spain 1650-1700 from North American Collections*, exhibition catalogue (Princeton, New Jersey, 1982), no. 23, 83-84 and plate 23.
4. Diego Angulo Iñiguez, "José Moreno," *Archivo español de arte* XXIX, no. 113 (1956): plate II opposite 67, and 70.
5. For whom see Javier Castro Mantecón and Manuel Zárate Aquino, *Miguel Cabrera, pintor oaxaqueño del siglo XVIII* (Córdoba, Mexico, 1958) and Francisco Diez Barroso, *El arte en Nueva España* (Mexico, 1921).
6. See Sullivan, *Painting in Spain*, no. 37, 100 and plate 37.
7. Manuel Romero de Terreros y Vincent, *El arte en Mexico durante el Virreinato* (Mexico, 1951), plate 93; see also its companion oval, the *Virgin as the Divine Shepherdess*, plate 94.
8. Diez Barroso, *El arte en Nueva España*, 313 (ill.).

UNKNOWN ARTIST

North European, Eighteenth Century

Holy Family (61.2)

Oil on panel, 16 x 22 in. (40.6 x 55.9 cm). Unsigned.

Provenance: Collection of Mr. and Mrs. Marc B. Rojtman; their gift to the University, 1961.

In an austere room, framed by an arch and a heavy green curtain, the Virgin sits with the Child upon her lap; Joseph, standing and gesturing, appears to speak with her. The three figures interact tenderly. Owing to its preciosity and prettiness, the panel would have been appreciated as a collector's image, rather than as a devotional one. Suggestive of Neo-Classicism are certain elements: the Virgin's sandals, her smoothly polished skin and crisp profile, Joseph's chiseled features, and the Child's exaggerated sweetness. These characteristics place the painting in the eighteenth century. The "fijnschilder" paint application indicates a north European artist, perhaps Dutch or Scandinavian.[1]

One artist whose name may be tentatively put forth as the author of this panel is Philip van Dyk (1680-1753).[2] A pupil of Arnold van Boonen in Amsterdam, van Dyk was active in Middelburgh and The Hague as a portraitist before becoming court painter to the Landgraf Wilhelm VIII of Hesse. Although he established himself in The Hague, van Dyk visited Cassel in 1726 and 1732. He was also sought after for portraits by the court of Willem IV, Prince of Orange. Typical of van Dyk's portraits are elegant figures, carefully blended brushstrokes, and rich, darkly glowing colors. These qualities are also apparent in his history pictures. One small panel, *Susanna and the Elders*, signed and dated 1721, offers comparison with the *Holy Family*.[3] Similarities include the fluidly rendered

The Holy Family, Northern European, Eighteenth Century, oil on panel

draperies and the features of the Elders and Joseph; the three men share squarely shaped noses, sunken eyes, and studied, emphasized gestures. If not certainly by van Dyk, the *Holy Family* may be placed within his circle.

A. G.

Notes:
1. The panel entered Marquette's collection as by Adriaen van der Werff; such authorship cannot be sustained, according to Barbara Gaehtgens in a letter (1984). Other artists who have been suggested are Willem van Mieris (Ian Kennedy, verbally, 1981) and Andries Lens (Julius S. Held, letter, 1983).
2. For an account of van Dyk's activities, see Ulrich Thieme and Felix Becker, *Allgemeines Lexikon der bildenden Künstler von der Antike bis zur Gegenwart* (Leipzig, 1907-1950), 9:275-276.
3. The *Susanna and the Elders* appeared in a sale at Christie's, New York, June 7, 1984, no. 71 (ill.).

NINETEENTH CENTURY

ALBERT BIERSTADT

German/American (1830–1902)

Born in Solingen, Germany, Bierstadt came to the United States at the age of two.[1] His family settled in New Bedford, Massachusetts, where he was raised and received his earlist artistic education. In 1853 he returned to Germany to train at the Düsseldorf Academy, at which he studied with Carl Friedrich Lessing, Emmanuel Leutze, and Andreas Achenbach.[2] Bierstadt traveled with Worthington Whittredge (with whom he shared a studio) and, later, Sanford Gifford throughout Germany, Switzerland, and Italy prior to his return home during the summer of 1857. The following year the artist joined the survey expedition to the West of General F. W. Lander, a trip (the first of four) that was to provide the majestic subject material with which Bierstadt became identified. In 1860 he moved to New York, and he was elected a member of the National Academy the same year. At his Tenth Street studio he painted the first of his very large Western landscapes. Bierstadt's grand paintings of mountainous scenes enjoyed considerable fame and both critical and popular approbation in the 1860s and 1870s, but later slowly fell out of popular favor. Although successful throughout his life, at the time of his death in 1902 he was largely forgotten in the art world.

Bierstadt's sizable and sometimes huge, paintings of cloud-enshrouded mountains brilliantly illuminated above still lakes and running torrents are highly dramatic, even awesome (but never bombastic) works. The artist's principal concerns seem to be the splendor of the native landscape, the limitless power of nature, and the relatively negligible status of man.

View in the Yosemite Valley   (83.48.1)

Oil on canvas, laid down on panel, 31 1/2 x 48 in. (80 x 122 cm). Signed l.l.: "ABierstadt."

Provenance: Collection of Brandt, Inc.; gift of Brandt, Inc. to the University, 1983, in memory of Earl William and Eugenia Brandt Quirk.

References:
John Wilmerding in a letter (1984), as looking like a Bierstadt.

Nancy Anderson, in a letter (1984), as related to *The Domes of the Yosemite* by Bierstadt.

Bierstadt made his first trip to California in 1863, and his paintings of the Yosemite Valley, based on sketches drawn then and on subsequent visits, have become perhaps his best-known works.[3] The largest of these, *The Domes of the Yosemite* (St. Johnsbury Atheneum, St. Johnsbury, Vermont), was commissioned, probably in late 1866, for the Norwalk (Conn.) mansion of Legrand Lockwood.[4] This painting, which measures nine and one-half by fifteen feet, was painted in 1867 in the studio of Bierstadt's mansion, Malkasten, in Irvington, New York. Upon its completion the *Domes* was publicly exhibited at Bierstadt's Tenth Street studio, where it evoked a tremendous variety of critical reaction; *The Tribune* found it "almost entirely destitute of grandeur," its author "common place," while another critic found it "the most remarkable landscape, in many respects, in the world," with the artist "ascending the throne...as the monarch of all landscape painters."[5]

The painting subsequently toured Philadelphia and Boston before arriving at the Lockwood house in Norwalk. After the patron's death in 1872, his widow (now financially ruined) auctioned the *Domes* for $5,100, considerably less than Bierstadt's $25,000 fee for painting it. It was later purchased by Horace Fairbanks, who installed it in the art gallery he constructed in his hometown of St. Johnsbury, Vermont, where, quipped the *Boston Globe*, "it will astonish the natives."[6]

Shortly after completing *The Domes of the Yosemite*, Bierstadt left for a European tour, during which he arranged for the reproduction of the painting in Düsseldorf. Serving as the source for the chromolithograph was a small version of the picture, which Bierstadt had painted from the original before it left his studio. That small painting has long been lost, the only proposed version (Private Collection, Boston) being of questionable authenticity.[7]

The Marquette painting, which has only recently come to light, is manifestly of the same subject as *The Domes of the Yosemite*, but, despite its relatively small size, would not seem to be the replica used for the chromolithograph: The composition is notably different from that of both the large canvas and the print. Rather this work appears to be an autonomous picture, perhaps painted slightly before the large *Domes*. In addition to the variations in composition (the absence of waterfall, disparate point of view further to the right, diminished panoramic effect), the varied treatment of numerous details (such as the foliage on the trees and arrangement of incidental rocks) underscores the independence of the Marquette picture. As such, it is an important addition to Bierstadt's work—one that may, with further study, shed light on the creation of the artist's largest and arguably greatest painting.

R. B. S.

View in the Yosemite Valley, Albert Bierstadt, oil on panel

Notes:
1. On Bierstadt, see, most accessibly, Gordon Hendricks, *Albert Bierstadt: Painter of the American West* (New York, 1974). Further on the artist, see Gordon Hendricks, *ABierstadt*, exhibition catalogue (Fort Worth, 1972); *Albert Bierstadt 1830-1902*, exhibition catalogue (Santa Barbara, 1964); and R. S. Trump, "Life and Works of Albert Bierstadt," unpub. diss. (Ohio State University, 1963). I am grateful to Nancy Anderson, Smithsonian Fellow at the National Museum of American Art, for her assistance in the preparation of this entry.
2. See Wend von Kalnein and Donelson Hoopes, *The Düsseldorf Academy and the Americans* (Atlanta, 1972), particularly 31-32, 41; and Wend von Kalnein, introduction to *The Hudson and the Rhine; Die Amerikanische Malerkolonie im Düsseldorf im 19. Jahrhundert* (Düsseldorf, 1976).
3. Bierstadt traveled with the writer Fitz Hugh Ludlow, whose description of the trip was published the following year; see F. H. Ludlow, "Seven Weeks in the Great Yo-Semite," *Atlantic Monthly XIII (1864): 739-754*. A fuller account, with Bierstadt's illustrations, later appeared in book form: F. H. Ludlow, *The Heart of the Continent* (New York, 1870).
4. Hendricks, *Albert Bierstadt* (1974), 159-165. See as well Gordon Hendricks, "Bierstadt's *The Domes of the Yosemite*," *American Art Journal* III, no. 2 (Fall 1971): 23-31, for a full discussion of the painting and its commission.
5. For these and other contemporary reviews, see Hendricks, "Bierstadt's *The Domes of the Yosemite*," 27-29.
6. Ibid., 30.
7. 22 1/2 x 33 1/4 in.; Hendricks, *ABierstadt*, 22, 24 (ill.), no. 45; the attribution is questioned by Theodore Stebbins, in *American Art Journal* V, no. 1 (May 1973). Another (?) version, measuring 22 x 33 in., was with the John Nicholson Gallery, New York, in 1957; reproduced in *Antiques* LXXII, no. 5 (November 1957): 398.

RALPH ALBERT BLAKELOCK

American (1847–1919)

Ralph Albert Blakelock was one of the most bizarre of American painters, in both his art and his life.[1] Born in New York in 1847, he appears to have been a self-taught artist, his education in public schools and the Free Academy (now City College) being of a general nature. He began exhibiting at the National Academy of Design in 1867 and continued to do so for the next seven years. Between 1869 and 1872 Blakelock traveled throughout the West; much of what he saw—of the wilderness and of Indian life—was to find a place in his pictorial vocabulary. During the 1880s, Blakelock exhibited at the National Academy and the Society of American Artists and received modest recognition and some patronage, although evidently not enough to support adequately his large family (which eventually included nine children). His first mental breakdown occurred in 1891, after a collector's refusal to pay the artist an expected amount, and strange and erratic behavior followed his apparent recovery. His condition had so worsened by 1889 that institutionalization became necessary. In that year he entered Long Island Hospital, where he stayed until 1902, when he was transferred to the Middletown (N.Y.) State Hospital for the insane.

Shortly after his hospitalization he began to receive the recognition and fame that had for so long eluded him—but neither he nor his family were in any position to benefit. One of his paintings (submitted by a collector) took first prize at the 1900 Universal Exhibition in Paris. Shortly afterwards, his first one-man show was arranged—one that was followed by a series of exhibitions and publications. Blakelock's pictures were in great demand and began to fetch impressive prices at auction. Almost immediately forgeries began to appear on the market, eventually in such quantities that their number far exceeds that of the authentic works. Although Blakelock was released briefly in 1916, he never regained his sanity. He died in a hospital in upstate New York in 1919.

Landscape at Sunset, Ralph Albert Blakelock, oil on panel

Landscape at Sunset (81.7)

Oil on panel, 11 1/2 x 14 7/8 in. (29.2 x 37.8 cm). Unsigned.

Provenance: Collection of H. M. Kitchell, Providence, R. I. (?); J. W. Young (Young's Art Galleries), Chicago (1928); Miss Mary Black, Deerfield, Ill.; her gift to the University, 1981, in memory of Mr. Harry Apple.

References:
Cora Blakelock (wife of the artist), in a certificate dated March 13, 1916 (not present but attested to in a document attached to verso of painting), as by Ralph Blakelock.

Blakelock's pictures are mysterious, poetic works— intense, fantastic, visionary. Although his earlier paintings are rendered in a more straightforward manner, they too are informed by a strange, quiet tone that is immediately perceptible in the artist's richly textured canvases. His mature works are, for the most part, variations on a limited group of subjects: forest landscapes, sunsets, nocturnes, and views of Indian encampments. Unfortunately, Blakelock's technique, which sometimes involved painting over incompletely dried areas, and his use of bitumen, a pigment that has proven unstable, has resulted in the darkening, deterioration, or destruction of many of his pictures. Although unsigned, *Landscape at Sunset* is a typical small work of Blakelock's maturity. A forest clearing is seen with a still pool in the foreground; a few figures, barely distinguishable, appear beneath the trees. A warm sunset glow fills the scene. The number of fraudulent Blakelocks naturally prompts one's doubts on any newly-encountered work attributed to the artist. Nor can a certificate from the artist's wife by itself be considered entirely without suspicion. Yet the early date of Mrs. Blakelock's approval of the picture (in March 1916, while the artist was still alive, but after fakes began appearing on the market), combined with the high quality of the picture itself suggests that the Marquette picture is indeed by Blakelock. Within a month of the date of Mrs. Blakelock's certificate an important Blakelock exhibition was held in Chicago at Young's Art Galleries.[2] Although Mrs. Blakelock collaborated with J. W. Young in the preparation of that exhibition (she wrote the foreword to the catalogue) and although Young later owned the Marquette picture, the painting does not appear to be identifiable among the works listed as on show.

R. B. S.

Notes:
1. On Blakelock, see Elliot Dangerfield, *Ralph Albert Blakelock* (New York, 1914); Lloyd Goodrich, *Ralph Albert Blakelock Centenary Exhibition*, catalogue of an exhibition (New York, 1947); D. Gebhart and P. Stuurman, *The Enigma of Ralph A. Blakelock 1847-1919* (Santa Barbara, et al., 1969). Blakelock is the subject of continuing research at the Nebraska Blakelock Archive. Preliminary findings have been presented in N. Geske, *Ralph Albert Blakelock; 1847-1919*, catalogue of an exhibition (Lincoln, Neb. and Trenton, N.J., 1975).

2. See *Catalog of the Works of R. A. Blakelock, N.A., and of his daughter Marian Blakelock, Exhibited at Young's Art Galleries, April 27-May 13, 1916* (Chicago, 1916).

RUDOLPH ERNST

Austrian (1854–1932)

Ernst was born in Vienna, where he began studies at the Akademie der bildenden Künste and was a pupil of the great German artist Anselm Feuerbach.[1] Although he is recorded as a portraitist, nearly all of his known works are oriental genre pictures—carefully wrought compositions drawn on the experiences of the artist's travels in Spain, Morocco, Italy, and Turkey. Ernst exhibited in both Munich and Vienna before moving, in 1876, to Paris, where he received a bronze medal at the Exposition Universelle three years later. He showed regularly at the Salon des Artistes Français and was well patronized, particularly by American collectors. Ernst's works, after years of relative neglect, are again the subject of broad collector interest.

A Moor Robing after the Bath (82.1.1)

Oil on panel, 21 3/4 x 18 1/4 in. (55.2 x 46.4 cm). Inscribed l.l.: "R. Ernst."

Provenance: Collection of J. O. Krumbholz, Milwaukee; Claire Hoff Toole, Milwaukee; gift of her estate to the University, 1982.

A Moor Robing after the Bath is a typical interior scene of Ernst's. A figure is seen stepping out of a bath as a servant assists him in his robing. The interior is a richly textured room with marble floors and wainscoting surmounted by decorative glazed tile. The cold surfaces are complemented by the pierced wood window, carved bench, foot mat, and oriental carpet. While it is basically a rich, sybaritic environment that is portrayed, the artist takes great delight in describing the elements of decay and discord in the room: fractured or missing tiles, cracked marble slabs, and the casual disarray of the rug and bathing bucket. Although these motifs reappear throughout the artist's oeuvre (and in fact the protagonists here may be thought of as somewhat stock figures), Ernst's paintings are remarkably varied in both subject and composition.

R. B. S.

Notes:
1. Little of a documentary nature has been written on Ernst. Further on him and on the entire Orientalist group see Heinrich Fuchs, *Die Österreichischen Maler des 19. Jahrhunderts* (Vienna, 1972), and Philippe Jullian, *The Orientalists* (Oxford, 1977).

AUGUST FRIEDRICH ALBRECHT SCHENCK

Danish (1828–1901)

Schenck was born in 1828 at Glückstadt, Duchy of Holstein. He worked in England and Portugal but is more closely associated with the French school. After a period of study at the École des Beaux-Arts in Paris (where one of his teachers was the noteworthy painter of romantic history subjects, Léon Cogniet), Schenck established his residence and studio at Ecouen, a town in the vicinity of Paris. The choice of this locale was typical of the landscapists and painters of rural life of the period who, following in the footsteps of the Barbizon painters, chose to live close by their source of subject matter and inspiration. After his debut at the Salon in 1857, Schenck was to attain both public and official approbation. In 1865 he was awarded a gold medal at the Salon and in 1885 was named *Chevalier de la Légion d'Honneur.* He was a popular and prolific artist whose works are still frequently seen at public auctions. He died at Ecouen in 1901.

Shepherd and Flock in Storm, August Friedrich Albrecht Schenck, oil on canvas

Shepherd and Flock in Storm   (65.14)

Oil on canvas, 24 x 34 3/4 in. (61 x 90.7 cm). Signed l.r.: "Schenck."

Provenance: Collection of Mrs. Fred A. Miller, Milwaukee; her gift to the University, 1965.

References:
Pick, *Marquette University Art Collection Supplement,* 11, as Schenck.

The subject matter of this work is typical of Schenck, who was noted for his winter landscapes with animals, usually sheep. His pictures tend to be formulaic, and this fact is consistent with the bourgeois taste to which he catered—a taste that desired recognizability and predictability. Depictions of shepherds and their flocks in a naturalistic setting were popularized in the 1850s and 1860s by the French painter of the Barbizon School, Charles-Émile Jacque. Though the subject matter here is the same as Jacque's, Schenck's interpretation is very different, perhaps because of his northern origins and temperament. Unlike Jacque's usually bucolic scenes, the prevailing mood in Schenck's works is one of profound melancholy. The same is also true of other Barbizon-influenced northerners such as the Dutch painter and contemporary of Schenck Anton Mauve (1838–1888). In this work Schenck expresses a sentiment, essentially romantic in its implications, of universal fatalism. The landscape is bleak, and the chill light of a winter sunset creates a powerful sense of foreboding. The intimations of mortality are very strong, and Schenck makes it clear that the rigors of rural life, and of life in general, are shared by man and beast alike.

In keeping with the melancholy mood of his work, Schenck limits his palette to tones of gray and brown. He therefore has a place in the study of the emergence of "tonal" painting (as exemplified by artists such as Eugène Carrière) in France. This tendency to tonalism comes together in Schenck's art with the Barbizon influence mentioned above and with that of Impressionism. The latter influence can be seen in Schenck's careful observation and naturalistic depiction of light effects as well as in his loose and rather aggressive brushwork. Schenck's works help document the merging of traditional subject matter and interpretation with some of the innovative stylistic trends in French art in the second half of the nineteenth century.

J. B.

ARNOLD-MARC GORTER

Dutch (1866–1933)

Arnold-Marc Gorter was born in 1866 at Ambt-Almelo, East Holland. In 1884 he traveled to Amsterdam, where he remained until 1890 as a student at the National Academy. After 1894 he exhibited in several European cities including Munich, Vienna, Berlin, and Paris. He also exhibited at the St. Louis World's Fair in 1903. He had considerable success, winning both critical acclaim and a gold medal at the Paris Salon of 1910. In 1923 he was named a "Membre Correspondent de l'Institut de France." His last years were spent in Amsterdam, where he died in 1933.[1]

Scene along the Riverbank, Arnold-Marc Gorter, oil on canvas

Scene Along a Riverbank (82.1.2)

Oil on canvas, 28 7/8 x 38 5/8 in. (73.3 x 90.6 cm).
Signed l.r.: "A.M. Gorter."

Provenance: Collection of Claire Hoff Toole; gift of her estate to the University, 1982.

This subject is typical of Gorter, who had a predilection for bucolic scenes set in his native East Holland. This is an indication of his affinities with the painters of the Hague School, who favored scenes that reflected the regional character of Dutch landscape. One can also point to the influence of the French Barbizon School, particularly in Gorter's naturalism and in his sensitivity to the "mood" of landscape. The autumnal landscape with cows recalls the works of both Théodore Rousseau and Constant Troyon. The low point of view, with a dark foreground giving way to a lighter background and the cloudy sky, are also Barbizon features associated, for the most part, with Rousseau; while Gorter's choice of a river view may show the influences of Charles Daubigny. To this generically Barbizon-style work Gorter added the agitated brushwork of Impressionism as well as the Impressionists' interest in reflected light. His mature works are also characterized by a preponderant green tonality. These factors indicate that this painting is an example of Gorter's mature style that shows rejection of the limited tonal range and traditional brushwork of the Hague School.

J. B.

Notes:
1. For a more thorough discussion of the life and career of Arnold-Marc Gorter, the reader is directed to W. Laanstra, "A. M. Gorter, Nature Seen Through Ordinary Eyes," *Tableau* VI (Sept./Oct. 1983): unpaginated.

JOZEF ISRAELS

Dutch (1824–1911)

Israels studied Hebrew and worked in his father's small business before turning his attention fully to art. He attended the Minerva Academy in Groningen for several years and went to Amsterdam in 1841, where he studied under the history painter Jan Kruseman. A three-year sojourn in Paris completed his formal training. Upon his return to Holland in 1846, he exhibited regularly and earned critical acclaim as a painter of historical themes. In 1850 he set up his own atelier in Amsterdam, and in 1871 he moved to The Hague, where he established his home and studio on the elegant Koninginnegracht. Marriage (1863), a son, and a daughter completed the generally bourgeois pattern of his life.[1] His son, Isaac (1865–1934), became a well-known painter of genre and landscape.[2]

Israels's early paintings concern subjects taken from the Bible, Shakespeare, and modern history, especially events connected with the founding of the Dutch States.[3] Such historical themes became rarer in his oeuvre as he focused upon genre and landscapes, and favored peasants and fishermen at work. Between 1870 and 1900 he made thirty-seven etchings, most of them scenes from daily life.[4] His portraits of friends and family reveal his interest in expressive physiognomy.

Israels belonged to the loosely knit group of artists called The Hague School.[5] While several of these painters, above all Maris, incorporated certain coloristic insights derived from the French Impressionists, Israels remained a painter of primarily dark sensibilities. Critics regarded him as the Dutch Millet[6] and credited him with reviving the genre themes and painterly emotion associated with certain Dutch seventeenth-century artists, especially Rembrandt.[7] During his lifetime Israels was considered the most important artist in Holland.[8] His art expressed the virtue of humble daily life and the inner, spiritual being of humanity. These are qualities perceived in much of the oeuvre of Holland's great Baroque artist Rembrandt. During the later nineteenth century, Rembrandt's reputation underwent a romantic revival. Much of Israels's popularity may have been due to his affinity with the values of Rembrandt's art. Contemporaries appeared to regard Israels as the artistic heir to Rembrandt. Rembrandt's influence on Israels is manifest in the viscous texture of paint, sensibility to values of light and shade within a limited tonal range, overall brownish tonality of many of his paintings, and choice of subject: from humble scenes of a mother and child to biblical subjects. In his *Saul and David*, Israels created a variation on a Rembrandt composition of the same subject.[9] Israels expressed his appreciation for Rembrandt in his short book about the artist.[10]

Israels's work, even as it was inspired by the art of Rembrandt, was admired by those critics who were themselves especially sensitive to Rembrandt's oeuvre. Carel Vosmaer, who authored a monograph on Rembrandt, and Jan Veth, who made insightful discoveries about Rembrandt's practice of borrowing motifs, wrote significant articles about Israels's paintings.[11] Not only did Israels emulate the art of Rembrandt, he also cultivated an appreciation of the parallels between his work and the Dutch Baroque master's.

Dutch Interior, Jozef Israels, oil on canvas

Dutch Interior (called Mother and Child), c. 1898   (59.13)

Oil on canvas, 38 1/4 x 52 in. (97.2 x 13.2 cm). Signed l.l.: "Jozef Israels."

Provenance: Apparently in the collection of Van Nievelt, The Hague, 1904; collection of Mr. I. A. Dinerstein; his gift to the University, 1959.

References:
Jan Veth, *Josef Israels und seine Kunst* (1906; reprint, The Hague, 1910), 15, plate 2.

Pick, *Marquette University Art Collection*, 16.

Carter, *Grain of Sand*, 6 (ill.), 9, no. 10.

Interior scenes of women and children occur often throughout Israels's oeuvre after the 1850s. While his immediate inspiration for such a subject may well have been daily life, his awareness of Dutch seventeenth-century genre played a significant role in his repeated depictions of such scenes. Israels recognized the nurturing qualities of certain Rembrandt etchings, which, he wrote, conveyed "motherly kindness, sweetness, and thoughtfulness...in every curve."[12] These were the values Israels sought to express in his images of mothers and children, including the Marquette painting.

This picture is apparently identical with that published in 1904 in an elephant portfolio edition of reproductions of fifty paintings by Israels with commentary by his friend, the art historian and amateur artist Jan Veth.[13] According to Veth's brief discussion, Israels completed the picture around 1898, having reworked it many times. Originally a boy stood near the hearth and rocked the baby's cradle; a dog stood in front of the youth. In finishing the painting, however, Israels painted out the boy and the dog and added, to the left, the seated woman, the table, and the fowl. Finally, Veth added that the artist had seen the interior setting in Zweeloo in Drente. The baby sleeping in the cradle occurs in reverse in the painting *Midday Meal in a Farmer's House*, c. 1885, in the Museum, Dordrecht.[14] Similar interior settings are used by Israels in paintings of the 1880s and 1890s; one such setting, which includes a woman knitting, is a painting of 1895–1900, formerly in the collection of Frank Stoop, London.[15]

The atmospheric depth and large size of the painting endow its tender subject with a gentle monumentality. Despite the composition's simplicity, the picture represents the elevation of the humble to the noble.

A. G.

Notes:
1. Basic bibliography about Israels's work and life includes G. Knuttel, in Ulrich Thieme and Felix Becker, *Allgemeines Lexikon der bildenden Künstler von der Antike bis zur Gegenwart* (Leipzig, 1907-1950), 19:255-261, and R. Muther, *The History of Modern Painting in Three Volumes* (New York, 1896), III, Chapter 39, esp. 233-246. See further M. Eisler, *Jozef Israels* (London, 1924), M. Lieberman, *Jozef Israels*, 7th ed. (Berlin, 1922), and C. L. Dake, *Jozef Israels* (Paris, n.d.).
2. See Knuttel, in Thieme and Becker, *Allgemeines Lexikon*, 19:261-262.
3. For Israels's position as a painter of Netherlandish historical themes, see *Het Vaderlandsch Gevoel*, catalogue of an exhibition at the Rijksmuseum (Amsterdam, 1978), cat. nos. 14 and 92.
4. Israels's etchings have been catalogued by H. J. Hubert, *The Etched Work of Jozef Israels* (Amsterdam, 1909).
5. See Josef de Gruyter, *De Haagse School*, 2 vols. (Rotterdam, 1968) and Ronald de Leeuw, et al, *The Hague School: Dutch Masters of the 19th Century*, catalogue of an exhibition at the Grand Palais (Paris, 1983).
6. Muther, *History of Modern Painting*, 234.
7. F. W. Gunsaulus, *Josef Israels, an address* (Toledo, 1912) unpaginated (XIII-XIV); and F. F. Dumas, *Illustrated Biographies of Modern Artists* (Paris, 1882-1888), I:125.
8. Knuttel, in Thieme and Becker, *Allgemeines Lexikon*, 259.
9. Israels's painting, completed 1898, is in the City Museum, Amsterdam. Rembrandt's large canvas is in the Mauritshuis, The Hague. See further Gunsaulus, *Josef Israels*, unpaginated (IV).
10. Jozef Israels, *Rembrandt* (London and New York, n.d.).
11. For their writings about Israels, see C. Vosmaer, *Onze hedendaagsche schilders*, I (The Hague, 1881); and Jan Veth, *Josef Israels und seine Kunst* (1906; reprint, The Hague, 1910).
12. Israels, *Rembrandt*, 55.
13. Veth, *Josef Israels und seine Kunst*, 15 and plate 2. The only difference between the painting and the reproduction is that the canvas includes a third fowl to the left.
14. Ibid., 17 and plate 8.
15. Ibid., 2 and plate 34.

SIR THOMAS LAWRENCE

English (1769–1830)

Lawrence was born at Bristol in 1769, the fourteenth of sixteen children. He showed a remarkable talent for drawing and by 1779, after his family had moved to Oxford, he made portrait drawings and had an engraving published after the likeness of William Hoare. By 1780 the family was living in the fashionable resort town of Bath, where Lawrence made profile portraits in pastel. It was there that he received his first instruction in oil painting, from Thomas Barker (Thomas Barker of Bath). In 1785 he won a prize at the Society of Artists in London for a drawn copy of Raphael's *Transfiguration*, and in 1786 he painted his first picture, *Christ Bearing the Cross*. By 1787 Lawrence had settled permanently in London and studied for three months at the Royal Academy, doing oil sketches. Soon after he began to execute full-length portraits and to make important social connections. From this point on his rise to prominence was meteoric. He was named A. R. A. (Associate of the Royal Academy) in 1791, R. A. (Royal Academician) in 1792, and, after the death of Sir Joshua Reynolds in 1792, Painter in Ordinary to the King. He also assumed Reynolds's position as the foremost portrait painter of his day, outshining his rivals John Hoppner and William Beechey.

Lawrence's fame rested equally on his attractive personality and dazzling skill as a painter. His suave and painterly technique and rich color (he was called the "English Titian"), combined with a highly individualized presentation of character, were well suited to a glamorous and dandified era. (His works also seemed, for some, the antidote to Reynolds's impersonal and intellectualized portrayals.) The influence of Lawrence's fluid style and psychological insight upon other national schools of portraiture was very great. (Among the French painters influenced by Lawrence are Delacroix and Manet.) He made his first trip to the Continent in 1815 to see the works collected by Napoleon in Paris. By 1818 his fame was such that he embarked on a Grand Tour to paint the crowned heads of Europe. The portraits from this period include the Emperor of Russia, the King of Prussia, and the Pope. In 1820 he succeeded Benjamin West as President of the Royal Academy, becoming the third person to hold that position. By this time he had achieved a level of fame and social status unequaled even by Reynolds, the first President of the Royal Academy. His great career ended with his death in 1830.

Portrait of Vincenzo Camuccini (?), Attributed to Sir Thomas Lawrence, oil on canvas

ATTRIBUTED TO SIR THOMAS LAWRENCE
Portrait of Vincenzo Camuccini (?) (73.18)

Oil on canvas, 29 x 24 1/2 in. (73.7 x 62.2 cm). Unsigned.

Provenance: Metropolitan Galleries, New York (1932); collection of Mr. and Mrs. James W. Bergstrom; their gift to the University, 1973.

References:
Illustrated in *The Art Digest* VI, no. 7 (Jan. 1932):13, as by Lawrence, a portrait of Camuccini, 1819.

J. Patrice Marandel, verbally (1976), as after Lawrence.

Ulrich Hiesinger, in a letter (1984), as not Camuccini.

The identification of the sitter in this picture is indeed problematic, as is the attribution to Lawrence. The work certainly reflects the style of Lawrence c. 1820. Half-length informal portraits of this type are characterized by a dramatic chiaroscuro with well-illuminated faces, in male portraits further heightened by a loosely painted white collar, set off against very dark clothing and backgrounds. (Very often the dark areas have a dull, flat look as a result of Lawrence's use of bitumen.) His technique is painterly, with sketchy backgrounds and occasional bold slashes of paint, especially in the clothing. He also presents his sitters, like the individual represented here, as bright, alert, and sensitive, with limpid and intelligent eyes.

The subject of the Marquette picture has traditionally been identified as Vincenzo Camuccini, a prominent Italian painter of the early nineteenth century.[1] Lawrence had met Camuccini during his visit to Rome in 1819—a trip prompted by a commission to paint portraits of Pope Pius VII and Cardinal Consalvi. Camuccini, who had held since 1814 the important papal post of Inspector of Public Paintings for Rome and the Papal States, had contact with Lawrence not only on an official but also on a personal level: His brother Pietro had befriended the English artist during an earlier residence in London.

Camuccini's features are known from at least three self-portraits. The earliest, formerly in the collection of the artist's heirs in Cantelupo Sabino, was destroyed during World War II.[2] An oil sketch portraying Camuccini at about the age of forty remains in the family palazzo at Cantelupo,[3] and a finished painting is in the self-portrait collection in the Uffizi Gallery in Florence.[4] From these works it would seem quite possible that the subject of the Marquette picture is indeed Camuccini—an identification rejected, however, by Hiesinger.[5] Further study following the cleaning and restoration of the picture should lead to some resolution regarding both the subject and the attribution of this intriguing portrait.

The portrait has been associated with one recorded by Armstrong in his catalogue of Lawrence's works; a portrait of Camuccini is described as, "Painted in Rome, 1819. Bust, facing, eyes to right. Short curly hair and whiskers. White cravat and collar. Eng[raved] by Pietro Bettellini (from picture by Cav. Tommaso Lawrence.)"[6] Although this description can be applied to the Marquette work, it more probably refers to Lawrence's portrait drawing of Camuccini, clearly the source of Bettelini's engraving and a work still extant in the Palazzo Camuccini in Cantelupo.[7]

J. B. / R. B. S.

Notes:
1. On Camuccini's career, see Ulrich Hiesinger, "The Paintings of Vincenzo Camuccini, 1771-1844," *Art Bulletin* LX, no. 2 (June 1978): 297-320.
2. Illustrated in *Enciclopedia Italiana* (Milan, 1930), VIII:620.
3. See *Vincenzo Camuccini, 1771-1844; Bozzetti e Disegni dallo Studio dell'artista*, exhibition catalogue (Rome, 1978), 96, no. 207.
4. Inv. 1890, #5173. Illustrated in *Gli Uffizi; Catalogo generale* (Florence, 1980), 826, no. A170.
5. Ulrich Hiesinger, in a letter (March 1984), as not representing Camuccini.
6. Sir Walter Armstrong, *Lawrence* (New York, 1913), 118.
7. Kenneth Garlick, *A Catalogue of the Paintings, Drawings and Pastels of Sir Thomas Lawrence*, Walpole Society, XXXIX (Glasgow, 1964), 220.

UNKNOWN ARTIST
British School, First Half of the Nineteenth Century

River Landscape (75.18)

Oil on canvas, 21 1/4 x 32 in. (54 x 81.3 cm). Unsigned.

Provenance: Collection of Elhanan Bicknell, until 1863 (?)[1]; Lord Armstrong, Cragside Hall, Rothbury (?)[2]; with David Carritt, London, 1972; Gertrude Bergstrom; gift of her estate to the University, 1975.

References:
Martin Butlin, in a letter (1972), as not by Turner.

A quiet river meanders through the valley seen in the middle ground, a classically proportioned bridge spanning it at center. The foreground is dominated by a fallen tree, beside which a small flock of sheep and two shepherds rest. In the distance mountains appear beneath gently undulating clouds, the depth and panoramic quality of the view accentuated by the "bracketing" of the scene's lateral edges by tall, dense trees.

This handsome landscape has traditionally been considered an early work by J. M. W. Turner (1775-1851), but it is painted in a manner wholly disparate from anything known by that artist. The picture is reminiscent of the classicial landscapes of Richard Wilson (1713-1782), although the descriptive quality and free handling suggest a somewhat later date. There might be as well a similarity with the landscape paintings of George Vincent (1796-1832), one of the Norwich school painters, but the resemblance seems on the whole too generic to sustain, at present, such an attribution.[3]

R. B. S.

Notes:
1. The reverse of the painting is inscribed as follows: "Turner, (Joseph M. W.) R.A./ Born 1775 Died 1851/ Turner was known to have visited Italy in 1819-1829 and about 1840-41. The view was painted during his last visit and was greatly admired during the private exhibition of his work in London in 1889 and came from the collection of M. E. Bixknells that was sold in 1863. The picture being bought privately." The collection in question would seem to be that of Elhanan Bicknell, whose sale at Christie's on April 25, 1863, contained several Turners, none of which can be identified with the present picture.
2. According to a label on the picture that reads: "A View of Naples/ J. M. W. Turner, R.A./ 1775 1851/ From the Collection of Lord Armstrong, Cragside Hall, Rothbury."
3. Compare Vincent's *View of Beach Head from Pevensey* (Castle Museum, Norwich); illustrated in Andrew Hemingway, *The Norwich School of Painters: 1803-1833* (Oxford, 1979), fig. 52.

River Landscape, British School, active Early Nineteenth Century, oil on canvas

VIRGILE NARCISSE DIAZ DE LA PEÑA

French (1808–1876)

Diaz was born of Spanish emigrant parents in Bordeaux in 1808.[1] Despite a personal history of childhood tragedy—he was orphaned at an early age and lost a leg in an accident—Diaz was a jocular and personable individual noted for his joie de vivre. Diaz's formal training consisted of only a short period of study with the painter Souchon. Like many artists of the nineteenth century (among them Renoir), Diaz began his artistic career as a porcelain painter. Throughout his career Diaz painted landscapes containing scenes of bathers, frolicking nymphs, or gypsies. He also consistently maintained his love of the naughty vignette and his affinity for the eighteenth-century *scène galante*. Diaz is, however, primarily appreciated for his landscapes reflecting the style and sensibility of the Barbizon painters. After about 1837 he was very closely associated with Corot, Troyon, Dupré, and especially Rousseau. He exhibited frequently at the Salon and never attained academic acceptance, though he was widely admired. He was in the vanguard of French artists working directly from nature, and his sensitive and naturalistic treatment of the effects of light and atmosphere was very influential for the next generation of landscapists, among them Sisley, Pissarro, and Monet. Diaz seldom traveled far afield, preferring to work in Fontainebleau and the region of Paris. He died at Menton in 1876.

Wooded Landscape   (62.4)

Oil on panel, 11 3/4 x 16 1/2 in. (30 x 41.8 cm). Inscribed l.l. "N. Diaz."

Provenance: Collection of Mr. William O. Goodrich; acquired by Dr. and Mrs. Francis J. Millen, 1956; their gift to the University, 1962.

References:
Pick, *Marquette University Art Collection*, 9, 10 (ill.), as Diaz.

Carter, *Grain of Sand*, no. 5, as Diaz.

Wooded Landscape, Virgile Narcisse Diaz de la Peña, oil on panel

This work is typical, in subject matter and composition, of Diaz's Forest of Fontainebleau subjects of the late 1860s and the 1870s.[2] It is, however, in all probability a partially finished study done before the motif.[3] As with the great majority of Diaz's views of forest interiors, there are trees at either side of the dark foreground and a view along a path toward a more brightly lit clearing in the distance. Typically, therefore, he creates a stage backdrop-like effect with an enclosed composition and a clear perspectival recession accentuated by the dynamics of light. Equally apparent is the sketchy technique employed by Diaz, with thinly painted areas and apparent brushstrokes. This technique exposes the underlying structure of Diaz's finished works. Here we see him laying down a patchwork of transparent strokes and "blocking out" the areas of light and shadow. From this starting point, as we can also observe in the present work, Diaz goes on to create a naturalistic view of nature with ever-changing light and sympathetic reflections. This aspect is particularly evident in the watery foreground, where one sees luminous reflections of the patches of blue in the cloudy sky. Diaz's special awareness of the constant change in nature is seen in the transient weather conditions reflected in his works; thus the present painting probably depicts the clearing skies after a storm. This sensitivity does not result simply from the climatic conditions he encountered in the Forest of Fontainebleau, though cloudy and damp weather are typical of that area. It is also a manifestation of Diaz's romanticism: The observation of nature's impermanence produces in the artist shifting, often contradictory, moods of joy and melancholy. This view of nature, as well as the choice of a marshy forest interior as subject matter, indicates the great influence of Théodore Rousseau upon Diaz's art.[4] The inclusion at the center of this composition of a rugged path leading into the distance also recalls a recurrent motif in the works of Rousseau. Like Rousseau, Diaz combines reverence for nature with an inherent romanticism. His interest in nature and luminous, flickering surfaces, also found in the art of Rousseau and other Barbizon painters, furthermore points the way to Impressionism.

J. B.

Notes:
1. David Croal Thomson, *The Barbizon School of Painters: Corot, Rousseau, Diaz, Millet, Daubigny* (London, 1891), 169-198.
2. By way of comparison, the reader is directed to Robert Herbert, *Barbizon Revisited* (New York, 1962), figs. 41, *The Forest of Fontainebleau*, Toledo Museum of Art; and 42, *Wood Interior*, Washington University, St. Louis.
3. Cf. ibid., fig. 43, *Landscape Sketch*, Anthony Bamfylde Collection.
4. One can also point to obvious parallels of style, subject matter, composition, etc. between the Marquette picture and well-known works by Rousseau such as *The Forest of Fontainebleau: Morning* in the Wallace Collection, London.

LOUIS METTLING
French (1847-1904)

Little is known of the life and career of Louis Mettling. He was born in Dijon in 1847 and worked initially in Lyon. He then became a student in the popular atelier of the prominent academician Alexandre Cabanal. His oeuvre includes portraits, genre, and some historical and religious subjects. He died at Neuilly in 1904.

Monk in Prayer (Saint Francis of Paola ?), Louis Mettling, oil on canvas

Monk in Prayer (Saint Francis of Paola?), 1885 (69.7)

Oil on canvas, 40 x 32 in. (101.5 x 81.2 cm). Inscribed l.l.: "L. Mettling .85."

Provenance: Collection of Dr. and Mrs. Alfred Bader, Milwaukee; their gift to the University, 1969.

The subject of this picture is, in all likelihood, the fifteenth-century Italian saint Francis of Paola. Francis, the founder of the Minim Friars, was born about 1416 in the Calabrian town of Paola. He was noted for his hermitic existence and is known to have dwelt for many years in isolation in a cave outside his native town.[1] In the visual arts he is traditionally represented bearded and garbed in a dark, hooded habit, much like that worn by Saint Francis of Assisi. Francis of Paola was frequently represented by seventeenth-century artists,[2] and Mettling's work shows the direct influence of seventeenth-century models.

The monk is seen kneeling in prayer, eyes uplifted, in a murky cavelike space. The mood of the work is exceedingly grave and reverential, a fact underscored by the somber palette oriented to shades of dark brown. The painting is lit by a single (but unspecified) light source. The light enters from the upper left and illuminates the most expressive elements of the composition—the monk's hands and face. This is a device taken directly from Baroque painting, probably indicating Mettling's study of Rembrandt. One also sees the influence of Spanish seventeenth-century painters, the most obvious being Jusepe de Ribera. Ribera's dramatic portrayal of Francis of Paola (Private Collection)[3] provides striking parallels to Mettling's asceticism as well as to his composition, dark palette, and highly textured surfaces. These neo-Baroque tendencies seen in the art of Mettling are characteristic of a wider-ranging development in French nineteenth-century academic painting. Baroque Old Masters were revered for their directness, dramatic intensity, and realism and were increasingly used as sources for portraits, genre subjects, and religious works. This imitation can be seen in the work of artists of the stature of Manet, but the nineteenth-century painter whom Mettling seems to be emulating is Théodore Ribot (1823–1891). Ribot executed many religious subjects in a comparably dark and "heavy" Baroque manner. Mettling's scumbled technique in the treatment of flesh seems in particular to have been derived from Ribot. Works such as this one, frequently overlooked as mere "straws in the art historical wind," shed light on the breadth of significant stylistic developments.

J. B. / R. B. S.

Notes:
1. See Herbert Thurston and Daniel Atwater, eds., *Butler's Lives of the Saints* (New York, 1956), II:10–13.
2. See, for example, Fontebasso's painting in the Louvre (ill. *Catalogue sommaire illustré des peintures* (Paris, 1981), II:175); Bencovich's in Ss. Trinità, Crema [ill. *Paragone*, XXVIII, no. 325 (Jan. 1977):88]; Caracciolo's *Immaculate Conception* from S. Maria della Stella, Naples [ill. *Painting in Naples from Caravaggio to Giordano*, catalogue of an exhibition at the Royal Academy (London, 1982), 112]; several works in S. Francesco di Paola, Venice [for which, see Martini in *Notizie da Palazzo Albani*, VIII, no. 1 (1979):93f.]; and Charles Mellin's representation [ill. in *Burlington Magazine* CXVIII, no. 885 (Dec. 1976): fig. 69].
3. Sold Sotheby Parke Bernet, New York, June 9, 1983, lot 93; ill. in catalogue.

PETER BAUMGARTNER
German (1834–1911)

Peter Baumgartner was born in Munich in 1834. Like Eduard Grützner, Baumgartner studied at the Munich Academy under Karl von Piloty and Hermann Anschütz, and he has been called a "worthy forerunner" or Grützner in her preference for humorous subject matter. Baumgartner's subjects, drawn from Bavarian popular customs and folk tales, do not have the satirical wit and insight found in the works of Carl Spitzweg. The great vogue that Baumgartner enjoyed was due more to his jovial and readily comprehended treatments of slightly naughty and amusing vignettes. He was even more popular in the United States than in Germany, and most of his later works entered American collections. After a long and productive career in Munich, Baumgartner died there in 1911.[1]

A Scene at the Cobbler's, 1869 (64.20)

Oil on canvas, 29 5/8 x 37 in. (75.2 x 94 cm). Signed l.r.: "P. Baumgartner, Munchen 1869."

Provenance: Purchased at auction at Parke Bernet Galleries, New York, by René von Schleinitz; René von Schleinitz Foundation; gift of the Foundation to the University, 1964.

References:
Letter of gift (1984) describes the painting as *A Game at the Cobbler's.*

Pick, *Marquette University Art Collection,* 5.

This charming and well-executed work is one of the gems of the Marquette University Fine Art Collection. It is one of two works by Baumgartner in Milwaukee collections (both at one time owned by René von Schleinitz). The other painting, *The Trusty Sentinel* (1861) in the Milwaukee Art Museum, is an outdoor scene with only one figure, but like the Marquette work it is very competently drawn and composed.[2] Baumgartner's highly developed sense of craft and his simple and direct presentation of humorous subject matter, evident in both works, are certainly in keeping with the "down to earth" character of Beidermeier painting in Munich.

An examination of Baumgartner's technique indicates that he was a typical product of the Munich Academy. One is immediately struck by his linear style and veristic approach to setting and detail. The cobbler's workshop is described with great precision, down to the bent nails in the wall and the crumpled piece of paper on the floor. Furthermore, the flat, glazed surface brings this wealth of detail into sharp focus. (These qualities are also apparent, at a later date in the art of Eduard Grützner.) Though Baumgartner's palette is low-keyed and modulated, areas of

A Scene at the Cobbler's, Peter Baumgartner, oil on canvas

brilliant color distributed throughout the painting work with the delicate detail to create a feeling of lightness and animation consistent with the subject matter.

A Scene at the Cobbler's falls into a tradition of interior genre scenes depicting popular manners and customs. Ultimately, this tradition can be traced back to seventeenth-century Dutch sources such as Jan Steen, the painter of humorous interior genre scenes. Of Baumgartner's contemporaries, the works of Ferdinand Georg Waldmüller can best be compared to the lighthearted genre of *A Scene at the Cobbler's*. Waldmüller's *Saint Nicholas Day* (1851, Milwaukee Art Museum), for example, clearly sets a precedent (though no direct connection is implied) for Baum-

gartner's work executed eighteen years later.[3] Baumgartner, like Waldmüller, treats his scene like a theatrical vignette, with the cast of characters arranged in a shallow stagelike space. Baumgartner also seems to follow Waldmüller in the very precise and formal manner in which his figures are drawn, posed, and grouped (note the pyramidal grouping at center) and in the use of a standardized repertoire of facial expressions conveying amusement, fear, and surprise. All these factors derive from Baumgartner's academic training.

The precise subject matter of *A Scene at the Cobbler's* is not known. A group of children has entered a cobbler's workshop, and one hands a book to the cobbler, who looks up in surprise from his workbench.

Given Baumgartner's interest in subjects relating to folk festivals, it is very likely that this depicts a scene during the festival *Fasching* (the Munich equivalent of Mardi Gras), a time of merrymaking and foolishness. The costumes worn by the children support this hypothesis. As with most of Baumgartner's pictures, the humor is based on irony. In this instance the ironic element is the boy at center wearing adult clothing, who is probably pretending to be a journeyman cobbler. Certainly Baumgartner's clientele had no difficulty in understanding the specific meaning of this scene.

J. B.

Notes:
1. For a biography and bibliography on Baumgartner see Rudolf M. Bisanz, *The René von Schleinitz Collection of the Milwaukee Art Center* (Milwaukee, 1980), 47.
2. Ill. ibid.
3. Ill. ibid., 261.

EDUARD GRÜTZNER

German (1846–1925)

Born in 1846 at Grosskarlowitz bei Neisse in Silesia, Grützner, the son of a farmer, showed an early talent for drawing. A career in the clergy had been planned for him, but following the counsel of the Munich architect Hirschberg, he decided to become a painter. In 1846 he traveled to Munich, a major artistic center, with the intention of studying with the renowned academician Karl von Piloty. After three years of preparatory study, for the most part in the painting class of Hermann Anschütz, he was admitted, in 1867, to Piloty's advanced class. He did not, however, share Piloty's taste for grand historical subjects, though he was considerably influenced by the older artist's technique. By 1869 he began to gain recognition with his pictures of monks, often engaged in harmless sensual pursuits such as drinking wine. While continuing to paint monks, Grützner enlarged his range of subject matter to include lighthearted scenes from the theater, for the most part taken from Shakespeare. He executed a great number of works either depicting Falstaff or with Falstaff as the central character. Also found in his repertoire are peasant and tavern scenes and some portraits and still lifes. With his mastery of humorous, subtly ironic subjects executed with great technical virtuosity, Grützner became one of the most wealthy and prolific artists of *Beidermeier* Munich. He spent his entire career in that city, dying there in 1925.[1]

Im Studierzimmer (In the Study), Eduard Grützner, oil on canvas

Im Studierzimmer (In the Study), 1891 (64.7)

Oil on canvas, 24 1/8 x 18 1/2 in. (61.3 x 47 cm). Signed l.r.: "Ed. Grützner, 91."

Provenance: Purchased at auction at Weinmüller Kunstversteigerhaus, Munich, by René von Schleinitz, Milwaukee; collection of the René von Schleinitz Foundation; the Foundation's gift to the University, 1964.

References:
Pick, *Marquette University Art Collection Supplement*, 5 (ill.), 6, as Grützner.

Garter, *Grain of Sand*, 9, no. 9, as Grützner.

To search for hidden psychological meaning or underlying social commentary in a work such as this one would be to search in vain. This is purely and simply an intimate and affectionate presentation of an aspect of the daily life of the friars in the monasteries of Munich. Here Grützner concentrates on an elderly monk enjoying a quiet moment of study from an old volume in the cloister library. This painting may be compared with Grützner's many other works depicting the Franciscan, Augustinian, and Benedictine friars of his native city. (Several of these works, also formerly owned by René von Schleinitz, are now in the collection of the Milwaukee Art Museum.) Here, as in paintings showing monks tasting wine, taking naps, eating meals, and so forth, there is a gently ironic inference that the brothers, despite their commitment to discipline and self-denial, still enjoyed some simple worldly pleasures. This idea, furthermore, was in conformity with the popular view of the monks—that they were quaint and eccentric but essentially benign and lovable individuals. A picture such as this one functioned in much the same manner as paintings of other types from the region or even of public buildings and civic and religious festivals. For bourgeois *Münchner* patrons such works reinforced civic pride and positive self-image. The life of Munich is consistently presented as being founded on solid values and traditions (e.g. Catholicism), as well as being essentially good-natured, prosperous, and fun-loving.

In this work there is great emphasis on utter clarity and legibility in both detail and content. Books, furniture, decorative elements, and assorted objects are all rendered with precision so as to create a believable setting. Precise details such as the torn back of the monk's chair are consistent with this acuity of vision and offer an inanimate parallel to the character of the monk—old and slightly disheveled yet still functioning. Grützner's evident skill at drawing also appealed to his patrons, who equated accuracy of representation with good craftsmanship. Therefore, despite the light-hearted mood of this work, it is very serious and high-minded from the standpoint of execution. In the academic tradition of Peter von Cornelius and Piloty, Grützner's art was founded on drawing rather than color (in academic terms, intellect as opposed to sensuality). As a result, all the parts of this work are precisely delineated, and the paint is applied flatly with an oil-glazing technique that eliminates evidence of brushstrokes. The tonal range, oriented to complementary earth tones of red and brown, is also very subdued and unified, as are the values of light and dark. Grützner's *Im Studierzimmer* is therefore the perfect reflection of both the bourgeois taste of the period and his own academic training.

J. B.

Notes:
1. For accounts of Grützner's life and work see Rudolf M. Bisanz, *The René von Schleinitz Collection of the Milwaukee Art Center. Major Schools of German Nineteenth-Century Popular Painting* (Milwaukee, 1980), 89-100; René von Schleinitz, "Grützner. Portrayer of Merry Art," *The American-German Review* XXIII, no. 2 (Dec.-Jan. 1956-1957):23-26. For a discussion of *Beidermeier* Munich see Bisanz, *The René von Schleinitz Collection*, 17-22.

WILHELM LAMPRECHT
German (1838-1906)

Wilhelm Lamprecht was born in the torn of Altenschönbach, near Würzburg.[1] He studied and worked in Munich from 1859 to 1867, at which time he went to America. Lamprecht painted several altarpieces, as well as mural and ceiling pictures, for churches in Boston, Chicago, Cincinnati, New York, and Philadelphia. He was active as well in Canada, where his most notable work was a cycle depicting the life of Saint Romuald in the parish church of the town of that name in Quebec province. By 1901 Lamprecht had returned to Munich, where he died five years later.

Père Marquette and the Indians, Wilhelm Lamprecht, oil on canvas

Père Marquette and the Indians, 1889   (00.3)

Oil on canvas, 43 1/2 x 53 in. (110.5 x 134.6 cm). Signed l.r.: "W. Lamprecht 1889."

Provenance: Said to have been purchased by the Rev. Stanislaus L. Lalumière, S.J., for Marquette College, c. 1889, from a Cincinnati collector who had won the picture in a raffle.

References:
Pick, *Marquette University Art Collection*, 16, 19 (ill.).

Marquette *Tribune*, Feb. 11, 1954.

Howard B. Wilder, Robert P. Ludlum and Harriet McCune Brown, *This Is America's Story*, 5th ed. (Boston, 1983), 61, 769.

Grand Dictionnaire (Paris, 1982-   ) (vol. in press).

In 1672 Father Jacques Marquette (1637–1675) was asked to accompany Louis Joliet on a journey to explore the Mississippi River.[2] The expedition got under way in the spring of 1673 with Father Marquette's departure from St. Ignace, Michigan. His route followed the northwest side of Lake Michigan to Green Bay and from there up the Fox River. Across a small land passage Marquette's party continued to the Wisconsin River, from which they entered the Mississippi.

The event recorded in Lamprecht's painting would seem to be Marquette's first viewing of the Wisconsin River.[3] The Miami Indians, who had been acting as guide to Father Marquette, are seen indicating the broad expanse of the Wisconsin across the portage from the Fox. Lamprecht's gestures and poses are rather academic, but his pictorial language is clear and his narrative ability evident.

This painting was reproduced on a one-cent postage stamp issued on June 17, 1898, to commemorate the Trans-Mississippi Exposition in Omaha. Although the stamp bears the motto "Marquette on the Mississippi" (the traditional title of the painting), the discovery of the Mississippi is known to have taken place in the company of Joliet and five other French travelers and without the direct assistance of local Indians.

R. B. S.

Notes:
1. The few known details of Lamprecht's career can be found in Ulrich Thieme and Felix Becker, *Allgemeines Lexikon der bildenden Künstler von der Antike bis zur Gegenwart* (Leipzig, 1907-1950), 22:277, and J. Russell Harper, *Early Painters and Engravers in Canada* (Toronto, 1970), 187.
2. See F. B. Steck, *The Joliet-Marquette Expedition, 1673* (New York, 1928).
3. See manuscript notes by Fr. McMahon in University Archives.

UNKNOWN ARTIST (RK)

Nineteenth Century

Academic Grisaille Study, 1881   (00.14)

Oil on canvas, 14 5/8 x 12 in. (37.2 x 30.5 cm). Inscribed: "1881" scratched in wet paint with wooden end of a brush, on the pedestal; "RK" in pencil, verso.

Provenance: Anonymous gift to the University.

Apparently painted from a plaster cast, this study depicts one of the four slaves on the base of the statue of the Grand-Duke Ferdinand I of Tuscany at Livorno (Leghorn). The marble statue of the Grand-Duke was completed by Giovanni Bandini in 1599 but erected only in 1617, and the base with its surrounding bronze statuary by Pietro Tacca was installed by 1624.[1] Each of the slaves is shown with hands bound behind him and with hands and ankles chained to the plinth of the

Academic Grisaille Study, Unknown Artist, Nineteenth Century, oil on canvas

base; each slave twists away from the base, adding an excitement to the otherwise stiff monument. Frequently reproduced in small bronze, the slaves present the virile, muscular male body in four slightly differing postures of dynamic movement.[2]

A. G.

Notes:
1. For the history of the monument, see John Pope-Hennessy, *Italian High Renaissance and Baroque Sculpture* (London, 1963), Text vol.:63–64; Catalogue vol.:92–93; and Plate vol.: Plate 96.
2. See, for example, the two slaves illustrated in *Apollo* 119 (1984):3 (advt.).

TWENTIETH CENTURY

FRANKLIN CHENAULT WATKINS

American (1894-1972)

Franklin Watkins is usually considered a Philadelphia artist, though one by adoption rather than birth. He was born in New York City in December 1894 but spent his early years in Kentucky and North Carolina. He attended the University of Virginia before moving to Philadelphia, where he was a student at both the University of Pennsylvania and the Pennsylvania Academy of the Fine Arts. He won two traveling fellowships, which he did not use until 1923—after Navy service in World War I and five years of work in commercial art. He traveled in Italy and France for a year and later (1926) returned to Europe and visited North Africa before settling permanently in Philadelphia.

Watkins worked in obscurity until 1931, when his painting *Suicide in Costume* (Philadelphia Museum of Art) won First Prize at the Carnegie International Exhibition in Pittsburgh. The picture, which depicts a man dressed as a clown holding a smoking gun, prompted much discussion, criticism, and admiration; Watkins's haunting brand of dramatic expression found response with critics and the public alike. The artist continued with a series of emotionally charged works, of which *The Crucifixion*—which depicts the event as a brutal, too-contemporary lynching—and *Poison for the King* (see below) are among the most noted. Watkins had his first one-man show at the Frank Rehn Gallery in 1934 and received numerous awards and prizes in subsequent years. His work became more varied in subject and tone as he adopted a somewhat more lyrical style that contrasts with that of his direct if rather unflattering portraits. Watkins taught and traveled in later years and was the recipient of major retrospective exhibitions in New York (1950) and Philadelphia (1966). He died while visiting Italy in 1972.

Poison for the King, 1934   (61.1)

Oil on canvas, 25 1/4 x 30 in. (64.1 x 76.2 cm). Unsigned.

Provenance: Frank K. M. Rehn Gallery, New York (1934); collection of Mr. Harry G. Sundheim, Jr., Philadelphia and Chicago; his gift to the University, 1961.

References:
Ernest Brace, "Franklin Watkins," *American Magazine of Art* XXIX (Nov. 1936): 723, 725, 728 (ill.).

Andrew C. Ritchie, *Franklin C. Watkins*, exhibition catalogue (New York, 1950), 45, no. 14.

Pick, *Marquette University Art Collection*, 27, 32 (ill.).

H. Clifford, *Franklin Watkins*, exhibition catalogue (Philadelphia, 1964), 10, no. 13 (ill.).

Ben Wolf, *Franklin C. Watkins: Portrait of a Painter* (Philadelphia, 1966), 78, no. 13 (ill.).

Carter, *Grain of Sand*, 9, no. 19.

Poison for the King, painted in 1934, is, like many of Watkins's paintings, a disturbing image. A seated figure holds a vial aloft in his right hand while grasping a scepter in his left. He is crowned and dressed in the all-too-familiar court dress of a playing-card king, actually the King of Hearts. His head is thrown back and his eyes appear bulbous as the whites stand out under evident strain. The skew position of the arms, as well as the brutal angularity of the contorted fingers, are underscored by the disquieting harshness of the artist's forceful style.

Poison for the King, Franklin Chenault Watkins, oil on canvas

Although the title suggests that the figure is a king and that he has just been poisoned, there is perhaps no more conspicuous a vehicle for poisoning than a vial. Ernest Brace, writing two years after the painting's completion, seems to have been responding to this difficulty when he described the work as representing a "court-jester brandishing a vial."[1] Watkins, however, referred to the figure as a king, although his recorded comments on the picture, made while viewing it again during his 1966 retrospective, are more jocular than illuminating: "Possibly this picture resulted from the

73

fact that I used to play bridge a great deal during those years. Probably someone had trumped my king!"[2] What would in fact seem to be the subject of the picture is the suicide of a king—the poison held in the vial having just been drunk. A hint at the artist's intentions might be had from the brief remark he made to Andrew Carnduff Ritchie at the time of the 1950 exhibition in New York: "Cards interested me briefly. *Poison for the King* was from a playing card."[3] That we are witnessing the self-inflicted death of a playing-card king, and specifically the King of Hearts, adds an ironic if not bitter note to the work. Watkins seems to suggest that even within the secure and apparently inviolable playing-card world passions and torments may appear that can lead one to the most desperate of acts.

R. B. S.

Flight into Egypt, Paul Berçot, oil on canvas

Notes:
1. Ernest Brace, "Franklin Watkins," *American Magazine of Art* XXIX (Nov. 1936):723.
2. Ben Wolf, *Franklin C. Watkins* (Philadelphia, 1966), 78.
3. Andrew C. Ritchie, *Franklin C. Watkins*, exhibition catalogue (New York, 1950), 8.

PAUL BERÇOT

French (1898-1970)

Paul Berçot was born in the French village of Bouligney in 1898.[1] He later moved to Paris, where he was a frequent and regular contributor to the various Salons from 1930. His style is vaguely representational, with geometrical abstractions determining shapes and compositional motifs. Berçot was relatively successful, if only locally; he received many prizes and commissions in France but few abroad. He died in 1970.

Flight into Egypt depicts a familiar subject, the flight of the Holy Family into Egypt, in Berçot's unfamiliar and unexpected style (for a painting of this traditional Christian theme). The figural elements have been reduced to their essentials, transformed by the artist into primitive geometric shapes. The faceless Virgin is cloaked in a pyramidal form that encloses and protects the Christ Child; they ride from right to left on the back of a donkey as Joseph deferentially walks beside, his comparatively advanced age indicated by the cane that he holds tightly in his hand.

R. B. S.

Notes:
1. See "Berçot," in E. Bénézit, *Dictionnaire critique et documentaire des Peintres, Sculpteurs, Dessinateurs et Gravures...*, new ed. (Paris, 1976), I:646.

Flight into Egypt, 1954   (57.3)

Oil on canvas, 39 1/4 x 31 7/8 in. (99.7 x 81 cm). Signed l.r.: "Berçot/-54-."

Provenance: Collection of Mr. and Mrs. Charles Zadok; their gift to the University, 1957.

References:
Pick, *Marquette University Art Collection*, 7, 8 (ill.).

Carter, *Grain of Sand*, 9, no. 2.

EUGÈNE PAUL, called GEN-PAUL

French (1895–1975)

Gen-Paul was born in Paris, the son of an embroider-ess and a cabaret musician.[1] His earliest works (at the age of eighteen) were decorated cigar boxes, his first oil painting not completed until three years later. In the interim World War I had begun and Paul became a soldier; he was wounded two times, the second requir-ing amputation of his right leg. On his demobilization in 1916 Paul took a job as a cornetist with the Cirque Bouglione in Paris—an activity reflected in later years by his many paintings of circus figures and magicians. His first picture, however, was a view of the Moulin de la Galette as seen from his studio window, one of numerous Paris views painted throughout his life.

Paul was largely self-taught and independent although not without close contacts with contempo-rary artists. His first signed work under the pseudonym "Gen-Paul" was painted in 1918. He exhibited at the Salon d'Automne in 1920, after which he traveled to France, Spain, and New York, making the last voyage as a stowaway. He exhibited at the Breckpod Gallery in Antwerp and the Saville Gallery in London before receiving his first one-man show in Paris, at the Gal-erie Bing, in 1926. His style, which he slowly elabo-rated in the 1920s, can be characterized generically as Expressionist, with bold masses of color drawn with force and vigor. His favorite subjects remained musi-cians, flowers, street scenes (especially of his native Montmartre), clowns, and portraits.

Following a visit to Spain in 1929 Paul suffered a severe mental breakdown. His recovery was slow, and his career as a painter only gradually resumed. He returned to the United States in 1934 and 1937 and after World War II moved to New York, where he remained until 1958. His last years were spent in Montmartre. Gen-Paul was the subject of a retrospec-tive exhibition at the Galerie Drouant-David in Paris in 1952.

The Cellist (57.2)

Oil on canvas, 45 5/8 x 29 1/8 in. (115.9 x 74 cm). Signed l.l.: "Gen Paul."

Provenance: Collection of Mr. and Mrs. Charles Zadok; their gift to the University, 1957.

References:
Exhibited Arts Club of Chicago (1952).

Exhibited Gen-Paul Retrospective Exhibition, Galerie Drouant-David, Paris (1952).

Pick, *Marquette University Art Collection*, 11, 15 (ill.).

The Cellist, Gen-Paul, oil on canvas

The Cellist represents a musician in the throes of a violent performance on his instrument. He bows the cello forcefully with his right hand while his left seems to dance along the fingerboard. The hands are particu-larly large as well as active, and their evident move-ment can be seen in contrast with the placid rigidity of the cellist's face. The boldly patterned background seems almost a response to the cellist's bowing. Gen-Paul did many paintings, drawings, and watercolors of cellists, of which the present picture appears to be the largest.

R. B. S.

Notes:
1. On Gen-Paul see Jean Miller, "Gen Paul," in E. Bénézit, *Diction-naire critique et documentaire des Peintres, Sculpteurs, Des-sinateurs et Graveurs* (Paris, 1976), IV:664–665.

JACQUES VILLON

French (1875-1963)

Born Gaston Duchamp, Jacques Villon chose the name by which he is known as an amalgam of the poet François Villon and the American nickname "Jack." Three of his younger siblings, Marcel Duchamp, Raymond Duchamp-Villon, and Suzanne Duchamp Crotti, followed his lead in pursuing an artistic career, and each became a painter or sculptor in his or her own right. Diverse personalities, they exerted much influence upon each other, especially in their early artistic formations.[1]

Villon began as an illustrator and a cartoonist and gradually developed into a painter and printmaker. Taking what he found of interest from the Neo-Impressionists, Cubists, and Futurists, he developed his own approach to line and color, in part using a grid system and module. His prints, often a combination of etching and drypoint, consistently examine objective reality through the discipline of a rigorously linear analysis of light and movement.[2] His paintings fuse the disciplined linear system of his graphic art with brilliant color, which suffuses his canvases with light.

Villon settled in Puteaux, near Paris, in 1906 and married Gabrielle Boeuf. In the early decades of the century he exhibited in the Salon d'Automne (1905) and Section d'Or (1912) in Paris. In 1913 he contributed eight paintings to the Armory Show in New York. In 1937 he was commissioned to paint a large mural entitled *Flight* for the Aeronautics section of the Exposition Internationale des Arts et Techniques. While his works were appreciated earlier by a number of connoisseurs in France, only after World War II did he have measurable success. Louis Carré bought the finished pieces in Villon's studio and gave him a solo exhibition in his Paris gallery in 1944; thereafter, Carré guided the swiftly growing reputation of Villon's art.

During the 1950s Villon exhibited widely and earned many prizes, among them Carnegie First Prize at the International Art Exhibition, Pittsburgh (1950), and the Grand Prix for Painting at the Twenty-Eighth Venice Biennale (1956). Retrospectives were held at the Musée National d'Art Moderne, Paris (1951), the Moderna Museet, Stockholm (1960) and the Kunsthaus, Zurich (1963). Honors were bestowed upon Villon: He was made Commander of the Legion of Honor and of Arts and Letters in France and an honorary member of the American Academy of Arts and Letters.

Villon's "Reflections on Painting" expresses his thoughts on the purpose of painting:

> Painting...why do I paint? How do I paint? I paint precisely because I want to discover of what painting consists. When I was young, I believed...that painting was a sort of reaction which reconstructed the spectacle before our eyes, preserving our memory of it...Now I think that painting is rather in the domain of philosophy. We paint in order to discover ourselves, to explain our deepest nature....[3]

Maternité, Jacques Villon, oil on canvas

Maternité (Maternity), c. 1948 (62.7)

Oil on canvas with some pen lines, 57 3/8 x 38 in. (145.7 x 96.5 cm) (sight). Signed l.r.: "Jacques Villon."

Provenance: Galerie Louis Carré, 1948; collection of Mr. and Mrs. Ira Haupt; their gift to the University, 1962.

References:
Dora Vallier, *Jacques Villon; oeuvres de 1897 à 1956* (Paris, 1957), 90.

Mother and Child in Modern Art, catalogue of an exhibition organized by the American Federation of Arts (New York, 1963), cat. no. 20 (ill.).

Pick, *Marquette University Art Collection*, 27.

Carter, *Grain of Sand*, 9, no. 17.

76

Images of children are exceedingly rare in Villon's oeuvre, and those of mothers with infants even more so. Nonetheless, in or about 1948 Villon made three works, similar in composition, of a mother and child. In addition to the Marquette canvas, he painted another version, entitled *Grande Maternité*, now in Oslo.[4] Whereas the dominant colors in the Marquette canvas are green, yellow, and blue, those in the Oslo painting are purples and mauves. An etching, *Maternité*, completes the trio of images.[5]

Villon's depiction of the mother and child is hardly sentimental in the Marquette painting. The chair functions as an architectonic support for the geometricized figure, who sits with crossed legs and cradles the baby close to her. Her features are chiseled of various yellows and pinks, and manifest no emotion. Swaddled in lozenges of yellow, the child lies as a bundle in her arms. Pen lines emphasize the woman's hands and the child's clothes. As an image of nurturing mother and babe, the painting inevitably recalls the theme of the Madonna and Christ Child. Yet Villon's fragmented pictorial language tends to discourage such association with traditional iconography.

Promethée libéré des ses chaînes (Prometheus Liberated from His Chains), Jacques Villon, oil on canvas

Promethée libéré des ses chaînes (Prometheus Liberated from His Chains), 1956 (60.11)

Oil on canvas with some pen lines, 35 7/8 x 25 3/8 in. (91 x 64.5 cm). Signed l.r.: "Jacques Villon / 56."

Provenance: Collection of Mr. and Mrs. Ira Haupt; their gift to the University, 1960.

References:
Dora Vallier, *Jacques Villon; oeuvres de 1897 à 1956* (Paris, 1957), 100-101.

Pick, *Marquette University Art Collection,* 27.

Carter, *Grain of Sand,* 9, no. 18, 5 (ill.).

In 1956 Villon was commissioned to make two large wall murals for the entrance hall of the École Technique in Cachan, south of Paris.[6] The two subjects concern Prometheus, who created the first man from clay and stole fire from the gods to give to man; he was chained to a rock on Zeus's orders and released by Hercules. Considered a clever inventor and a metaphor for the artist, who receives inspiration from divine sources, Prometheus is thematically appropriate for decoration at a technical school. The Marquette painting is an oil sketch for one of these panels. The present whereabouts of the other oil sketch, *L'Aigle Quitté Promethée,* is unknown. While the commission for the École Technique de Cachan has received passing mention in literature about Villon, the paintings themselves have been published only once as oil sketches.[7]

A. G.

Notes:
1. Basic bibliography concerning Villon includes Dora Vallier, *Jacques Villon oeuvres de 1897 à 1956* (Paris, 1957); *Les Duchamps: Jacques Villon (1875-1963), Raymond Duchamp-Villon (1876-1918), Marcel Duchamp (1887-   ), Suzanne Duchamp (1889-1963),* catalogue of an exhibition at the Musée des Beaux-Arts de Rouen (Rouen, 1967); *Jacques Villon,* catalogue of an exhibition at the Musée de Peinture, Rouen, and Grand Palais, Paris (1975); Pierre Cabanne, *The Brothers Duchamp* (Boston, 1976); and Daniel Robbins, ed., *Jacques Villon,* catalogue of an exhibition at the Fogg Art Museum (Cambridge, 1976).
2. For Villon's graphic oeuvre, see especially *Jacques Villon: Master of Graphic Art (1875-1963),* catalogue of an exhibition at the Museum of Fine Arts (Boston, 1964); and Colette de Ginestet and Catherine Pouillon, *Jacques Villon: les estampes et les illustrations catalogue raisonné* (Paris, 1979).
3. This passage is published in full in *Jacques Villon/Lyonel Feininger with "Reflections on Painting" by Jacques Villon,* with essays by George Heard Hamilton, Thomas B. Hess, and Frederick S. Wight, catalogue of an exhibition at the Institute of Contemporary Art (Boston, 1950), 7.
4. For this second version, also dated 1948, in the collection of Sonja Henie, Oslo, see *Jacques Villon,* catalogue of an exhibition at the Kunstnernes Hus (Olso, 1960), cat. no. 44.
5. For the etching, see *Jacques Villon, Master of Graphic Art (1875-1963),* cat. no. 116, and de Ginestet and Pouillon, *Jacques Villon, les estampes et les illustrations,* cat. no. E. 534.

6. For mention of this commission, see Cabanne, *The Brothers Duchamp*, 237, and J. P. Crespelle, *Villon* (Paris, 1958), 1. The finished paintings each measure approximately seven by six meters.
7. Both studies were published with brief commentary by Vallier, *Jacques Villon*, between pages 100 and 101.

SALVADOR DALÍ

Spanish (1904–   )

Salvador Dalí was born in Figueras, a tiny village in the Spanish province of Catalonia.[1] While he began painting as a young child (and with the encouragement of the Impressionist painter and family friend Ramón Pitchot), Dalí enrolled for his formal training in 1921 at the Fine Arts Academy in Madrid. His controversial personality, with manifest tendencies toward anarchism, led to his suspension from the Academy in 1923 for walking out of an assembly convened to announce the appointment of a professor whom Dalí and other students considered incompetent. Dalí returned to the school in 1924 but was permanently expelled in 1926 when he declared that his professors were unqualified to examine him.

Perhaps the most lasting influence of these school years was his associations with avant-garde writers and artists such as Federico García Lorca and Luis Buñuel, and his own experiments with a variety of traditional and modern approaches to painting. During his student years, Dalí explored the pictorial vocabularies of painters ranging from the Spanish masters (Velázquez, El Greco, Goya) to "the successive stages of European modernism" (Post-Impressionism, Fauvism, Cubism, the fantasy painting of Chagall and Kandinsky, and the Purism of Ozenfant and Jeaneret, known as Le Corbusier).[2] The influence of Picasso was an important force in Dalí's formative years, especially during the late twenties.

The mature painting of Dalí has been profoundly influenced by the Surrealists and by his admiration for the Renaissance painters, especially Piero della Francesca and Raphael. Surrealism, founded in 1924 by the French poet André Breton and inspired by the discoveries of Sigmund Freud, favors the creative and imaginative forces of mind over reason. Thought "in the absence of all control exercised by reason and outside all aesthetic or moral preoccupations" (Breton) is the motto of Surrealist art.[3]

Although Surrealist images began appearing in his works around 1926, Dalí first met the Surrealists on a visit to Paris in 1928. In contrast to other Surrealist painters (Giorgio De Chirico, Max Ernst, and René Magritte), Dalí's imagery presents the extremes of unconscious experience. In this respect the outpourings of his unrestrained personality exemplify Surrealism in its most complete form and content. Dalí's relations with the Surrealists were nevertheless punctuated with differences on questions of theory, taste, and politics.[4] In his writings of 1927 he identifies a fundamental distinction between himself and the surrealists based on a realist approach to seeing objective reality.[5] Even after he "joins" the Surrealist movement in 1929, the range of Dalí's interest never quite matches that of the Surrealists. Despite their concurrent interests in Freud and the irrational imagination, Dalí remained indifferent to the social and political concerns of the Surrealists, and his attraction to Catholicism and the painterly values of classical Renaissance artists led to interim quarrels between Breton and Dalí (1934) and to a complete break by 1940.

His intermittent years from 1940 to the period of the religious paintings (the Marquette *Madonna of Port Lligat*, 1949, is the first) were mainly spent in the United States, where he attracted worldwide attention for the eccentric behavior that has perhaps unduly drawn attention from his brilliance as painter and theorist.

Madonna of Port Lligat, 1949   (59.9)

Oil on canvas, 19 1/2 x 15 1/16 in. (49.5 x 38.3 cm). Signed l.r.: "Dalí."

Provenance: Carstairs Gallery, New York; collection of Mr. and Mrs. Ira Haupt; their gift to the University, 1959.

References:
Exhibition of the "Madonna of Port Lligat" by Salvador Dalí, catalogue of an exhibition at the Carstairs Gallery (New York, 1950).

New York Herald Tribune, March 23, 1956.

A. Reynolds Morse, *Dalí. A Study of His Life and Work* (New York, 1958), 62–63, ill. no. 63.

The Milwaukee Journal, October 13, 1959 (ill.).

Isodor Montiel, "Madonna of Port Lligat," *Hobbies* 66 (August 1961), 45 (ill.), 57.

Mother and Child in Modern Art, catalogue of an exhibition organized by the American Federation of Arts (New York, 1963), cat. no. 6.

Pick, *Marquette University Art Collection,* 9, cover ill.

A Guide to Works by Salvador Dalí in Public Museum Collections (Cleveland, 1974), 23 (ill.).

Robert Descharnes, *Salvador Dalí* (New York, 1976), 148.

Claude Pallene, "Comment les servitudes de son inspiration ont amené Dalí à la grandeur," *Journal de l'amateur d'art,* no. 654 (December 1, 1979): 15 (ill.).

Le Point, no. 378 (December 17, 1979): (ill.).

Guido Almansi, "Quel libidinoso pennello di Dalí," *La Republica,* Milan, December 31, 1979.

Carter, *Grain of Sand,* 4 (ill.), 9, no. 4.

Ramón Gomez de la Serna, *Dalí* (New York, 1979), 121.

Salvador Dalí rétrospective 1920-1980, catalogue of an exhibition at the Centre Georges Pompidou, Musée National d'Art Moderne (Paris, 1979), cat. no. 311, 375 (color ill.).

La Libre Belgique, January 4, 1980 (ill.).

The Guardian, January 5, 1980 (ill.).

Die Rheinptolz, January 5, 1980 (ill.).

Jeanine Baron, "Dalí ou la guerre du plaisir et de la réalité," *La Croix*, January 5-6, 1980.

The Financial Times of London, January 15, 1980 (ill.).

Basler Zeitung, February 5, 1980 (ill.).

La Montagne, February 5, 1980 (ill.).

Gazetta del Popolo, February 6, 1980 (ill.).

Le Democrate, March 26, 1980 (ill.).

Hugh Adams, "In Praise of Folly," *Art and Artists* 14 (March 1980):15 (ill.).

Art News 79, no. 4 (April 1980):91 (ill.).

The Milwaukee Journal, August 20, 1980 (ill.).

"O Sonho domesticado," *Journal do Brazil* (1980):18.

Salvador Dalí, catalogue of an exhibition at the Tate Gallery (London, 1980), cat. no. 213 (color ill.).

Art: Das Kunstmagazin nr. 11 (November 1981):57 (ill.).

Omni 4, no. 3 (December 1981):81 (ill.).

Dawn Ades, *Dalí* (London, 1982), 8, 175, ill. no. 151, 187.

Ignacio Gomez de Liano, *Dalí* (Barcelona, 1982), plate no. 99.

Retrospective Salvador Dalí 1982, catalogue of an exhibition at the Isetan Museum of Art, Tokyo, Daimaru Art Museum, Osaka, Kitakyushu Municipal Museum of Art, Kitakyushu, and Hiroshima Prefectural Museum of Art, Hiroshima (Tokyo, 1982), cat. no. 18 (color ill.).

400 Obras de Salvador Dalí de 1914 a 1983, catalogue of an exhibition at the Museo Español de Arte Contemporaneo, Madrid, and Palau Real de Pedralbes, Barcelona (Madrid, 1983), cat. no. 380, color ill. facing 216.

Treasures of the Vatican, catalogue of an exhibition at the New Orleans Vatican Pavilion at the 1984 Louisiana World Exposition (New Orleans, 1984), 49-51 (color ill.).

Dalí painted this first version of *The Madonna of Port Lligat* (1949) in his beloved Port Lligat, a tiny fishing village on the Spanish coast between Barcelona and the French border, shortly after he returned from the United States, where he had lived during World War II. A preliminary sketch, called a "Study for the Madonna of Port Lligat" (1949), is in a private collection.[6] A larger painting of the same title, with notable differences in the rendering of the subject and an expansion of the symbolism, was formerly in the collection of Lady Beaverbrook of New Brunswick, Canada.[7]

Dalí traveled to Rome with the earlier *Madonna of Port Lligat* during 1949, where he met with Pope Pius XII. The Pope showed great interest in Dalí's Surrealist interpretation of the Madonna and Child. In the spirit of a Holy Year, the Pope accepted the sincerity of Dalí's pilgrimage and blessed the work.

The 1949 *Madonna of Port Lligat* marks several important transitions in Dalí's career: a gradual break with the Surrealists with whom he had been identified for many years, a public identification with Catholicism symbolized by his visit to Pius XII, and the beginning of a series of important religious works that he was to produce over the next several years. Within an artistic framework representing a merging of classical and surrealist ideas of painting, Dalí manifests his religious mysticism, which can be traced to the Spaniards St. John of the Cross and St. Teresa of Ávila.[8]

In these works, and especially in the *Madonna*, Dali combines a tradition of classical Western painting with the mystical and surrealist experiences of his life. He was influenced by classical painters, notably by Piero della Francesca and Raphael. Dalí himself refers to Piero's *The Virgin and Child with Saints and Angels* (Pinacoteca Di Brera, Milan) as the inspiration for his *Madonna of Port Lligat*. Similarities do exist between the two paintings. Both Madonnas are seated on thrones with their hands clasped together and forming an arch above the Christ Child. Both are prominently centered under an arch beneath which a white egg hangs by a string from a large seashell. Even a casual survey of Raphael's Madonnas will show that Dalí's *Madonna of Port Lligat* (1949) belongs to the same classical tradition of painting. Raphael's *The Madonna Di Foligno*, now in the Vatican Museum Pinacoteca, also shows the Madonna and Child suspended in space above the earth. Other Raphael paintings represent the Madonna seated on a throne within an architectural or landscape setting, for example, *Virgin and Child with Saints* (Metropolitan Museum of Art, New York) and *Ansidei Madonna* (National Gallery, London).

Dalí's use of the concept of "dematerialization" illustrates the impact the atomic age had made upon him. He explains its meaning: The changes in matter resulting from an atomic explosion are parallel to his spiritual transformation of the Madonna. Because of her unique role, her physical body is "dematerialized." The open space cut through her torso, as depicted in *The Madonna of Port Lligat*, becomes a "mystical and virginal tabernacle" wherein the Christ Child is suspended in space. Her masklike face and head are suspended above dismembered hands and arms.

Dalí's allusions to the atomic age, in combination with his use of surrealist imagery, shows his intention to produce a modern painting, not a mere working of a familiar theme according to an earlier style. The modernity of the *Madonna of Port Lligat* is also sustained in his use of modern optics. A remarkable sense of spatial depth is achieved here by introducing three-dimensional stereoscopic qualities. The colors of striking clarity suggest the medium of modern color photography, which may also have influenced Dalí's approach to the painting.

Although Dalí uses the pictorial images of Christianity and the Renaissance, his symbolism in *The Madonna of Port Lligat* (1949) is more complex than it first appears. His Madonna is intended to be doubly understood, first as the Madonna of the mystical spirit and then as Dalí's tribute to his beloved wife, Gala, who is the model. For Dalí, Gala, as the guiding force in his life, was both Helen of Troy and Madonna, the sensuous and spiritual ideal in one.[9]

Although in a visually subordinate role, the Christ Child (Juan Figueras, a fisherman's son from Cadaques is the model) has a central place in the meaning of the painting. His placement in the tabernacle carved out of the Madonna's body, near where her heart would otherwise be, symbolizes his central role in the iconography. The cross and globe signify his intended dominion over the world.

The egg and seashell trace back to Piero della Francesca's *Brera Altarpiece* in Milan, as noted earlier, except that Dali inverts the seashell in the manner of the inverted seashell in Carlo Crivelli's *Madonna and Child Enthroned* (National Gallery, Washington).[10] The egg in Piero's painting is a symbol that has occasioned much debate, both as to the kind of egg it is and as to its possible meanings: as a reliquary, a symbol of Virgin birth, death and resurrection, or of the four elements of the earth.[11] Dalí discusses Piero's and his own uses of the egg at length in his book *Fifty Secrets of Magic Craftsmanship*. He compares it to a world suspended from heaven and also uses it to represent the unity of the Catholic Church in the world. Its placement over the Madonna signals her prominence in that world sphere. Or, as we have indicated, the egg may additionally represent the central role of Gala in the artist's personal world.

Seashells, in particular scallop shells, may represent pilgrimage or baptism, while the fish represents Christ and the lemons are associated with fidelity in love. Dalí's use of these symbols apparently follows the conventions of Christian tradition.

The sea urchin (especially prominent in this painting) has a unique meaning for Dalí. He invites any painter to view his own paintings through the microscopic world of the sea urchin's skeleton fitted with a crystal lens, as a measure of perfection. Dalí also compares the "architectural" structure of the skeleton of a sea urchin to the finest of man-made architectural structures and likens the sea urchin's role in the life of a painter to the role of a human skeleton in the life of a saint. The saint, who periodically experiences ecstasies and is drawn by "otherworldly" concerns, is reminded of his earthly condition by a human skull. The painter, whose ecstasies are primarily related to the material world, requires the skeleton of the sea urchin to remind him of the celestial regions beyond the sensuality of his oils.[12]

Important to a complete reading of this painting is the role of architectural symbolism. From the Middle Ages on, architecture has been used in paintings to express essential thoughts. Dalí follows the Renaissance painters, particularly Piero della Francesca, in his use of an architectural structure to enclose the Madonna and Child (Piero's *Brera Altarpiece*).[13] The architecture is intended to express a synthesis of humankind and the world and is the point of view from which a painter perceives people and nature itself. In this instance Dalí shows the human figures suspended in space, fragmented and dismembered; what he seems to be saying, then, is that they are mystically transcendent and dematerialized in respect to the world.

C. L. C.

Notes:
1. The sources for studying the life and work of Salvador Dalí include a growing number of scholarly catalogues and books. Principal sources for this biography are: Dawn Ades, *Dalí and Surrealism* (New York, 1982); *400 Obras de 1914 a 1983 Salvador Dalí*, exhibition catalogue, 2 vols. (Barcelona, 1983) with extensive chronology and bibliography; *Salvador Dalí rétrospective 1920-1980*, exhibition catalogue (Paris, 1979); *Salvador Dalí*, exhibition catalogue (London, 1980); A. Reynolds Morse, *Dalí. A Study of His Life and Work* (New York, 1958) and other texts by Morse. Dalí's own writings are not to be ignored in an approach to his life and work: *Conquest of the Irrational* (New York, 1935); *The Secret Life of Salvador Dalí* (New York, 1942); *Fifty Secrets of Magic Craftsmanship* (New York, 1948), and numerous other books and articles listed in the Barcelona catalogue, 1983.
2. Ades, *Dalí and Surrealism*, 14-16.
3. André Breton, *Manifeste du Surréalism* (Paris, 1924).
4. Ades, *Dalí and Surrealism*, chapter 3, especially 45, 46, 96.
5. Dalí, "My pictures at the Autumn Salon," *L'Amie de les Arts* (Oct. 1927), cited in Ades, *Dalí and Surrealism*, 46.
6. "Study for the Madonna of Port Lligat," (1949), collection of Gala Dalí. Reproduced in Robert Descharnes, *The World of Salvador Dalí* (Lausanne and London, 1979), 1976.
7. The present location of the 1950 *Madonna of Port Lligat* is unknown. According to a letter from Ian G. Lumsden, Curator, Beaverbrook Art Gallery (May 24, 1984), it was sold from the collection of Lady Beaverbrook in St. Andrews, New Brunswick, Canada, several years before the date of his letter.
8. G. A. Gevasco, *Salvador Dalí* (Charlottesville, N.Y., 1981), 16.
9. Max Gérard, ed., *Dalí*, Eleanor Morse, trans. (New York, 1958). Also, Dalí, *Fifty Secrets of Magic Craftsmanship*, 79.
10. George W. Ferguson, *Signs and Symbols in Christian Art* (New York, 1954).
11. Millard Meiss, *La Sacra Conversazione de Piero della Francesca* (Florence, 1971). Also, Marilyn Aronberg Lawn, "Piero della Francesca's Montefeltro Altarpiece: A Pledge of Fidelity," *Art Bulletin* LI, no. 4 (Dec. 1969): 367-371, et al.
12. Dalí, *Fifty Secrets of Magic Craftsmanship*, 76, 174-176.
13. Henri Focillon, *Piero della Francesca* (Paris, 1952), 135-137. Also, Rudolf Wittkower, *Architectural Principles in the Age of Humanism* (New York, 1962).

I. *Madonna of Port Lligat, 1949 version, Salvador Dalí, oil on canvas*

II. *Adoration of the Magi, Claude Vignon, oil on canvas*

III. *A Moor Robing after the Bath, Rudolph Ernst, oil on panel*

IV. *Bowl, Sevres, porcelain, after a painting by Teniers*

V. *Vase, Wedgwood, designed by Daisy Makeig-Jones,*
faience with Fairyland luster

WORKS ON PAPER

SIXTEENTH CENTURY

HENDRIK GOLTZIUS

Dutch (1558–1617)

Goltzius first studied glass painting in his father's workshop and then engraving with Dirk Volkertsz. Coornhert; he accompanied Coornhert upon his return to Haarlem in 1577. Together with Carel van Mander and Cornelis van Haarlem, Goltzius was one of the chief proponents of the Mannerist aesthetic, inspired above all by Bartholomaeus Spranger, in the north Netherlands. Until 1600 Goltzius was active and famous as an engraver; after that year, apparently because of failing eyesight, he began to paint. His Italian sojourn of 1590–1591 had a decisive influence upon his art, for during this journey he turned from the artifice of Mannerism toward the observation of nature. This shift in style is clearly evident in his drawings. He excelled in depiction of historical subjects, mythologies, and portraits.[1]

Mucius Scaevola, Hendrik Goltzius, engraving

Titus Manlius Torquatus, Hendrik Goltzius, engraving

Mucius Scaevola   (83.32.3)

Engraving, 22 1/4 x 17 1/2 in. (56.5 x 44.4 cm). Inscribed l.l.: "HG fecit/3" with four lines of verse beneath the image.

Provenance: Collection of Dr. and Mrs. Sidney M. Boxer; their gift to the University, 1983.

Titus Manlius Torquatus   (83.32.4)

Engraving, 20 1/4 x 15 in. (51.4 x 38.1 cm). Inscribed l.l.: "HG fecit/5" with four lines of verse beneath the image.

Provenance: Collection of Dr. and Mrs. Sidney M. Boxer; their gift to the University, 1983.

In 1586 Goltzius published a series of ten engravings depicting eight Roman heroes, plus a title page and concluding allegory of Fame and History.[2] Walter Strauss has posited that these prints were intended to inspire the young men of the present by presenting heroic examples from Roman history.[3] Indeed, the heroes represented are often exemplars of physical as well as moral strength.

After mistakenly killing the secretary to King Porsenna instead of the King himself, Mucius Scaevola was sentenced to be burned alive. However, he thrust his right hand into the fire and steadfastly watched it burn; after this display of courage, King Porsenna freed him.[4] Titus Manlius Torquatus killed single-handedly a giant Gaul, thereby proving his own bravery in battle.[5] In both of these engravings, Goltzius has shown the hero himself, heavily muscled, contorted, and armored, in the foreground, while including his valorous deed in the background.

A. G.

Notes:
1. For Goltzius's life and work, see above all. Carel van Mander, *Het Schilderboeck* (Haarlem, 1604; reprint Utrecht, 1969, and New York, 1980), fols. 281v–287; E. K. J. Reznicek, *Die Zeichnungen von Hendrick Goltzius*, 2 vols. (Utrecht, 1961); Frederick den Breder, *Hendrik Goltzius and the Printmakers of Haarlem*, catalogue of an exhibition at the Museum of Art, the University of Connecticut (Storrs, 1972); and P. van Thiel, in *Gods, Saints and Heroes: Dutch Painting in the Age of Rembrandt*, catalogue of an exhibition at the National Gallery of Art (Washington, 1980), 94ff.
2. The series has been catalogued by F. W. H. Hollstein, *Dutch and Flemish Etchings, Engravings and Woodcuts, ca. 1450-1700* (Amsterdam, 1949-   ), 8:36, cat. nos. 161–170, and by Walter L. Strauss, *Hendrik Goltzius, 1558-1617: The Complete Engravings and Woodcuts* (New York, 1977), 1:370ff., cat. nos. 230–239. The series is mentioned by van Mander, *Het Schilderboeck*, fol. 284v.
3. Strauss, *Hendrik Goltzius*, 1:370.
4. Hollstein, *Dutch and Flemish Etchings, Engravings and Woodcuts*, 8:36, cat. no. 164; Strauss, *Hendrik Goltzius*, 1:390, cat. no. 233.
5. Hollstein, *Dutch and Flemish Etchings, Engravings and Woodcuts*, 8:36, cat. no. 166; Strauss, *Hendrik Goltzius*, 1:394, cat. no. 235.

MARTEN VAN HEEMSKERCK
Dutch (1498-1574)

The son of a farmer, Heemskerck learned painting from Cornelius Willemsz in Haarlem, from Jan Lucasz in Delft, and finally from Jan van Scorel. Between 1532 and about 1536 he lived in Italy, where he assiduously studied ancient and contemporary art and architecture in Venice and Rome. Upon his return to Haarlem, he became one of that city's leading and most prolific artists, painting altarpieces, designing tapestries, and making drawings that served for engravings.[1]

His fame, according to contemporary sources, may have been due chiefly to his designs for prints, which were engraved for the most part by the best engravers then active in the Netherlands—Bos, Coornhert, Galle, Müller, and Cort.[2] Heemskerck specialized in series of prints, often illustrating a sequence of events from the Bible and adding Latin verses that interpret or summarize the depicted action. Heemskerck's imagery is often iconographically complex. From his contact with learned humanists, especially Coornhert and Hadrianus Junius, Heemskerck designed his allegorical prints with a rare depth of knowledge, both religious and secular.

Esther Crowned by Ahasuerus   (67.5.1)

(No. 1 of the series)

Engraving, 9 x 11 3/8 in. (22.9 x 28.9 cm). Inscribed l.l.: "I." and "Martynus Heemskerck Inventor 1564 / P. Gallus Fecit."

Mordecai Overhearing the Treason of Bigthan and Teresh   (67.5.2)

(No. 2 of the series)

Engraving, 9 5/16 x 11 1/16 in. (23.7 x 28.1 cm). Inscribed l.l.: "MHEE.IN."; "2."

Ahasuerus Giving His Ring to Haman   (67.5.3)

(No. 3 of the series)

Engraving, 10 9/16 x 13 7/8 in. (26.8 x 35.2 cm). Inscribed l.l.: "MHEE.IN."; and l.r.: "3."

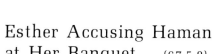

Ahasuerus Giving His Ring to Haman, from the Story of Ahasuerus and Esther, Marten van Heemskerck, engraving

Ahasuerus Consulting with Haman, from the Story of Ahasuerus and Esther, Marten van Heemskerck, engraving

Esther Preparing to Intercede for the Jews (67.5.4)

(No. 4 of the series)

Engraving, 9 11/16 x 12 7/16 in. (24.6 x 31.6 cm). Inscribed l.c.: "MHEE.IN."; and l.r.: "4."

Esther before Ahasuerus (67.5.5)

(No. 5 of the series)

Engraving, 10 3/4 x 13 3/4 in. (27.3 x 34.9 cm). Inscribed l.c.: "MHEE.IN."; and l.l.: "5."

Ahasuerus Consulting the Records by Night (67.5.6)

(No. 6 of the series)

Engraving, 10 11/16 x 13 1/2 in. (27.1 x 34.3 cm). Inscribed l.l.: "MHEE.IN."; and "6."

Ahasuerus Consulting with Haman (67.5.7)

(No. 7 of the series)

Engraving, 10 9/16 x 13 1/2 in. (26.8 x 34.3 cm). Inscribed l.c.: "MHEE.IN."; and "7."

Esther Accusing Haman at Her Banquet (67.5.8)

(No. 8 of the series)

Engraving, 10 3/16 x 13 7/8 in. (27.5 x 35.2 cm). Inscribed l.c.: "MHEE.IN."; and "8."

Provenance: Collection of Mr. and Mrs. Philip Pinsof; their gift to the University, 1967.

This group of eight prints was engraved in 1563 by Philips Galle after Heemskerck's drawings, which are now in the State Museum of Art, Copenhagen.[3] The engravings, as usual, reproduce the drawings in reverse; otherwise, the prints are faithful translations of Heemskerck's compositions. Such biblical stories as that of Esther, Ahasuerus, and Haman are typical of Heemskerck's choice of subjects for graphic reproduction. He generally followed the biblical text quite closely in his pictorial inventions, but selected moments of high drama.

This series illustrates the eight episodes of the story of Esther that are both essential to the narrative and most revealing of the motives and feelings of the characters. After casting out his queen, Vashti, for disobedience, King Ahasuerus sought a replacement by holding a kind of contest among all available virgins. As his new queen, he chose Esther. His crowning of Esther (Esther 2:17) is shown in Heemskerck's first composition.

Shortly thereafter, Esther's Jewish uncle and guardian, Mordecai, overheard two of the king's chamberlains, Bigthan and Teresh, plot against him (Esther 2:21). Ahasuerus soon afterward gave Haman a promotion and a ring, and also empowered him to seek out the king's enemies (Esther 3:10-11). Unaware that Esther herself was Jewish, and angered by Mordecai, who refused to honor him sufficiently, Haman began a campaign against all Jews. Esther then prepared to intercede for her people (Esther 5:1). She pleaded before Ahasuerus that he and Haman should come to a banquet that she would prepare (Esther 5:2-5). The night before the banquet, the king could not sleep and read the chronicles of his reign (Esther 6:1); he thus learned that Mordecai had been responsible for discovering the treason of Bigthan and Teresh, and he considered rewarding Mordecai. Ahasuerus consulted Haman about a just reward for one whom the king wished to honor (Esther 6:6-10). Haman mistakenly believed that the king wished to honor him and was incensed that Ahasuerus had Mordecai in mind; Mordecai was then paraded through the city upon a horse led by Haman. At Esther's banquet (Esther 7:6), at which only the king, the queen, and Haman were present, Esther accused Haman of being an enemy to her people. Ahasuerus then condemned Haman to death, and he was hanged. Heemskerck's designs depict the psychological states of the characters as these are manifested in their actions.

A. G.

Notes:
1. An essential source for the life and work of Heemskerck is still Carel van Mander, *Het Schilderboeck* (Haarlem, 1604, fol. 247; reprint eds., (Utrecht, 1969 and New York, 1980). See also Ilya M. Veldman, *Maarten van Heemskerck and Dutch Humanism in the Sixteenth Century* (Maarssen, 1977), which provides full bibliography.
2. Veldman, *Maarten van Heemskerck*, 16.
3. The prints are catalogued by F. W. H. Hollstein, *Dutch and Flemish Etchings, Engravings and Woodcuts, c. 1450-1700* (Amsterdam, 1949-), 8:243, cat. nos. 248-255. For Heemskerck's drawings, see Jan Garff, *Tegninger af Maerten van Heemskerck* (Copenhagen, 1971), cat. nos. 72-79.

ALBRECHT DÜRER
German (1471-1528)

From his early training by his goldsmith father, Dürer became familiar with the tools and meticulous workmanship that would serve him well when he would engrave upon copper. From an apprenticeship to the painter Michael Wolgemut during the years 1486-1490, Dürer learned the materials and craft of painting upon panel, watercolor, and drawing; Wolgemut also supervised the production of woodcuts for illustrated books. Thus, Dürer thoroughly learned the various techniques of the engraver, woodcutter, and painter. Three years of travel completed his training. In 1493 he returned to Nuremberg and married Agnes Frey. In 1494-1495 and again in 1505-1506 he visited Italy; in 1521 he visited the Netherlands. His travels and his friendships with foremost intellectuals, most especially Willibald Pirckheimer, put Dürer in close contact with the leading currents of European scholarly and artistic life. He exchanged drawings with Raphael and enjoyed the patronage of the Emperors Maximilian and Charles V.[1]

Even as Dürer was himself influenced by Italian Renaissance art, his own influence was strong upon the artists of his time in Germany, the Netherlands, and Italy and upon the art of subsequent centuries. His prints transformed the techniques of woodcutting and engraving, as well as the vocabulary of images available, secular and devotional.[2] While his paintings did not circulate as widely as his printed work, they were nonetheless treasured by patrons and collectors in Nuremberg and throughout Europe.[3]

St. John before God and the Elders   (56.9)

Woodcut, 15 1/2 x 11 7/8 in. (39.4 x 30.2 cm).

Provenance: Collection of Mrs. Otto H. Falk; her gift to the University, 1956.

References:
Pick, *Marquette University Art Collection*, 9.

Worship of the Lamb   (56.1)

Woodcut, 11 7/16 x 8 3/16 in. (29.1 x 20.8 cm).

Provenance: Collection of Mrs. Otto H. Falk; her gift to the University, 1956.

References:
Pick, *Marquette University Art Collection*, 9.

St. John before God and the Elders, Albrecht
Dürer, woodcut

Four Horsemen, Albrecht Dürer, woodcut

Worship of the Lamb, Albrecht Dürer, woodcut

St. Michael Fighting the Dragon, Albrecht
Dürer, woodcut

Nativity, Albrecht Dürer, woodcut

Assumption and Coronation of the Virgin, Albrecht Dürer, woodcut

Flight into Egypt, Albrecht Dürer, woodcut

The Glorification of the Virgin, Albrecht Dürer, woodcut

Four Horsemen (56.2)

Woodcut, 15 1/2 x 11 in. (39.4 x 27.9 cm).

Provenance: Collection of Mrs. Otto H. Falk; her gift to the University, 1956.

References:
Pick, *Marquette University Art Collection*, 9.

St. Michael
Fighting the Dragon (56.7)

Woodcut, 15 1/2 x 11 in. (39.4 x 27.9 cm).

Provenance: Collection of Mrs. Otto H. Falk; her gift to the University, 1956.

References:
Pick, *Marquette University Art Collection*, 9.

These woodcuts are four of the fifteen that comprise Dürer's series illustrating the Book of Revelation, first published in 1498 in editions with German and Latin texts, and again in 1511 with only the Latin text. By causing the text to be printed on the verso of each woodcut, Dürer effectively separated the written word from his grand pictorial renditions of the apocalyptic visions of St. John on Patmos. His condensation of the twenty-two-chapter narrative into fifteen images further focuses the attention of the viewer and reader upon the woodcuts, rather than upon the text.[4]

In *St. John before God and the Elders* (Rev. 4:1-8), the door opens to Heaven, and John beholds the vision of the enthroned Lord, who is surrounded first by a rainbow and then by twenty-four elders.[5] Flashes of lightning burst forth. The seven-horned, seven-eyed lamb prepares to take the book from the knees of the Lord. Dürer contrasts this powerful heavenly vista with a seemingly realistic German landscape below, thus showing both John's origin on earth and his destiny in Heaven.

The *Worship of the Lamb* (Rev. 5:6-13) follows *St. John before God and the Elders*.[6] Among the elders, the lamb, standing "as it had been slain" and with seven horns and seven eyes, appears. All present sing to this creature, "for thou wast slain and hast redeemed us to God by thy blood." Dürer makes the comparison between the lamb and Christ crucified even more explicit by including the chalice into which the lamb's blood spills.

The *Four Horsemen* of the Apocalypse (Rev. 6:1-8) signify War, Pestilence, Famine, and Death.[7] Hell's mouth opens at the left to devour the victims. Panofsky has pointed out that the text describes how each horseman goes forth at the opening of one of the first four seals and how the horsemen do not have direct contact with humanity; Dürer, departing from the narrative, shows the horsemen "as a closed squadron charging upon a crowd of helpless victims."[8]

St. Michael Fighting the Dragon (Rev. 12:7-9) describes the battle in Heaven in which St. Michael, with the help of three angels, fights the forces of darkness, represented by the dragon and his angels.[9] St. Michael, victorious over these evils, casts the dragon and his angels down to the earthly world.

Nativity (56.8)

Woodcut, 10 3/4 x 8 1/8 in. (27.3 x 20.6 cm).

Provenance: Collection of Mrs. Otto H. Falk; her gift to the University, 1956.

References:
Pick, *Marquette University Art Collection*, 9.

Carter, *Grain of Sand*, 11, no. 35.

Flight into Egypt (56.3)

Woodcut, 11 3/4 x 8 1/4 in. (29.9 x 21 cm).

Provenance: Collection of Mrs. Otto H. Falk; her gift to the University, 1956.

References:
Pick, *Marquette University Art Collection*, 9, 11 (ill.).

Carter, *Grain of Sand*, 11, no. 33.

Assumption and Coronation
of the Virgin (56.10)

Woodcut, 11 1/2 x 8 1/8 in. (29.2 x 20.6 cm).

Provenance: Collection of Mrs. Otto H. Falk; her gift to the University, 1956.

References:
Pick, *Marquette University Art Collection*, 9.

Glorification
of the Virgin (56.6)

Woodcut, 11 9/16 x 8 1/4 in. (29.4 x 21 cm).

Provenance: Collection of Mrs. Otto H. Falk; her gift to the University, 1956.

References:
Pick, *Marquette University Art Collection*, 11.

These four sheets belong to the series called *The Life of the Virgin*, which was published as a bound edition of nineteen woodcuts and a title page with Latin text in 1511; seventeen scenes had been printed c. 1504–1505, and the remaining three prints were made in 1510.[10] In contrast to the cathartic and expressive fervor of the *Apocalypse* (see above), the *Life of the Virgin* concerns itself with intimate human relationships. The requisite domestic and ecclesiastic settings afforded Dürer the opportunity to compose large interior spaces, as in the *Nativity*, or to design naturalistic landscapes, as in the *Flight into Egypt*. Taken together, the series illustrates the best known and theologically important events of the Virgin's life.

In the *Nativity*, the Virgin, protected by a ramshackle stone shelter, kneels in humility and awe before the newborn Child.[11] Joseph, wearing archaic robes and headdress, enters at the left as two shepherds, in German peasant costume, step in at the right. At the distant right a third shepherd receives the news of the Savior's birth from an angel.

The forested landscape in the *Flight into Egypt* serves as a rich tapestry-like background for the figures of the Virgin and Child, who ride on the donkey, and for Joseph, who leads the animal.[12] The Holy Family is about to cross a small bridge. Texturally lush, the landscape also controls the pictorial space. The large palm at the left establishes the foreground, and the trees recede toward the dense woods at the distant center.

The *Assumption and Coronation of the Virgin*, dated 1510, is one of the three blocks added to the original seventeen woodcuts in order to complete the series for the 1511 edition.[13] As the Apostles, standing in the lower half, behold the Virgin's ascent, she bows her head to receive the crown, held by Christ and God the Father. The dove hovers above.

Appearing last in the bound 1511 edition, the *Glorification of the Virgin* was among the first woodcuts made by Dürer for the series.[14] Among the saints who adore the Virgin are Catherine, patroness of virgins and brides, Paul, Jerome, Anthony, and the Baptist; Joseph humbly stands to the right. Moses, symbolic of the Old Law, is seen above in a lunette.

Melencolia I, 1514   (56.5)

Engraving, 9 1/2 x 7 1/4 in. (24.1 x 18.4 cm).

Provenance: Collection of Mrs. Otto H. Falk; her gift to the University, 1956.

References:
Pick, *Marquette University Art Collection*, 11.

Carter, *Grain of Sand*, 11, no. 34 (cover ill.).

One of Dürer's three master engravings, *Melencolia I* is also among his most complex.[15] A brooding, winged female, Melancholy sits among scientific and manual tools, a sleeping dog, and a millstone; nearby are a

Melencolia I, Albrecht Dürer, engraving

magic number square, a bell, scales, and an hourglass. With one hand she aimlessly holds a compass against a closed book, and with the other she supports her head. Her own ponderous mental state contrasts with that of the putto, who, perched upon the millstone, scribbles upon a tablet. The objects surrounding Melancholy are symbolic of the realm in which she dwells, that of the imagination. She represents the creative, intellectual soul burdened by despair.

Her keys and purse symbolize power and wealth, and her wings, her superiority over mortals. The bat, a dweller in lonely places, is traditionally associated with Melancholy. Moonlight, coming from the right, casts a cool glow over the scene; the comet, in the sky to the left and encircled by a lunar rainbow, signifies astronomy. The tools strewn about Melancholy are emblematic of geometry and of the craft of the artist— whose task of representing man was closely aligned with mathematics and perspective. The sphere of wood and the truncated rhombo-hedron of stone are emblems of the scientific principles allied with the artist's profession. Melancholy, one of the four humors, was further associated with cold, dryness, earth, autumn, and evening. None of the layers of meaning inherent in her character has escaped Dürer's elaborate invention.

St. Jerome in His Study, Albrecht Dürer, engraving

Virgin and Child Crowned by Two Angels,
Albrecht Dürer, engraving

St. Jerome
in His Study, 1514   (64.3)

Engraving, 9 3/4 x 7 1/2 in. (24.8 x 19.1 cm).

Provenance: Collection of Dr. and Mrs. John Pick; their gift to the University, 1964.

References:
Pick, *Marquette University Art Collection*, 11.

Carter, *Grain of Sand*, 11, no. 36.

Dürer's engraving of St. Jerome presents the Saint busily writing in his study, a light-filled, well-ordered cell.[16] A calm, scholarly mood pervades the space, extending to the drowsy lion and sleeping dog. Death and man's transient existence are represented by the skull on the windowsill and the hourglass on the wall. *St. Jerome* is one of the three master engravings by Dürer; the other two are *Melencolia I* (see above) and *Knight, Death and the Devil,* of 1513; taken together, the three represent man's intellectual pursuits, man's creative and imaginative life, and man's physical strength.[17] St. Jerome is the exemplar of "a life in the service of God" leading to the "peaceful bliss of divine wisdom."[18]

Virgin and Child Crowned
by Two Angels, 1518   (56.4)

Engraving, 5 11/16 x 3 7/8 in. (14.4 x 9.8 cm).

Provenance: Collection of Mrs. Otto H. Falk; her gift to the University, 1956.

References:
Pick, *Marquette University Art Collection*, 11.

Among Dürer's later devotional images, the *Virgin and Child Crowned by Two Angels* manifests his concern with balance.[19] Two symmetrical, yet not identical, angels hold the crown above the Virgin's head. The Madonna, cradling the Child in one hand and an apple in the other, looks out, youthful and serious. Her voluminous drapery is deftly designed in sculptural folds. The sturdy Child, too, appears sculptural. Such a substantially developed formal language bespeaks Dürer's absorption of certain tenets of Italian Renaissance art.

A. G.

Notes:

1. The authoritative study of Dürer's life and work remains Erwin Panofsky, *The Life and Art of Albrecht Dürer*, 3rd ed. Princeton, 1955).
2. The standard catalogues of Dürer's prints include those by Joseph Meder, *Dürer-Katalog* (Vienna, 1932) and Walter L. Strauss, ed., *The Illustrated Bartsch (Commentary), 16th Century German Artists, Albrecht Dürer* (New York, 1981).
3. For Dürer's paintings, see, above all, Fedja Anselewsky, *Albrecht Dürer: das malerische Werk* (Berlin, 1971).
4. Excellent discussions of the place of the Apocalypse in Dürer's art are provided by Panofsky, *Albrecht Dürer*, 51ff.; by Wilhelm Waetzoldt, *Dürer and His Times* (London, 1950), 29ff., and by Charles Talbot, ed., *Dürer in America: His Graphic Work*, catalogue of an exhibition at the National Gallery of Art (Washington, 1971), 164ff.
5. Catalogued by Meder, *Dürer-Katalog*, cat. no. 166, and by Strauss, *Dürer*, cat. no. .263; both give additional references.
6. Catalogued by Meder, *Dürer-Katalog*, cat. no. 176, and by Strauss, *Dürer*, cat. no. .267; both give additional references.
7. Catalogued by Meder, *Dürer-Katalog*, cat. no. 167, and by Strauss, *Dürer*, cat. no. .264.
8. Panofsky, *Albrecht Dürer*, 53.
9. Catalogued by Meder, *Dürer-Katalog*, cat. no. 174, and by Strauss, *Dürer*, cat. no. .272; both give additional references.
10. For discussion of the *Life of the Virgin* in Dürer's oeuvre, see Panofsky, *Albrecht Dürer*, 96ff., and Waetzoldt, *Dürer and His Times*, 100ff.
11. Catalogued by Meder, *Dürer-Katalog*, cat. no. 197, and by Strauss, *Dürer*, cat. no. .285; both give additional references.
12. Catalogued by Meder, *Dürer-Katalog*, cat. no. 201, and by Strauss, *Dürer*, cat. no. .289; both give additional references.
13. Catalogued by Meder, *Dürer-Katalog*, cat. no. 206, and by Strauss, *Dürer*, cat. no. .294; both give additional references.
14. Catalogued by Meder, *Dürer-Katalog*, cat. no. 207, and by Strauss, *Dürer*, cat. no. .295; both give additional references.
15. The engraving is catalogued by Meder, *Dürer-Katalog*, cat. no. 75, and by Strauss, *Dürer*, cat. no. .074; both give further bibliography. The most extensive analysis of the iconography of *Melencolia I* is that provided by Panofsky, *Albrecht Dürer*, 156ff. See further D. Pingree, "A New Look at Melancholia I," *Journal of the Warburg and Courtauld Institutes* 43 (1980):257f., and Philip L. Sohm, "Dürer's 'Melancholia I': The Limits of Knowledge," *Studies in the History of Art* 9 (1980):13–32.
16. The engraving is catalogued by Meder, *Dürer-Katalog*, cat. no. 59, and by Strauss, *Dürer*, cat. no. .060; both give additional references. While the Marquette impression is somewhat worn, it nonetheless conveys the sparkling glow of Dürer's invention.
17. Panofsky, *Albrecht Dürer*, 154ff., discussed the three images, which may be considered a loose series depicting complementary and opposing ideas.
18. Ibid., 156.
19. The engraving is catalogued by Meder, *Dürer-Katalog*, cat. no. 38, and by Strauss, *Dürer*, cat. no. .039; both give additional references. See further Panofsky, *Albrecht Dürer*, 199.

SEVENTEENTH CENTURY

PETER PAUL RUBENS

Flemish (1577–1640)

Classically educated and apprenticed to the Antwerp painter Otto van Veen, Rubens went to Italy and, briefly, to Spain between 1600 and 1608. Upon his return to Antwerp, he quickly became recognized as that city's leading artist. He received commissions from the leading monarchs and aristocrats of Europe and was ennobled by Charles I of England and Philip IV of Spain. For the archduchess Isabella, Regent of the Spanish Netherlands, Rubens served as diplomat and confidential adviser. Perhaps no other artist had such a pervasive role in both the art and politics of his time, and few were so well versed in classical history and literature and ancient and contemporary art as Rubens.[1]

Marcus Brutus, 1638   (00.224)

Engraving, 11 1/2 x 7 7/8 in. (29.2 x 20 cm). Inscribed in the plate l.c.: "M. BRVTVS IMP./Ex marmore antiquo."; and l.l.: "P P Rubens delin./L. Vorstermans sculpsit A.° 1638."; and l.r.: "Cum privilegiis...."

Provenance: Collection of Mrs. Joseph D. Patton; her gift to the University, 1961.

M. Tullius Cicero, 1638   (00.234)

Engraving, 14 7/16 x 9 15/16 in. (36.7 x 25.2 cm). Inscribed in the plate l.c.: "M. TVLLIVS CICERO./Ex marmore antiquo."; and l.l.: "P P Rubens delin./H. Withouc Sculp. A.° 1638."; and l.r.: "Cum privilegiis...."

Provenance: Collection of Mrs. Joseph D. Patton; her gift to the University, 1961.

Rubens trained and supervised a group of engravers who worked expressly for him; Lucas Vorsterman and Hans Witdoeck are two such printmakers. Rubens also made a number of designs whose final form was intended to be a published print or series of prints. These two prints of Marcus Brutus and M. Tullius Cicero belong to a series of twelve engravings after ancient marble busts of statesmen and philosophers, six Greek and six Roman.[2] The other prints represent Sophocles, Socrates, Democritus, Hippocrates, Plato, Demosthenes, Scipio Africanus, Caesar, Seneca, and

Nero. Although Rubens may have begun planning the publication of the series as early as 1624, he did not bring the project to completion until 1638.[3]

A. G.

Notes:
1. Excellent sources for the life and work of Rubens include Julius S. Held and Donald Posner, *Seventeenth and Eighteenth Century Art* (Englewood Cliffs and New York, n.d.), 196–212; Julius S. Held, *The Oil Sketches of Peter Paul Rubens: A Critical Catalogue*, 2 vols. (Princeton, 1980); R. S. Magurn, ed., *The Letters of Peter Paul Rubens* (Cambridge, Mass., 1955); and C. V. Wedgwood, *The World of Rubens* (New York, 1967).
2. The series is catalogued by C. G. Voorhelm Schneevoogt, *Catalogue des estampes gravées d'après P. P. Rubens* (Haarlem, 1873), 223–224, nos. 25.1–12; for the *Cicero*, see no. 8, and for the *Brutus*, no. 10. For the *Brutus*, see further Didier Bodart, *Rubens e l'incisione*, catalogue of an exhibition at the Gabinetto Nazionale delle Stampe (Rome, 1977), 80, cat. no. 149.
3. Bodart, *Rubens e l'incisione*, 80.

Marcus Brutus, Peter Paul Rubens, engraving

M. Tullius Cicero, Peter Paul Rubens, engraving

EIGHTEENTH CENTURY

RICHARD WILSON
English (1713?–1782)

After receiving a classical education, Wilson went to London in 1729 and served as an apprentice to the portraitist Thomas Wright. His interest soon turned to landscape, although he also painted portraits. Between 1750 and 1756 he lived in Italy, chiefly in Rome, and absorbed both the atmosphere and culture of classical landscape and antiquity. Upon his return to London, Wilson established a studio and attracted the patronage of important landed gentry. He became extremely successful during the 1760s as a painter of Italian views and classical literary landscapes. One of the founding members of the Royal Academy, he was appointed librarian of the Academy in 1776, as a partial remedy for his financial difficulties, which may have been caused by alcoholism. In the following years his reputation declined, and he died in obscurity, tended by relatives in his native north Wales.[1]

Wilson himself apparently did not engage in printmaking. A total of thirty-eight etchings after his invention were published during his lifetime;[2] many of these prints reproduce some of his grandest canvases, but others reproduce drawings made by the artist, presumably expressly for the etcher. The series "Twelve Original Views of Italy" is discussed below. Wilson's sketches of Roman views and monuments were appreciated by collectors during his lifetime and after his death; one volume of sketches made during his Roman years was published in 1811.[3] Another sketchbook of his Italian sojourn was issued in facsimile in 1968.[4]

Banks of the Tiber   (00.296.11)

Etching, 10 3/16 x 14 7/16 in. (27.5 x 36.7 cm). Inscribed in the plate l.l.: "R. Wilson del."; and l.r.: "Jas. Gandon sc."

Provenance: Anonymous gift to the University.

Baths of Diocletian   (00.296.7)

Etching, 10 3/4 x 14 3/8 in. (27.3 x 36.5 cm). Inscribed in the plate l.l.: "R. Wilson del."; and l.r.: "Jas. Gandon sc."

Provenance: Anonymous gift to the University.

Bridge of Augustus at Rimini   (00.296.6)

Etching, 10 3/4 x 14 1/2 in. (27.3 x 36.8 cm). Inscribed in the plate l.l.: "R. Wilson del."; and l.r.: "Jos. Farington sc."

Provenance: Anonymous gift to the University.

Castle of Ischia   (00.296.8)

Etching, 10 3/4 x 14 3/8 in. (27.3 x 36.5 cm). Inscribed in the plate l.l.: "R. Wilson del."; and l.r.: "Jas. Gandon sc."

Provenance: Anonymous gift to the University.

Circus of Caracalla   (00.296.1)

Etching, 10 3/4 x 14 3/8 in. (27.3 x 36.5 cm). Inscribed in the plate l.l.: "R. Wilson del."; and l.r.: "E. Rooker, sc."

Provenance: Anonymous gift to the University.

In the Strada Nomentana   (00.296.5)

Etching, 10 3/4 x 14 1/4 in. (27.3 x 36.2 cm). Inscribed in the plate l.l.: "R. Wilson del."; and l.r.: "J. Farington sc."

Provenance: Anonymous gift to the University.

Pompey's Bridge at Terni   (00.296.10)

Etching, 14 3/8 x 10 3/4 in. (36.5 x 27.3 cm). Inscribed in the plate l.l.: "R. Wilson del."; and l.r.: "Ja. Gandon sc."

Provenance: Anonymous gift to the University.

Temple of Peace   (00.296.3)

Etching, 10 3/4 x 14 7/16 in. (27.3 x 36.7 cm). Inscribed in the plate l.l.: "R. Wilson del."; and l.r.: "M. Rooker sc."

Provenance: Anonymous gift to the University.

In the Strada Nomentana, from the series Twelve Original Views of Italy, Richard Wilson, etching

Temple of Romulus and Remus (00.296.9)

Etching, 10 1/2 x 14 3/8 in. (26.7 x 36.5 cm). Inscribed in the plate l.l.: "R. Wilson del."; and l.r.: "Jas. Gandon sc."

Provenance: Anonymous gift to the University.

Torre delle Grotte (00.296.4)

Etching, 10 3/4 x 14 7/16 in. (27.3 x 36.7 cm). Inscribed in the plate l.l.: "R. Wilson del."; and l.r.: "W. Hodges sc."

Provenance: Anonymous gift to the University.

Pompey's Bridge at Terni, from the series Twelve Original Views of Italy, Richard Wilson, etching

Villa of Maecenas at Tivoli, from the series Twelve Original Views of Italy, Richard Wilson, etching

Villa of Maecenas at Tivoli   (00.296.2)

Etching, 14 1/4 x 10 3/4 in. (36.2 x 27.3 cm). Inscribed in the plate l.l.: "R. Wilson del."; and l.r.: "M. Rooker sc."

Provenance: Anonymous gift to the University.

These eleven etchings belong to a series of twelve views of ancient ruins situated, for the most part, in and around Rome.[5] The prints were published in 1776 by Boydell, under the title "Twelve Original Views of Italy."[6] Not only would these compositions have been recognizable by connoisseurs as depicting some of the most renowned Roman monuments; they also would have been appreciated for Wilson's novel viewpoints and placement of the ruins within ideal landscapes. Such etchings, made under the publisher's supervision and by etchers no doubt selected by him, would have been produced from drawings by Wilson himself. Although the precise drawings that were reproduced in this series are not identified, they and the finished etchings are closely related to oil paintings made by Wilson in his London studio from drawings made during his Italian sojourn.[7]

A. G.

Notes:
1. Essential bibliography about Wilson includes David H. Solkin, *Richard Wilson: The Landscape of Reaction,* catalogue of an exhibition at The Tate Gallery (London, 1982); W. G. Constable, *Richard Wilson* (London, 1953); and T. Wright, *Some Account of the Life of Richard Wilson, Esq., R. A.* (London, 1824).
2. Wright, *Life of Richard Wilson,* 274–275, provides a summary of the principal prints made after Wilson's designs.
3. Anonymously edited, *Studies and Designs, by Richard Wilson, Done at Rome in the Year 1752* (Oxford, 1811); the plates reproduce sketches belonging to the late Oldfield Bowles, Esq.
4. Denys Sutton, ed., and Ann Clements, catalogue, *An Italian Sketchbook by Richard Wilson R. A.* (London, 1968).
5. Missing from the Marquette series is *In the Villa Adriana,* inscribed "M. Rooker sc."
6. Constable, *Richard Wilson,* 202.
7. Brinsley Ford, *The Drawings of Richard Wilson* (London, 1951), 33, discussed the difficulties involved in connecting Wilson's drawings to specific paintings. Nonetheless, we may remark that the etching *Torre delle Grotte* may be related in subject if not precise composition to the drawings in the collection of A. P. Oppé, ill. ibid., 57 and plate 43, and to the painting in the Molesworth St. Aubyn collection, discussed by Constable, *Richard Wilson,* 199 and plate 78a. The etching *In the Strada Nomentana* is related to the painting of the same subject in the Russell-Cotes Art Gallery and Museum, Bournemouth; see Solkin, *Richard Wilson,* 230, and Constable, *Richard Wilson,* 210–211, where several versions of this design are discussed.

NINETEENTH CENTURY

NATHANIEL CURRIER
American (1813–1888)
JAMES MERRITT IVES
American (1824–1895)

In 1835 Currier founded his own lithographic firm in New York; in 1857 Ives became a partner in the company. Between 1835 and 1895 the firm published over 7,000 lithographs. Currier retired in 1880, and in 1895 Ives died. The firm, however, closed only in 1907.[1]

Lithography, the process of printing upon a polished stone surface, permitted a nearly unlimited number of prints to be made from a single stone image. The resultant prints were often hand-colored, and, even then, sold at extremely low prices. Currier and Ives employed specialized draftsmen to draw designs upon the stones, skilled printers, and a group of girls who applied color after the black "drawings" were printed. The publishing activities of Currier and Ives produced a nearly comprehensive pictorial record of American nineteenth-century life and history.

THE SOLDIER'S GRAVE, 1862   (82.7.10)

Hand-colored lithograph, 13 7/8 x 10 in. (35.2 x 25.4 cm).

Provenance: Collection of Dr. Kenneth Maier; his gift to the University, 1982.

A modest memorial to a soldier who died during the Civil War, this print carries an inscription upon the tombstone:[2]

IN MEMORY OF

Dwight W. Eddy

OF THE

First Regt. Vt. Volunteers

WHO DIED AT

Tinmouth, Vermont

November 19th 1862

A BRAVE AND GALLANT SOLDIER

AND A TRUE PATRIOT

His toils are past, his work is done;
And he is fully blest;
He fought the fight, the victory won,
And enters into rest.

Such a printed memorial would have been relatively inexpensive and probably would have hung in the home of the deceased's immediate family. The mourning woman, weeping willows, and roses belong to the traditional iconography of tombs and memorials; however, the soldiers marching in the distant right clearly allude to the circumstances of the Civil War.

A. G.

Notes:
1. The prolific production of the Currier and Ives firm has been catalogued by Harry T. Peters, *Currier and Ives: Printmakers to the American People* (New York, 1929 and 1976), and by Frederic A. Conningham, *Currier and Ives Prints: An Illustrated Checklist* (New York, 1949). See further Russel Crouse, *Mr. Currier and Mr. Ives: A Note on Their Lives and Times* (New York, 1937).
2. The name of the deceased, his regiment, and the place and date of his death have been inscribed in pen. The print has been catalogued by Conningham, *Currier and Ives Prints*, 242, no. 5597. A close variant of this print, made slightly larger, was published by Currier and Ives in 1865, undoubtedly because the prolonged Civil War necessitated the availability of such inexpensive memorials.

The Soldier's Grave, Nathaniel Currier and James Merritt Ives, hand-colored lithograph

FREDERIC LEIGHTON

English (1830–1896)

One of five children of an intellectually and pedagogically enlightened physician, Federic Leighton was given an independent schooling under the supervision of his father.[1] Several extended sojourns on the Continent from 1839 onward continued his education, primarily in the museums and art academies of Italy, Germany, and France. In 1846 he entered the Städelsches Kunstinstitut in Frankfurt, and he completed his formal training in Rome and Paris. In 1859 he settled permanently in London and in the middle 1860s built an eccentric house on Holland Park.[2]

In 1855 his *Cimabue's Madonna*, exhibited at the Royal Academy, brought him critical acclaim; Queen Victoria purchased the picture for the Royal Collection and thereby eased his path toward financial success, which came a few years later.[3] He was elected an Associate of the Royal Academy in 1864 and became its president in 1878. Shortly before his death in 1896, he was named a peer.

Many of his grand historical paintings depicted events in the lives of Italian Renaissance artists taken from Vasari's *Le Vite* (1568); he also painted subjects from the Bible, classical mythology, Shakespeare's plays, and other literary sources. Thoroughly familiar with the art of antiquity, the Renaissance, and the Baroque, he adapted compositional and stylistic components to suit his own romantic and dramatic aesthetic.

Head of Venus   (00.239)

Charcoal, 13 5/8 x 10 1/2 in. (34.7 x 26.8 cm). Signed in ink l.l.: "F. Leighton"; watermark "J. Whatman."

Provenance: Collection of Mr. and Mrs. Philip Pinsof; their gift to the University.

References:
Carter, *Grain of Sand*, 11, no. 4, as Athena by Leighton.

Richard Ormond, in a letter (1983), as Leighton.

Obviously made from a cast, this broadly drawn charcoal sheet is apparently a youthful work, perhaps drawn, as Ormond has suggested, during the artist's early years at the Städelsches Kunstinstitut in Frankfurt, 1846–1848. The original of the cast is the head of the *Medici Venus* (Uffizi, Florence), one of the most famous of antique statues.[4] Leighton almost certainly knew the marble first-hand from his sojourn in Florence in 1844–1845. However, the precise view of the head represented in the drawing would have been difficult to draw from the original. Although the classical features of the statue's head might appear somewhat generic, the tight band and small bobbed hair are par-

Head of Venus, Frederic Leighton, charcoal

Drawings and Studies in Pencil, Chalk, and Other Mediums by the Late Lord Leighton of Stretton, P.R.A. (London, 1898).
2. Ormond and Ormond, *Lord Leighton*, 62ff.
3. The picture's full title is *Cimabue's Celebrated Madonna Is Carried in Procession through the Streets of Florence*; see ibid., 26–31.
4. On the *Medici Venus* and its influence, see Francis Haskell and Nicholas Penny, *Taste and the Antique; the Lure of Classical Sculpture 1500–1900* (New Haven-London, 1981), 325–328.
5. John Ruskin, *Works*, E. T. Cook and E. Wedderburn, eds. (London, 1903), I:433.
6. Ormond and Ormond, *Lord Leighton*, no. 370, plate 171.

UNKNOWN ARTIST

British, Nineteenth Century

No Escape! My God!, 1889   (00.377)

Graphite, 10 x 6 5/8 in. (25.4 x 16.8 cm) (sight). Inscribed l.c.: "No Escape! My God!"; and l.r.: "July 1889."

Provenance: Lane Collection; collection of V. Winthrop Newman; sold American Art Galleries, New York, May 8, 1923, lot 25; Mr. and Mrs. Philip Pinsof; their gift to the University.

References:
Carter, *Grain of Sand*, 11, no. 31, 12 (ill.), as William Blake.

Possibly a self-portrait, this is an image of true despair. Not only do the eyes, brow, and mouth express exaggerated terror and dismay, but also the inscription, below the head, "No Escape! My God!" leaves no doubt as to the depth of the emotion. The drawing's purpose, however, is apparently not that of an ordinary portrait, but probably illustrative, although a specific literary source has not yet been identified.

The date, most likely to be read as "July 1889," rules out an attribution to William Blake, under whose name the drawing passed while in the Newman and Lane collections, and as it was known when it entered Marquette's collection.[1] Nonetheless, the bold, firm yet impetuous strokes are stylistically somewhat akin to those of Blake.

A. G.

Notes:
1. The date may also be read as July, 1809, 1804, 1864, 1869, and 1884.

ticular to the *Medici Venus*. Since its discovery in the early seventeenth century, the sculpture had been admired, studied, and copied by artists throughout Europe; casts were and are legion. Adulation of the figure was no longer universal at the time Leighton made this drawing; nevertheless, in 1840 Ruskin could still find the original "one of the purest and most elevated incarnations of woman conceivable."[5]

Leighton never directly used the head of the *Medici Venus* in any of his paintings; however, its inspiration can be perceived in many of his classical heroines. Particularly striking in this regard is the woman seen in profile in the artist's late *At the Fountain*, now in the Milwaukee Art Museum.[6]

A. G.

Notes:
1. The authority for Leighton's life and work is Leonée Ormond and Richard Ormond, *Lord Leighton* (New Haven, 1975), which includes a catalogue of oil paintings, frescoes, and life-size statues. See further Richard Ormond, *Leighton's Frescoes in the Victoria and Albert Museum* (London, 1975); Richard Dorment et al., *Victorian High Renaissance*, catalogue of an exhibition at the Manchester Gallery and Minneapolis Institute of Arts (Manchester and Minneapolis, 1978), 95–127; Edgcumbe Staley, *Lord Leighton of Stretton, P.R.A.* (London, 1906); S. Pepys Cockerell,

No Escape! My God!, British, Nineteenth Century, graphite

working for a printer and publisher as a general secretary; when he was eighteen he set up his own framing and stationery shop with a partner. In his spare time, he drew. The shop brought as customers several Parisian artists who summered in Le Havre: Isabey, Troyon, Couture, and Millet. Perhaps acting upon their examples, Boudin determined to follow painting as a career; he soon left the shop and concentrated on painting and sketching the activities of the port and the nearby peasants. In 1850 his efforts were rewarded with a stipend from the municipal council of Le Havre to study in Paris for three years, and, after struggling in the next decade, he thereafter achieved moderate success as a painter of marine and beach scenes. Durand-Ruel, the gallery owner famous for his patronage of the Impressionists, gave Boudin one-man shows in Paris in 1883, 1889 and 1891, in Boston in 1891, and in New York in 1898.[1]

A painter of plein air landscape, Boudin influenced Claude Monet, whose friend he became in Le Havre in 1858. In 1859 Boudin met Courbet and Baudelaire, who later would review exhibitions of his work. Realizing that Paris was the artistic center of France, Boudin moved to that city for the winters and back to the coast for the summers. A simple and modest man, Boudin was content to observe and record the nuances of sea and sky. Figures populate his beach paintings, but rarely are they individualized except through clothing. His work has great affinity with that of the Dutch seascape painter Jongkind, whom he met in Paris, and also with the Dutch landscapists of the seventeenth century. Yet his uniqueness lies in his ability to translate his observations with fresh immediacy into paint and in his rendering of a cool, marine light. Boudin was called "le Roi des Ciels" by Corot, an extremely apt title.[2]

EUGÈNE BOUDIN

French (1824–1898)

Since Boudin's father and many relatives were sailors and he himself was raised in the ports of Honfleur and Le Havre, it is not surprising that beach, harbor, and ships dominate the artist's imagery. Yet his only first-hand experience of the sea was somewhat disastrous: at the age of ten he acted as cabin boy on his father's boat and fell overboard. Two years later Boudin began

Women in Gowns (82.10.1)

Watercolor, 4 x 7 3/8 in. (10.2 x 18.7 cm). Signed l.r.: "EB."

Provenance: Anonymous gift to the University, 1982.

Boudin would have made a drawing such as this one out-of-doors, perhaps along a street or promenade near the beach. He was apparently fascinated with the stiff, gaily colored crinoline gowns worn by the fashionably dressed ladies of his day, and he made many such sketches. Often the sketches were incorporated, with changes, into his oil paintings. The present sheet may be compared with the watercolor *Crinolines on Trouville Beach* of 1865 and with *The Crinolines* of about the same date.[3] Finished oils that contain similarly dressed and posed women include *Trouville Beach* of 1863 and *Deauville Beach* of 1864.[4] Such comparable works may indicate a date of the mid-1860s for the Marquette drawing.

Women in Gowns, Eugène Boudin, watercolor

City Street Scene, Eugène Boudin, watercolor

City Street Scene   (82.10.2)

Watercolor, 4 x 7 3/8 in. (10.2 x 18.7 cm). Signed l.r.: "EB."

Provenance: Anonymous gift to the University, 1982.

The scene appears to be a street along which awnings are erected over market stalls, and along which many passersby stop to examine displayed wares or goods. Behind the stalls is a large, possibly permanent, structure. While Boudin has not provided many clues to the actual location, he did paint several oils of the Fish Market in Trouville in 1868 and 1871, and, by analogy with the permanent structure in the present drawing, we may tentatively suggest that it represents the exterior of the Trouville Fish Market.[4]

A. G.

Notes:
1. Essential bibliography concerning the life and work of Boudin includes G. Jean-Aubry, *La Vie et l'oeuvre d'après les lettres et les documents inédits d'Eugène Boudin* (Paris, 1968); idem, *Eugène Boudin* (London, 1969); Gilbert de Knyff, *Eugène Boudin raconté par lui-même: sa vie, son atelier, son oeuvre* (Paris, 1976); Robert Schmit, *Eugène Boudin 1824–1898*, 3 vols. (Paris, 1973). All these publications contain extensive bibliography.
2. Claude Roger-Marx, *Eugène Boudin 1824–1898* (Paris, 1927), 5.
3. Jean-Aubry, *Eugène Boudin*, 197, and 55.
4. Ibid., 31 and 43.
5. Two such paintings are dated 1868 and 1871; see ibid., 199.

HONORÉ DAUMIER

French (1808-1879)

Daumier was born in Marseilles in 1808. In 1815 his father, a glassmaker and an amateur poet, decided to move the family to Paris. As a boy Daumier worked from 1820-1821 as a messenger in the law courts and as a clerk in a bookstore. These occupations made a lasting impression on him, as his paintings of lawyers and bookshops done in later years attest. By 1822 he had decided on a career as an artist, and he received his first formal instruction from the painter Alexandre Lenoir. In that same year he enrolled at the Académie Suisse, where he drew from models. Of even greater significance, however, for Daumier's development as an artist and social critic was his interest in the relatively new medium of lithography. He did his first lithographs in 1820 and later went to work in the shop of Belliard, a publisher of contemporary portraits.

Daumier's artistic interests at this time were turning inexorably toward caricature and social and political criticism. In the early 1830s he began to publish his works in new satirical publications that featured lithographic illustrations. He attacked Charles X, the Church, and the authorities in *La Silhouette, La Caricature,* and *Le Charivari.* Daumier was particularly venomous in his attacks on Louis Philippe and the members of the Legislative Assembly (who were also grotesquely caricatured in sculpture). Daumier's prints, which essentially established the form and mission of the modern political cartoon, were much too radical for the time, with the result that he was imprisoned for six months, and *La Caricature* was suppressed by the state. After his release Daumier became more moderate, choosing to satirize contemporary customs and manners, rather than specific individuals, in *Le Charivari.*

Daumier's political consciousness was not given full artistic expression again until 1848, when he was chosen one of the finalists in the competition to create a new symbol of the Republic. The Republic was shortlived, however, and Daumier never completed this work. During the period of Napoleon III, Daumier's antimonarchist views resulted in his being unable to sell his works to the state. In the early years of Napoleon III's region Daumier had briefly resumed direct political commentary, but he soon abandoned that in favor of an indirect approach in the form of lithographs and sculptures on the theme of *Ratapoil* (a secret agent of the Emperor).

In the 1850s and 1860s Daumier, under the influence of the Realists, executed paintings depicting the dreary life of the Parisian working class. Such works as his *Washerwoman* (1862) and *Third Class Carriage* (1856) are among the landmark Realist works that he produced in the later years of his career. Those late years (the 1870s) were very difficult ones for Daumier. He remained a staunch opponent of Napoleon III, so much

so in fact that he refused to accept an appointment to the Légion d'Honneur. His imagery during the period of the Franco-Prussian war was particulary bitter in its indictment of the regime and of the war. Until his death Daumier staunchly maintained his republican, antiestablishment convictions. He died in debt and nearly blind in Paris in 1879 and was buried in a pauper's grave.

Les Représentans Représentés Series
Altaroche   (00.301.23)

Lithograph on newsprint, 14 3/8 x 9 5/16 in. (36.5 x 23.7 cm). Inscribed in the stone l.l.: "h.D."; l.r.: "20"; u.c.: "LES REPRÉSENTANS REPRÉSENTÉS"; l.c.: "ALTAROCHE" with text below.

Provenance: Collection of Mr. and Mrs. Philip Pinsof; their gift to the University, 1960.

Bastide   (00.301.7)

Lithograph on newsprint, 14 3/8 x 9 1/16 in. (36.5 x 23 cm). Inscribed in the stone l.l.: "h.D."; l.r.: "1363"; u.r.: "12"; u.c.: "LES REPRÉSENTANS REPRÉSENTÉS"; l.c.: "BASTIDE" with text below.

Provenance: Collection of Mr. and Mrs. Philip Pinsof; their gift to the University, 1959.

Berger   (00.301.4)

Lithograph on newsprint, 14 5/16 x 9 5/8 in. (36.4 x 24.4 cm). Inscribed in the stone l.l.: "h.D."; l.r.: "19"; u.r.: "30"; u.c.: "LES REPRÉSENTANS REPRÉSENTÉS"; l.c.: "BERGER" with text below.

Provenance: Collection of Mr. and Mrs. Philip Pinsof; their gift to the University, 1959.

Boulay (de la Meurthe)   (00.301.16)

Lithograph on newsprint, 14 3/8 x 9 1/2 in. (36.5 x 24.1 cm). Inscribed in the stone l.l.: "h.D."; l.r.: "17"; u.r.: "24"; u.c.: "LES REPRÉSENTANS REPRÉSENTÉS"; l.c.: "BOULAY (DE LA MEURTHE)" with text below.

Provenance: Collection of Mr. and Mrs. Philip Pinsof; their gift to the University, 1960.

Berger, Honoré Daumier, lithograph on newsprint

Buffet (00.301.3)

Lithograph on newsprint, 14 3/8 x 9 11/16 in. (36.5 x 24.6 cm). Inscribed in the stone l.l.: "h.D."; l.r.: "35"; u.r.: "40"; u.c.: "LES REPRÉSENTANS REPRÉSENTÉS"; l.c.: "BUFFET" with text below.

Provenance: Collection of Mr. and Mrs. Philip Pinsof; their gift to the University, 1959.

Buvignier (00.301.22)

Lithograph on newsprint, 14 1/4 x 10 1/4 in. (36.2 x 26 cm). Inscribed in the stone l.l.: "h.D."; l.r.: "39"; u.r.: "44"; u.c.: "LES REPRÉSENTANS REPRÉSENTÉS"; l.c.: "BUVIGNIER" with text below.

Provenance: Collection of Mr. and Mrs. Philip Pinsof; their gift to the University, 1960.

Changarnier (00.301.10)

Lithograph on newsprint, 14 3/8 x 9 11/16 in. (36.5 x 24.6 cm). Inscribed in the stone l.l.: "h.D."; l.r.: "27"; u.r.: "33"; u.c.: "LES REPRÉSENTANS REPRÉSENTÉS"; l.c.: "CHANGARNIER" with text below.

Provenance: Collection of Mr. and Mrs. Philip Pinsof; their gift to the University, 1960.

Denjoy (00.301.1)

Lithograph on newsprint, 14 3/8 x 9 1/2 in. (36.5 x 24.1 cm). Inscribed in the stone l.l.: "h.D."; l.r.: "32"; u.r.: "41"; u.c.: "LES REPRÉSENTANS REPRÉSENTÉS"; l.c.: "DENJOY" with text below.

Provenance: Collection of Mr. and Mrs. Philip Pinsof; their gift to the University, 1959.

Denjoy, Honoré Daumier, lithograph on newsprint

Boulay (de la Meurthe), Honoré Daumier, lithograph on newsprint

Drouin de L'Huys   (00.301.6)

Lithograph on newsprint, 14 3/8 x 9 3/4 in. (36.5 x 24.8 cm). Inscribed in the stone l.l.: "h.D."; l.r.: "36"; u.r.: "46"; u.c.: "LES REPRÉSENTANS REPRÉSENTÉS"; l.c.: "DROUIN DE L'HUYS" with text below.

Provenance: Collection of Mr. and Mrs. Philip Pinsof; their gift to the University, 1960.

Ducoux   (00.301.14)

Lithograph on newsprint, 14 1/4 x 10 5/16 in. (36.2 x 26.2 cm). Inscribed in the stone l.l.: "h.D."; l.r.: "29"; u.r.: "39"; u.c.: "LES REPRÉSENTANS REPRÉSENTÉS"; l.c.: "DUCOUX" with text below.

Provenance: Collection of Mr. and Mrs. Philip Pinsof; their gift to the University, 1960.

Felix Pyat   (00.301.19)

Lithograph on newsprint, 14 1/4 x 9 5/8 in. (36.2 x 24.4 cm). Inscribed in the stone l.l.: "h.D."; l.r.: "1351"; u.r.: "9"; u.c.: "LES REPRÉSENTANS REPRÉSENTÉS"; l.c.: "FELIX PYAT" with text below.

Provenance: Collection of Mr. and Mrs. Philip Pinsof; their gift to the University, 1960.

Ferdinand Flocon   (00.301.8)

Lithograph on newsprint, 14 3/8 x 9 1/4 in. (36.6 x 23.6 cm). Inscribed in the stone l.l.: "h.D."; l.r.: "18"; u.r.: "25"; u.c.: "LES REPRÉSENTANS REPRÉSENTÉS"; l.c.: "FERDINAND FLOCON" with text below.

Provenance: Collection of Mr. and Mrs. Philip Pinsof; their gift to the University, 1959.

Laboulie   (00.301.12)

Lithograph on newsprint, 14 1/4 x 9 1/4 in. (36.2 x 23.5 cm). Inscribed in the stone l.l.: "h.D."; l.r.: "53"; u.c.: "LES REPRÉSENTANS REPRÉSENTÉS"/ASSEMBLÉE LÉGISLATIVE. 15"; l.c.: "LABOULIE" with text below.

Provenance: Anonymous gift to the University.

Lanjuinais   (00.301.11)

Lithograph on newsprint, 14 1/4 x 10 1/4 in. (36.2 x 26 cm). Inscribed in the stone l.l.: "h.D."; l.r.: "41"; u.r.: "48"; u.c.: "LES REPRÉSENTANS REPRÉSENTÉS"; l.c.: "LANJUINAIS" with text below.

Provenance: Collection of Mr. and Mrs. Philip Pinsof; their gift to the University, 1960.

Larabit   (00.301.18)

Lithograph on newsprint, 14 1/4 x 9 1/4 in. (36.2 x 23.5 cm). Inscribed in the stone l.l.: "h.D."; l.r. "59"; u.c.: "LES REPRÉSENTANS REPRÉSENTÉS"/ASSEMBLÉE LÉGISLATIVE 14"; l.c.: "LARABIT" with text below.

Provenance: Collection of Mr. and Mrs. Philip Pinsof; their gift to the University, 1960.

Larabit, Honoré Daumier, lithograph on newsprint

Odilon Barrot, Honoré Daumier, lithograph on newsprint

Lebreton   (00.301.21)

Lithograph on newsprint, 14 1/4 x 10 1/16 in. (36.2 x 25.6 cm). Inscribed in the stone l.l.: "h.D."; l.r.: "45"; u.c.: "LES REPRÉSENTANS REPRÉSENTÉS"/ASSEMBLÉE LÉGISLATIVE. 3."; l.c.: "LEBRETON" with text below.

Provenance: Collection of Mr. and Mrs. Philip Pinsof; their gift to the University, 1960.

Leon Faucher   (00.301.9)

Lithograph on newsprint, 14 3/8 x 9 1/2 in. (36.5 x 24.1 cm). Inscribed in the stone l.l.: "h.D."; l.r.: "42"; u.r.: "45"; u.c.: "LES REPRÉSENTANS REPRÉSENTÉS"; l.c.: "LEON FAUCHER" with text below.

Provenance: Collection of Mr. and Mrs. Philip Pinsof; their gift to the University, 1960.

Odilon Barrot   (00.301.2)

Lithograph on newsprint, 14 1/8 x 9 7/8 in. (35.9 x 25.1 cm). Inscribed in the stone l.l.: "h.D."; l.r.: "1368"; u.r.: "15"; u.c.: "LES REPRÉSENTANS REPRÉSENTÉS"; l.c.: "ODILON BARROT" with text below.

Provenance: Collection of Mr. and Mrs. Philip Pinsof; their gift to the University, 1960.

Pagnerre   (00.301.15)

Lithograph on newsprint, 14 3/8 x 9 1/2 in. (36.5 x 24.1 cm). Inscribed in the stone l.r.: "1306"; u.r.: "13"; u.c.: "LES REPRÉSENTANS REPRÉSENTÉS"; l.c.: "PAGNERRE" with text below.

Provenance: Collection of Mr. and Mrs. Philip Pinsof; their gift to the University, 1960.

Rateau   (00.301.20)

Lithograph on newsprint, 14 3/8 x 9 3/4 in. (36.5 x 24.8 cm). Inscribed in the stone l.l.: "h.D."; u.r.: "27"; u.c.: "LES REPRÉSENTANS REPRÉSENTÉS"; l.c.: "RATEAU" with text below.

Provenance: Collection of Mr. and Mrs. Philip Pinsof; their gift to the University, 1960.

Vaulabelle   (00.301.5)

Lithograph on newsprint, 14 1/4 x 10 1/8 in. (36.2 x 25.7 cm). Inscribed in the stone u.r.: "38"; u.c.: "LES REPRÉSENTANS REPRÉSENTÉS"; l.c.: "VAULA-BELLE" with text below.

Provenance: Collection of Mr. and Mrs. Philip Pinsof; their gift to the University, 1960.

Volouski, Honoré Daumier, lithograph on newsprint

Volouski   (00.301.17)

Lithograph on newsprint, 14 1/4 x 9 11/16 in. (36.2 x 48.4 cm). Inscribed in the stone l.l.: "h.D."; l.r.: "8"; u.r.: "29"; u.c.: "LES REPRÉSENTANS REPRÉSENTÉS"; l.c.: "VOLOUSKI" with text below.

Provenance: Collection of Mr. and Mrs. Philip Pinsof; their gift to the University, 1960.

Les Représentans (sic) Représentés (The Representatives Represented), a series of eighty-nine lithographic caricatures of the parliamentarians of the Second Empire, appeared in *Le Charivari* from November 1848 through August 1850. It marks a return to the kind of political criticism, directed at specific individuals, that Daumier had engaged in during the reign of Louis Philippe and prior to his arrest for sedition. The prototypes for these images were Daumier's own lithographic and sculptural depictions of members of the Legislative Assembly, other public officials, and the King, done from 1832 to 1835. In these earlier works Daumier treated his subjects as grotesque, almost dehumanized creatures who embodied qualities such as greed, stupidity, avarice, malevolence, and the like. In *Les Représentans Représentés* Daumier treats the objects of his scorn and derision with less obvious cruelty than he had fifteen years earlier. (This was no doubt due to his having been imprisoned.) The exaggerations of the peculiar physical characteristics of the representatives are far less grotesque than in earlier works, and Daumier now relies on a new device—the big head on the little body—as his standard anatomical distortion. (This is particularly effective in works such as *Volouski*, (number 8 of the series), where Daumier wants to express the individual's self-importance). Daumier compensates for the abandonment of gross physical distortion by creating a highly individualized and insightful portrait caricature through the careful study of pose, costume, gesture, and facial characterization. His *Léon Faucher* (number 42 of the series), for example, exudes arrogance and duplicity. It was works of this kind, much more than the earlier ones, that set both the tone and look of much of the political cartooning from the mid-nineteenth century on. Daumier above all others comprehended the potential of art as a political weapon and used his art to warn the public of the dangers of dictatorship and demagoguery.

J. B.

TWENTIETH CENTURY

JOHN TAYLOR ARMS

American (1887-1953)

Arms studied law at Princeton University for several years before transferring in 1907 to study architecture at the Massachusetts Institute of Technology. He worked as an office draftsman with Carrere and Hastings in New York, where he contributed to the firm's designs for the mansion of Henry Clay Frick; he then practiced architecture with Cameron Clark. He dissolved this partnership in 1916 in order to enter the Navy, where he served as a navigation officer on convoy duty during World War I. In 1913 he married Dorothy Frothingham Noyes, a writer, with whom he would later collaborate on publications of European architecture. It was she who determined the direction of Arms's talents in etching—she gave him a small etching kit as a Christmas gift shortly after their marriage.[1]

He soon began to copy prints by Jongkind and others, as well as make prints of his own design—chiefly scenes in New York and France, where part of his war years were spent. After Arms's discharge from the Navy, he decided to pursue etching as a career and settled in Fairfield, Connecticut. Maintaining a studio there, he frequently traveled to Europe and New York.

Two themes dominate Arms's etchings: architecture and ships. His passion for Gothic churches inspired several publications, written by Dorothy Noyes Arms and illustrated with heliogravure reproductions of Arms's etchings.[2] He made two series of sailing ships, one of seven plates, 1921-1925, and another, 1943-1947, of four plates of ships "U.S. Navy ships built during World War II."

In numerous lectures and in a book about printmaking, Arms demonstrated the technique of etching and its historical importance.[3] He was influenced by those nineteenth-century etchers who contributed to the revival of the medium, above all Charles Meryon, James Abbot McNeil Whistler, and Joseph Pennell.

Ugly Devil, 1924   (00.261)

Etching, 9 1/8 x 8 1/8 in. (23.2 x 20.6 cm). Inscribed in pencil l.l.: "To Mr. Harry Simmons/with my compliments/John Taylor Arms"; and l.r.: "John Taylor Arms 1924"

Provenance: Collection of Mr. and Mrs. Philip Pinsof; their gift to the University, 1959.

Ugly Devil, John Taylor Arms, etching

During Arms's visits to France, both during World War I and afterward, he made numerous sketches of French cathedrals. This print belongs to a series recording the gargoyles that form part of the roof decoration of Nôtre Dame of Paris.[4] It was published in Dorothy Noyes Arms's *Churches of France.*[5] Inspired by Charles Meryon's prints of Nôtre Dame, which often featured the gargoyles, Arms decribed the gargoyles as "those queer, grim grotesques, often humorous, sometimes tragic and always entirely fascinating, which constitute such telling decorative accents on all the great Gothic buildings in France."[6]

Chartres in Miniature, 1939   (83.3.1)

Etching, 6 3/4 x 8 3/4 in. (17.2 x 22.2 cm). Inscribed in pencil l.r.: "John Taylor Arms 1939."

Provenance: Collection of Florence Rossbach; gift of her estate to the University, 1983.

In the Gothic cathedrals Arms found a subject not only suitable to his meticulous training as a draftsman, but also symbolic of man's highest spiritual values. He saw in such monuments as Chartres "all that was most beautiful in man-made building—grandeur of scale, beauty of proportion and abundant wealth of detail."[7] Even in the small scale of this 1939 etching of Chartres, Arms's reverence for the Gothic is apparent.[8]

Chartres in Miniature, John Taylor Arms, etching

Chartres the Magnificent, John Taylor Arms, etching

Chartres
the Magnificent, 1948 (83.3.2.)

Etching, 4 x 4 3/4 in. (10.2 x 12.1 cm) (comp.). Inscribed in pencil l.r.: "John Taylor Arms 1948."

Provenance: Collection of Florence Rossbach; gift of her estate to the University, 1983.

This etching and the preceding one are among seven prints by Arms of the Cathedral of Chartres or its architectural details. This etching was published in a book by Dorothy Noyes Arms, *French Churches.*[9] Arms summarized his thoughts and feelings for Gothic art thus:

> To me the Gothic represents the most spiritual and significant expression of his aspirations that man has yet created in terms of stone and glass and metal, and so for years I have followed its trail, through France and England, Italy and Spain, and, in the presence of these mighty monuments, sought to perpetuate for times to come the ideals and the spirit they embody.[10]

Chartres may well have signified for Arms the most complete expression of the Gothic.

A.G.

Notes:

1. Essential bibliography about Arms includes Ben L. Bassham, *John Taylor Arms, American Etcher,* catalogue of an exhibition at the Elvehjem Art Center (Madison, Wisconsin, 1975), and W.D. Fletcher, *John Taylor Arms: A Man for All Times* (New Haven, 1982).

2. For example, Dorothy Noyes Arms, *Churches of France* (New York, 1929) and *Hill Towns and Cities of Northern Italy* (New York, 1932).
3. See, above all, Arms's book, *Handbook of Printmaking and Printmakers* (New York, 1934).
4. Fletcher, *John Taylor Arms,* cat. no. 148.
5. Dorothy Noyes Arms, *Churches of France,* plate 6.
6. Quoted in Gabriel P. Weisberg and Ronnie L. Zakon, *Between Past and Present: French, English, and American Etching 1850-1950,* catalogue of an exhibition at the Cleveland Museum of Art (Cleveland, n.d.), 61.
7. Arms's words are here quoted from ibid., 61.
8. *Chartres in Miniature* is catalogued by Fletcher, *John Taylor Arms,* cat. no. 330, and by Bassham, *John Taylor Arms,* cat. no. 335.
9. Published in 1948; the etching is no. 49, and it is catalogued by Fletcher, *John Taylor Arms,* cat. no. 411, and by Bassham, *John Taylor Arms,* cat. no. 422.
10. Quoted from Arms's essay in *John Taylor Arms,* catalogue of an exhibition at the Grand Central Art Galleries (New York, 1937), 10.

FRANK WESTON BENSON

American (1862-1951)

Benson studied at the School of the Boston Museum of Fine Arts and in Paris, and lived for several years in Portland, Maine, before settling down as a teacher at the Boston Museum School.[1] His early success was based upon his paintings, which were exhibited with the group of artists known as The Ten, between 1898 and 1918.[2] He painted primarily portraits, landscapes, and genre scenes, all with careful study of the effects of sunlight and harmonic color. In 1906 he was elected to the National Academy of Design. Although he made his first etching in 1882, it was not until 1912 that he began to etch seriously. By 1930 he had made 310 prints.[3] An avid outdoorsman, he drew much of the subject matter for his etchings from his activities as a hunter and birdwatcher.

skill as a draftsman and etcher all come into play. In the diminutive *Two Crows*, the birds appear to have been resting on the branch, yet one readies for flight while the other turns its head to take notice of what has prompted the first to move.[4]

Two Crows, Frank Weston Benson, etching with drypoint and roulette

Old Tom, Frank Weston Benson, etching

Two Crows, 1920   (83.3.4)

Etching with drypoint and roulette, 2 1/2 x 3 1/4 in. (6.4 x 8.3. cm) (comp.). Inscribed l.l. in pencil: "Frank W. Benson"; and in the plate: "FWB '20."

Provenance: Collection of Florence Rossbach; gift of her estate to the University, 1983.

Two Crows is among Benson's many etchings of birds of all kinds—geese, ducks, wild swans, egrets, eagles, pelicans, and yellowlegs. Since his youth he had been an amateur ornithologist, and later, hunting and fishing were to become his favored sports. The fruits of his activities outdoors are best observed in his prints of birds, for his powers of patient observation and his

Old Tom, 1926   (83.3.3)

Etching, 15 1/2 x 10 1/4 in. (39.4 x 26 cm) (comp.). Inscribed in pencil l.l.: "Frank W. Benson."

Provenance: Collection of Florence Rossbach; gift of her estate to the University, 1983.

This image of the rugged hunter, bearing rifle in one hand and game in the other, would very much have been part of Benson's daily experience. He often hunted duck himself—though more often he portrayed birds in flight than as hunter's trophy. In *Old Tom*, the hunter's weatherbeaten, rugged strength proclaims his victory over both fowl and terrain.[5]

A.G.

Notes:

1. For accounts of Benson's life and activity, with emphasis upon his printmaking, see Malcolm C. Salaman, *Modern Masters of Etching: Frank W. Benson* (London, 1925), and Samuel Chamberlain, "Frank W. Benson: The Etcher," *Print Collector's Quarterly* 25 (1938):167ff.
2. See Donelson F. Hoopes and Melinda M. Mayer, *The Ten*, catalogue of an exhibition at the Art Museum of South Texas (Corpus Christi, 1977), and Marvin D. Schwartz, *The New Vision: American Styles of 1876-1910*, catalogue of an exhibition at the Museum of Fine Arts (St. Petersburg, Florida, 1976).
3. For Benson's etched oeuvre, see Adam E. M. Paff, *Etchings and Drypoints by Frank W. Benson: An Illustrated and Descriptive Catalogue*, 4 vols. (Boston and New York, 1917-1920), and Charles Lemon Morgan, introduction to *Frank W. Benson, N.A., The Crafton Collection, Inc.* (New York, 1931).
4. Morgan, *Benson: The Crafton Collection*, cat. no. 175.
5. Ibid., cat. no. 246.

AUDREY FLACK

American (1931-   )

Educated at Cooper Union, Yale University, and New York University's Institute of Fine Arts, Audrey Flack is now recognized as one of the foremost American New Realist or Photo-Realist painters.[1] She uses the camera as a means of transferring imagery to the canvas and also as a way of organizing her compositions. Since 1971 she has used the air brush to apply acrylic pigment to canvas, thus achieving a smoothly finished surface. She draws her inspiration from art of past masters as well as contemporary history. A series of *vanitas* still-life paintings pays homage to the work of the Dutch seventeenth-century artist Maria van Oosterwyck.[2] Her most recent paintings, also still life in theme, are of more personal iconography, yet retain references to Dutch masters. Other, earlier paintings concern modern historical personages: Adolf Hitler, John F. Kennedy, and Marilyn Monroe. European travel prompted Flack to paint such subjects as the cathedrals of Siena and Amiens and such recognized masterpieces as Michelangelo's *David*. In contrast to other artists who have been called New Realist or Photo-Realist, who seek the "familiarity of the everyday" and who also make use of a painting style that transforms the seen world through the camera and air brush, Flack seeks out "the familiarity of the enduring" monuments of past centuries.[3]

Esperanza, or Macarena of Miracles, 1973   (80.29)

Lithograph, 34 x 24 in. (86.4 x 61 cm). Inscribed in colored pencil l.r.: "Audrey Flack 54/150."

Provenance: Collection of Mr. Michael H. Lord; his gift to the University, 1980.

Esperanza or Macarena of Miracles, Audrey Flack, lithograph

In composition, this lithograph is closely related to Flack's paintings of the *Macarena Esperanza*, a statue in a church in Seville by the Spanish Baroque sculptress Luisa Roldán.[4] In 1970 Flack went to Spain, and her encounter with the bejeweled, weeping Madonna inspired her to make several works based on the Roldán sculpture.[5] In both the paintings and the print, Flack conveys the sense of the hard, brilliantly hued polychrome surface of Roldán's *Macarena Esperanza*.

Between 1973 and 1978 Flack made four prints: the *Esperanza* lithograph, and three serigraphs that depict still-life compositions.[6] In both medium and theme, the Madonna, the earliest of the prints, is the most traditional.

A.G.

Notes:

1. Major publications include Audrey Flack, *On Painting*, introduction by Lawrence Alloway and contributions by Ann Sutherland Harris and Jeanne Hamilton (New York, 1981), which contains extensive bibliography; and Louis K. Meisel, *Photo-Realism* (New York, 1980), 241-272.

2. Flack, *On Painting*, 26 and 76f.
3. Alloway, in ibid., 24.
4. Roldán, while famous in Spain, is little known in the United States; see Beatrice Gilman Proske, "Luisa Roldán at Madrid, Part 1," *Connoisseur* 155 (1964):128ff. and "Part 2," 199ff.; and Flack, *On Painting*, 34.
5. For related paintings, see *Macarena of Miracles*, 1971, Metropolitan Museum of Art, New York, ill. in Flack, *On Painting*, 38, fig. 36, and in Meisel, *Photo-Realism*, fig. 559; *Lady Madonna*, 1972, Whitney Museum of American Art, New York, ill. in Flack, *On Painting*, 40, fig. 38, and Meisel, *Photo-Realism*, fig. 558; *Dolores of Cordoba*, 1971, Private Collection, ill. in Meisel, *Photo-Realism*, fig. 560; and *Macarena Esperanza*, 1971, Hoffman Collection, Illinois, ill. in Meisel, *Photo-Realism*, fig. 561.
6. See Susan Pear Meisel, *Complete Guide to Photo-Realist Print-making* (New York, 1978), unpaginated, where each of Flack's prints is illustrated and catalogued among all prints by Photo-Realists produced between 1968 and 1978.

PAUL STARRETT SAMPLE

American (1896-1974)

Born in Kentucky and raised in various states of the West and Midwest, Paul Sample graduated from Dartmouth College in 1921. Shortly afterward he was treated for tuberculosis at Saranac Lake, New York. There, encouraged by his physician and by the painter Jonas Lie, he began to draw and paint. After his cure in 1925, he studied at the Greenleaf Art School, New York, and the Otis Art Institute, Los Angeles. In 1926 he joined the faculty of the University of Southern California, where he taught until 1936, when he took a year off to travel throughout Europe. In 1938 he received the prestigious appointment of Artist-in-Residence at Dartmouth College, a post he held until his

retirement in 1962. During World War II, Sample was an artist correspondent for *Life* magazine and covered the South Pacific in 1943 and 1944. He painted in oils, watercolor, and egg tempera and exhibited extensively in the United States.[1]

Two distinct phases characterize Sample's oeuvre. His works produced before 1940 may be considered largely Regionalist and as belonging to those by the loose group of artists who "devoted their efforts to depicting the rural American landscape and celebrating the lives of ordinary citizens."[2] Often such works manifest sympathy for the poor and the unemployed and express a critical view of current social conditions. After about 1940 Sample turned primarily to the landscape of New England for his subject matter and apparently abandoned the social commentary of his earlier work.

Whistle Stop, c. 1940   (83.3.20)

Watercolor, 14 x 21 in. (35.6 x 53.3 cm). Inscribed in pencil l.l.: "Paul Sample."

Provenance: Collection of Florence Rossbach; gift of her estate to the University, 1983.

References:
Paul Sample, in a letter (1954), discusses this work.

John Haletsky, in a letter (1984), dates it ca. 1940.

Sample identified the locale of *Whistle Stop* as the outskirts of the town of Wells River, Vermont, and the railroad as the old Wells River line.[3] The watercolor was most probably painted around 1940.[4] The town of Wells River is some forty miles north along the Connecticut River from Norwich, the town just across the

Whistle Stop, Paul Starrett Sample, watercolor

river from Hanover, New Hampshire, where the Samples settled when he became Artist-in-Residence at Dartmouth.

In 1928, while teaching at the University of Southern California, Sample married Sylvia Ann Howland of Montpelier, Vermont. Every summer the Samples drove east to visit the Howland family. That annual pilgrimage, Sample's own undergraduate education at Dartmouth, and his appointment as Artist-in-Residence in 1938 at his alma mater contributed to his affection for the terrain of central Vermont and New Hampshire.

Deceptively simple in its components, *Whistle Stop* reveals its painter's mastery of composition. The blue-brown hill towers behind the placid river as the train appears to pass the tiny station. The train, river, and station buildings would seem to establish a dominant horizontal force, yet the hill provides a balance, creating interest in both depth and height. Sample's own words may be aptly suited to the combination of man-made and natural elements in *Whistle Stop:*

> The whole of a painting contributes to an expression of this: its entire organizational structure of color, mass, and pattern, as well as its allegiance to its source—which is nature...An artist's mission is his search for reality, and in his painting he aspires to a communication charged with the essence of it.[5]

A.G.

Notes:
1. I wish to thank Guy Colston of the Hood Museum of Art, Dartmouth College, and John Haletsky of the Lowe Art Museum, University of Miami, for their kind help in researching the life and work of Sample. For Sample's place in American art, see John T. Haletsky, *Paul Sample, Ivy League Regionalist*, catalogue of an exhibition at the Lowe Art Museum, University of Miami (Coral Gables, 1984). See further Sidney Chandler Hayward, "Paul Sample Vermont Artist," *Vermont Life* 14, no. 2 (Winter 1959-1960):46f.
2. Haletsky, *Paul Sample, Ivy League Regionalist*, 8.
3. Correspondence, Paul Sample to Mr. Rossbach, April 16, 1954 (files).
4. Correspondence, John Haletsky, 1984.
5. Hayward, "Paul Sample Vermont Artist," 50.

FRANK LLOYD WRIGHT

American (1869-1959)

Wright followed an undergraduate course in civil engineering at the University of Wisconsin at Madison, and, before graduating, left school to work in the Chicago architectural firm of J.L. Silsbee, and then that of Louis H. Sullivan. In 1893 he opened his own office, and he soon began to design houses and other buildings in Illinois and Wisconsin. In 1911 he built Taliesin in Spring Green, Wisconsin, as a place of both residence and business (rebuilt 1914 and 1925); he opened

a school for architects there in 1932. Several visits to Arizona prompted him to build a second establishment near Scottsdale, called Taliesin West, in 1938.[1]

If Wright's professional success came to him fairly surely and steadily, his personal life was occasionally tempestuous and tragic. In 1889 he married Catherine Lee Tobin, and they settled in Oak Park. Six children were born of that marriage, which was dissolved in 1909 when Wright fell in love with Mamah Borthwick Cheney; their liaison lasted until 1914, when she and her two children perished in a disastrous fire, which, set by an employee, destroyed Taliesin. Wright soon fell in love again, this time with Maud Miriam Noel; they married in 1923 and stayed together until 1924. Then, a year later, he was captivated by Olga Milanoff, known affectionately as Olgivanna; they married in 1926.

Of some 400 buildings that were designed and built by Wright, among the most famous are the Midway Gardens (1913; demolished 1929), a pleasure palace in Chicago;[2] Fallingwater (1936), a small vacation home in Bear Run, Pennsylvania, built for the Kaufmann family;[3] and the Guggenheim Museum (design begun 1943, completed 1956) in New York.[4] These three further demonstrate the variety of structures designed by Wright: amusement and leisure hall, private domicile, and public museum.

Wright's ideas about architecture were expressed both in his buildings and in his writings, which comprise over a dozen books.[5] From his earliest years as an independent architect, he endeavored to incorporate the organic forms found in nature with those used in buildings. Consistently he considered the settings of his buildings as intrinsic to the aesthetic as well as functional meanings of his structures.

Plan of Pavilion for the Leesburg Floating Gardens, 1952   (78.4.1)

Colored pencil and ink on tracing paper, 36 x 48 3/4 in. (91.4 x 123.8 cm) (sight). Signed l.r.: "FLW/Q115/52."

Provenance: Collection of Mrs. George Raab; Mr. and Mrs. Kirby Raab; their gift to the University, 1978.

References:
Carter, *Grain of Sand*, 13, no. 51.

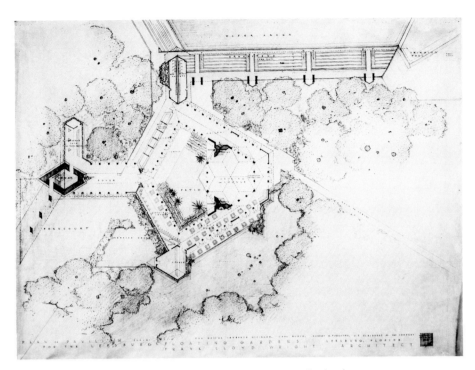

Plan of Pavilion for the Leesburg Floating Gardens, Frank Lloyd
Wright, colored pencil and ink on tracing paper

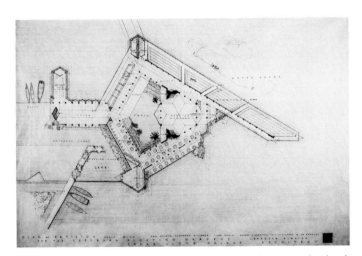

Plan of Pavilion for the Leesburg Floating Gardens, Frank Lloyd
Wright, colored pencil and ink on tracing paper

Plan of Pavilion
for the Leesburg
Floating Gardens, 1952 (78.4.4)

Colored pencil and ink on tracing paper, 35 x 48 in.
(88.9 x 121.9 cm) (sight). Unsigned.

Provenance: Collection of Mrs. George Raab; Mr. and Mrs. Kirby
Raab; their gift to the University, 1978.

References:
Carter, *Grain of Sand*, 13, no. 51.

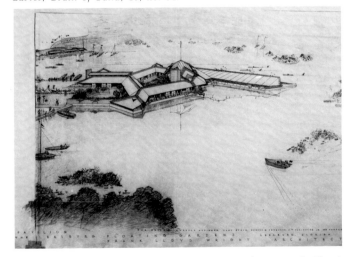

Perspective Rendering, Leesburg Floating Gardens, Frank Lloyd
Wright, colored pencil and ink on tracing paper

Perspective Rendering, Leesburg Floating Gardens, 1952   (78.4.3)

Colored pencil and ink on tracing paper, 36 x 49 1/2 in. (91.4 x 125.7 cm) (sight). Unsigned.

Provenance: Collection of Mrs. George Raab; Mr. and Mrs. Kirby Raab; their gift to the University, 1978.

References:
Carter, *Grain of Sand*, 13, no. 51.

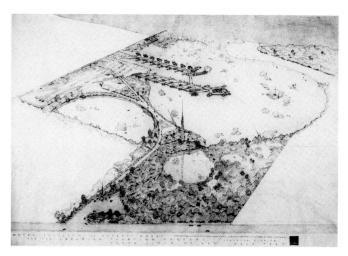

Site Perspective Rendering, Leesburg Floating Gardens, Frank Lloyd Wright, colored pencil and ink on tracing paper

Site Perspective Rendering, Leesburg Floating Gardens, 1952   (78.4.2)

Colored pencil and ink on tracing paper, 34 3/4 x 51 1/2 in. (88.3 x 130.8 cm) (sight). Signed l.r.: "FLW/ July 20/52."

Provenance: Collection of Mrs. George Raab; Mr. and Mrs. Kirby Raab; their gift to the University, 1978.

The plans, made in 1952, for the Leesburg Floating Gardens comprised a resort motel with an office, a dining pavilion for dancing and music, and an entertainment area, the whole to be built upon and around a lake in central Florida.[6] The clients, Messrs. Ottinger, Byoir, Furguson, and Claiborne, Jr., may have desired these four grand drawings for promotional purposes to secure financing.[7] On the architect's part, there had been some concern about the practicality of building upon the lake and about the permanence of the lake itself; "several lakes in the vicinity had drained them-

selves upon perforations of the lake beds, leaving dry arid pits where lakes had been."[8] Whether from lack of financial support or out of concern for the lake itself, the project was abandoned in the mid-1950s.

Wright's interest in and designs for pleasure pavilions date back to the 1890s; perhaps his most famous such project was the Midway Gardens (built 1913; demolished 1929). The design for the Leesburg Floating Gardens recalls another of Wright's unexecuted projects, that for the Wolf Lake Amusement Park (1895).[9] Both projects incorporate a lake setting, and geometrical forms control the organization of the building in its relation to the site. The irregular polygons of the Leesburg building's general shape and its patio, kitchen, and grandstand are crowned by the nearly central hexagon of the dancing lounge. Wright favored the hexagon, or honeycomb, as a structural form found in nature.

The Raabs had acquired the drawings in a trade with Wright. When Midway Gardens was demolished, Mr. George Raab had bought a number of statues and fragments from that project and placed them on the grounds of the family estate near the Wisconsin Dells. Much later, Wright and his chief architect, William Wesley Peters, learned of the whereabouts of the statues. Mrs. Helen Raab agreed to give Wright two of the Midway statues and, subsequently, agreed to trade the rest of the Midway sculpture for the four drawings of the Leesburg Floating Gardens.

A.G.

Notes:
1. For Wright's life, see the architect's *An Autobiography* (1st ed., 1932; New York, 1977), and *A Testament* (New York, 1957); see further Olgivanna Lloyd Wright, *Frank Lloyd Wright: His Life, His Work, His Words* (New York, 1966), and Robert C. Twombly, *Frank Lloyd Wright: An Interpretive Biography* (New York, 1973). For Wright's works, see, *inter alia, Frank Lloyd Wright: Writings and Buildings,* selected by Edgar Kaufman and Ben Raeburn (New York, 1960), and William Allin Storrer, *The Architecture of Frank Lloyd Wright: A Complete Catalogue,* 2nd ed. (Cambridge, Mass., 1978). All these publications contain extensive bibliography.
2. Storrer, *Complete Catalogue,* cat. no. 180.
3. Ibid., cat. nos. 230–232.
4. Ibid., cat. no. 400.
5. For a bibliography of Wright's own writings, see Twombly, *An Interpretive Biography,* 343ff.
6. Although the drawings have not been previously published, they have been listed in Patrick Meehan, *Frank Lloyd Wright: A Research Guide to Archival Sources* (New York, 1983), 47. The four drawings were exhibited at Marquette University, *Grain of Sand,* cat. no. 51, p. 13. Indira Berndtson, Assistant to the Director of the Archives, The Frank Lloyd Wright Memorial Foundation, Taliesin West, greatly facilitated my research into the circumstances surrounding the commission for the Leesburg Floating Gardens, and William Wesley Peters was especially kind to furnish his recollections about the project, including the trade of the drawings for the Midway Gardens sculpture.
7. William Wesley Peters, correspondence, 1984.
8. Ibid.
9. See Grant Carpenter Manson, *Frank Lloyd Wright to 1910: The First Golden Age* (New York, 1958), 85. I am grateful to Professor Mary Woods of Pennsylvania State University for discussing with me the context of the Leesburg project within Wright's work.

EDMUND BLAMPIED

English (1886–1966)

Born and raised in Jersey, Blampied studied art and lived in London between 1903 and 1916, when he returned to the isolated, rugged island to settle permanently with his wife. He practiced painting in both oil and watercolor, printmaking, etching, drypoint, and lithography; he exhibited widely in England and the United States.[1]

When Blampied began lithography in 1920, by drawing on transfer paper with lithographic chalk, he was already an experienced printmaker in etching and drypoint. His lithographs are quite faithful translations of his drawings. Occasionally he reworked his designs directly upon the stone, and he even made one print, *The Stream*, with ink wash alone upon stone.[2] With the cooperation of a skilled printer, Blampied achieved great tonal depth and fine detail in his completed prints, which were often published in small editions. Predominant in his oeuvre are the farmers and animals of Jersey, landscape, and people at work. His prints have been compared to those of Daumier in their blending of humor and dignity, and to those of Millet, Ostade, and Bega in their humanity and earthiness.[3]

Farmer Dentist, Edmund Blampied, etching with drypoint

Farmer Dentist   (83.3.7)

Etching with drypoint, 10 1/2 x 15 5/8 in. (26.7 x 39.7 cm). Inscribed in pencil l.r.: "E. Blampied"; and in the plate l.r.: "Blampied."

Provenance: Collection of Florence Rossbach; gift of her estate to the University, 1983.

Gaston the Chef, Edmund Blampied, lithograph

Gaston the Chef, 1931   (83.3.5)

Lithograph, 10 x 14 1/4 in. (25.4 x 36.2 cm). Inscribed in pencil l.r.: "E. Blampied"; and in the stone l.l.; "Blampied 1931."

Provenance: Collection of Florence Rossbach; gift of her estate to the University, 1983.

A Baker and a Woman, Edmund Blampied, etching

A Baker and a Woman   (83.3.6)

Etching, 11 x 8 1/4 in. (28 x 21 cm). Inscribed l.r.: "E. Blampied"; and l.l.: "37/100"; and in the plate l.l.: "Blampied."

Provenance: Collection of Florence Rossbach; gift of her estate to the University, 1983.

While not intended as a series, these three prints complement one another in their depiction of daily life. In the first, *Gaston the Chef*, published in 1932, the corpulent cook contrasts with the two women, also cooks, as he receives the joking attentions of one of them.[4] In the second, *Farmer Dentist*, a man undergoes a painful tooth extraction by apparently, a farmer who may be more familiar with the same operation performed on a horse; a woman holds the patient's head and another man grasps his knees. In the third, *A Baker and a Woman*, a paunchy baker confronts a woman who, resting one hand akimbo and the other upon her broomhandle, gazes at him teasingly. In each, Blampied treated his subjects with affectionate humor as he delineated their homely features.

These three prints also demonstrate the range of Blampied's graphic style. *Gaston the Chef* is a fully toned lithograph, with much use of dramatic shading to create a suggestive interior atmosphere. *Farmer Dentist* is a sparely rendered drypoint with some etching. *A Baker and a Woman*, another etching with drypoint, contains heavy contrasts between darks and lights, which reinforce the distinctions in character and physique between the two figures.

A. G.

Notes:
1. Sources for Blampied's life and work include Campbell Dodgson, *A Complete Catalogue of the Etchings and Drypoints of Edmund Blampied, R.A.* (London, 1926); Malcolm C. Salaman, "Blampied's Paintings in Oil and Watercolours," *Apollo* 9 (1929): 281-284; idem, introduction *Edmund Blampied,*" (London, 1926); E.L. Allhusen, "The Etchings of Edmund Blampied," *Print Collector's Quarterly* 13 (1926):69-94; and Harold J. Bailey, "Blampied: Artist and Philosopher," *Print Collector's Quarterly* 24 (1937): 363-393.
2. Malcolm C. Salaman, "The Lithographs of Edmund Blampied," *Print Collector's Quarterly* 19 (1932):312.
3. F.A. Phillips, "The Isle of Jersey's Venerable Master: Edmund Blampied," *American Artist* 30 (1966):42.
4. This print was briefly discussed by Salaman, "The Lithographs of Edmund Blampied," 319.

GEORGE CLAUSEN
English (1852-1944)

After he had worked in a firm of decorators for six years, Clausen's talent was recognized by the painter Edwin Long, whose house the young man decorated.[1] Through Long's efforts, Clausen attended art school. In 1874 he began to exhibit regularly in London, and he became a successful artist in that city during the next few decades. In 1895 he was elected to the Royal Academy, and in 1903 he was appointed Professor of Painting at the Royal Academy schools. Many of the lectures he delivered at the Academy were published.[2] Essentially an academician, Clausen was influenced by artistic developments on the Continent, where he spent many summers. His early landscapes with figures seem to depend partly upon contemporary French and Dutch art, especially the work of Israels, Maris, Legros, Millet, and Bastien-Lepage. Predominant in his oeuvre are images of laborers in landscape settings, whether farmers or fishermen. Such compositions, combining pastoral elements with men at work, embody the moral values associated with both hard labor and nature's bounty.[3]

The Great Hammer, 1917   (00.132)

Lithograph, 15 1/4 x 20 in. (38.7 x 50.8 cm). Inscribed in pencil l.r.: "George Clausen"; and in the stone l.r.: "G. Clausen, 1917."

Provenance: Collection of Mr. and Mrs. Philip Pinsof; their gift to the University, 1959.

Making Guns: Lifting an Inner Tube, 1917   (00.133)

Lithograph, 20 1/8 x 15 3/8 in. (51.1 x 39.1 cm). Inscribed in pencil l.r.: "George Clausen"; and in the stone l.r.: "G. Clausen/1917."

Provenance: Collection of Mr. and Mrs. Philip Pinsof; their gift to the University, 1959.

The Mill, 1917   (00.183)

Lithograph, 20 1/16 x 15 1/4 in. (51 x 38.7 cm). Inscribed in pencil l.r.: "George Clausen"; and in the stone l.r.: "G. Clausen 1917."

Provenance: Collection of Mr. and Mrs. Philip Pinsof; their gift to the University, 1959.

The Great Hammer, George Clausen, lithograph

Making Guns: Lifting an Inner Tube, George Clausen, lithograph

The Mill, George Clausen, lithograph

These three lithographs belong to a series entitled "Britain's Efforts and Ideals in the Great War."[4] The project's purposes were to illustrate all aspects of the war from the battlefields to the home front, to serve as a record of war, and to inspire patriotism of present and future generations. Among the other seventeen artists who contributed to the series were Brangwyn, Bone, Nevinson, and Rothenstein. The full set of lithographs was first exhibited at the Fine Art Society, London, in July, 1917,[5] and in 1919 the series was shown at the Worcester Art Museum and elsewhere in the United States.[6]

Several of Clausen's lithographs were apparently based on drawings that he made at Woolwich Arsenal near London. His contribution to the series resulted in a commission from the Ministry of Information for a large painting, *In the Gun Factory at Woolwich Arsenal*, completed in 1918.[7] In his lithographs and in the large painting of Woolwich Arsenal, Clausen rendered the figures with little specific description and the machinery with accuracy and precision. Clearly, his focus was to show the industrial power utilized for the war effort.

A.G.

Notes:

1. For accounts of Clausen's life and activities, see N. Peacock, in Ulrich Thieme and Felix Becker, *Allgemeines Lexikon der bildenden Künstler von der Antike bis zur Gegenwart* (Leipzig, 1907-1950), 8:64-66, and Kenneth McConkey, *Sir George Clausen, R. A., 1852-1944*, catalogue of an exhibition at the Bradford City Art Gallery (Bradford, 1980).
2. George Clausen, *Lectures on Painting* (London, 1904); *Aims and Ideals in Art: Eight Lectures* (London, 1907), and *Vermeer of Delft and Modern Painting* (London, 1925).
3. Michael Rosenthal, *British Landscape Painting* (Ithaca, 1982), 160-162.
4. For discussion of this series, see McConkey, *Sir George Clausen, R. A., 1852-1944*, 89-91.
5. This exhibition was reviewed by Malcolm Salaman, "The Great War: Britain's Efforts and Ideals Depicted by British Artists," *The Studio* 71 (1917):103-117.
6. Christian Brinton, introduction, and R. Wyer, foreword, *War: Paintings and Drawings by British Artists*, catalogue of an exhibition at the Worcester Art Museum (Worcester, Mass., 1919).
7. McConkey, *Sir George Clausen, R. A., 1852-1944*, 92, cat. no. 123; the painting is now in the Imperial War Museum.

AUGUSTE BROUET

French (1872-1941)

Brouet was born into a family of extremely modest means. For a number of years his mother managed a circus; such childhood memories of the circus affected his art, and circus imagery appears in his etchings (see below). When he was eleven years old, Brouet was apprenticed to a music printer, then to a lute maker, and finally to a lithographer. While he earned his living engraving for a music printer in the afternoons, he worked for Gustave Moreau at the École des Beaux-Arts in the mornings. At fifteen he began to study etchings and often visited the Bibliothèque Nationale, where he looked particularly at the prints of Rembrandt. When he was nineteen years old, he fulfilled his military duty; upon his return from the military, he made the acquaintance of the printmaker and printer Eugène Delâtre; under that master's direction, he concentrated on etching. During the 1920s he contributed illustrations to a number of books by such authors as Ed. de Goncourt, J.-K. Huysmans, and M. Barrès.[1]

Brouet's etched oeuvre comprises about 300 prints. He frequently combined drypoint and etching, thereby achieving a rich texture. Although he enjoyed a measure of success during the 1920s and 1930s, his reputation had apparently fallen into relative obscurity until only recently; at present his work is enjoying renewed appreciation.[2]

Le Cirque Pinder (The Pinder Circus) (83.3.11)

Etching, 8 x 14 1/4 in. (20.2 x 36.2 cm) (sight). Inscribed in pencil l.r.: "A. Brouet"; and l.l.: "22/70."

Provenance: Florence Rossbach Collection; gift of her estate to the University, 1983.

One of five prints of circus subjects in Brouet's work,[3] this one juxtaposes the backstage activities of the players with the on-stage performance of an acrobat; the audience fades into the distance. Brouet has compiled a panorama of contrasting performers: at the left, two small dancers sit, one completing her costume; two boys stand patiently; in the center, a small accordionist plays to a seated clown; to the right, a seeming giant prepares two monkeys to drive a carriage on stage. At the center, a horse and rider leave the arena for the wings; to the left, a groom tends a horse. Drums, horns, and other paraphernalia clutter the floor and walls.

La Relève (The Relief), 1914 (83.3.8)

Etching, 5 1/2 x 8 3/4 in. (14 x 22.2 cm). Inscribed in pencil l.r.: "A. Brouet"; and l.l.: "(?)5/10."

Provenance: Collection of Florence Rossbach; gift of her estate to the University, 1983.

Dated 1914, this print is one of about a dozen depicting scenes of World War I;[4] another is *Peeling Potatoes*, discussed below. Brouet's own experience in the military, during the 1890s, may have fostered his sympathies for the plight of the soldiers in World War I. Yet his natural predilection for low-life genre, too, may have attracted him to subjects of troops marching and wartime preparations. This modest image, nonetheless, evokes all the weariness and determination of the marching relief troops.

L'Épluchage des pommes de terre (Peeling Potatoes) (83.3.9)

Etching, 6 3/4 x 6 1/2 in. (17.2 x 16.5 cm). Inscribed in pencil l.r.: "A. Brouet"; and l.l.: "9/15."

Provenance: Collection of Florence Rossbach; gift of her estate to the University, 1983.

This print, like the preceding one, *La Relève*, depicts a scene of World War I. Here, weary soldiers prepare a meager dinner of potatoes.[5] By working the foreground deeply and the background sketchily, Brouet created a marked contrast between the two areas: In the foreground five men gather around a table and peel potatoes; to the distant right a man, seen from the back, sits, perhaps already eating his rations. In both subject and technique, this print is reminiscent of several etchings by Rembrandt.[6]

La Relève (The Relief), Auguste Brouet, etching

L'Épluchage des pommes de terre (Peeling Potatoes), Auguste Brouet, etching

Après la danse (After the Dance), Auguste Brouet, roulette engraving

Après la danse (After the Dance)   (00.13)

Roulette engraving, 12 3/4 x 15 in. (32.5 x 38 cm). Inscribed in pencil l.r.: "A Brouet"; and l.l.: "37/100."

Provenance: Collection of Mr. and Mrs. Philip Pinsof; their gift to the University, 1959.

One of Brouet's sixteen prints of ballet dancers, this is among the more intimate.[7] As in other compositions, Brouet here juxtaposed a distant and a foreground scene; unlike many of these compositions, however, the foreground scene is brilliantly lit while the background scene is heavily shaded. As one ballerina ties her shoe, the other fixes her hair. The marginalia sketches elaborate three aspects of ballet—a dancer, apparently bending to curtsy, a pair of feet in relevé, and a dancer seen from the back. Such incidental details in the margins recall the prints of Félix Buhot, whose elaborate and often reworked prints contributed to Brouet's technique and composition.[8]

L'Habilleuse (The Dresser)   (83.3.10)

Roulette engraving, 6 3/4 x 8 1/2 in. (17.2 x 21.6 cm). Inscribed in pencil l.r.: "A. Brouet"; and l.l.: "19/75."

Provenance: Collection of Florence Rossbach; gift of her estate to the University, 1983.

References:
Geffroy, *L'oeuvre gravé de Auguste Brouet, cat. no. 121.*

A. G.

117

Notes:

1. Essential bibliography about Brouet includes Gustave Geffroy, *L'oeuvre gravé de Auguste Brouet* (Paris, 1923); Raymond Hesse, *Auguste Brouet* (Paris, 1930); and Arsène Alexandre, "De la gravure originale et d'un graveur original: Auguste Brouet," *La Renaissance de l'art français*, 5, no. 3 (1922):107-114.
2. See, for example, Merrill Chase Galleries, *Rediscovered Printmakers of the Nineteenth Century* (Chicago, 1978), 11. More recently, Brouet received a one-man exhibition at Martin Sumers Graphics, New York, January, 1984.
3. Geffroy, *L'oeuvre gravé de Auguste Brouet*, cat. no. 88.
4. Ibid., cat. no. 128.
5. Ibid., cat. no. 140.
6. As, for example, *Old Woman with Onions*, 1631, and *The Pancake Woman*, 1635; Gary Schwartz, *Rembrandt: All the etchings reproduced in true size* (London and Maarssen, 1977), B. 134 and B. 124, respectively.
7. Geffroy, *L'oeuvre gravé de Auguste Brouet*, cat. no. 233.
8. See Gustave Bourcard and James Goodfriend, *Félix Buhot, Catalogue descriptif de son ouevre gravé* (New York, 1979), for examples, cat. nos. 85-95.

GASTON LACHAISE

French (1882-1935)

Lachaise's family background determined his interest in sculpture. His father, a cabinetmaker, designed and crafted the woodwork for Eiffel's private apartments at the top of the iron tower. The young Gaston carved wood and ornamental plaster in his father's shop. He received a thorough training in sculpting various materials and in mastering the techniques of drawing, painting, and anatomy in the rigorous French tradition, first at the École Bernard Palissy and then at the Académie Nationale des Beaux-Arts. While a student at the Académie, Lachaise met an American woman, Isabel Dutaud Nagle, and left Paris for Boston in 1906 in order to be near her; they married in 1917. In Boston, Lachaise became an assistant to the sculptor Henry Hudson Kitson, who moved his studio to New York in 1912; Lachaise followed Kitson there and soon after left his studio for that of Paul Manship. For both Kitson and Manship, Lachaise specialized in the meticulous ornamental detail in decorative sculpture for which his background had so well prepared him.[1]

At the same time, Lachaise developed his personal aesthetic. Inspired by Isabel, he began to sculpt in clay images of woman. One of his figurines, *Woman*, of 1912, was exhibited at the Armory Show of 1913.[2] In 1918 he held his first one-man show at the Bourgeois Gallery in New York, and other exhibitions ensued at the Kraushaar Gallery, at Stieglitz's The Intimate Gallery, and elsewhere. His critical success was established in reviews and articles by the young writers Henry McBride and E. E. Cummings for the reorganized journal *The Dial*.

Commissions for architectural reliefs and public sculptures provided Lachaise with a substantial if erratic income. He contributed reliefs, friezes, and free-standing sculpture to the American Telephone and Telegraph building and to Rockefeller Center in New York and to the Chicago World's Fair, the Coast Guard Memorial at Arlington Cemetery, and the Fairmount Park Memorial in Philadelphia.[4] His numerous portraits included many of those writers who were involved in *The Dial*: its publishers Scofield Thayer and James Sibley Watson, Jr., its art critic Henry McBride, its editors Marianne Moore and Gilbert Seldes, and its contributor E.E. Cummings.[5] Artist friends portrayed by Lachaise included Alfred Stieglitz, John Marin, Georgia O'Keeffe, and Carl van Vechten. Patrons of the arts whose features Lachaise sculpted included Edward M. M. Warburg, various members of the Rockefeller family, and Lincoln Kirstein. Lachaise's connections to such powerful patrons and critics in literature and the arts assured him of an appreciative audience during the 1920s and 1930s. The retrospective at the Museum of Modern Art, due largely to the efforts of Lincoln Kirstein, who organized the exhibition and wrote the catalogue, both secured Lachaise's reputation and, occurring shortly before his death in 1935, served as a memorial to him.[6]

Reclining Nude Seen from Behind, Gaston Lachaise, graphite on envelope

Reclining Nude Seen from Behind (80.3.3.1)

Graphite on envelope, 3 5/8 x 6 1/4 in. (9.2 x 15.9 cm) (sight). Signed in ink l.r.: "G. Lachaise."

Povenance: Collection of Mr. Joseph P. Antonow; his gift to the University, 1980.

Reclining Nude Seen from the Front, Gaston Lachaise, graphite on envelope

Reclining Nude Seen from the Front (80.3.3.2)

Graphite on envelope, 3 3/8 x 6 1/4 in. (8.6 x 15.9 cm) (sight). Unsigned.

Provenance: Collection of Mr. Joseph P. Antonow; his gift to the University, 1980.

Two Reclining Nudes Seen from Behind, Gaston Lachaise, graphite on envelope

Two Reclining Nudes Seen from Behind (80.3.3.3)

Graphite on envelope, 3 7/8 x 6 3/4 in. (9.8 x 17.2 cm) (sight). Unsigned.

Provenance: Collection of Mr. Joseph P. Antonow; his gift to the University, 1980.

Most consistently and passionately, Lachaise sculpted the female nude; his involvement with this form went together with his meeting Isabel and his love for her. It is difficult, if not impossible, to separate Lachaise's passion for his wife from his vision of womanhood. All Lachaise's renderings of the female nude express his preoccupation with Isabel's sensuality and her femininity. As small intimate images, these three drawings appear as musings for sculptural ideas. Gerald Nordland has dated the three sketches 1912-1914.[7] The second drawing, *Reclining Nude Seen from the Front*, approaches compositionally the sculpture *The Mountain*, first made in clay, cast in plaster in 1913 and later in bronze, and finally in cement in 1934.[8] Of this piece, Lachaise stated:

> You may say that the model [of *The Mountain*] is my wife. It is a large, generous figure of great placidity, great tranquility.... What I am aiming to express is the glorification of the human being, of the human body, of the human spirit with all that there is of daring, magnificence. . . .[9]

Diminutive though they are, these three sketches nonetheless project the exuberant, fecund, and vital power of Lachaise's more grandly scaled sculpture.

A. G.

Notes:
1. For Lachaise's life and work, see Gerald Nordland, *Gaston Lachaise, 1882-1935, Sculpture and Drawings*, catalogue of an exhibition at the Los Angeles County Museum and the Whitney Museum of American Art (Los Angeles, 1963), and idem, *Gaston Lachaise: The Man and His Work* (New York, 1974). For Lachaise's drawings of the nude, see Jeanne L. Wasserman, *Three American Sculptors and the Female Nude*, catalogue of an exhibition at the Fogg Art Museum (Cambridge, 1980). For assessments of Lachaise's place in American sculpture, see Joan M. Marter, Roberta K. Tarbell, and Jeffrey Wechsler, *Vanguard American Sculpture 1913-1939*, catalogue of an exhibition at the Rutgers University Art Gallery (New Brunswick, 1979), and Dore Ashton, *Modern American Sculpture* (New York, n. d.), 12.
2. Nordland, *Gaston Lachaise: The Man and His Work*, 62, fig. 5.
3. For Lachaise's involvement with *The Dial*, see ibid., 22-25.
4. Ibid., 25ff. for the AT&T building, 46ff. for Rockefeller Center, 44ff. for the Chicago World's Fair, and 28f. for the Coast Guard Memorial.
5. For Lachaise's portraiture, see ibid., 31ff., 43ff., and 89-102.
6. Lincoln Kirstein, *Gaston Lachaise: Retrospective Exhibition*, catalogue of an exhibition at the Museum of Modern Art (New York, 1935), reprinted in *Five American Sculptors*, catalogue of an exhibition at the Museum of Modern Art (New York, 1969).
7. I am grateful to Gerald Nordland, Director of the Milwaukee Art Museum, for his evaluation of the three sketches.

8. For the monumental concrete version of this work, commissioned by G. L. K. Morris for his estate in Lenox, Massachusetts, see Nordland, *Gaston Lachaise: The Man and His Work*, plate 56; for other versions of the sculpture in bronze and stone see ibid., plates 53-55, and see Nordland, *Gaston Lachaise, 1882-1935, Sculpture and Drawings*, cat. no. 82.

9. Interview with Lachaise, published in *Arts Digest*, February 2, 1935, and cited by Nordland, *Gaston Lachaise: The Man and His Work*, 50.

GEORGES ROUAULT

French (1871-1958)

A frail child born into a family of skilled artisans, Rouault was encouraged by his grandfather to become an artist. His father was a wood finisher for the Pleyel Piano Company, and his aunts were painters of porcelain. Apprenticed at first to a stained glass maker and then to a restorer of medieval stained glass, the young Rouault completed his artistic training by night courses at the École Nationale des Arts Décoratifs and later at the École des Beaux-Arts, where he studied with Gustave Moreau. Following that master's death, Rouault became Director of the Musée Gustave Moreau. He exhibited at the official Salon between 1895 and 1901, from 1905 to 1912 in the Salon des Indépendants, and in 1903 and following years in the Salon d'Automne.[1]

Although Rouault does not belong to any single movement, his painting style is generally considered Expressionist in its use of color and emotional subjects, and akin to the Fauves only in its use of brilliant color.[2] The heavy black outlines containing vibrant hues in Rouault's paintings and prints are inspired by medieval stained glass. Clowns, prostitutes, and Christ dominate his imagery. His artistic maturity is inseparable from his intense piety, which was fostered by several French Catholic writers, especially Léon Bloy.

Rouault turned seriously to printmaking in 1912; under the direction of the art dealer Ambroise Vollard, Rouault made a number of series of intaglios and lithographs, including *Miserere* (see below), as well as less formidably gloomy subjects: circus themes, landscapes, and several literary works, including *Père Ubu* and *Fleurs du Mal*.[3] His prints translate his painterly vision into ink upon paper and are distinctive for the depth of plate biting in his copper plates and for the complicated and virtuoso techniques in his lithographs.

Miserere   (58.1.1-.58)

Series of fifty-eight prints in aquatint, drypoint, and etching; dimensions vary. Some works inscribed in the plate. Inscriptions vary.

Provenance: Collection of Mr. Leonard Scheller; his gift to the University, 1958.

Originally intended as a series of 100 plates in two volumes, with text by André Suarès under the title *Miserere et Guerre*, the series was published as *Miserere* and consisted of only fifty-eight plates. It was begun in 1914 under the encouragement and supervision of the dealer Ambroise Vollard. The copper plates were worked on between 1916-1918 and 1920-1927; although the plates were printed in 1927, they were officially published in 1948. The original agreement with Vollard, made in 1916 and resolved with the dealer's death in 1939 and after a lawsuit of 1947, called for the 100 plates. During the 1920s it became apparent to Rouault that the magnitude of the project would preclude the completion of the whole as planned.[4]

Rouault transformed his original ink drawings into

Have Mercy on Me, God, According to Thy Great Mercy, Georges Rouault, aquatint, drypoint and etching

120

Who Does Not Wear a Mask?, from the Miserere Series, Georges Rouault, aquatint, drypoint and etching

Peace seems never to reign
Over this anguished world
Of shame and shadows

Jesus on the cross will tell you better than I,
Jeanne in her brief and sublime replies at her trial
As well as other saints and martyrs
Obscure or consecrated.[7]

As bold images withimal use of words, the *Miserere* belongs to the tradition of medieval block-books and of devotional prints of the fifteenth and sixteenth centuries. Rouault's images, iconic and mystical, are powerful testimony to his own spirituality as a Catholic and tenacious expressions of his faith as an artist.

A. G.

Notes:
1. Basic sources for Rouault's life and work include Lionello Venturi, *Georges Rouault* (Paris, 1948), and James Thrall Soby, *Georges Rouault Paintings and Prints*, catalogue of an exhibition at the Museum of Modern Art, 1945 (New York, 1947).
2. A concise assessment of Rouault's achievement is given by George Heard Hamilton, *Painting and Sculpture in Europe 1880 to 1940* (Baltimore, 1967), 110ff.
3. François Chapon and Isabelle Rouault, *Ouevre gravé Rouault* (Monte Carlo, 1978), and Alan Wofsy, *Georges Rouault: The Graphic Work* (San Francisco, 1976).
4. For discussion of the circumstances surrounding the inception and appearance of the *Miserere*, see the essay by Chapon in Chapon and Rouault, *Oeuvre gravé Rouault*, 73ff.
5. The techniques used in the *Miserere* are discussed by Monroe Wheeler, in his introduction, and by the artist himself in his preface, Georges Rouault, *Miserere* (New York, 1952), unpaginated.
6. Wheeler, introduction to *Miserere*, unpaginated.
7. Rouault, preface to *Miserere*, unpaginated.

gouache or oil paintings. These were then transferred by photogravure onto large copper plates, averaging 21 x 18 inches. Rouault then reworked the plates, making as many as 15 states of a single design, in order to arrive at the desired effects of depth and tone. He used a variety of techniques: aquatint, drypoint, roulette, and acid applied directly to the metal.[5]

Rouault's *Miserere* commences and ends with Christ's sorrows; between these clearly Christian icons are compositions concerned with secular cruelties of the human condition, above all, war. The *Miserere* series expresses the message that man's fate upon earth is tragic.[6] The artist himself introduced a facsimile edition of *Miserere* with these lines:

Form, color, harmony
Oasis or mirage
For the eyes, the heart, and the spirit
Toward the moving ocean of pictorial appeal

"Tomorrow will be beautiful," said the shipwrecked man
Before he disappeared beneath the sullen horizon

PAUL CASSIRER, BERLIN
(Publisher)

German

Kriegszeit. Künstlerflugblätter (Wartime. Artists' Pamphlets), August 1914/March 1916 (81.15.3.1-.57)

Series of fifty-seven offset lithographs on newsprint, 19 x 12 3/4 in. (48.3 x 32.3 cm), each

Provenance: Collection of Mr. and Mrs. Marvin L. Fishman; their gift to the University, 1981.

References:
Orrel P. Reed, Jr., *German Expressionist Art: The Robert Gore Rifkind Collection,* catalogue of an exhibition at the Frederick S. Wright Art Gallery, University of California, Los Angeles (Los Angeles, 1977), 222-226.

Max Liebermann in seiner Zeit, catalogue of an exhibition at the Nationalgalerie, Berlin (Berlin, 1979), 667, no. 480.

R. Jentsch, *Max Beckmann. Radierungen. Lithographien. Holzschmitte* (New York, 1981), 29.

Kriegszeit und der Bildermann, catalogue of an exhibition at Ernst Barlach Haus, Hamburg (Hamburg, 1984).

Kriegszeit. Künstlerflugblätter is in the tradition of early twentieth-century German periodicals intended to serve as a forum of information, criticism, and debate about art, literature, and politics.[1] It functioned, along with many other such periodicals, including *Der Sturm* (founded and edited by Herwarth Walden beginning in 1910) and *Die Action* (founded and edited by Franz Pflemfert beginning in 1911), to serve the needs of a sizable reading public of pre-war Germany. These publications, though individuated according to their different causes and ideologies, shared a common theme of "Expressionism" encompassing art, literature, and politics and ranging from the more avant-garde to conservative tendencies in all three.[2]

Founded and edited by Paul Cassirer and Alfred Gold, the sixty-five issues of *Kriegszeit* appeared at first weekly and then less regularly over a two-year period between August, 1914, and March, 1916, at the beginning of World War I. Cassirer was a publisher and an art dealer who exhibited Secession artists, who had parted from the Academy, the Brücke group of artists, and the French Impressionists. Cassirer was also responsible for several other publications of the time, including *Pan* magazine and *Der Bildermann.* Gold, the associate editor of *Kriegszeit,* was a conservative art critic trained as well in philosophy.[3]

Kriegszeit appeared during the early stages of the war when Germany was amassing wide popular support for her battle against England, France, and Russia. Early issues of the periodical show support for German imperialist efforts, including the submarine campaign, as well as praise for the sinking of the *Lusi-*

Cover Illustration, September 7, 1914, Max Liebermann, offset lithograph, from *Kriegszeit. Künstlerflugblätter* (Wartime. Artists' Pamphlets), Paul Cassirer, Publisher

tania, an unarmed passenger ship. German soldiers are depicted as "noble custodians of culture" and as "bastions against the British" and other Western opposition.

Cassirer drew upon the major Expressionist artists of the day including Ernst Barlach, Max Beckman, August Gaul, Rudolf Grossmann, Franz Heckendorf, Otto Hettner, Willi Jaeckel, Käthe Kollwitz, Max Liebermann, Hans Meid, Mopp, J.A. Nerlinger, Karl Petersen, Max Slevogt, E. R. Weiss, and others totaling fifty-two. Many of these were Cassirer's gallery artists.

Throughout the collection of illustrations there appears an explosive ambience generated by thick lines and highly energized picture surfaces. These pictorial elements are often used to celebrate military glory, as in Liebermann's *Der Kaiser (the Emperor)* (No. 2, September 7, 1914), and Hettner's *Zerschossene*

Bildnis des verwundeten Schwagers Martin Tube (Portrait of the Wounded Brother-in-Law Martin Tube), Max Beckmann, lithograph, from *Kreigszeit. Künstlerflugblätter (Wartime. Artists' Pamphlets)*, Paul Cassirer, publisher

Batterie (Destroyed Battery) (No. 9, October 21, 1914). A more hesitant response to war is reflected in the image of a young boy in Grossmann's *Wer will unter die Soldaten (Who Wants to Be a Soldier)*, suggesting a lessening of enthusiasm for war as its realities are better understood. Though often grim in subject matter, the images are not without humor, as in Petersen's *Russischer Katzenjammer (Russian Hangover)* (No. 56, November 1, 1915). Here the Russian Czar appears surrounded by broken boxes and miscellaneous rubble, possibly meant to represent a shipwreck, sprawling forward on his hands and looking very foolish in his "collapsed" world. Barlach displays a similar ironic humor in his jibe at the Church in a work titled *Und wenn die Welt voll Teufel wär (And If the World Were Full of Devils)* where he shows a fiendish figure sidling up an ecclesiastical personage in a taunting manner as if to ask the question implied in the title (No. 46, July 1, 1915).

The styles represented in the illustrations published in *Kriegszeit* vary from minimal cartoonlike caricatures (Petersen's *The Fairy Tale of Bird Grey*, No. 49,

July 28, 1915) to fully developed Expressionist images of Beckmann's *Untitled/Bildnis des verwundeten Schwagers Martin Tube (Portrait of the Wounded Brother-in-Law Martin Tube)*, No. 11, November 4, 1914) (see ill. p. 123 and Barlach's intense peasantlike figures (*An der Ostgrenze (On the Eastern Frontier)*, No. 12, November 11, 1914 (see ill. p. 123), and others). Barlach's forms do not fail to reflect the tragic emotive effects of war and the social upheaval of the times, often with an implied social message, as in *Strassenecke in Warschau (Street Corner in Warsaw)* (No. 28, February 24, 1915), where two heavy souls rest in the street while a battle ensues in the background, or in *Die Bethlehem Steel Company in Amerika* (No. 49, July 28, 1950), where an old bent-over crone carries metal bells with clappers in the form of human skulls.

Overall, the illustrations in *Kriegszeit* reflect the merging of art and politics common to similar periodicals of the time; there is a distinct shifting of views from the beginning, where war and German imperialism are enthusiastically touted, to disenchantment as the artists realized that any victories resulting from the war were too costly in human sacrifice (Kollwitz's

An der Ostgrenze (On the Eastern Frontier), Ernst Barlach, lithograph, from *Kriegszeit. Künstlerflugblätter (Wartime. Artists' Pamphlets)*, Paul Cassirer, publisher

son was killed in the war) and incompatible with their humanist ideals. Cassirer ended *Kriegszeit* in 1916 and began another journal, *Der Bildermann*, that reflected the change from nationalist to internationalist views and from support of to opposition against the war.

The Marquette volumes acquired in 1981 are complete except for nos. 50, 51, 59, 62–65. A complete set consisting of sixty-five issues plus a separate print by Max Oppenheimer is in the Robert Gore Rifkind Collection (see *German Expressionist Art*, exhibition catalogue listed in References; for a complete listing of artists and illustrations; see also, Busch-Reisinger Museum Collection, Harvard University).

C.L.C.

Notes:
1. The principal secondary source used in preparing this essay is Orrel P. Reed, Jr.'s *German Expressionist Art: The Robert Gore Rifkind Collection*, catalogue of an exhibition at the Frederick S. Wright Art Gallery, University of California, Los Angeles (Los Angeles, 1977). See also *Max Lieberman in seiner Zeit*, catalogue of an exhibition at the Nationalgalerie, Berlin (Berlin, 1979), 667, no. 480; R. Jentsch, *Max Beckmann. Radierungen. Lithographien. Holzschnitte* (New York, 1981), 29; *Kriegszeit und der Bildermann*, catalogue of an exhibition at Ernst Barlach Haus, Hamburg (Hamburg, 1984).
2. German Expressionism is a parallel development to Fauve art in France. It reflects a new freedom of color and shape, as initiated by the Cubists. In German Expressionism these non-realist developments are manifest in a particular way, reflecting an intensified emotional character and a tradition of German painting that is reminiscent of the Renaissance artists Mattias Grünewald and Albrecht Dürer. (For this capsule view I wish to thank Rudolf Arnheim, Professor Emeritus, Carpenter Center, Harvard University, who was living in Germany at the time *Kriegszeit* was being published.) To this interpretation Ida Rigby adds that the personal inner vision of each German Expressionist artist provides a link between the artists and their political and social worlds. (Reed, *German Expressionist Art*, 1.)
3. Reed, *German Expressionist Art*, 222, 270.

BENVENUTO DISERTORI

Italian (1887–1967)

Although Disertori was trained as a graphic artist, his career crossed the lines of the pictorial arts into musicology.[1] Between 1906 and 1915 he studied art in Venice, Munich, Rome, Berlin, Vienna, and Perugia; in 1914 he exhibited at the Venice Biennale. He lived in Rome (1915–1923), Florence (1923–1931), Milan (1931–1950), and Parma (1950 and later). At the Accademia di Brera in Milan he taught etching (1931–1950), and at the University of Parma, early Renaissance music (1950 and after). His scholarly inclinations led him to write a brief history of Italian printmaking.[2] His expertise as a historian of Italian graphics of the fifteenth and sixteenth centuries is evident from his own etchings, which are often stylistically and thematically rooted in Italian Renaissance art and iconography. From Nicoletto da Modena and Marcantonio Raimondi, Disertori adapted allegorical subjects; he

also incorporated the consistent, firm, and functional language of those early engravers into his own decorative and solid linear schema. His prints include city views, architectural monuments, nudes, and genre scenes, as well as planetary and allegorical images derived from Renaissance engravings.[3] For the most part he pulled small editions of his etchings, and he often printed only about twenty impressions from a single plate.

La Fortuna ed Apollo (Fortune and Apollo), 1928 (00.136)

Engraving and etching, 14 1/2 x 13 in. (36.8 x 33 cm). Inscribed in the plate l.l. with monogram; and in pen, l.r.: "Benvenuto Disertori."

Provenance: Anonymous gift to the University.

As Apollo prepares to bow his viol, Fortune points to a wheel spinning in the air; just as Apollo is concerned only with making music, Fortune indicates the precarious nature of the world. An allegory in the tradition of Marcantonio Raimondi and Nicoletto da Modena, Disertori's image juxtaposes the world's folly with the redeeming power of art.[4]

Il Piede della dea Giunone (The Foot of the Goddess Juno), 1919 (00.64)

Engraving and etching, 17 3/8 x 13 3/4 in. (44.1 x 34.9 cm). Inscribed in the plate l.c.: "BD"; and in pen l.r.: "Benvenuto Disertori."

Provenance: Anonymous gift to the University.

Disertori's image of this ancient fragment of a monumental statue both evokes the power of time to destroy man's endeavors and affirms the power of art to survive such destruction. The foot of Juno has tenaciously withstood the vicissitudes of centuries; Disertori has recorded the fragment as it stood, in sunlit clarity, in the cloister of the Church of Sta. Maria degli Angeli in Rome.[5]

A.G.

Il Piede della Dea Giunone (The Foot of the Goddess Juno), Benvenuto
Disertori, engraving and etching

La Fortuna ed Apollo (Fortune and Apollo), Benvenuto Disertori,
engraving and etching

Notes:

1. For information concerning Disertori's biography and activity as
   an etcher, see Riccardo Maroni, "Benvenuto Disertori, Incisore e
   umanista," in *Collana Artisti Trentini* 8:238–315. See further Cle-
   lia Alberici, *Benvenuto Disertori Professore di Incisione presso
   l'Accademia di Brera* (Milan, 1979).
2. Benvenuto Disertori, *L'Incisione Italiane* (Florence, 1931).
3. For Disertori's etchings see Augusto Calabi, "The Etchings of Benvenuto Disertori," *The Print Collector's Quarterly* 22 (1935):41–
   61; for his entire oeuvre of 138 prints in various media, see Paolo
   Bellini, "Benvenuto Disertori: a complete catalogue of his engravings," *Print Collector* 3 (1973):24–41.
4. See Maroni, "Benvenuto Disertori, Incisore e umanista," 242;
   Calabi, "The Etchings of Benvenuto Disertori," 45 and 55, cat. no
   3; and Bellini, "Benvenuto Disertori: a complete catalogue of his
   engravings," cat. no. 53.
5. See Maroni, "Benvenuto Disertori, Incisore e umanista," 286;
   Calabi, "The Etchings of Benvenuto Disertori," 58, no. 26; and
   Bellini, "Benvenuto Disertori: a complete catalogue of his engravings," cat. no. 32.

ALEXANDER ARCHIPENKO

Russian (1887–1964)

Archipenko attended art school in Kiev 1902–1905, but was expelled for criticizing his professors as too academic. Thereafter he spent several years in Moscow, and in 1908 he went to Paris. There he exhibited with the Section d'Or, the Salon des Indépendants, and the Société Anonyme and established a studio in Montparnasse, where his students included Modigliani and Gaudier-Brzeska. In 1913 his work was included in the New York Armory Show, and his reputation in Europe and in the United States was secured with a one-man exhibition that toured major European cities in 1919–1920. After a brief stay in Berlin, he moved to the United States in 1924 and remained there for most of his life, returning to Europe only for visits. In Woodstock, New York, he opened a summer art school; he taught at various colleges throughout the country during the ensuing decades, residing in New York, Los Angeles, and Chicago.[1]

Considered a "pioneer Cubist sculptor," Archipenko consistently explored the interaction of the surrounding space with the cavities and convexities of his sculptural materials.[2] He strove to fuse concave forms with color and movement and used substances as varied as wood, sheet metal, glass, cloth, and lucite. He favored terra-cotta and bronze and frequently endowed the surfaces of his sculptures with patinas, glazes, and lacquers. The organically geometric and polished forms of his sculpture, evident in his first mature works made in Paris, remain constant elements in his oeuvre. In 1924 he invented and patented a movable painting machine, called "Archipentura," a contraption containing 110 horizontal metal strips that could be moved to change 110 canvases and thereby achieve an enormous variety of visual configurations.[3] Most prevalent in Archipenko's oeuvre are depictions of the female nude; on occasion he turned to still life, portraiture, and genre figures.

In his autobiography, published 1960, he expounded his theory of analogous, creative forces throughout the universe and explained his own art as a spiritual progression, arising from his vision of movement in plastic form. His inspirations included the Gothic, Hindu, and Egyptian transformations of the human body toward spiritual ends.

Madonna and Child, Alexander Archipenko, colored pencil, crayon and ink

Madonna and Child   (55.4)

Colored pencil, crayon and ink, 15 1/2 x 13 in. (39.4 x 33 cm) (sight). Signed in blue ballpoint pen, l.r.: "Archipenko."

Provenance: Presented to the University by the artist through the friendship of Dr. Roman S. Smal-Stocki, 1955.

References:
Pick, *Marquette University Art Collection*, 7 (ill.).

Carter, *Grain of Sand*, 11, no. 28.

This drawing is unusual in Archipenko's graphic work in that it is so carefully rendered. The majority of his works on paper, which constitute numerous drawings and fifty-three prints, are sketchier in style. According to the artist, there were fundamentally two categories of drawing. One type of drawing served as a notation for further development, and the other, which could be either rough or finished in workmanship, functioned as a completed statement. In this category, "the essence remains in its transformative character, which evolves into a style expressive of the personality of the artist, through specific forms, lines, patterns and techniques."[4] The *Madonna and Child* clearly belongs to the second category.

As an explicit image of the *Madonna and Child*, so titled by the artist, the present drawing is rare in his oeuvre. It is, however, related thematically to several religious images made in the late 1940s and early 1950s.[5] The Marquette drawing is more closely related to Archipenko's non-Christian images of woman, which he often imbued with a spiritual interpretation. His fascination with the female form is exemplified by his life-size terra-cotta of a seated woman, entitled *Ma-meditation* (meaning in Hungarian the creative and mystic power in woman, not the English colloquial term for mother). It is inscribed:

> Ma is dedicated to every mother; to everyone who is in love and suffers from love; to everyone who creates in the arts and science; to every hero; to everyone who is lost in problems; to everyone who knows and feels Eternity and Infinity.[6]

The small *Madonna and Child* drawing expresses this secular sentiment as well as the traditional Christian meaning invested in the image of Mary and the Christ Child.

A. G.

Notes:
1. Essential bibliography about Archipenko includes his autobiography, *Archipenko: Fifty Creative Years, 1908-1958* (New York, 1960), which contains extensive references to early exhibitions, catalogues, and critical writings. Recent exhibition catalogues include: Donald H. Karshan, ed., *Archipenko: International Visionary*, Smithsonian Institution (Washington, 1969); Katherine Kuh, et al., *Alexander Archipenko* (Los Angeles, 1967); Jeanne L. Wasserman, *Three American Sculptors and the Female Nude*, catalogue of an exhibition at the Fogg Art Museum (Cambridge, 1980); and Joan M. Marter, Roberta K. Tarbell, and Jeffrey Wechsler, *Vanguard American Sculpture 1913-1939*, catalogue of an exhibition at the Rutgers University Art Gallery (New Brunswick, 1979).
2. Kuh, *Alexander Archipenko*, 7.
3. For an account of "Archipentura," see Archipenko's autobiography, *Archipenko: Fifty Creative Years, 1908-1958*, 65-66 and figs. 290, 291.
4. Ibid., 63.
5. Ibid., plate 196: *Religious Motif*, 1948, and plate 197: *Ascension*, 1950.
6. Kuh, *Alexander Archipenko*, 9.

MARC CHAGALL
Russian (1887–   )

As a young boy Chagall was struck with the ambition to become a painter; he eagerly practiced drawing even as a child. In 1907 he began to attend art school in St. Petersburg. Between 1910 and 1914 he lived in Paris, where he studied the Old Master paintings in the Louvre and came into contact with the most recent developments of modern painting at various exhibitions, especially those at the Salon des Indépendants. In the early summer of 1914 he went to Berlin; shortly thereafter he returned to Vitebsk, where he married his longtime fiancée, Bella. After the Revolution he was appointed Commissar of Fine Arts for the district of Vitebsk. However, the proliferation of revolutionary art and its overtly propagandist aims did not appeal to him. In 1922 he went to Berlin, where he and his wife stayed for a year, and then to Paris, where they spent most of their time until World War II. In 1941 they fled to New York, where Bella died in 1944. After the war Chagall returned to France and settled in Vence. He married Valentina Brodsky in 1952.[1]

In Paris Chagall absorbed variously the currents of Fauvism and Cubism; from the Fauves, he gained an understanding of the power of intense color, and from the Cubists, a means of endowing form with underlying structure. His pictorial language, heavily dependent upon his village upbringing and fantasy, is wholly his own. Recognition came swiftly and strongly to Chagall. His first one-man show was held at the Sturm Gallery in Berlin in 1914, and after that he exhibited regularly. In 1946 major exhibitions of his work were held at the Museum of Modern Art, New York, at the Art Institute of Chicago, and at the Musée National d'Art Moderne, Paris; in 1950 a retrospective was held at the Kunsthaus, Zurich.

Commissions for theatrical sets, murals, stained glass, and mosaics occupied much of Chagall's time after 1942, when he designed the sets for the Tchaikowsky-Pushkin ballet *Aleko*, produced in Mexico, and Stravinsky's *The Firebird*, produced in New York, 1945. Once established in southern France, he made sculpture in marble and bronze, and ceramics. His involvement with printmaking began in 1922, when he made twenty etchings, entitled *Mein Leben*, which were published by Cassirer in Berlin. The series, essentially autobiographical, combined Chagall's fantasy with his own experiences and related closely to the imagery of his paintings. Ambroise Vollard encouraged him to make more prints, and, under Vollard's supervision, Chagall made 107 etchings for an edition of Gogol's *Dead Souls* (1923-1927; 1948). Again prompted by Vollard, Chagall made 100 gouaches for an edition of La Fontaine's *Fables* (1926-1927; 1952). In 1931 he began the biblical series, published only in 1957 (see below). Much later he would illustrate *Daph-*

nis and Chloë and experiment with lithographs and monotypes.[2] His oil paintings, done before World War II, however, may well be considered his most enduring works; in any case, they provided much of the imagery and formal structure for his later paintings, prints, and sculpture.

The Young Shepherd Joseph, from the Bible Series, Marc Chagall, hand-colored etching

The Bible Series   (80.7.1-.105)

105 hand-colored etchings, each about 24 x 18 in. (61 x 45.7 cm). Each inscribed in the plate, l.r. or l.l.: "Chagall" and inscribed in pencil, l.l.: "65/100"; and l.r.: "M. Ch."

Provenance: Collection of the Aldrich Museum of Contemporary Art, Ridgefield, Conn.; sold to Mr. and Mrs. Patrick Haggerty; their gift to the University, 1980.

Like his etchings for Gogol's *Dead Souls* (1923-1927; published 1948) and those for La Fontaine's *Fables* (1926-1927; published 1952), Chagall's *The Bible* was a project conceived with the collaboration of Ambroise Vollard. However, the three series were published only after Vollard's death, by his heir, Tériade. In 1931 Vollard suggested that Chagall do a series based upon the Bible.[3] In preparation for the series, the artist, with his wife and daughter, went to Palestine for three months. Upon his return to Paris he made the gouaches that would serve as models for the etchings, which, printed in black ink, were then hand-colored; the series was finally published in 1957.

In Palestine Chagall drew and painted landscapes, Bedouin, and specific buildings and sites; these motifs appear in his work, in the etched series as well as in his paintings. Yet it was especially the brilliantly clear atmosphere of the Holy Land that influenced Chagall's handling of light in the biblical series. Shortly after his sojourn in Palestine, Chagall said, "The air of the land of Israel makes men wise—we have old traditions."[4]

Chagall's choice of subjects for inclusion in the series is personal. As his primary theme he focused upon

The Song of David, from the Bible Series, Marc Chagall, hand-colored etching

Promise to Jerusalem, from the Bible Series, Marc Chagall, hand-colored etching

Elijah's Vision, from the Bible Series, Marc Chagall, hand-colored etching

man: "Man who remains the same through the centuries, man whom God looked upon, with whom God spoke, who thus received his rank and dignity."[5] He selected the patriarchs: Noah, Abraham, Isaac, Jacob, Joseph; Moses and the Exodus; Joshua; Samson; David, Solomon, and the prophets: Elijah, Jeremiah, and Ezekiel. Meyer Schapiro perceived this choice as divisible into three groups, which, taken together, compose a "characteristic unity of Jewish awareness."[6] These three groups are the ancestors who founded the Jewish community and received the covenant and law; those who founded the nation of Israel; and the prophets. In the series Chagall achieved a singular unity between text and image, for only with the biblical narrative in mind does the full meaning of many of these images become fully understood.

In 1931 Chagall himself expressed his approach to the biblical series: "I didn't see the Bible, I dreamt it. I never work from my head. When I had to illustrate the

Bible for Vollard, he told me: 'Go to the Place Pigalle.' But I wanted to see Palestine, I wanted to touch the earth."[7]

A. G.

Jeremiah in the Pit, from the Bible Series, Marc Chagall, hand-colored etching

The Creation of Man, from the Bible Series, Marc Chagall, hand-colored etching

Notes:

1. For Chagall's life and work, see, above all, the artist's autobiography, *My Life* (New York, 1960; Werner Haftmann, *Marc Chagall Life and Work* (New York, 1963); Werner Haftmann, *Marc Chagall* (New York, n.d. (1973?)); and Charles Sorlier, ed., *Chagall by Chagall* (New York, 1979). All these publications contain extensive bibliography.

2. For Chagall's graphics, see *Marc Chagall: His Graphic Work*, introduction and selections by Franz Meyer, documentation by Hans Bolliger (New York, 1957); Julien Cain and Fernand Merlot, *The Lithographs of Chagall*, 3 vols. (New York and Boston, 1960-1969); and Eberhard W. Kornfeld, *Verzeichnis der Kupferstiche, Radierungen, and Holzschnitte von Marc Chagall, Vol. I: Werke 1922-1966* (Bern, 1970).

3. For the circumstances of the series's inception, see *Marc Chagall: His Graphic Work*, xxiii–xxvi. The complete series was illustrated in *Verve* 33/34 (September 1956) with an introduction by Meyer Schapiro.

4. Meyer, *Marc Chagall, Life and Work*, 385.

5. H. M. Rotermund, quoted in ibid., 386.

6. Schapiro, in *Verve*, unpaginated.

7. Sorlier, ed., *Chagall by Chagall*, 243.

SCULPTURE
AND
DECORATIVE ARTS

SIXTEENTH CENTURY

ANDREA DELLA ROBBIA
Italian (1435-1525)

"Della Robbia" is a term so frequently encountered for glazed terra-cotta sculpture that its origin is often overlooked. Luca di Simone di Marco della Robbia (1399/1400-1482) was a Florentine sculptor of great distinction who sculpted in bronze and marble in addition to the enameled terra-cotta for which he has become best known. His nephew, Andrea, who became Luca's pupil and the successor to his workshop, seems to have worked almost exclusively in terra-cotta. Andrea's son, Giovanni (1469-1529), together with other more obscure members of the family, continued the workshop well into the sixteenth century.

Andrea worked as an assistant to his uncle, but from early in his career he received numerous independent commissions.[1] The most important and imposing of these are the large altarpieces undertaken for Tuscan churches—in particular the series of the *Incarnation*, *Annunciation*, *Assumption of the Virgin*, *Ascension*, and *Crucifixion* at La Verna. These multifigure compositions for public display were paralleled by the artist's small-scale terra-cottas, most often of the Madonna and Child, which were clearly conceived for private devotion. These works were extremely popular in his own time—Andrea evidently became quite successful in their production—and after. Variations and copies have been produced in Italy from the sixteenth century to today.

FOLLOWER OF ANDREA DELLA ROBBIA
Madonna and Child with Angels   (49.1)

Glazed terra-cotta, 43 x 23 1/8 in. (109.2 x 58.7 cm). Unsigned.

Provenance: Collection of the Marchese Niccolini di Camugliano, Camugliano (Florence) [?]; Boston Store of Milwaukee; gift of Richard P. Herzfeld, President of the Boston Store, to the University, 1949.

References:
Pick, *Marquette University Art Collection*, 42 (ill.), 43, as Della Robbia.

Carter, *Grain of Sand*, 17, no. 84 (ill.), as School of Della Robbia.

Madonna and Child with Angels, Follower of Andrea della Robbia, glazed terra-cotta

In this enameled terra-cotta relief the Madonna is seen seated holding the Christ Child, who stands on her lap as he wraps his left arm around his mother for support. Christ is quite childlike, even a bit playful; the Virgin, holding him tenderly, stares pensively into the distance, certainly aware of his destiny. Three seraphim, bodiless winged angel heads, hover about the figures while a fourth appears in the decorative base below. A swag of flowers and fruit surrounds the composition.

Marquette's *Madonna and Child with Angels* is ultimately derived from one of Andrea della Robbia's most beautiful works, the *Madonna of the Architects* (Bargello, Florence) of 1475.[2] The precise pose of the Madonna and Child appear, however, in several reliefs from Andrea's workshop, the best of which is perhaps the *Madonna and Child with Angels* at Baragazza.[3] Marquette's *Madonna* would rather seem to be a later derivation from these works. The composition lacks the tight organization and the figures the vivid presence found in Andrea's autograph works and those of his workshop.

R. B. S.

Notes:
1. John Pope-Hennessy, "Thoughts on Andrea della Robbia," in *The Study and Criticism of Italian Sculpture* (New York, 1980), 173. The standard reference to the artist's works is still Allan Marquand, *Andrea della Robbia and his Atelier* (Princeton, 1922); see as well Maud Cruttwell, *Luca and Andrea della Robbia and Their Successors* (London, 1901) and I. B. Supino, "Andrea della Robbia," in Ulrich Thieme and Felix Becker, *Allgemeines Lexikon der bildenden Künstler von der Antike bis zur Gegenwart* (Leipzig, 1907-1950), 28:414.
2. Pope-Hennessy, "Thoughts on Andrea della Robbia," fig. 13.
3. Marquand, *Andrea della Robbia and his Atelier*, II: no. 173 (ill.).

NINETEENTH CENTURY

VICTOR-CONSTANTINE DELAIGUE

French (act. late nineteenth-early twentieth century)

No biographical information has been found on Delaigue, who is thought to have been active in the early part of this century.[1]

Dante in the Inferno   (64.2)

Bronze and ivory, 30 x 15 x 17 1/2 in. (76.2 x 38.1 x 44.5 cm). Inscribed c.r.: "Delaigue."

Provenance: Anonymous gift to the University, 1964.

References:
Pick, *Marquette University Art Collection*, 13 (ill.).

Carter, *Grain of Sand*, 15, no. 68.

The figure of Dante is seen striding forcefully down into the underworld, his left hand clenched in a fist as his right arm raises his cloak in a gesture of protection. The ground on which he walks is more than a rendering of a craggy rock; it is an emblematic representation of Dante's Hell, with tormented souls emerging from the crags of the stone's surface. No specific moment in Dante's *Divine Comedy* seems to be illustrated here; rather the subject is the poet himself.

Portraits of Dante and illustrations of his work, which began to appear in Renaissance Italy, flourished in the nineteenth century, especially in France. Delacroix, Géricault, Gerome, Scheffer, and Ingres all treated notable Dantesque subjects, as did the sculptors Carpeaux, Rodin, Félicie de Fauveau, Etex, and Triqueti—to mention only a few. Perhaps most influential were the engraved illustrations of Gustave Doré, whose *Inferno* appeared in 1862.[3] Delaigue's Dante is very much of the Doré type, in physiognomy as well as conception—a terrific figure and, as both subject and author, a Romantic hero.

While *Dante in the Inferno* is basically a bronze statuette, the face and hands are executed in ivory. Chryselephantine sculpture, as this type of work is known, often included precious metals and jewels as well; this combination of disparate materials, relatively popular in nineteenth-century France, was actually inspired by literary descriptions of lost ancient works of art.[4]

R. B. S.

Dante in the Inferno, Victor-Constantine DeLaigue, bronze and ivory

Notes:
1. Harold Berman, *Bronzes: Sculptors and Founders* (Chicago, 1974-1980), III:788, where another example of the bronze, entitled *Dante's Inferno*, is illustrated as no. 2925 with a date of c. 1910.
2. On Dante's iconography see, generally, Richard Thayer Holbrook, *Portraits of Dante* (London, 1911); F. J. Mather, Jr., *The Portraits of Dante* (Princeton, 1924); and, mostly concerning nineteenth-century German representations, Ludwig Volkmann, *Iconographia Dantesca* (London, 1899).

3. *L'Enfer de Dante Alighieri avec les dessins de Gustave Doré*, trans. Pier-Angelo Fiorentino (Paris, 1862); see *Gustave Doré; 1832-1883*, exhibition catalogue (Strasbourg-Paris, 1983), 239-241.
4. Of these the most famous is the lost *Athena Parthenos* of Phidias, the colossal cult statue of the Parthenon. See Gisela M. A. Richter, *The Sculpture and Sculptors of the Greeks* (London-New Haven, 1929), 219f. On the media see G. Bapst, "La Sculpture Chryséléphantine," *La Revue de famille* II (1892):334-343.

G. VIVIANO or VIVIANI

Italian, Nineteenth Century

No biographical information has been found on this sculptor, who, on the basis of the signature and inscription, would seem to have been a late nineteenth-century Florentine professor of fine arts, perhaps at the Accademia del Disegno.

Rebecca at the Well   (79.19)

Marble, 43 x 14 1/2 x 12 in. (109.2 x 36.8 x 30.5 cm). Inscribed on the rear of the sculpture: "Prof. G. Viviano [or Viviani]" and "Galleria P. Bazzanti Firenze."

Provenance: Galleria P. Bazzanti, Florence; collection of Miss Frances F. Gumina; her gift to the University, 1979, in memory of her parents, Sam and Concetta Gumina.

This work is an especially attractive example of a type of popular sculpture most current in the late nineteenth century. In it the single medium (of, most usually, white marble) is abandoned in favor of a variety of white and colored stone. The desired effect is to increase the verisimilitude of the sculpture by utilizing different stone to simulate disparate materials—in this case, drapery, jewelry, rope, and a pitcher.

The story of Rebecca is related in the twenty-fourth chapter of Genesis. Abraham sent his servant Eliezer to Mesopotamia to find a wife for his son Isaac. At a well at which he stopped to water his camels, Eliezer was met by Rebecca "with her pitcher upon her shoulder."

> And the damsel was very fair to look upon, a virgin, neither had any man known her: and she went down to the well, and filled her pitcher, and came up. And the servant ran to meet her, and said, Let me, I pray thee, drink a little water of thy pitcher. And she said, Drink, my lord: and she hasted, and let down her pitcher upon her hand, and gave him drink. And when she had done giving him drink, she said, I will draw water for thy camels also, until they have done drinking (Genesis 24:16-19).

Rebecca at the Well, G. Viviano (Viviani ?), marble

Rebecca's generosity and humility—later interpreted as an Old Testament type for the Virgin Mary—demonstrated to Eliezer her destiny as the wife of Isaac.

In the present work—as in so many of its kind—the subject seems to be incidental to the artist's purpose. The sculpture seems not so much a portrayal of the scene of Rebecca at the Well as it is a representation of any beautiful and somewhat timid young woman. Although the multicolored marbles perhaps do not increase the viewer's belief in the sentience of the figure, they do both convey a sense of luxury by their extravagant use and heighten the effect of the smoothness and purity of the face, arms, and feet of Rebecca.

R. B. S.

TWENTIETH CENTURY

PETER STEYER

Czechoslovakian (1927-   )

Peter Steyer was born in Senica, near Pressburg, Czechoslovakia, in 1927.[1] His artistic education began at the Akademie der bildenden Künste in Vienna, which he attended from 1944 to 1945. After the war Steyer became a pupil of Richard Scheibe at the Hochschule für bildende Künste in Berlin. He received the Georg Kolbe Prize for sculpture in 1953 and has exhibited extensively in Germany since then. An archaeologist as well as a sculptor, Steyer participated in the important digs at Uruk-Warka in Iraq (1954-1956) and at Hattusa-Boggazköy in Turkey. From 1957 to 1965 Steyer lived in Istanbul, where he was attached to the Deutsches Archäologische Institut. Since 1965 he has practiced exclusively as a sculptor in Germany.

Porträt Amir (Portrait of Amir), 1955
(80.25.1)

Bronze, 16 1/2 x 9 1/2 x 9 1/2 in. (41.9 x 24.1 x 24.1 cm). Inscribed center left with initials, "P.S."; and stamped lower left at base with the foundry mark of H. Noack, Berlin.

pathy and perhaps affection, which is underscored by an introspective mood heightened by the simple planes and classical format of the bust.

R. B. S.

Notes:
1. Albert Steyer, *Peter Steyer*, exhibition catalogue (Cologne, n.d.).

Porträt Amir (Portrait of Amir), Peter Steyer, bronze

Provenance: Galerie Abels, Cologne (?); collection of Mr. Joseph P. Antonow; his gift to the University, 1980.

References:
Hermann Noack, in a letter (1981), confirming the attribution to Steyer.

Peter Steyer, in a letter (1981), affirming his authorship of the work.

The *Portrait of Amir* (*Porträt Amir*) was modeled by Steyer during his stay in Iraq in 1955. It is a sensitive rendering of an Arab youth, whose pensive features are contained beneath the smooth contours of his hooded dress. Steyer's subject is handled with sym-

RÉNÉ LALIQUE

French (1860–1945)

Réné Lalique was born in the village of Ay (Marne).[1] From his youth his artistic interests were devoted to the medium of glass, but recognition of his innovative work came much later, beginning with his taking prizes at the Salons of 1895, 1896, and 1897. Lalique initially worked at the École des Arts Décoratifs, and his success eventually brought him his own glassworks, which survives to this day. He was the first modern figure to utilize glass in jewelry, and he developed a variety of techniques to create the frosted, etched, and opalescent glass for which he became best known. Lalique was a pioneer in developing the architectural use of glass, fabricating doors, windows, fountains, even complete furnished environments. He is best known, however, for small elegant glass objects, from bottles, glasses, lamps, and automobile mascots to devotional pieces.

The Crucifixion (81.24)

Glass, 12 5/8 x 6 9/16 x 1 1/2 in. (32.1 x 16.7 x 3.8 cm). Inscribed (stamped) l.r. margin: "R. Lalique France."

Provenance: Collection of Mr. and Mrs. Robert L. Pagel, Sr.; their gift to the University, 1981.

The Crucifixion is one of several glass plaques of religious subjects made by Lalique; others include representations of the Virgin and Child, St. Theresa, and the Last Supper.[2] The precise date of the *Crucifixion* is not known but would seem to be around 1930, about the time that Lalique was involved with a number of religious projects. The most prominent of these were two complete chapels in glass. The first, exhibited at the Salon d'Automne in 1930, was made for the high altar of the Chapelle de la Vierge Fidèle at the Convent of Delivrande in Caen (Calvados).[3] A larger chapel, with a cross but no crucifix, was commissioned in 1932 for St. Matthew's Church at St.-Helier on the Isle of Jersey.[4]

R. B. S.

The Crucifixion, Réné Lalique, glass

Notes:
1. On Lalique, see Marc and Marie-Claude Lalique, eds., *Lalique par Lalique* (Lausanne, 1977); Christopher Vane Percy, *The Glass of Lalique; a collector's guide* (New York, 1977); and Katharine M. McClinton, *Lalique for Collectors* (New York, 1975).
2. McClinton, *Lalique for Collectors*, 77. Another example of the *Crucifixion*, illustrated by McClinton, is in the Toledo Museum of Art.
3. Lalique and Lalique, eds., *Lalique par Lalique*, 159f.
4. Ibid., 146f.

WILHELM LEHMBRUCK

German (1881–1919)

The son of a miner, Wilhelm Lehmbruck was born in 1881 in the German village of Meiderich near Duisberg.[1] At fourteen he entered the School of Arts and Crafts in Düsseldorf and six years later began work at the Düsseldorf Academy, where he ultimately served as the chief assistant to the sculptor Karl Janssen. He visited Paris in 1908 and moved his studio there two years later. Lehmbruck's work at the time was deeply indebted to Rodin's, an influence that seems to have ended abruptly following the young sculptor's meeting with his hero.

His first work in Paris, the *Standing Female Figure* (*Die grosse Stehende*) of 1910, was conservative and still somewhat academic in nature. With his major sculpture of the following year, the *Kneeling Woman* (*Die Knieende*), Lehmbruck's style underwent a dramatic change: All robustness vanished in that conception of a spidery kneeling figure with elongated limbs—an ideal human figure, but one conceived outside of the classical tradition.[2] The *Kneeling Woman* was exhibited at the Salon d'Automne in 1911; it was instantly controversial and evoked strong critical comment, both enthusiastic and negative. It appeared in many exhibitions in the years following, including the famous New York Armory Show of 1913 and the Cologne Sonderbund Exhibition in 1912, where it was called the "symbol of Expressionism."[3]

With the outbreak of World War I, Lehmbruck was obliged to leave France. He lived in Berlin from 1914 to 1917, then in Zurich. Through the exhibition of his works at many important shows, Lehmbruck became internationally celebrated. He returned to Berlin, where, at the peak of his fame, he committed suicide in March 1919.

It has been suggested that Lehmbruck's art is "best understood through comparison with modern dance or ballet, in which emotional states are symbolized through pose and dramatic gesture."[4] This introspective, unheroic quality was ill-suited to the artistic taste of Nazi Germany, and many of Lehmbruck's works were banned, sold or destroyed. The *Head of a Kneeling Woman* (literally, *Inclined Head of a Woman*) was included in the notorious exhibition of "degenerate art" (Entartete Kunst) held in Munich in 1937. At the same time the work became a symbol of the repression of artistic freedom in Europe.[5]

Geneigter Frauenkopf (Called Head of a Kneeling Woman), 1911   (64.15)

Bronze, 16 1/2 x 16 x 9 in. (41.9 x 40.6 x 22.9 cm). Inscribed on the back: "W.Lehmbruck" and "5/1."

137

Geneigter Frauenkopf (Head of a Kneeling Woman), Wilhelm Lehmbruck, bronze

Provenance: Collection of Mr. Joseph P. Antonow, Chicago; his gift
to the University, 1964.

References:
Pick, *Marquette University Art Collection*, 13 (ill.), 14.

German Expressionism from Milwaukee Collections, catalogue of an
exhibition at the Fine Arts Galleries, University of Wisconsin-
Milwaukee (Milwaukee, 1979), no. 85 (ill.).

Carter, *Grain of Sand*, 4, 15 (ill.), no. 69.

The *Geneigter Frauenkopf* is a bust-length version,
devised by the artist, of *The Kneeling Woman* (*Die
Knieende*), Lehmbruck's most famous and perhaps
most influential work.[6] The full-length figure exists in
several examples. What is probably the oldest, in cast
stone, is in the Albright-Knox Gallery in Buffalo.[7]

Another stone example, formerly in the Mannheim
Kunsthalle, is at the Museum of Modern Art in New
York. A third stone cast, sold from the Dresden Alber-
tinum, is currently in the Collection of Walter Chrysler
(New York). A stone version once in Munich was de-
stroyed by the Nazis. Bronze casts of the work are in the
Wilhelm Lehmbruck Museum in Duisberg and the Lan-
desmuseum in Mainz; a recent bronze cast is at the
Metropolitan Opera House in New York. Two plaster
versions survive—one in Duisberg and another, a frag-
mentary sketch model, in the Nationalgalerie in East
Berlin.[8]

The *Head*, which is essentially the *Kneeling Woman*
truncated at her breasts, also survives in several casts.
A cast stone example is in the Art Institute of Chicago,[9] and another was formerly in the Museum at

Chemnitz. Terra-cotta versions are in Duisberg, Buffalo, Frankfurt, and recently, on the art markets of Cologne and Düsseldorf.[10] A bronze from the family of the artist is in the collection of the Lehmbruck Museum in Duisberg, and another cast is in the Österreichische Galerie in Vienna.[11]

The *Kneeling Woman* is an eerie, spiritual work; although its "limb architecture," the attenuated representation of a figure kneeling, seems its most prominent feature, it is Lehmbruck's theoretical conceptualization that was so revolutionary. This has been characterized as an attempt to "express thought and emotion through movement and expressive distortion...; here, tallness is combined with exaggerated slenderness, [and] the mood becomes otherworldly, introspective, even melancholy."[12]

The large scale and uneasy pose of the *Kneeling Woman* suggest not only external movement but also the contained activity of growth.[13] Such nuance might necessarily seem lost in the smaller *Head*, although the reduction was carefully conceived by Lehmbruck to create "a concentrated variation on the melancholy, contemplative, ethereal existence of the full figure."[14]

R. B. S.

Notes:

1. On Lehmbruck see, most recently, Dietrich Schubert, *Die Kunst Lehmbrucks* (Worms, 1981); *Hommage à Lehmbruck; Lehmbruck in seiner Zeit*, catalogue of an exhibition (Duisberg, 1981-1982); and Reinhold Heller, *The Art of Wilhelm Lehmbruck*, catalogue of an exhibition (Washington, 1972). See as well Werner Hofmann, *Wilhelm Lehmbruck* (London, 1958); August Hoff, *Wilhelm Lehmbruck; Leben und Werk* (Berlin, 1961), and Paul Westheim, *Wilhelm Lehmbruck* (Potsdam, 1922).

2. On this work, see as well Eduard Trier, introduction to *Wilhelm Lehmbruck: Die Knieende*, Reclams Werkmonographien, 32 (Stuttgart, 1958).

3. H. Hildebrandt, as the "Sinnbild des Expressionismus," quoted in Trier, *Wilhelm Lehmbruck*, 6.

4. Andrew C. Ritchie, ed., *Catalogue of Contemporary Paintings and Sculpture; The Buffalo Fine Arts Academy; Albright Art Gallery* (Buffalo, 1949), 186.

5. *Hommage à Lehmbruck*, 44.

6. Schubert, *Die Kunst Lehmbrucks*, 8.

7. Ritchie, *Catalogue of Contemporary Paintings and Sculpture*, 186, 211. The Buffalo example was the one exhibited at the Armory Show.

8. Schubert, *Die Kunst Lehmbrucks*, 143f; Trier, *Wilhelm Lehmbruck*, 7.

9. Acc. no. 39.406; illustrated in the *Art Institute of Chicago Bulletin* (March 1940):41-42. I wish to thank Ian Wordropper of the Art Institute for his assistance in obtaining information on this example.

10. *Wilhelm Lehmbruck; Aristide Maillol*, catalogue of an exhibition (New York, 1930), no. 2. Westheim, *Wilhelm Lehmbruck*, 48, fig. 31. Sale Lempertz, Cologne, November 24, 1972. With Galerie Wilhelm Grosshennig, Düsseldorf, 1979.

11. Heller, *Art of Wilhelm Lehmbruck*, no. 23 (ill.), for the Duisberg bronze; inv. no. 4371 for the Vienna example.

12. Ritchie, *Catalogue of Contemporary Paintings and Sculpture*, 186.

13. W. R. Valentiner, "The Simile in Sculptural Composition," *Art Quarterly* X, no. 4 (Autumn 1947):264.

14. Heller, *Art of Wilhelm Lehmbruck*, 26.

PAUL SPECK

Swiss (1896–1966)

Paul Speck was born in 1896 in the Swiss town of Hombrechtikon.[1] From 1914 to 1924 he lived in Munich, until 1919 as a student of the painter Stanislaus Stückgold. He began working in ceramics about the age of sixteen and became quite proficient in subsequent years. By 1924 he was teaching ceramics at the State Majolica factory in Karlsruhe and sculpture at the Badischen Landeskunstschule. In 1934 he returned to Switzerland; the year before he had received a major commission for the altarpiece in white majolica of St. Karls Kirche in Lucerne. From 1956 until his death ten years later he lived in Tegna (Tessin) and Zurich.

Speck was a sculptor, ceramicist, and draftsman of some distinction, but his fame has been largely local. His style can be generically termed "semirepresentational," incorporating as it does figural elements into massive, abstract forms. He worked in a variety of media—as a sculptor, largely in plaster, granite, and bronze.

Death Mask of James Joyce, After Paul Speck, bronze

AFTER PAUL SPECK
Death Mask of James Joyce   (77.10)

Bronze, 12 x 7 x 6 1/2 in. (30.5 x 17.8 x 16.5 cm). Unsigned.

Provenance: Collection of Mr. Paul J. Polansky; his gift to the University, 1977.

References:
Paul Polansky, in a letter (1978), as taken from the original plaster cast by Paul Speck and cast in bronze by sculptor John Beehan.

James Joyce died in the Red Cross Hospital of Zurich on January 13, 1941. The task of taking a death mask of the writer was given to Paul Speck. From the direct casting of Joyce's features, the sculptor then finished the head, completing and refining minor details such as the hair and ears.

Sculptors have traditionally taken death masks from the noted and noble, often to serve as models for subsequent portraits.[2] Speck's mask of Joyce is a relatively straightforward translation of his subject's final visage, but one that is, for those familiar with Joyce's features, nonetheless unexpected:

> The death mask of James Joyce, taken by the sculptor Paul Speck, at first surprises one, the face seems so unfamiliar. This is because the thick glasses, which he seldom removed, are no longer there. The face is that of a weary man; the two lines of his forehead are deep, the cheeks are sunken; the face is not relaxed in death, but about the tightly closed lips there seems to be the faint flicker of a smile.[3]

The Marquette bronze was taken from the original plaster mask owned by Dublin architect Michael Scott, who with John Houston founded the James Joyce Museum (Martello Tower) in Dublin.[4] (The Museum and its contents were subsequently sold to the Ireland Eastern Regional Tourism Organization, and it is not known whether the original mask was included in the sale.)

Apparently very few casts of Joyce's death mask exist today. Two masks were done by Speck at the time of Joyce's death. Joyce's son, Georgio, has one, as does his grandson Stephen. Other existing casts are located at the Abbey Theater in Dublin; the private collection of Carla Gideon;[5] and the Crossman Collection of the University of Southern Illinois Library.[6] Another cast is reproduced as the frontispiece to the memorial volume that appeared shortly after his death.[7]

R. B. S. / C. L. C.

Notes:
1. On Speck's career see *Paul Speck; Monographie* (Zurich, 1974); Felix Baumann, *Paul Speck 1896-1966,* exhibition catalogue (Zurich, 1970); and "Paul Speck," in *Künstler Lexikon der Schweiz; XX.Jahrhundert* (Frauenfeld, 1958-1967), II:912-914.
2. The history of death masks is treated in Ernest Benkard, *Das Ewige Antlitz* (Berlin, 1926), and Rosemarie Clausen, *Die Vollendeten* (Stuttgart, 1941).
3. *James Joyce: A Portrait* (New York, 1957), 39.
4. Correspondence from Paul Polansky, April 13, 1978.
5. Ibid.
6. Reproduced in Chester G. Anderson, *James Joyce and His World* (London, 1967), 127.
7. *In Memoriam: James Joyce* (Zurich, 1941).

SPECIAL
COLLECTIONS

THE NORBERT J. BEIHOFF COLLECTION OF IVORIES

The use of ivory as a sculptural medium is as old as our civilization. Paleolithic artifacts, carved from elephant and mammoth tusks, attest to its antiquity, and its use has been both universal and continuous since. Partly as a function of its rarity (and durability), ivory sculpture has always been sought after, and thus it is not surprising that, in addition to its connotations of luxury, the material has been associated with magical and religious properties in various cultures. Marquette is fortunate in having a fascinating collection of works in ivory, a group that in its variety can serve as an introduction to sculptural art in the medium.

UNKNOWN ARTIST

Flemish, 19th century (?)

Libation Cup   (63.11)

Ivory, 7 1/16 x 1 3/4 x 1 3/4 in. (18.1 x 4.5 x 4.5 cm). Unsigned.

UNKNOWN ARTIST

Goan, early 19th century

Madonna and Child   (63.15)

Ivory, 20 1/2 x 4 1/2 x 4 in. (52.1 x 11.4 x 10.2 cm). Unsigned.

Reference:
Norbert J. Beihoff, *Ivory Sculpture through the Ages* (Milwaukee, 1961), 78 (ill.)

UNKNOWN ARTIST

Spanish/Portuguese, 18th–19th century

Mary Magdalene   (63.14)

Ivory, 7 7/8 x 2 3/8 x 2 in. (20 x 6 x 5.1 cm). Unsigned.

Reference:
Norbert J. Beihoff, *Ivory Sculpture through the Ages* (Milwaukee, 1961), 22 (ill.), as a Madonna.

Libation Cup, Flemish, Nineteenth Century (?), ivory

142

St. Anthony of Padua and Christ Child, Italian, Eighteenth Century, ivory

Monk, Spanish, Seventeenth Century, ivory

St. Sebastian, French, Nineteenth Century, ivory·

UNKNOWN ARTIST

Spanish, 17th century

Monk   (63.16)

Ivory, 19 7/8 x 5 3/4 x 4 in. (50.5 x 14.6 x 10.2 cm).
Unsigned.

Reference:
Robert J. Beihoff, *Ivory Sculpture through the Ages* (Milwaukee,
1961), 78 (ill.).

UNKNOWN ARTIST

Italian, 18th century

St. Anthony of Padua and Christ Child   (63.13)

Ivory, 5 x 1 1/2 x 1 1/8 in. (12.7 x 3.8 x 2.9 cm).
Unsigned.

UNKNOWN ARTIST

French, 19th century

St. Sebastian   (63.9)

Ivory, 6 1/4 x 1 5/8 x 1 3/8 in. (15.9 x 4.1 x 3.5 cm).
Unsigned.

Reference:
Robert J. Beihoff, *Ivory Sculpture through the Ages* (Milwaukee,
1961), 22 (ill.).

UNKNOWN ARTIST

French, mid-19th century

Seated Moon Sprite   (63.10)

Ivory, 17 1/16 x 8 x 6 1/4 in. (43.3 x 20.3 x 15.9 cm).
Unsigned.

Provenance: Collection of Mr. Norbert J. Beihoff; his gift to the University, 1963.

One of the most striking works is the large *Madonna and Child* (back cover ill.), whose elongated, slightly curved shape reflects the original contour of the tusk from which it was carved. Patterned after fourteenth-century French Burgundian types, this elegant figure holds nonetheless an oriental flavor, its repeating stylized drapery folds complementing the subtle round forms of its model. This combination of Eastern and

Western styles suggests that the *Madonna* may have originated in the Portuguese colony of Goa in India, where in the seventeenth century an ivory carving school was established by Jesuit missionaries. Somewhat similar in style, although not based on a medieval prototype, is the *Monk* (see ill. p. 143), a figure no doubt meant to represent a Franciscan saint. More in keeping with traditional Spanish and Portuguese styles is the standing *Mary Magdalene* (Acc. No. 63.14), seen with her arms held together in prayer, her long hair distinguishing her from an image of the Madonna.

Two figures of saints of roughly contemporary date illustrate the variety of sculptural styles employed. In the *St. Anthony of Padua and Christ Child* (see ill. p. 143), a traditional iconographic type is rendered in a blocky, straightforward manner, its rigidity perhaps meant to accentuate the religious purpose. The *St. Sebastian*, in contrast, seems to have been carved less as an object of veneration than as one of delectation—the sensuousness of the youth's body emphasized by the polished surface of the ivory.

Among secular items one might mention the small *Libation Cup* (see ill. p. 142), with its fanciful rendering of dancing putti surmounting the grotesque figure of a naked woman. And, perhaps the most beautiful among the purely decorative pieces, the *Seated Moon Sprite*, a mid-nineteenth-century French work, who gazes pensively into the distance as she sits enveloped in a variety of intricately carved vegetation.

R. B. S.

Seated Moon Sprite, French, Mid-nineteenth Century, ivory

THE A. J. CONROY COLLECTION OF MINIATURE PAINTINGS

Portrait miniatures originated in fifteenth-century Europe, a combination of the form of portrait medals and the technique of illuminated manuscripts. The term itself connotes its medieval ancestry: *minium* is the term for the red lead pigment used in writing the rubrics in manuscripts. The earliest autonomous portrait miniatures—those not done as part of books or manuscripts—appeared in Flanders, but it was not until the emigration to England of one of the most noted practitioners of the art, Gerard Horenbout, that the miniature portrait became established as a form. At the court of Henry VIII Horenbout and his family, together with the great portraitist Hans Holbein the Younger, initiated the long tradition of English miniature painting, an art form that did not wane in popularity until the advent of photography.

American miniature painting began in the second half of the eighteenth century, essentially as a provincial offshoot of the English school. Its history is relatively short, beginning in cities with the work of Charles Willson Peale and his son Rembrandt Peale in the late 1700s and ending in rural areas with the arrival of itinerant portrait photographers at the end of the nineteenth century.

ATTRIBUTED TO RICHARD COSWAY

English (1742-1821)

Portrait of a Woman in a White Ruffled Gown and Hat (81.28.5)

Watercolor on ivory, 2 x 2 3/4 in. (5.1 x 7 cm). Unsigned.

Provenance: Collection of A. J. Conroy; anonymous gift to the University, 1981.

ATTRIBUTED TO RICHARD CROSSE

English (1742-1810)

Portrait of a Gentleman (81.28.1)

Watercolor on ivory, 1 1/2 x 1 3/4 in (3.8 x 4.5 cm). Unsigned.

Provenance: Collection of A. J. Conroy; anonymous gift to the University, 1981.

Portrait of a Woman in a White Ruffled Gown and Hat, Attributed to Richard Cosway, watercolor on ivory

AFTER CARLO DOLCI

Italian (1616-1686)

Mater Dolorosa (Mother of Sorrows) (80.28.1)

Enamel on porcelain, 4 1/2 x 3 1/2 in. (11.4 x 8.9 cm). Unsigned.

Provenance: Collection of A. J. Conroy; anonymous gift to the University, 1980.

Portrait of a Gentleman, Attributed to Richard Crosse, watercolor on ivory

include miniatures by or attributed to the English limners Richard Cosway, Richard Crosse, and the American Charles Willson Peale.

In addition to portraits a variety of other miniature paintings are included in the Conroy Collection, ranging from devotional images to copies of Old Master paintings. These, like the portraits, are mounted in a variety of ways that help to indicate the social function of the miniature. As a brooch, as a locket, a framed piece for the wall, or a bibelot on the mantlepiece—a miniature often had a use other than decorative: to memorialize a person, to substitute for a distant loved one, as something to keep close to one's heart.

The techniques of miniature painting vary somewhat but generally involve a watercolor medium on parchment or, after 1700, ivory. The related form of enameling, which involves fired paints on supports of copper and, later, ceramic, is represented as well in the Collection; one nineteenth-century example in an elaborate wooden frame is the oval plaque after Carlo Dolci's so-called *Blue Madonna*.

R. B. S.

Portrait of a Man in a Houndstooth Check Vest, Attributed to Charles Willson Peale, watercolor on ivory

ATTRIBUTED TO CHARLES WILLSON PEALE

American (1741–1827)

Portrait of a Man in a Houndstooth Check Vest (81.28.4)

Watercolor on ivory, 1 3/4 x 2 1/4 in. (4.5 x 5.7 cm). Unsigned.

Provenance: Collection of A. J. Conroy; anonymous gift to the University, 1981.

The A. J. Conroy Collection of Miniature Paintings provides a splendid introduction to the specialized world of the miniature. There are several hundred examples in the Collection, which is particularly strong in British and American portraits. Highlights

THE BARBARA MORGAN COLLECTION OF PHOTOGRAPHS

American-born photographer Barbara Morgan (1900-   ) resolved to become an artist when she discovered painting as a child.[1] Her studies at the University of California at Los Angeles (1919-1923), which included realist and abstract approaches to art, prepared her for a career in painting. She was introduced to photography by her late husband, Willard, a photographer and writer, whom she married in 1925. As a young instructor in art at U.C.L.A. in 1926, Morgan assisted Edward Weston in hanging an exhibition of his photographs and became a friend of Weston. Her own first realization that photography could be art came as a result of her husband's urgings and this experience with Weston's photographs. As an abstract painter Morgan experienced difficulty accepting the realism of photography as a legitimate art form. But she saw in Weston's realist photographs the potential for abstract symbolism.

In 1930 Morgan moved to New York; there she continued to paint, and in 1935 she established a photography studio and gradually moved into her work as an artist-photographer. In 1941 she moved her studio and home from New York City to Scarsdale, New York.

Morgan's photographic subjects include modern dance, photomontage, light drawings, people, nature, "junk," photograms, and miscellaneous experiments. Her work in all of these categories has been widely published in a series of books: *Martha Graham*, 1941; *Prestini's Art in Wood*, 1950; *Summer's Children*, 1951; *Barbara Morgan*, 1972, and *Barbara Morgan Photomontage*, 1980, as well as in many articles and books throughout the world.

Barbara Morgan is best known for her photographs of modern dancers taken primarily between 1935 and 1945, especially the photographs of Martha Graham, Merce Cunningham, Doris Humphrey, José Limón, Charles Weidman, and Valerie Bettis. The dance photographs were initially inspired by Morgan's having experienced Southwest Hopi and Navajo Indian ceremonial rituals during summer vacation periods between 1925 and 1930 with her husband Willard. The Indians' use of dance to unify their people in accordance with the fundamental "life forces of rhythm and motion," and not merely as entertainment, was a major influence. Morgan saw in Martha Graham's dances a similar interest in the Southwest Indian experiences.[2] This mutual interest between Morgan and Graham eventually led to collaboration on Morgan's first book of photographs: *Martha Graham: Sixteen Dances in Photographs*. Morgan's unique insight into the dances of Graham reveals their common interest in philosophical as well as movement aspects of dance. Morgan sees Graham first as a philosopher who "dances because philosophically this is the way she sees life or wants to interpret life."[3] The dance photographs can be appreciated for their high artistic merit as well as for their documentation of this important period of American dance.

Photomontage (combining two or more images through combination printing, sandwiching negatives together, pre-planned double exposure, re-photographing of collaged photographs, and/or a combination of these according to a visual concept) provided the vehicle for Morgan's initial transition from abstract painting to artistic photography. Again her interest in photomontage comes basically from a philosophical interest in metaphoric comparisons, showing for instance a fossil or a shell against the forms of a city as in *Fossil in Formation, 1965*, and *City Shell, 1938*. Photomontage allowed Morgan to express the complexities of the world, often juxtaposing nature, made environments, and people to convey whimsical or playful or sharply critical or ironic social commentary, as in the photographs, *Brainwashed, 1966* and *Nuclear Fossilization, 1979*.

Morgan's experiments with light drawings derive from Oriental ink drawings that she encountered as a student and teacher, and from her childhood experiences of "making pictures" by manipulating sun rays through the holes of a sun hat. Her photographic light drawings are images of light patterns created with a flashlight tied to the moving wrist and projected on a black cloth. Varying the rhythmic patterns and speeds of the wrist motion created lines of different widths and shapes.

In photographing people, Morgan thinks of them in relation to the world and not merely as individuals. Her photographs of people express a concern with human values in a mechanical world and sometimes reveal ironic comparisons. Her interest in the universal themes of human behavior is expressed in photographs showing a vast cross-section of the emotional, philosophical, and practical dimensions of life in so many different stages: youth and age, the fearful and the joyous, the emotive and the contemplative. Instead of emphasizing physiognomy, Morgan tries to create "visual representations of the inner activities of the human mind."[4] The photographs of children as represented in the book *Summer's Children*, 1951, are primarily from a period of her own life when her children Douglas (1932-   ) and Lloyd (1935-   ) were growing up. Several were photographed at Camp Treetops near Lake Placid, New York, "where children of varied backgrounds were in touch with nature."[5]

Many of Morgan's nature photographs reveal a strong sense of organic rhythmic form and motion. She sees her photographs of nature as "metaphors of cosmic dances: the corn leaf, for example, exhibits in rhythmic metre nature's life force."[6]

"Junk," as in *Broken Light Bulb, 1934* or *Battered Tin Can, 1942*, represents the inevitable metabolism of life as it is seen through Morgan's eyes.

The remaining corpus of Morgan's photographs falls into the miscellaneous categories of photograms (silhouette photographs made by placing objects directly upon sensitized paper and exposing it to light), "Southwest" pictures taken primarily between 1925 and 1930 before Morgan had decided to pursue photography as an art, and "experiments." Her works in all of the categories discussed here represent "a search for the invisible energies of life." She tries to express these inner life forces through the exterior visual forms of photography.

Morgan used many cameras to produce these photographs, but the principal ones were the 4 x 5 Speed Graphic, used in the dance photographs, and the Leica, used for photographing children. "The Speed Graphic is my choice when the pictures are to be built with light as are the dance photographs for my book, *Martha Graham*, and other work in that field."[7] (Morgan's husband Willard wrote the first Leica manual and was instrumental in promoting its use.)

Morgan's photographs have been exhibited in major museums across the world and are represented in such collections as the Museum of Modern Art, New York; the Smithsonian Institution, Washington, D.C.; the International Museum of Photography, Rochester; the collection of the Library of Congress, Washington, D.C.; the Lincoln Center Library and Museum of Performing Arts, New York; the Philadelphia Museum of Art, Philadelphia; and in many other museum, university, and private collections.

A retrospective exhibition of 113 Barbara Morgan photographs constituted the President's Exhibition at Marquette University, October 2-30, 1977. Morgan was awarded an honorary Doctor of Fine Arts degree from Marquette University in 1978. In 1983 a collection of approximately 400 vintage prints was acquired by an anonymous patron, intended for donation to the art museum at Marquette. When the transfer is completed the Marquette collection will represent the major existing assemblage of Morgan's vintage works.

In addition to the promised gift mentioned above the collection at Marquette presently includes a limited edition dance portfolio given by Mr. and Mrs. John Ogden (discussed below) and forty miscellaneous prints of dance, photomontage, and people given by Douglas and Lloyd Morgan.

At age eighty-four Morgan maintains an active schedule of exhibitions, lectures, and archival printing as she prepares her book, *Dynamics of Composition*.

Barbara Morgan
Dance Photographs,
1935–1944   (78.1.1-.10)

Limited edition portfolio of ten photographs, published by Morgan and Morgan, Dobbs Ferry, New York, 1977; portfolio size: 17 3/8 x 21 7/8 x 1 3/4 in (44.1 x 55.6 x 4.4 cm); archivally printed; individually signed.

Martha Graham—
Frontier, 1935   (78.1.1)

10 5/8 x 13 9/16 in. (27 x 34.5 cm). Signed in pencil l.r.: "Barbara Morgan 1935"; l.l.: "Martha Graham Frontier."

Martha Graham—
Lamentation (Oblique), 1935   (78.1.2)

13 1/8 x 10 7/16 in. (33.3 x 26.5 cm). Signed in pencil l.r.: "Barbara Morgan—1935"; l.l.: "Martha Graham Lamentation."

Martha Graham—
Letter to the World
(Kick), 1940   (78.1.3)

10 1/4 x 13 1/4 in. (26 x 33.7 cm). Signed in pencil l.r.: "Barbara Morgan—1940"; l.l.: "Martha Graham— Letter to the World."

Martha Graham—
Letter to the World
(Duet with Merce Cunningham
"Dear March Come In"), 1940   (78.1.4)

10 3/16 x 13 3/8 in. (25.9 x 34 cm). Signed in pencil l.r.: "Barbara Morgan 1940"; l.l.: "Martha Graham— Letter to the World (Duet with Cunningham—'Dear March Come In')."

Martha Graham-Letter to the World (Kick), Barbara Morgan, photograph

Martha Graham—
Ekstasis (Torso), 1938   (78.1.5)

13 1/4 x 10 1/8 in. (33.7 x 25.7 cm). Signed in pencil
l.r.: "Barbara Morgan—1938"; l.l.: "Martha Graham—
Ekstasis."

Martha Graham—
El Penitente (Solo—Erick
Hawkins—El Flagellante),
1940   (78.1.6)

13 3/8 x 10 3/8 in. (34 x 26.4 cm). Signed in pencil
l.r.: "Barbara Morgan 1940"; l.l.: "Martha Graham—
El Penitente—(Solo—Hawkins—El Flagellante)."

Charles Weidman—Lynchtown (Humphrey-Weidman Group), 1938   (78.1.7)

9 3/4 x 13 1/2 in. (24.8 x 34.3 cm). Signed in pencil l.r.: "Barbara Morgan—1938"; l.l.: "Charles Weidman-Lynchtown (Humphrey-Weidman Group)."

José Limón—Mexican Suite (Peon), 1944   (78.1.8)

10 3/16 x 13 1/2 in. (25.9 x 34.3 cm). Signed in pencil l.r.: "Barbara Morgan—1944"; l.l.: "José Limón—Mexican Suite—Peon."

Pearl Primus—Speak to Me of Rivers, 1944   (78.1.9)

10 3/8 x 13 1/2 in. (26.4 x 34.3 cm). Signed in pencil l.r.: "Barbara Morgan 1944"; l.l.: "Pearl Primus—Speak to Me of Rivers."

Doris Humphrey— Passacaglia, 1938   (78.1.10)

13 1/4 x 10 1/2 in. (33.7 x 26.7 cm). Signed in pencil l.r.: "Barbara Morgan—1938"; l.l.: "Doris Humphrey-Passacaglia."

Provenance: Purchased from the artist by Mr. and Mrs. John Ogden; their gift to the University, 1978.

References:
Barbara Morgan, *Martha Graham: Sixteen Dances in Photographs* (1941; reprint, Dobbs Ferry, N.Y., 1980), ill. 21, 34, 125, 120, 41, 91.

Barbara Morgan, *Barbara Morgan* (Hastings-on-Hudson, N.Y., 1972), ill. 42, 48, 54, 35.

The portfolio consists of a limited selection of Morgan's dance photographs executed between 1935 and 1944. Martha Graham's dances are represented in six of the ten images, with the dances of Charles Weidman, José Limón, Pearl Primus, and Doris Humphrey occupying the remaining four prints. Two of Morgan's most famous photographs, *Letter to the World (Kick)*, 1940 and *Lamentation (Oblique)*, 1935, are included. Morgan's photographs as represented here constitute a major record of American dance during the 1930s and 1940s. Her photographs capture the moods, expression, and philosophical ideas incorporated into the dances as well as their rhythmic and other movement aspects.

None of the photographs was taken during public performances; they were conceived and lighted by Morgan and produced entirely in Morgan's studio or in a theater at Columbia University. "Before I would ever photograph, I would get Martha Graham to tell me her inspiration for the dance. Then I would be invited by Martha to see the dances in small and large theaters." These experiences enabled Morgan to select from a dance of twenty or thirty minutes the crucial moments and gestures to express the emotional, philosophical, and aesthetic aspects of the dances. These selected moments were photographed as the dancers performed privately before Morgan's camera and were done in a spirit of mutual artistic collaboration, particularly in the relationship of Morgan and Graham.

This limited edition portfolio is the only such project that Morgan has assembled in her entire career. Apparently she has little interest in such projects, preferring instead to concentrate on the artistic and conceptual aspects of her work. The selection of photographs for the portfolio was made in consultation with Martha Graham and other members of the dance community, curators of photography, and family members.

C. L. C.

Notes:
1. Much of the information presented here is taken directly from personal interviews between 1975 and 1984 by the author. Other principal sources include Morgan's books and articles (see References and the bibliographies of included items), and articles about Barbara Morgan from 1938 to the present (see bibliographies listed in works contained in the References here). Sources of particular relevance are: Leonard N. Amico and Stephen Ross Edidin, *The Photographs of Barbara Morgan*, catalogue of an exhibition at Williams College Museum of Art (Williamstown, Mass., 1978); Doris Hering, "Barbara Morgan: One of America's Great Dance Photographers Reflects on a Decade of Dance 1935-1945," *Dance Magazine* (July 1971):43-56; Beaumont New-Hall, *The History of Photography from 1839 to the Present Day* (New York, 1949), 158-159; *Encyclopedia of Photography* (New York, 1964), 13:2373-2375; Curtis L. Carter, *Barbara Morgan: Exhibition of Photographs*, catalogue of an exhibition at Marquette University, Milwaukee, Wis. (Milwaukee, 1977).
2. Carter, *Barbara Morgan: Exhibition of Photographs*, 2.
3. Amico and Edidin, *Photographs of Barbara Morgan*, 7.
4. Ibid., 6.
5. Barbara Morgan, "Working Thoughts," *Barbara Morgan* (Hastings-on-Hudson, New York, 1972), 155.
6. Carter, *Barbara Morgan: Exhibition of Photographs*, 2.
7. Amico and Edidin, *Photographs of Barbara Morgan*, 15.
8. Conversation with Barbara Morgan, June 24, 1984.

Martha Graham—Lamentation (oblique), Barbara Morgan, photograph

CATALOGUE CHECKLIST

Notes on the Catalogue Checklist

The works listed below represent a selection from the Marquette University Fine Art Collection and do not constitute a complete listing.

The listing is arranged first by medium; then alphabetically by artist. The works of each artist appear alphabetically by title.

Works that have not been attributed are listed under Unknown Artist and are arranged alphabetically by title.

Artist's nationality indicates country of birth. Dual nationalities have been given for artists born in one country who primarily worked in another.

The accession number assigned to a work is listed to the right of the title and date.

Dimensions are given in feet and inches and in centimeters. Height precedes width, and depth is also given for three-dimensional works. The abbreviation d. stands for diameter. Size is actual for paintings, sculptures, and decorative arts objects, and sheet for works on paper, unless otherwise noted.

A single asterisk next to a title indicates that the work is illustrated in the checklist section.

A double asterisk next to an artist's name indicates that a work or works by that artist are discussed and illustrated in the essay section.

Trial of Jan Hus, Karl-Friedrich Lessing, oil on canvas

Execution of Jan Hus, Karl-Friedrich Lessing, oil on canvas

Omegas Augen (The Eyes of Omega), Edvard Munch, lithograph

Jester Playing Guitar, Gino Severini, ink on paper

155

Domestic Shrine with Scene of the Marriage of St. Catherine,
Unknown Artist, oil on lapis lazuli with marble and semi-precious
stones

PAINTINGS

ALLOT, R.
Nationality Unknown (n.d.)
Wharf Scene   (00.421)
Oil on canvas, 29 3/8 x 39 3/4 in.
  (74.6 x 101 cm)
Anonymous Gift

BABCOCK, Richard E.
American (1887-   )
Père Marquette   (67.10)
Oil on canvas, 62 1/2 x 43 3/4 in.
  (158.8 x 111.1 cm)
Gift of Mr. and Mrs. Richard L. Kronzer

BARUCCI, Pietro, Attributed to
Italian (1845-1917)
Bulls in Roman Landscape   (63.20)
Oil on canvas, 24 7/8 x 43 3/4 in.
  (63.2 x 111.1 cm)
Gift of Mrs. George Raab

**BASSANO, Francesco
(Francesco da Ponte Il
Giovane), After ****
Italian (1549-1592)
*The Exodus of Moses and the
  Israelites*   (60.4)
Oil on canvas, 29 x 35 in. (73.7 x
  88.9 cm)
Gift of Mr. and Mrs. Marc B. Rojtman

**BAUDESSON, Nicolas,
Attributed to ****
French (1611-1680)
Still Life with Flowers   (66.11)
Oil on panel, 24 3/4 x 33 in. (62.9 x
  83.8 cm)
  Gift of Miss Paula Uihlein

BAUMGARTNER, Peter **
German (1834-1911)
A Scene at the Cobbler's, 1869
  (64.20)
Oil on canvas, 29 5/8 x 37 in. (75.2 x
  94 cm)
Gift of the René von Schleinitz
  Foundation

La Dolorosa (Our Lady of Sorrows),
Fr. Pedro Bedón, oil on canvas

BEDÓN, Fr. Pedro
Peruvian (c. 1556-1621)
*La Dolorosa (Our Lady of Sorrows)**
  (66.10)
Oil on canvas, 11 3/8 x 9 in. (28.9 x
  22.9 cm)
Gift of Dr. Miguel Valverde Ramis

BELLINI, Giovanni (?), After
Italian (1430-1516)
Madonna and Child   (66.16)
Oil on canvas, 25 x 18 3/4 in. (63.5
  x 47.6 cm)
Gift of Mr. and Mrs. Richard B. Flagg

BENT, Johannes van der **
Dutch (c. 1650-1690)
Wooded Landscape with Figures
  (63.19)
Oil on canvas, 23 1/2 x 32 1/8 in.
  (59.7 x 81.6 cm)
Gift of Mrs. George Raab

BERÇOT, Paul **
French (1898-1970)
Flight into Egypt, 1954   (57.3)
Oil on canvas, 39 1/4 x 31 7/8 in.
  (99.7 x 81 cm)
Gift of Mr. and Mrs. Charles Zadok

BERTIN, Roger
French (1915-   )
*Haut Montmartre (High on
  Montmartre)*   (80.17.16)
Oil on canvas, 19 3/4 x 39 1/4 in.
  (50.2 x 99.7 cm)
Gift of Mr. Paul P. Lipton

**BERTOJA, Jacopo Zanguidi,
  Attributed to**
Italian (1544-1574)
Madonna and Child with St. John
  (59.1)
Oil on panel, 21 3/4 x 18 3/4 in.
  (55.3 x 47.6 cm)
Gift of Mr. and Mrs. Marc B. Rojtman

BIERSTADT, Albert **
German/American (1830-1902)
View in the Yosemite Valley
  (83.48.1)
Oil on panel, 31 1/2 x 48 in. (80 x
  121.9 cm)
Gift of Brandt, Inc., in memory of Earl
  William and Eugenia Brandt Quirk

BLAKELOCK, Ralph Albert **
American (1847-1919)
Landscape at Sunset   (81.7)
Oil on panel, 11 1/2 x 14 7/8 in.
  (29.2 x 37.8 cm)
Gift of Miss Mary Black in memory of
  Mr. Harry Apple

BLANCH, Arnold
American (1896-1968)
Seashells and Flowers   (75.11.1)
Oil on canvas, 22 1/4 x 36 in.
  (56.5 x 91.4 cm)
Gift of Mrs. Irene Gayas Jungwirth

BOCCACCI, Marcello
Italian (1914-   )
Florence II   (61.19)
Oil on paperboard, 23 1/2 x 35 1/2 in.
  (59.7 x 90.2 cm)
Gift of Mr. David M. Solinger

BOGGS, Franklin
American (1914-   )
Interval of Adjustment, 1950
  (55.18)
Oil on masonite, 35 x 54 1/4 in.
  (88.9 x 137.8 cm)
Gift of Gimbel Brothers

BONFILE, S.
French (late 19th century-early 20th
  century)
Leisure Moments   (73.19)
Oil on canvas, 22 x 19 1/4 in.
  (55.9 x 48.9 cm)
Gift of Dr. and Mrs. Michael F.
  McCanles

BOSBOOM, Johannes
Dutch (1817-1891)
*Church Interior **   (71.5)
Oil on canvas, 19 x 15 in. (48.3 x
  38.1 cm) (sight)
Gift of Dr. and Mrs. Alfred Bader

Church Interior, Johannes Bosboom, oil on canvas

BRADLEY, Dorothy
American (1920-   )
Sundance Beach   (81.26.7)
Acrylic on canvas, 54 x 54 in. (137.2 x
   137.2 cm)
Gift of Mr. Frederick D. Gore

BRAMER, Leonard, Attributed to *
Dutch (1596-1674)
Discovery of Deuteronomy   (81.36)
Oil on panel, 14 1/2 x 19 1/2 in.
   (36.8 x 49.5 cm)
Gift of Mr. and Mrs. Eckhart G.
   Grohmann

BRINK, Guido P.
American (1913-   )
Portrait of Father Wade   (60.8)
Oil on canvas, 60 1/4 x 48 in. (153 x
   121.9 cm)
Gift of the artist

CABRERA, Miguel, Attributed to *
Mexican (1695-1768)
*The Holy Family During the Journey
   into Egypt*   (72.20)
Oil on copper, 26 1/8 x 19 3/4 in.
   (66.4 x 50.2 cm)
Gift of Dr. and Mrs. Alfred Bader

CALOGERO, Jean
Italian (1922-   )
Portrait of a Young Girl   (77.2)
Acrylic on canvas, 13 1/4 x 10 1/8 in.
   (33.7 x 25.7 cm)
Gift of Mr. and Mrs. Raymond F.
   Newman

CARNEO, Antonio, Attributed to *
Italian (1637-1692)
*Abimelech Restores Sarah to
   Abraham*   (81.23)
Oil on canvas, 49 5/8 x 46 in. (126.1 x
   116.8 cm) (sight)
Gift of Mr. and Mrs. Eckhart G.
   Grohmann

CECCONI, A.
Italian (1910-   )
Old Fisherman   (80.11.1)
Oil on canvas, 32 1/2 x 24 in. (82.6 x
   61 cm)
   Gift of Mr. and Mrs. Bernard Soref

**CLAEISSENS, Anthuenis, Attributed
to ***
Flemish (1536-1613)
The Story of Elijah   (60.3)
Oil on panel, 26 1/2 x 45 in. (67.3 x
   114.3 cm)
Gift of Mr. and Mrs. Marc B. Rojtman

CLEMENS, Paul Lewis
American (1911-   )
Portrait of Eliot Fitch   (70.3)
Oil on canvas, 48 x 39 3/4 in. (121.9
   x 101 cm)
Anonymous Gift

Portrait of Father O'Donnell   (73.9)
Oil on canvas, 45 x 35 1/2 in. (114.3
   x 90.2 cm)
Gift of the Marquette University
   Faculty and Staff

CORBELLINI, Luigi
Italian (1901-1968)
Girl with Black Headdress
   (75.16)
Oil on canvas, 8 3/4 x 10 3/4 in.
   (22.2 x 27.3 cm)
Gift of Mr. and Mrs. Raymond F.
   Newman

Young Girl with Cat   (75.19)
Oil on canvas, 11 3/8 x 10 1/4 in.
   (28.9 x 26 cm)
Gift of Mr. and Mrs. Raymond F.
   Newman

CORREA DE VIVAR, Juan *
Spanish (active 1539-1562)
The Lamentation of Mary over the Body of Christ with Angels Holding the Symbols of the Passion (58.5)
Oil on panel, 56 1/2 x 47 in. (143.5 x 119.4 cm)
Gift of Mr. and Mrs. Marc B. Rojtman

DALÍ, Salvador *
Spanish (1904-)
Madonna of Port Lligat, 1949 (59.9)
Oil on canvas, 19 1/2 x 15 1/16 in. (49.5 x 38.3 cm)
Gift of Mr. and Mrs. Ira Haupt

DIAZ DE LA PEÑA, Narcisse Virgile *
French (1808-1867)
Wooded Landscape (62.4)
Oil on panel, 11 3/4 x 16 1/2 in. (29.9 x 41.9 cm)
Gift of Dr. and Mrs. Francis J. Millen

DIX, Charles
American (1939-)
The Far Reaches of Infinity, 1967 (83.30)
Acrylic on masonite, 36 x 48 in. (91.4 x 121.9 cm)
Gift of Mrs. Geraldine Powers

Rose Space (68.3)
Acrylic on masonite, 48 x 36 1/8 in. (121.9 x 91.8 cm)
Gift of Mrs. Myra Peache

DOLCI, Carlo, After
Italian (1616-1686)
Madonna and Child (75.1)
Oil on canvas, 32 x 42 1/4 in. (81.3 x 107.3 cm)
Gift of Mr. and Mrs. Charles B. McCanna

DYCK, Anton van, After
Flemish (1599-1641)
Madonna and Child (70.6)
Oil on canvas, 41 x 33 1/2 in. (104.1 x 85.1 cm)
Gift of Dr. and Mrs. Alfred Bader

The Mocking of Christ (58.8)
Oil on canvas, 43 x 38 7/8 in. (109.2 x 98.7 cm)
Gift of Mr. and Mrs. Marc B. Rojtman

EBEFING (?)
Nationality Unknown (n.d.)
Bucolic Scene with Cattle (64.37)
Oil on canvas, 14 5/8 x 23 in. (37.2 x 58.4 cm)
Gift of Mr. Gardiner Dalton

EDIE, Stuart
American (1908-1974)
Viaduct
Oil on canvas, 9 1/4 x 11 1/4 in. (23.5 x 28.6 cm)
Promised gift of Mr. and Mrs. Marvin L. Fishman

ELLE, Louis I (called Ferdinand the Elder) *
French (1612-1689)
Portrait of Françoise Bertaut, 1664 (79.3)
Oil on canvas, 70 3/16 x 35 7/8 in. (178.3 x 91.1 cm)
Anonymous Gift

ERNST, Rudolph *
Austrian (1854-1932)
A Moor Robing after the Bath (82.1.1)
Oil on panel, 21 3/4 x 18 1/4 in. (55.2 x 46.4 cm)
Gift of the Estate of Claire Hoff Toole

FALKENBACH, Joseph F.
German (b. 1883)
Nativity Scene, 1949 (83.25.3S)
Oil on canvas, 56 x 34 1/2 in. (142.2 x 87.6 cm)
Gift of Mrs. Colet Coughlin

Return to Christ, 1956 (83.25.2S)
Oil on masonite, 45 5/8 x 26 7/8 in. (115.9 x 68.3 cm)
Gift of Mrs. Colet Coughlin

FESSLER, Sr. Mary Thomasita
American (1912-)
St. Josaphat Basilica, 1976 (82.14)
Mixed media collage on canvas, 52 1/2 x 44 in. (133.4 x 111.8 cm)
Gift of Mr. and Mrs. George E. Vander Beke

FIEDLER, Herbert
German (1891-1962)
Dorfstrasse mit rotem Haus (Village Street with Red House), 1924 * (83.26.1)
Oil on canvas, 20 1/4 x 24 1/4 in. (51.4 x 61.6 cm)
Gift of Mr. and Mrs. Marvin L. Fishman

Dorfstrasse mit rotem Haus (Village Street with Red House), Herbert Fiedler, oil on canvas

FRANCKEN, Ambrosius the Elder, Attributed to **
Flemish (1544-1618)
The Holy Family with Saints John the Baptist and Elizabeth (61.3)
Oil on canvas, 44 1/8 x 55 in. (112.1 x 139.7 cm)
Gift of Mr. and Mrs. Marc B. Rojtman

FRIEBERT, Joseph
American (1908-)
Street Workers (55.24)
Oil on masonite, 20 3/4 x 33 1/4 in. (52.7 x 84.5 cm)
Gift of Gimbel Brothers

FRIED, Otto
German (20th century)
Steel Workers (77.9)
Oil on canvas, 60 3/8 x 48 1/8 in. (153.4 x 122.2 cm)
Gift of Mrs. W. W. Busby

GAMP, Baron Botho von
German (b. 1894)
Rotes Gehöft (The Red Farm House), 1921
Oil on canvas, 33 x 38 5/8 in. (83.8 x 98.1 cm)
Promised gift of Mr. and Mrs. Marvin L. Fishman

GANSHEROFF, Samuel
American (1910-)
Homer's Odyssey and the World (65.7)
Oil on panel, 48 x 72 in. (121.9 x 182.9 cm)
Gift of the artist

GEN-PAUL (Eugène Paul) **
French (1895-1975)
The Cellist (57.2)
Oil on canvas, 45 5/8 x 29 1/8 in. (115.9 x 74 cm)
Gift of Mr. and Mrs. Charles Zadok

GERE, Byron
American (1896-1962)
Time Out, 1950 (55.22)
Oil on masonite, 18 7/8 x 40 in. (47.9 x 101.6 cm)
Gift of Gimbel Brothers

GHEZZI, Pier Leone **
Italian (1674-1755)
The Singing Monks (Matins) c. 1715-1730 (60.2)
Oil on canvas, 32 1/2 x 18 3/4 in. (82.6 x 47.6 cm)
Gift of Mr. and Mrs. Marc B. Rojtman

GHEZZI, Pier Leone, Attributed to **
Italian (1674-1755)
Portrait of Cardinal Giuseppe Renato Imperiali, c. 1710-1715 (73.17)
Oil on canvas, 51 1/4 x 38 1/2 in. (130.2 x 97.8 cm)
Gift of Schroeder Hotels, Inc.

GIRARD, André
French (1901-1968)
Christ's Instruction to the Disciples (58.10)
Oil on panel, 85 x 120 in. (215.9 x 304.8 cm)
Gift of the Boegner Foundation

The Twelve Apostles (58.11-.22)
Series of twelve oils on panel, 34 1/2 x 16 1/2 in. (87.6 x 41.9 cm)
Gift of the Boegner Foundation

GIRARD MASTER (possibly Pedro Girard) **
Spanish (active 15th century)
Saint Julian of Toledo (84.7.1)
Oil on panel, 54 x 18 in. (137.2 x 45.7 cm)
Gift of the Rojtman Foundation

GOOD, John R.
American (20th century)
Red Barn (61.16)
Oil on paperboard, 9 x 18 1/8 in. (22.9 x 46 cm)
Gift of Mr. Harry G. Sundheim, Jr.

GORTER, Arnold-Marc **
Dutch (1866-1933)
Scene along a Riverbank (82.1.2)
Oil on canvas, 28 7/8 x 35 5/8 in. (73.3 x 90.5 cm)
Gift of the Estate of Claire Hoff Toole

GOYEN, Jan van, After
Dutch (1596-1665)
The Meuse at Dordrecht (66.9)
Oil on canvas, 39 x 26 5/8 in. (99.1 x 67.6 cm)
Gift of Mr. and Mrs. Malcolm K. Whyte in memory of William Merrill Chester

GRIMM, J. P. P.
American (active mid-19th century)
St. Patrick, 1861 (83.25.1S)
Oil on canvas adhered to panel, 56 3/4 x 26 5/8 in. (144.2 x 67.6 cm)
Gift of Mrs. Colet Coughlin

GRÜTZNER, Eduard **
German (1846-1925)
Im Studierzimmer (In the Study), 1891 (64.7)
Oil on canvas, 24 1/8 x 18 1/2 in. (61.3 x 47 cm)
Gift of the René von Schleinitz Foundation

HADDON, Arthur Trevor
English (1864-1941)
Neapolitan Fountain (80.11.2)
Oil on canvas, 20 1/4 x 30 in. (51.4 x 76.2 cm)
Gift of Mr. and Mrs. Bernard Soref

HALLÉ, Noël, Attributed to
French (1711-1781)
Untitled (Scene with Two Cherubs) (72.3)
Oil on canvas, 15 1/4 x 11 1/4 in. (38.7 x 28.6 cm)
Gift of Mrs. Jetta Muntain Smith in memory of her son, Aurel Muntain

Untitled (Scene with Two Cherubs and Leopard) (72.4)
Oil on canvas, 15 1/4 x 11 1/4 in. (38.7 x 28.6 cm)
Gift of Mrs. Jetta Muntain Smith in memory of her son, Aurel Muntain

HARING, Keith
American (1958-)
Untitled (Mural for the Patrick and Beatrice Haggerty Museum of Art Construction Site), 1983 (83.12.3)
Oil on plywood, 96 x 8 ft. (29.3 x 2.4 m)
Gift of the artist

HEALY, George P. A.
American (1808-1894)
Portrait of William E. Cramer, 1884 (22.1)
Oil on canvas, 46 1/4 x 35 3/8 in. (117.5 x 89.9 cm)
Gift of the Estate of Harriet L. Cramer

HECKENDORF, Franz
German (1888-1964)
Dorfweiher (Village Pond), 1922
Oil on canvas, 31 7/8 x 39 3/4 in. (81 x 101 cm)
Promised gift of Mr. and Mrs. Marvin L. Fishman

HEINE, Frederick Wilhelm
German (1845-1921)
Untitled (Desert Caravan) (81.19.1)
Oil on canvas, 13 x 20 1/2 in. (33 x 52.1 cm)
Gift of Mr. Edward J. O'Keefe

HENDRICKSON, Russell
American (1927-   )
Father Marquette Mural   (53.2)
Oil on canvas, 9 ft. 4 in. x 20 ft. 5 in.
   (2.8 x 6.2 m)
Gift of Gimbel Brothers

HERMANN, Leo
English (b.1853)
The Cardinal   (60.6)
Oil on canvas, 11 7/8 x 9 1/8 in.
   (30.2 x 23.2 cm)
Gift of Mr. and Mrs. Clifford A.
   Randall

HLAVACEK, Joseph F.
American (1926-1982)
Warriors Return   (66.21)
Oil on masonite, 45 1/4 x 66 in.
   (114.9 x 167.6 cm)
Gift of the artist

HUET, Jean Baptiste
French (1745-1811)
Peasant Family
Oil on panel, 43 x 32 in. (109.2 x
   81.3 cm)
On extended loan from Mr. and Mrs.
   E. James Quirk

HÜTHER, Julius
German (1881-1954)
Winterfreude (Pleasures of Winter),
   1931*
Oil on canvas, 39 1/2 x 27 1/2 in.
   (100.3 x 69.9 cm)
Promised gift of Mr. and Mrs.
   Marvin L. Fishman

INGWERSEN, James Jay
American (20th century)
Portrait of Russell V. Brown
   (83.16)
Oil on canvas, 29 1/8 x 23 3/8 in.
   (74 x 59.4 cm) (sight)
Gift of the Marquette University
   Dental School and Faculty

INNESS, George, After
American (1824-1911)
Wooded Landscape with Cattle
   (61.17)
Oil on canvas, 20 1/2 x 16 1/2 in.
   (52.1 x 41.9 cm)
Gift of Mr. I. A. Dinerstein

ISRAELS, Jozef **
Dutch (1824-1911)
*Dutch Interior (called Mother and
   Child)*, c. 1898   (59.13)
Oil on canvas, 38 1/4 x 52 in.
   (97.2 x 132.1 cm)
Gift of Mr. I. A. Dinerstein

**JONES, Bolton Hugh, Attributed
to**
American (1848-1927)
Russian Troika in Snowy Landscape
   (82.17.1)
Oil on canvas, 30 x 50 1/8 in.
   (76.2 x 127.3 cm)
Gift of Mr. Eckhart G. Grohmann

JUNGWIRTH, Irene Gayas
American (1913-   )
Collection of Paintings   (63.25;
   64.24-.27; 67.2-.4; 70.1)
Oil and egg tempera on panel;
   dimensions vary
Gift of the artist

Winterfreude (Pleasures of Winter), Julius Hüther, oil on canvas

KAISER, Charles James
American (1939-   )
The Bobbin   (83.49.2)
Acrylic on canvas, 16 1/8 x 26 1/8 in.
   (41 x 66.4 cm)
Gift of Mr. Frederick D. Gore

The Bubbler   (83.49.1)
Acrylic on canvas, 24 x 12 1/4 in.
   (61 x 31.1 cm)
Gift of Mr. Frederick D. Gore

KAMLOOKHINE, Xenia
American (1894-1980)
Untitled   (81.8S)
Oil on canvas, 39 3/4 x 29 3/4 in.
   (101 x 75.6 cm)
Gift of Mr. and Mrs. Igor Kamlukin

KERN, James W. (Jaya)
American (1944-   )
Dark Night Descending   (77.13)
Acrylic on Plexiglas, 47 7/8 x
   35 15/16 in. (121.6 x 91.3 cm)
Gift of the artist

KLEINHOLZ, Frank
American (1901-   )
Children at Play, 1956   (59.10)
Tempera on canvas, 88 x 61 in.
   (223.5 x 154.9 cm)
Gift of Mr. Joseph P. Antonow

Park Scene   (62.1)
Acrylic on canvas, 22 1/4 x 18 1/4 in.
   (56.5 x 46.4 cm)
Gift of Mr. and Mrs. George H.
   Struthers

KNELLER, Sir Godfrey *
English (1646-1723)
Self-Portrait with (?) James Huckle,
   c. 1705   (61.14)
Oil on canvas, 22 x 22 in. (55.9 x
   55.9 cm)
Gift of Mr. I. A. Dinerstein

KNOPF, Hermann
Austrian (b. 1870)
Scenes of Village Life
   (58.28.1&.2)
Oil on canvas, 37 1/2 x 30 in.
   (95.3 x 76.2 cm), each
Gift of Mrs. Norman J. Kopmeier

LALANDE, Jacques
French (20th century)
*Innocent sur la plage (Innocent on
   the Beach)*, 1963   (83.29.1)
Oil on canvas, 21 1/2 x 18 7/8 in.
   (54.6 x 47.9 cm)
Gift of Mr. Paul P. Lipton

Lovers, 1960   (83.29.3)
Oil on canvas, 24 x 18 1/4 in.
   (61 x 46.4 cm)
Gift of Mr. Paul P. Lipton

*Young Girl in Red Sweater Seated
   on Beach with Bird*   (83.29.2)
Oil on canvas, 21 3/4 x 18 1/4 in.
   (55.3 x 46.4 cm)
Gift of Mr. Paul P. Lipton

LAMPRECHT, Wilhelm *
German (1838-1906)
Père Marquette and the Indians,
   1889   (00.3)
Oil on canvas, 43 1/2 x 53 in.
   (110.5 x 134.6 cm)
Gift of Rev. Stanislaus L.
   Lalumière, S.J.

Portrait of a Man, André Lanskoy, acrylic
on canvas

LANSKOY, André
French (1902-1976)
*Portrait of a Man**   (00.4)
Acrylic on canvas, 25 3/4 x
   21 1/2 in. (65.4 x 54.6 cm)
Gift of Mr. and Mrs. Charles Zadok

**LAWRENCE, Sir Thomas,
   Attributed to ***
English (1769-1830)
Portrait of Vincenzo Camuccini (?)
   (73.18)
Oil on canvas, 29 x 24 1/4 in.
   (73.7 x 61.6 cm)
Gift of Mr. and Mrs. James W.
   Bergstrom

LE BRUN, Charles, After *
French (1619-1690)
Deposition of Christ   (76.60)
Oil on canvas, 18 1/8 x 11 5/8 in.
   (48.6 x 29.5 cm)
Gift of Dr. John M. Gules

LESSING, Karl-Friedrich
German (1808-1880)
*Trial of Jan Hus**
Oil on canvas, 40 x 60 in. (101.6 x
   152.4 cm)
On extended loan from Ms. Joanna
   Sturm

*Execution of Jan Hus**
Oil on canvas, 40 x 60 in. (101.6 x
   152.4 cm)
On extended loan from Ms. Joanna
   Sturm

LEWANDOWSKI, Edmund D.
American (1914-   )
Industrial Structures, 1950
   (55.21)
Oil on masonite, 40 x 20 in.
   (101.6 x 50.8 cm)
Gift of Gimbel Brothers

Railroad Jungle, 1952*   (80.22)
Oil on canvas, 20 1/4 x 36 1/8 in.
   (51.4 x 91.8 cm)
Gift of Mr. and Mrs. Richard R.
   Teschner

LEWIS, William Lee
American (20th century)
Desert Country   (77.1)
Oil on canvas, 20 1/4 x 26 1/8 in.
   (51.4 x 66.4 cm)
Gift of Mr. and Mrs. Raymond F.
   Newman

LINDERUM, Richard
German (b. 1851)
Scene of Clerical Life   (56.13)
Oil on canvas, 21 1/2 x 17 7/8 in.
   (54.6 x 45.4 cm)
Gift of Mrs. Charles P. Vogel

LOCCA, Bernard
French (1927-   )
Young Boy in a Storm, 1963
   (83.29.5)
Oil on canvas, 38 5/8 x 18 7/8 in.
   (98.1 x 47.9 cm)
Gift of Mr. Paul P. Lipton

*Young Girl with Blonde Hair in Pink
   Blouse*, 1964   (83.29.6)
Oil on canvas, 38 5/8 x 18 7/8 in.
   (98.1 x 47.9 cm)
Gift of Mr. Paul P. Lipton

Madonna and Child, Karl Priebe, casein on board

Youngster Kneeling with Apple in Hand, 1961 (83.29.4)
Oil on canvas, 25 3/4 x 21 1/4 in.
(65.4 x 54 cm)
Gift of Mr. Paul P. Lipton

LOCKWOOD, David
American (20th century)
The Power of the Green, 1960
(61.18)
Acrylic on canvas, 32 1/8 x 24 1/4 in.
(81.6 x 61.6 cm)
Gift of Mr. Harry G. Sundheim, Jr.

LOMBARD, Lambert, School of *
Flemish (1506-1566)
The Birth of St. John the Baptist
(59.4)
Oil on panel, 47 1/2 x 35 1/2 in.
(120.7 x 90.2 cm)
Gift of Mr. and Mrs. Marc B. Rojtman

MAINARDI, Sebastiano, After *
Italian (c. 1455-1513)
The Nativity of Christ (59.3)
Oil on canvas, transferred from
panel, 35 5/8 x 25 3/4 in.
(90.5 x 65.4 cm)
Gift of Mr. and Mrs. Marc B. Rojtman

Railroad Jungle, Edmund D. Lewandowski, oil on canvas

163

MARASCO, Frank
American (1893/94-1980)
Portrait of Stanley Lowe, 1970
(70.14)
Oil on canvas, 20 3/8 x 20 1/4 in.
(51.8 x 51.4 cm)
Gift of the Marquette University
Athletic Department

MASSOPUST, Leo Carl
American (1893-1970)
Portrait of Harriet Cramer   (29.2)
Oil on canvas, 46 1/4 x 36 1/4 in.
(117.5 x 92.1 cm)
Gift of the artist

Portrait of Louis F. Germain
(29.1)
Oil on panel, 22 5/8 x 17 3/4 in.
(57.5 x 45.1 cm)
Gift of the artist

MENTI, C.
American (1929-   )
Crucifixion, 1959   (63.1)
Oil on panel, 36 1/4 x 48 1/4 in.
(92.1 x 122.6 cm)
Gift of Mrs. Joseph C. O'Hearn

MERIPOL, A. A.
American (d. 1939)
Portrait of Mrs. Sarah Olwell
(67.9)
Oil on canvas, 36 x 28 1/4 in.
(91.5 x 71.6 cm)
Gift of Miss Alice Olwell

METTLING, Louis *
French (1847-1904)
*Monk in Prayer (Saint Francis of
Paola ?),* 1885   (69.7)
Oil on canvas, 40 x 32 in. (101.6 x
81.3 cm)
Gift of Dr. and Mrs. Alfred Bader

MILLER, Albert
American (20th century)
Agony, 1948   (64.21)
Oil on panel, 30 1/4 x 24 1/8 in.
(76.8 x 61.3 cm)
Gift of Dr. and Mrs. Louis Maxey

MITCHELL, James E.
American (1926-   )
Atlantic Surf, 1971   (83.52)
Oil on canvas, 36 1/2 x 48 in.
(92.7 x 121.9 cm)
Gift of Mrs. Lloyd H. Pettit

**MORLAND, George and William
Anderson**
English (1763-1804); English
(1757-1837)
Fisherman with Nets   (84.9.3)
Oil on panel, 16 13/16 x 14 in.
(42.7 x 35.6 cm)
Gift of Mr. and Mrs. Donald B. Abert

MOSTAERT, Gillis *
Flemish (1534-1598)
The Passion of Christ   (58.9)
Oil on canvas, 43 1/2 x 50 1/2 in.
(110.5 x 128.3 cm)
Gift of Mr. and Mrs. Marc B. Rojtman

MYTENS, Daniel, Follower of *
Dutch (c.1590-1647)
*Portrait of a Man, possibly Edward,
2nd Viscount Conway*   (60.7)
Oil on canvas, 26 1/16 x 22 1/4 in.
(66.2 x 56.5 cm)
Gift of Mr. I. A. Dinerstein

ORTLIEB, Frederich
German (1839-1909)
Girl with Hat   (84.9.4)
Oil on canvas, 21 1/2 x 25 3/4 in.
(54.6 x 65.4 cm)
Gift of Mr. and Mrs. Donald B. Abert

PETER, George
American (1860-1950)
Father Marquette and the Indians
(00.419)
Oil on canvas, 48 x 144 in. (121.9 x
365.8 cm)
Gift of the Milwaukee Public Museum

PLOCHMANN, Carolyn
American (1926-   )
Old Woman Seated in a Chair
(76.64)
Oil on panel, 23 3/4 x 17 3/4 in.
(60.3 x 45.1 cm) (sight)
Gift of Mr. and Mrs. Raymond F.
Newman

**POST, William Merritt,
Attributed to**
American (1856-1935)
Landscape   (58.26)
Oil on canvas, 30 1/4 x 40 1/4 in.
(76.8 x 102.2 cm)
Gift of Mr. George L. N. Meyer, Sr.

PRIEBE, Karl
American (1914-1976)
Madonna and Child, 1941*   (77.14)
Casein on board, 41 x 33 in. (104 x
84 cm)
Gift of Mr. Emil Priebe

PROVOST, Jan II
Flemish (1462/65-1529)
*Madonna and Child with Saints and
Angels,* c. 1510
Oil on panel, 31 x 25 1/2 in. (78.7 x
64.8 cm)
On extended loan from Mr. and Mrs.
E. James Quirk

PRUNIER, Marcel
French (20th century)
Bar Interior, c. 1961   (80.17.17)
Oil on canvas, 10 1/2 x 8 1/2 in.
(26.7 x 21.6 cm)
Gift of Mr. Paul P. Lipton

PUCCI, Silvio, Attributed to
Italian (1899-   )
Nun with Hula Hoop   (76.2)
Oil on panel, 14 1/4 x 6 3/4 in.
(36.2 x 17.2 cm)
Gift of Mr. and Mrs. Raymond F.
Newman

Priest with Flying Hat   (76.3)
Oil on panel, 14 1/4 x 6 7/8 in.
(36.2 x 17.5 cm)
Gift of Mr. and Mrs. Raymond F.
Newman

**PYNE, James Baker, Attributed
to**
English (1800-1870)
*View of the Tiber River, Rome,
Looking to the Southwest*
(83.48.2)
Oil on canvas, 33 1/2 x 53 1/2 in.
(85.1 x 135.9 cm)
Gift of Brandt, Inc., in memory of
Earl William and Eugenia Brandt
Quirk

RATTNER, Abraham
American (1895-1978)
Pillar of Fire   (63.22)
Oil on panel, 16 x 19 7/8 in.
(40.6 x 50.5 cm)
Gift of Dr. and Mrs. Gerhard D.
Straus

RAU, Emil
German, (b. 1858)
*Besuch der Sennerin (Visit of the
Alpine Milkmaid),* 1901   (64.32)
Oil on canvas, 47 1/4 x 38 in.
(120 x 96.5 cm)
Gift of the René von Schleinitz
Foundation

REYNOLDS, Sir Joshua, Attributed to *
English (1723-1792)
Portrait of an Officer in a Red Jacket, c. 1755 (61.13)
Oil on canvas, 30 x 25 in. (76.2 x 63.5 cm)
Gift of Mr. I. A. Dinerstein

RICO Y ORTEGA, Martin
Spanish (1833-1908)
Venice Canal (65.1)
Oil on canvas, 31 1/4 x 49 1/4 in. (79.4 x 125.1 cm)
Gift of Mrs. Fred A. Miller

ROTH, Etienne
Nationality Unknown (20th century)
Three Young Girls (83.29.7.1-.3)
Oil on canvas, 10 3/4 x 8 3/4 in. (27.3 x 22.2 cm), each
Gift of Mr. Paul P. Lipton

RUBENS, Peter Paul, After
Flemish (1577-1640)
Adoration of the Shepherds (81.35)
Oil on copper, 26 x 19 in. (66 x 48.2 cm)
Gift of Grohmann Industries, Inc.

Salome with the Head of John the Baptist (65.11)
Oil on canvas, 21 1/4 x 21 1/4 in. (54 x 54 cm)
Gift of Mr. and Mrs. Richard B. Flagg

RUBENS, Peter Paul, Circle of *
Flemish (1577-1640)
Noli Me Tangere (59.2)
Oil on panel, 18 x 27 3/16 in. (45.7 x 69.1 cm)
Gift of Mr. and Mrs. Marc B. Rojtman

RUDOLPH, Wilhelm
German (1899-1982)
Droschke und Pferd (Horse and Carriage), c. 1925*
Oil on canvas, 27 3/4 x 51 1/4 in. (70.5 x 130.2 cm)
Promised gift of Mr. and Mrs. Marvin L. Fishman

SALISBURY, Frank O.
English (1874-1962)
Portrait of Frank J. Sensenbrenner (72.23)
Oil on canvas, 43 3/4 x 33 5/8 in. (111.1 x 85.4 cm)
Gift of Mrs. James W. Bergstrom

Droschke und Pferd (Horse and Carriage), Wilhelm Rudolph, oil on canvas

SALVI, Giovanni Battista (called Sassoferrato), After
Italian (1609-1685)
Madonna (58.4)
Oil on canvas, 25 5/8 x 20 1/2 in. (65.1 x 52.1 cm)
Gift of Mr. and Mrs. Marc B. Rojtman

Madonna and Child (58.6)
Oil on panel, 26 1/2 x 20 3/8 in. (67.3 x 51.8 cm)
Gift of Mr. and Mrs. Marc B. Rojtman

SCHENCK, August Friedrich Albrecht *
Danish (1828-1901)
Shepherd and Flock in Storm (65.14)
Oil on canvas, 24 x 35 3/4 in. (61 x 90.8 cm)
Gift of Mrs. Fred A. Miller

SCHLEPPEGRELL, Walter
German (b. 1891)
Marschlandschaft (Marsh Landscape) (83.34)
Oil on panel, 23 x 28 1/2 in. (58.4 x 72.4 cm)
Gift of Mr. and Mrs. Marvin L. Fishman

CONRAD SCHMITT STUDIOS
American (20th century)
Landscape and Flowers (00.456)
Oil on canvas, 31 x 71 5/8 in. (78.7 x 181.9 cm)
Gift of Conrad Schmitt Studios

SCHNEIDER, G. W.
Nationality Unknown (20th century)
Church Interior, 1930 (62.11)
After a painting by Marius François Granet
Oil on canvas, 33 3/4 x 39 3/4 in. (85.7 x 101 cm) (sight)
Gift of Miss Dorothy Riedl

SCHOEVAERDTS, Mathys *
Flemish (c. 1665-after 1694)
Village Festival (64.16)
Oil on canvas, 18 x 22 7/8 in. (45.7 x 58.1 cm)
Gift of Mr. and Mrs. Richard B. Flagg

SCHOLZ, Max
German (b. 1855)
*Monks and Musicians** (64.19)
Oil on canvas, 21 1/8 x 26 1/2 in. (53.7 x 67.3 cm)
Gift of Mr. and Mrs. Ray Smith, Jr.

SCHWAR, Wilhelm
German (b. 1860)
Portrait of a Man with Pipe and Stein, 1893 (82.1.3)
Oil on panel, 11 1/8 x 9 1/4 in. (28.3 x 23.5 cm)
Gift of the Estate of Claire Hoff Toole

SCHWARTZ, Lester O.
American (1912-)
Drama, 1953 (53.12)
Oil on canvas, 7 ft. 7 in. x 29 ft. 9 in. (2.3 x 9.1 m)
Gift of Gimbel Brothers

Monks and Musicians, Max Scholz, oil on canvas

Fox Farm Fantasy   (55.19)
Oil on panel, 30 x 48 in. (76.2 x
    122 cm)
Gift of Gimbel Brothers

Pony Performance   (83.49.3)
Acrylic and encaustic on paperboard,
    12 x 16 1/2 in. (30.5 x 41.9 cm)
Gift of Mr. Frederick D. Gore

SCHWICHTENBERG, Martel
German (1896-1945)
*Landschaft mit rotem Berg (Land-
    scape with Red Mountain),* c. 1925
Oil on canvas, 23 9/16 x 29 1/2 in.
    (60 x 75 cm)
Promised gift of Mr. and Mrs.
    Marvin L. Fishman

San Gimignano, c. 1925
Oil on canvas, 29 1/2 x 23 5/8 in.
    (74.9 x 60 cm)
Promised gift of Mr. and Mrs.
    Marvin L. Fishman

SEGALL, Julius
American (1860-1925)
George Washington, 1909   (59.14)
Oil on canvas, 56 1/4 x 39 7/8 in.
    (142.9 x 101.3 cm)
Gift of Mr. William M. Lamers, Sr.

SERRIER, Jean Pierre
French (1934-   )
*La Jeune fille au bouquet de fleurs
    (Young Girl with Bouquet of
    Flowers)*   (83.29.8)
Oil on canvas, 38 5/8 x 18 7/8 in.
    (98.1 x 47.9 cm)
Gift of Mr. Paul P. Lipton

L'Arlequine (Harlequin), 1966
    (83.29.9)
Oil on canvas, 28 5/8 x 36 1/8 in.
    (72.2 x 91.8 cm)
Gift of Mr. Paul P. Lipton

*L'Arlequine assise avec bouquet de
    fleurs (Seated Harlequin with
    Bouquet of Flowers),* 1964
    (83.29.11)
Oil on canvas, 38 3/4 x 19 1/4 in.
    (98.4 x 48.9 cm)
Gift of Mr. Paul P. Lipton

Seated Young Girl in Red Dress,
    1964   (83.29.10)
Oil on canvas, 38 3/4 x 19 1/4 in.
    (98.4 x 48.9 cm)
Gift of Mr. Paul P. Lipton

**SOLIMENA, Francesco ** **
Italian (1657-1747)
*The Christ Child Contemplating His
    Future Passion,* c. 1720-1730
    (61.4)
Oil on canvas, 19 3/4 x 25 7/8 in.
    (50.2 x 65.7 cm)
Gift of Mr. and Mrs. Marc B. Rojtman

**SOLIMENA, Francesco, Circle
    of ** **
Italian (1657-1747)
*St. Bruno Refusing the Arch-
    bishopric,* c. 1725-1750   (73.16)
Oil on canvas, 18 3/8 x 14 1/8 in.
    (46.7 x 35.9 cm)
Gift of Dr. and Mrs. John E. Cordes

SPERL, Johann
German (1840-1914)
Return from the Hunt   (57.4)
Oil on canvas, 26 3/8 x 34 3/8 in.
    (67 x 87.3 cm)
Gift of Mrs. Charles P. Vogel

SPICUZZA, Francesco
American (1883-1962)
Portrait of Edward J. O'Donnell, S.J.
    (62.16)
Oil on canvas, 30 3/8 x 24 in. (77.2
    x 61 cm)
Gift of Mr. I. A. Dinerstein

STAHL, Ben
American (?) (20th century)
The Moment of Silent Prayer
    (69.10)
Oil on canvas, 80 1/4 x 37 3/4 in.
    (203.8 x 95.9 cm)
Gift of Mr. and Mrs. Donald T.
    McNeill

STANLEY, Robert
American (1932-   )
Beatles Recording, 1965   (82.4.1)
Acrylic on canvas, 45 x 38 in.
    (114.3 x 96.5 cm)
Gift of Mrs. Lloyd H. Pettit

SZERNER, Vladyslav
Polish (1836-1915)
Cossack Men with Horses   (63.23)
Oil on canvas, 23 1/4 x 20 in.
    (59.1 x 50.8 cm)
Gift of Mr. and Mrs. Clifford A.
    Randall

THOMPSON, Richard Earl
American (1914-   )
Meditation on a College Campus
    (72.7)
Oil on canvas, 24 1/2 x 30 1/4 in.
    (62.2 x 76.8 cm)
Gift of Mr. Jack M. Horner

THWAITES, Charles W.
American (1904-   )
*Henry L. Banzhaf, Dean Emeritus
(1902-1944), 1944   (44.1)*
Oil on canvas, 31 5/8 x 23 1/2 in.
(80.3 x 59.7 cm)
Gift of Gimbel Brothers

Steel, 1950   (55.20)
Oil on masonite, 47 1/4 x 36 in.
(120 x 91.4 cm)
Gift of Gimbel Brothers

TREVISANI, Francesco *
Italian (1656-1746)
St. Francis in Penitence, c. 1695-1700
(59.5)
Oil on canvas, 52 7/8 x 38 7/16 in.
(134.3 x 97.6 cm)
Gift of Mr. and Mrs. Marc B. Rojtman

St. Mary Magdalen in Penitence,
c. 1710-1715   (59.6)
Oil on canvas, 39 x 30 in. (99.1 x
76.2 cm)
Gift of Mr. and Mrs. Marc B. Rojtman

UNKNOWN ARTIST *
Nationality Unknown (19th century)
Academic Grisaille Study, 1881
(00.14)
Oil on canvas, 14 5/8 x 12 in.
(37.2 x 30.5 cm)
Anonymous Gift

Portrait of Christ, Flemish School, Sixteenth Century, oil on panel

UNKNOWN ARTIST *
German School, Middle Rhine (16th
century)
The Adoration of the Magi   (66.5)
Oil on panel, 12 5/8 x 9 1/2 in.
(32.1 x 24.1 cm)
Gift of Dr. and Mrs. Joseph E.
Halloin

UNKNOWN ARTIST *
Veneto-Byzantine School (16th
century)
Adoration of the Magi   (84.7.2)
Tempera on panel, 29 x 40 in.
(73.7 x 101.6 cm)
Gift of the Rojtman Foundation

UNKNOWN ARTIST *
Emilian School (16th century)
Adoration of the Shepherds
(64.14)
Oil on panel, 20 3/8 x 15 1/8 in.
(51.8 x 38.4 cm)
Gift of Dr. and Mrs. Joseph E.
Halloin

UNKNOWN ARTIST
American (late 19th - early 20th
century)
Bishop John M. Henni   (00.401)
Oil on canvas, 32 x 26 in. (81.3 x
66 cm)
Anonymous Gift

**UNKNOWN ARTIST (Roman
Master) ***
Italian (17th century)
Bust-Length Portrait of a Cardinal,
c. 1600-1625   (75.17)
Oil on canvas, 23 1/8 x 18 in. (58.7 x
45.7 cm)
Gift of Mr. and Mrs. Raymond F.
Newman

UNKNOWN ARTIST
Italian (?) (mid 18th century)
Four Seasons-Fall   (75.13)
Oil on canvas, 32 1/2 x 26 in.
(82.6 x 66 cm)
Gift of Mrs. Malcolm K. Whyte

Four Seasons-Spring   (75.15)
Oil on canvas, 32 3/8 x 26 in.
(82.2 x 66 cm)
Gift of Mrs. Malcolm K. Whyte

Four Seasons-Summer   (75.12)
Oil on canvas, 32 3/8 x 26 in.
(82.2 x 66 cm)
Gift of Mrs. Malcolm K. Whyte

Four Seasons-Winter   (75.14)
Oil on canvas, 32 3/8 x 26 in.
(82.2 x 66 cm)
Gift of Mrs. Malcolm K. Whyte

UNKNOWN ARTIST
European (late 19th-early 20th
century)
Head of a Girl   (69.8)
Oil on canvas, 17 5/8 x 15 in.
(44.8 x 38.1 cm)
Gift of Mrs. Douglass Van Dyke

UNKNOWN ARTIST *
Northern European (18th century)
The Holy Family   (61.2)
Oil on panel, 16 x 22 in. (40.6 x
55.9 cm)
Gift of Mr. and Mrs. Marc B. Rojtman

UNKNOWN ARTIST
Bolognese School (17th century)
Mary Magdalene   (76.61)
Oil on canvas, 25 1/4 x 21 1/4 in.
(64.1 x 54 cm)
Gift of Dr. John M. Gules

UNKNOWN ARTIST *
Flemish (17th century)
Mary Magdalene in Penitence,
c. 1630   (61.5)
Oil on panel, 14 1/2 x 22 in. (36.8 x
55.9 cm)
Gift of Mr. and Mrs. Marc B. Rojtman

UNKNOWN ARTIST *
British School (late 18th-early 19th
century)
Moses Breaking the Tablets
(79.13)
Oil on canvas, 50 1/4 x 40 1/2 in.
(127.6 x 102.9 cm)
Gift of Mr. and Mrs. Eckhart G.
Grohmann

UNKNOWN ARTIST *
North Italian School (?) (early 16th
century)
The Nativity of Christ   (58.7)
Oil on panel, 57 1/8 x 30 3/4 in.
(145.1 x 78.1 cm)
Gift of Mr. and Mrs. Marc B. Rojtman

UNKNOWN ARTIST
English (?) (late 19th-early 20th
century)
Pair of Pastoral Scenes
(81.27.4.1&.2)
Oil on glass, 16 1/4 x 24 in. (41.3 x
61 cm), each
Gift of Dr. Kenneth Maier

UNKNOWN ARTIST
American (20th century)
Portrait of Charles L. Coughlin
(00.515)
Oil on canvas, 30 1/2 x 24 1/4 in.
(77.5 x 61.6 cm)
Gift of Mrs. Colet Coughlin

UNKNOWN ARTIST
Flemish School (16th century)
Portrait of Christ* (82.17.2)
Oil on panel, 32 3/8 x 21 1/2 in.
(82.3 x 54.6 cm)
Gift of Mr. Eckhart G. Grohmann

UNKNOWN ARTIST **
German School, Middle Rhine (16th century)
The Presentation in the Temple
(66.4)
Oil on panel, 12 3/8 x 9 1/2 in.
(31.4 x 24 1 cm)
Gift of Dr. and Mrs. Joseph E. Halloin

UNKNOWN ARTIST
Retreat of Napoleon (62.13)
Oil on canvas, 23 3/4 x 29 5/8 in.
(60.3 x 75.3 cm)
Gift of Messrs. Carl W. Moebius, Jr., Frank R. Moebius, Howard E. Moebius, and Kenneth D. Moebius

UNKNOWN ARTIST
Flemish (16th-17th century)
Revelation of St. John on Patmos
(82.3)
Oil on copper, 12 5/8 x 9 7/8 in.
(32.1 x 25.1 cm)
Gift of Mr. and Mrs. Eckhart G. Grohmann

UNKNOWN ARTIST **
British School (active early 19th century)
River Landscape (75.18)
Oil on canvas, 21 1/4 x 32 in.
(54 x 81.3 cm)
Gift of the Estate of Gertrude Bergstrom

UNKNOWN ARTIST
Italian (early 18th century ?)
Ruins in Landscape (63.18)
Oil on canvas, 29 x 23 3/4 in.
(73.7 x 60.3 cm)
Gift of Mrs. George Raab

UNKNOWN ARTIST
Flemish (17th century ?)
The Sacrifice of Isaac (83.44)
Oil on panel, 32 3/4 x 24 3/4 in.
(83.2 x 62.9 cm)
Gift of Mr. Eckhart G. Grohmann

UNKNOWN ARTIST
*The Sacrifice of the Women of Rome
to the Government of Rome during
the War with Hannibal* (69.2)
Oil on canvas, 70 1/2 x 95 in.
(179.1 x 241.3 cm)
Gift of Mr. Paul A. Frederick on behalf of Frederick and Company, Inc.

UNKNOWN ARTIST
English (18th century)
St. Ignatius (81.33)
Oil on copper, 4 3/8 x 3 1/2 in.
(11.1 x 8.9 cm)
Gift of Mr. and Mrs. Richard F. C. Kegel

UNKNOWN ARTIST **
Dutch (17th century)
St. Jerome (64.33)
Oil on panel, 9 1/4 x 8 1/8 in.
(23.5 x 20.6 cm)
Gift of Mrs. William P. Hayes

UNKNOWN ARTIST **
Byzantine School (17th century)
*Scenes from the Life of St. Elias
(The Prophet Elijah)* (84.7.3)
Tempera and oil on panel, 50 x 38 in.
(127 x 96.5 cm)
Gift of the Rojtman Foundation

UNKNOWN ARTIST
American (late 19th century)
Three Children on a Veranda
(65.17)
Oil on canvas, 33 1/4 x 28 in.
(84.5 x 71 cm)
Gift of Mrs. Fred A. Miller

UNKNOWN ARTIST
Mexican (late 19th-early 20th century)
*La Virgen de los Remedios (Our
Lady of Healing)* (66.13)
Oil on copper, 7 1/8 x 8 in. (18.1 x 20.3 cm)
Gift of Mrs. Herbert Polacheck

VERNA, Germaine
French (1908-1975)
Frederika, 1958 (83.41.1)
Oil on canvas, 28 1/2 x 36 in. (72.4 x 91.4 cm)
Anonymous Gift

Les Garçons, 1960 (83.40.2)
Oil on canvas, 33 1/2 x 25 in. (85.1 x 63.5 cm)
Anonymous Gift

Lady with Blue Hat, 1960
(83.40.1)
Oil on canvas, 36 x 24 1/2 in. (91.4 x 62.2 cm)
Anonymous Gift

Portrait of Paulette Goddard, 1974
(81.20.2)
Oil on canvas, 28 3/4 x 21 in. (73 x 53.3 cm)
Anonymous Gift

Seated Gentleman, 1959 (83.41.2)
Oil on canvas, 31 11/16 x 25 1/4 in.
(80.5 x 64.1 cm)
Anonymous Gift

Untitled (Red Boats in Harbor)
(81.20.1)
Oil on canvas, 21 3/8 x 28 7/8 in.
(54.3 x 73.3 cm)
Anonymous Gift

Woman in Blue with Bracelet, Germaine Verna, oil on canvas

Woman in Blue with Bracelet, 1967*
(82.21.2)
Oil on canvas, 34 7/8 x 20 3/8 in.
(88.6 x 51.8 cm)
Anonymous Gift

Woman with Shoes Off, 1955
 (82.21.1)
Oil on canvas, 38 5/8 x 19 1/4 in.
 (98.1 x 48.9 cm) (sight)
Anonymous Gift

VIGNON, Claude *
French (1593-1670)
Adoration of the Magi, c. 1625-1630
 (60.5)
Oil on canvas, 36 x 46 in. (91.4 x
116.8 cm)
Gift of Mr. and Mrs. Marc B. Rojtman

VILLON, Jacques *
French (1875-1963)
Maternité, c. 1948   (62.7)
Oil on canvas, 57 3/8 x 38 in. (145.7 x
 96.5 cm)
Gift of Mr. and Mrs. Ira Haupt

*Promethée libéré de ses chaînes
 (Prometheus Freed from His
 Chains)*, 1956   (60.11)
Oil on canvas, 35 7/8 x 25 3/8 in.
 (91.1 x 64.4 cm)
Gift of Mr. and Mrs. Ira Haupt

VON NEUMANN, Robert
American (1888-1976)
The Mending of the Trout Net, 1945*
 (79.16)
Oil on panel, 28 x 36 3/8 in. (71.1 x
 92.4 cm)
Gift of Mrs. Mortimer P. Allen

WASSERMAN, Helene
American (1929-   )
Reclining Figure   (80.17.18)
Oil on masonite, 24 x 18 in. (61 x
45.7 cm)
Gift of Mr. Paul P. Lipton

Still Life with Artist Reading, John Wilde, oil on panel

WATKINS, Franklin Chenault *
American (1894-1972)
Poison for the King, 1934   (61.1)
Oil on canvas, 25 1/4 x 30 in.
 (64.1 x 76.2 cm)
Gift of Mr. Harry G. Sundheim, Jr.

WATROUS, James*
American (1908-   )
After the Concert   (55.25)
Oil on masonite, 21 1/2 x 13 1/2 in.
 (54.6 x 34.3 cm)
Gift of Gimbel Brothers

WELLER, Eric
American (20th century)
Untitled   (80.8)
Acrylic on canvas with wood and
 glass, 46 3/4 x 46 3/4 in. (118.8 x
 118.8 cm)
Anonymous Gift

WILDE, John
American (1919-   )
Cucumber, 1962   (65.10)
Oil on panel, 8 x 10 1/16 in. (20.3 x
 25.6 cm)
Gift of Mr. and Mrs. Raymond F.
 Newman

July 25, 1949   (55.17)
Oil on panel, 14 x 20 in. (35.6 x
 50.8 cm)
Gift of Gimbel Brothers

*Still Life with Artist Reading**
 (76.62)
Oil on panel, 14 x 20 in. (35.6 x
 50.8 cm)
Gift of Mr. and Mrs. Raymond F.
 Newman

The Mending of the Trout Net, Robert von Neumann, oil on panel

169

Still Life with Purple Raspberries,
1964   (77.3)
Oil on panel, 7 5/8 x 9 1/2 in. (19.4 x
24.1 cm) (sight)
Gift of Mr. and Mrs. Raymond F.
Newman

WILLS, T. Anthony
American (20th century)
Portrait of C. Frederic (Todd) Wehr,
1965   (65.20)
Oil on canvas, 41 1/4 x 35 1/4
(104.8 x 89.5 cm) (sight)
Anonymous Gift

WOUWERMAN, Philips *
Dutch (1619-1668)
*Dutch Cavalry before a Sutler's
Tent,* c. 1640-1650   (71.4)
Oil on canvas, 10 3/4 x 13 7/8 in.
(27.3 x 35.2 cm)
Gift of Mrs. Jetta Muntain Smith in
memory of her son, Aurel Muntain

ZINGALE, Santos
American (1908-   )
University Sports   (53.13)
Oil on canvas, 7 ft. 7 in. x 27 ft. 6 in.
(2.3 x 8.4 m)
Gift of Gimbel Brothers

Wisconsin Construction, 1950
(53.1)
Oil on canvas, 43 1/8 x 30 1/4 in.
(109.5 x 76.8 cm)
Gift of Gimbel Brothers

ZWAAN, (?)
Dutch (n.d.)
Interior with Mother and Child
(62.12)
Oil on canvas, 22 1/4 x 28 1/4 in.
(56.5 x 71.8 cm)
Gift of Mr. and Mrs. Clifford A.
Randall

MINIATURE PAINTINGS

Unless otherwise noted, all miniature paintings are part of the A. J. Conroy Collection and were given anonymously to the University.

AMANS, Jacques, Attributed to
American (1801-1888)
*Portrait of a Gentleman—Mr. Della
Ronde*   (80.28.10)
Watercolor on ivory, 3 x 2 1/2 in.
(7.6 x 6.4 cm)

BOIT, Charles, Attributed to
Swedish (1663-1727)
Portrait of a Woman   (81.28.19)
Watercolor on ivory, 2 1/2 x 3 1/2 in.
(6.4 x 8.9 cm)

**BURET, Marguerite
(Madame Cresty)**
French (b. 1841)
Portrait of King Stanislaus of Poland
(80.28.14)
Watercolor on ivory, 3 3/8 x 2 5/8 in.
(8.6 x 6.7 cm)

**COLLAS, Louis Antoine,
Attributed to**
French/American (active 1798-1829)
*Portrait of a Woman Wearing a
White Gown with Veil*
(80.28.13)
Watercolor on ivory, 2 5/8 x 2 1/2 in.
(6.7 x 6.4 cm)

*Portrait of a Woman Wearing a
White Lace Gown*   (80.28.19)
Watercolor on ivory, 1 3/4 x 1 1/2 in.
(4.5 x 3.8 cm)

**CORNEILLE DE LYON, Claude,
Attributed to (called Corneille
de la Haye)**
Flemish (d. 1474)
Portrait of Mary, Queen of Scots
(82.20.1)
Watercolor on ivory, 3 3/8 x 2 5/8 in.
(8.6 x 6.7 cm)

**COSWAY, Richard, Attributed
to ***
English (1742-1821)
*Portrait of a Woman in a White
Ruffled Gown and Hat*   (81.28.5)
Watercolor on ivory, 2 x 2 3/4 in.
(5.1 x 7 cm)

**CROSSE, Richard, Attributed
to ***
English (1742-1810)
Portrait of a Gentleman   (81.28.1)
Watercolor on ivory, 1 1/2 x 1 3/4 in.
(3.8 x 4.5 cm)

DOLCI, Carlo, After *
Italian (1616-1686)
Ecce Homo   (80.28.2)
Enamel on porcelain, 4 3/4 x 3 5/8 in.
(12.1 x 9.2 cm)

Mater Dolorosa (Mother of Sorrows)
(80.28.1)
Enamel on porcelain, 4 1/2 x 3 1/2 in.
(11.4 x 8.9 cm)

DOUMANT, (?)
European (18th century)
Lady with a Plumed Hat   (81.28.14)
Watercolor on ivory, 2 5/8 x 3 3/8 in.
(6.7 x 8.6 cm)

DRESSEL (?), L. L.
German (late 19th century)
Portrait of a Woman in a Red Gown
(80.28.9)
Watercolor on celluloid, 3 1/4 x 2 7/8
in. (8.3 x 7.3 cm)

DUBILLO, (?)
European (19th century)
Suzanna before the Elders
(80.28.18)
Watercolor on ivory, after Anton van
Dyck, 4 3/4 x 3 5/8 in. (12.1 x 9.2
cm)

ENGLEHART, George, After
English (late 18th-early 19th
century)
*Portrait of Mrs. Mills, Duchess of
Devonshire*   (81.28.3)
Watercolor on ivory, 3 x 3 in. (7.6 x
7.6 cm)

HALL, Peter Adolph, Attributed to
Swedish (1739-1793)
Portrait of a Young Woman
(81.28.6)
Watercolor on ivory, 2 1/4 in x 3 in.
(5.7 x 7.6 cm)

**HIPPIUS, Gustav Adolph,
Attributed to**
Russian (1792-1856)
*Portrait of Maria Theresia, Queen
of Hungary* (83.38.5)
Watercolor on ivory, 3 3/8 x 2 3/8 in.
(8.6 x 6 cm)

HOFFMAN (?), After
Nationality Unknown (early 20th
century)
Head of Christ (81.28.22)
Watercolor on ivory, 1 1/4 x 1 1/2 in.
(3.2 x 3.8 cm)

**ISABEY, Jean Baptiste, School
of**
French (19th century)
*Portrait of a Gentleman (possibly
Axel Oxenstierna, Swedish Count)*
(82.20.3)
Watercolor on ivory, after Thomas
Cooper, 2 7/8 x 2 1/2 in. (7.3 x
6.4 cm)

**ISABEY, Jean Baptiste,
Attributed to**
French (1767-1858)
Portrait of a Lady (83.38.2)
Watercolor on ivory, 1 15/16 x 1 1/2
in. (4.9 x 3.8 cm)

LOIZZLO, Karpoithy (?)
Russian (late 19th-early 20th
century)
*Portrait of the Son of the Last
Czar* (80.10.3)
Oil on porcelain, 2 1/8 x 1 3/8 in.
(5.4 x 3.5 cm)
Gift of Dr. Kenneth Maier

**PEALE, Charles Willson,
Attributed to ****
American (1741-1827)
*Portrait of a Man in a Houndstooth
Check Vest** (81.28.4)
Watercolor on ivory, 1 3/4 x 2 1/4 in.
(4.5 x 5.7 cm)

REY, Arthur de, Attributed to
French (1797-1886)
*Portrait of a Gentleman in a Blue
Uniform* (80.28.4)
Watercolor on ivory, 3 1/4 x 2 3/8 in.
(8.3 x 6 cm)

**ROBERTSON, Alexander, or
RICHARD COSWAY,
Attributed to**
English (1768-1841); English
(1742-1821)
*Portrait of a Gentleman in a Dark
Jacket* (80.28.11)
Watercolor on ivory, 2 1/4 x 2 5/8 in.
(5.7 x 6.7 cm)

ROLAND, Octave, Attributed to
French (1799-1886)
Portait of Princiss de Lamballe
(83.38.6)
Watercolor on ivory, 2 in. d. (5.1
cm d.)

ROY, JOSÉ
Nationality Unknown (18th century)
Portrait of Marquis de Lafayette
(81.28.16)
Watercolor on ivory, 1 5/8 x 2 1/8 in.
(4.1 x 5.4 cm)

**RUSSELL, Moses B., Attributed
to**
American (1810-1884)
Portrait of Albert Alden (81.28.2)
Watercolor on ivory, 2 x 2 1/2 in.
(5.1 x 6.4 cm)

UNKNOWN ARTIST
American (late 18th-early 19th
century)
*Portrait of a Gentleman in a Blue
Jacket* (80.28.7)
Watercolor on ivory, 2 1/8 x 1 3/4 in.
(5.4 x 4.5 cm)

UNKNOWN ARTIST
European (late 18th-early 19th
century)
*Portrait of a Gentleman in a Blue
Jacket* (81.28.7)
Watercolor on ivory, 1 3/4 x 2 1/4 in.
(4.5 x 5.7 cm)

UNKNOWN ARTIST
English or American (18th century)
*Portrait of a Gentleman in Profile,
c. 1785* (81.28.24)
Watercolor on ivory, 1 5/8 x 2 in.
(4.1 x 5.1 cm)

UNKNOWN ARTIST
French (late 18th century)
Portrait of a Russian Princess
(81.28.20)
Watercolor on ivory, 2 1/2 x 3 1/4 in.
(6.4 x 8.3 cm)

UNKNOWN ARTIST
European (late 19th century)
Portrait of a Woman (65.18.2)
Oil on ivory, 4 3/8 x 3 1/4 in.
(11.1 x 8.3 cm) (sight)
Gift of Mrs. Jetta Muntain Smith, in
memory of her son, Aurel Muntain

UNKNOWN ARTIST
American (early 19th century)
*Portrait of a Young Woman in a
White Gown* (81.28.12)
Watercolor on ivory, 1 7/8 x 3 1/4 in.
(4.8 x 8.3 cm)

UNKNOWN ARTIST (C.H.)
European (19th century)
*Portrait of Bismarck, Chancellor of
Germany, 1830-1835* (82.20.2)
Watercolor on ivory, 2 1/2 x 2 1/8 in.
(6.4 x 5.4 cm)

UNKNOWN ARTIST
European (late 19th century)
Portrait of Cardinal Mundelein
(81.28.17)
Watercolor on ivory, 2 x 2 3/4 in.
(5.1 x 7 cm)

UNKNOWN ARTIST
European (19th century)
*Portrait of Duchess de Nemours,
1840-1850* (83.38.1)
Watercolor on ivory, 2 3/8 in. d.
(6 cm d.)

UNKNOWN ARTIST
American (late 18th-early 19th
century)
*Portrait of a Gentleman, John
Adams, Wearing a Blue Coat*
(80.28.12)
Watercolor on ivory, 1 5/8 x 1 1/8 in.
(4.1 x 2.8 cm)

UNKNOWN ARTIST
American (?) (19th century)
Portrait of Joseph H. Wheeler
(81.28.23)
Watercolor on ivory, 1 3/4 x 2 in.
(4.5 x 5.1 cm)

UNKNOWN ARTIST
European (19th century?)
Portrait of King Louis XVI
(81.28.10)
Watercolor on ivory, 2 1/4 x 3 1/2
in. (5.7 x 8.9 cm)

UNKNOWN ARTIST
European (19th century?)
Portrait of Louis XV (80.28.16)
Watercolor on paper, 3/4 x 5/8 in.
(1.9 x 1.6 cm)

UNKNOWN ARTIST
French (18th century?)
Portrait of Madame de Montesen
(80.28.17)
Watercolor on ivory, 3 3/4 x 3 1/8 in.
(9.5 x 7.9 cm)

UNKNOWN ARTIST
European (18th century?)
*Portrait of Marie Louise of Prussia
in a Pink Gown with Jeweled
Crown** (81.28.9)
Watercolor on ivory, 2 3/4 x 2 in.
(7 x 5.1 cm)

Portrait of Marie Louise in a Pink Gown with Jeweled Crown, European, Eighteenth Century, watercolor on ivory

Portrait of Mary, Queen of Scots, Dutch, Eighteenth Century, watercolor on ivory

UNKNOWN ARTIST
Dutch (18th century)
*Portrait of Mary, Queen of Scots**
(81.28.15)
Watercolor on ivory, 2 5/8 x 3 1/4 in.
(6.7 x 8.3 cm)

UNKNOWN ARTIST
Nationality Unknown (18th century)
Portrait of Mary, Queen of Scots
(81.28.18)
Watercolor on ivory, 2 x 2 1/4 in.
(5.1 x 5.7 cm)

UNKNOWN ARTIST
European (18th century)
Portrait of Peter the Great of Russia
(80.28.15)
Watercolor on ivory, 2 1/4 x 2 1/4 in.
(5.7 x 5.7 cm)

UNKNOWN ARTIST
French (17th century)
Portrait of Phillipe de Clarnibault, Marshall of France, 1650
(81.28.8)
Watercolor on ivory, 2 1/2 x 3 in.
(6.4 x 7.6 cm)

UNKNOWN ARTIST
German (19th century)
Portrait of Marie Louise of Austria
(80.28.8)
Watercolor on porcelain, 5 1/4 x 3 3/4
in. (13.3 x 9.5 cm)

UNKNOWN ARTIST
American (?) (18th century)
Portrait of the Count of von Hessen-Darmstadt (81.28.11)
Watercolor on vellum, 2 1/4 x 2 3/4
in. (5.7 x 7 cm)

UNKNOWN ARTIST
European (19th century)
Portrait of a Woman in a Lavender Gown (81.28.21)
Watercolor on ivory, 1 3/8 x 1 7/8 in.
(3.5 x 4.8 cm)

UNKNOWN ARTIST
Nationality Unknown (19th–20th century)
Portrait of a Young Woman with a Rose-Decorated Hat (65.18.3)
Oil on ivory, 3 3/4 x 2 3/4 in.
(9.5 x 7 cm) (sight)
Gift of Mrs. Jetta Muntain Smith, in memory of her son, Aurel Muntain

UNKNOWN ARTIST
Nationality Unknown (19th century)
Reclining Nude (80.28.3)
Watercolor on ivory, after Jean-Auguste-Dominique Ingres, 4 1/2 x 6 1/4 in. (11.4 x 15.9 cm)

VAUGHAN, M.
Scottish (19th century)
Portrait of a Woman (80.28.6)
Watercolor on ivory, 2 1/2 x 1 7/8 in.
(6.4 x 4.8 cm)

VIGÉE-LE BRUN, Marie Louise Elisabeth, Attributed to
French (1755-1842)
Portrait of Countess Skowranksy
(83.38.3)
Watercolor on ivory, 2 x 1 5/8 in.
(5.1 x 4.2 cm)

Portrait of Graf Skowranksy, Russian (83.38.4)
Watercolor on ivory, 2 x 1 5/8 in.
(5.1 x 4.1 cm)

VILLERNE, (?)
European (19th century)
Portrait of the Duchess of Devonshire (81.28.13)
Watercolor on ivory, after Thomas Gainsborough, 2 5/8 x 3 3/8 in.
(6.7 x 8.6 cm)

WILLIAMS, Alyn, Attributed to
English (1865-1941)
Portrait of a Young Woman
(80.28.5)
Watercolor on ivory, 2 1/8 x 1 5/8 in.
(5.4 x 4.1 cm)

WORKS ON PAPER

AIKEN, Patricia
American (20th century)
Flight of the Dragonfly   (00.437)
Watercolor, 25 3/4 x 32 3/4 in.
    (65.4 x 83.2 cm) (sight)
Gift of the Artist

ALTMAN, Harold
American (1924-   )
Mother and Child   (83.27.10)
Ink, 24 1/8 x 20 in. (61.3 x 50.8 cm)
    (sight)
Gift of Mr. and Mrs. Ray Smith, Jr.

Sunny Street   (83.27.4)
Etching, 11 x 12 3/4 in. (27.9 x 32.4
    cm)
Gift of Mr. and Mrs. Ray Smith, Jr.

ALVAREZ, Carlos Hermosilla
Chilean (1905-   )
Gabriela Mistral   (84.6.2)
Woodcut, 21 3/4 x 18 1/4 in. (55.3 x
    46.4 cm)
Gift of Mr. and Mrs. Joel H.
    Rosenthal

Juan XXIII, 1978   (84.6.1)
Woodcut, 21 3/4 x 15 1/8 in. (55.3 x
    38.4 cm)
Gift of Mr. and Mrs. Joel H.
    Rosenthal

AMICI, Domenico
Italian (b. 1808)
*Grande Cascata dell' Aniene (Large
    Waterfall at Aniene),* 1847
    (80.17.2)
Hand-colored engraving, 6 3/4 x
    9 3/8 in. (17.2 x 23.8 cm) (comp.)
Gift of Mr. Paul P. Lipton

*Sepolcro Detto di Nerone (Said to Be
    Nero's Tomb),* 1835   (80.17.35)
Hand-colored engraving, 8 5/8 x
    10 1/2 in. (21.9 x 26.7 cm) (comp.)
Gift of Mr. Paul P. Lipton

ANGUIANO, Raul
Mexican (1915-   )
*Cado chango en su mecate (Each
    Monkey in His Sack)*   (00.170)
Lithograph, 13 11/16 x 18 in. (34.8 x
    45.7 cm)
Gift of Mr. and Mrs. Philip Pinsof

Leper Women, 1939   (00.166)
Lithograph, 17 15/16 x 21 1/8 in.
    (45.6 x 53.7 cm)
Gift of Mr. and Mrs. Philip Pinsof

Untitled (Men Working)   (00.107)
Lithograph, 15 1/8 x 16 7/8 in.
    (38.4 x 42.9 cm)
Anonymous Gift

ARCHIPENKO, Alexander *
Russian (1887-1964)
Madonna and Child   (55.4)
Colored pencil, crayon and ink,
    15 1/2 x 13 in. (39.4 x 33 cm) (sight)
Gift of the artist through the friend-
    ship of Mr. Roman S. Smal-Stocki

ARMS, John Taylor *
American (1887-1953)
Chartres in Miniature, 1939
    (83.3.1)
Etching, 6 3/4 x 8 3/4 in. (17.2 x
    22.2 cm)
Gift of the Estate of Florence
    Rossbach

Chartres the Magnificent, 1948
    (83.3.2)
Etching, 4 x 4 3/4 in. (10.2 x 12.1 cm)
    (comp.)
Gift of the Estate of Florence
    Rossbach

Ugly Devil, 1924   (00.261)
Etching, 9 1/8 x 8 1/8 in. (23.2 x
    20.6 cm)
Gift of Mr. and Mrs. Philip Pinsof

Untitled (Woman Sleeping in Field), Robert
Austin, ink and charcoal

AUSTIN, Robert
English (b. 1895)
*Untitled (Woman Sleeping in Field)**
    (00.232)
Ink and charcoal, 8 11/16 x 12 3/8
    in. (22.1 x 31.4 cm)
Anonymous Gift

AVERY, Milton
American (1893-1965)
Untitled (Reclining Woman), 1960
    (00.240)
Linoleum engraving, 7 11/16 x 15 1/4
    in. (19.5 x 39.7 cm)
Anonymous Gift

BACHER, Otto-Henry
American (1856-1909)
*Farmhouse Scene**   (82.11.2)
Etching, 11 1/4 x 14 1/8 in. (28.6 x
    35.9 cm)
Gift of Mr. and Mrs. Marvin L.
    Fishman

BACON, Peggy, Attributed to
American (1895-   )
Maybe You Stole It   (00.31)
Pen and ink on tracing paper, 11 3/4
    x 9 in. (29.9 x 22.9 cm)
Anonymous Gift

Untitled (Old Woman in Chair)
    (00.221)
Pen and ink on tracing paper, 11 7/8
    x 9 1/2 in. (30.2 x 24.1 cm)
Anonymous Gift

Untitled (Black Woman in Forest)
    (00.222)
Pen and ink on tracing paper, 11 1/4
    x 7 in. (28.6 x 17.8 cm)
Anonymous Gift

BAKER, Samuel H.
English (1824-1909)
Ribbesford Church   (00.34)
Etching printed in brown ink, 10 3/4
    x 15 in. (27.3 x 38.1 cm)
Anonymous Gift

BAKHUIZEN, Ludolf
Dutch (1631-1708)
Untitled (The Fishwife), 1701
    (00.36)
Etching, 7 5/8 x 10 1/2 in. (19.4 x
    26.7 cm)
Anonymous Gift

BANDINI, Enrico
Italian (n.d.)
General Lafayette   (00.53)
Engraving, 14 3/4 x 10 7/8 in. (37.5
    x 27.6 cm)
Anonymous Gift

BANNERMAN, Alexander
English (1730-1780)
George Lambert   (00.284)
Engraving, 9 5/16 x 6 11/16 in.
    (23.7 x 17 cm)
Anonymous Gift

Farmhouse Scene, Otto-Henry Bacher, etching

BARRAUD, Maurice
Swiss (1889–1955)
Untitled (Embrace)   (80.25.3)
Graphite, 10 1/8 x 8 in. (25.7 x 20.3
    cm) (sight)
Gift of Mr. Joseph P. Antonow

Untitled (Embrace)   (80.25.4)
Conté crayon, 10 x 6 3/4 in. (25.4 x
    17.2 cm) (sight)
Gift of Mr. Joseph P. Antonow

BARTOLOZZI, Francesco
Italian (1725/27–1815)
Earl of Mansfield, 1786   (00.245)
Engraving after Sir Joshua
    Reynolds, 19 7/16 x 14 in. (49.4 x
    35.6 cm)
Gift of Mrs. Joseph D. Patton

BARTSCH, Adam von
Austrian (1757–1821)
Portrait of Ferdinand Bol   (00.216)
Etching, 7 1/2 x 5 13/16 in. (19.1 x
    14.8 cm)
Anonymous Gift

BAYER, Herbert
German (1900–   )
Colorado Landscape, 1949
    (83.50.1)
Serigraph, 14 1/8 x 19 in. (35.9 x
    48.3 cm)
Gift of Mr. and Mrs. Marvin L.
    Fishman

Free Arrangement of Four Equal Parts, Herbert Bayer, serigraph

*Free Arrangement of Four Equal
    Parts*, 1973*   (80.24.19)
Serigraph, 33 7/8 x 33 1/8 in. (86 x
    84.1 cm)
Gift of Mr. Robert Layton

Seven Convolutions Series, 1948*
    (83.50.2.1–.7)
Suite of seven lithographs, 18 x 22 1/8
    in. (45.7 x 56.2 cm), each
Gift of Mr. and Mrs. Marvin L.
    Fishman

Untitled from the Seven Convolutions Series, Herbert Bayer, lithograph

BAYES, Alfred Walter
English (1832–1909)
John Phillip, R.A.   (00.22)
Etching, 15 1/8 x 10 7/8 in. (38.4 x
    27.6 cm)
Gift of Mrs. Joseph D. Patton

BELTRÁN, Juan
Nationality Unknown (20th century)
Untitled   (00.98)
Linoleum engraving, 6 1/2 x 10 5/8 in.
    (16.5 x 27 cm)
Gift of Mr. and Mrs. Philip Pinsof

Untitled (The Sugar Cane Press)
    (00.101)
Lithograph, 15 1/4 x 16 1/2 in. (38.7 x
    42 cm)
Anonymous Gift

BENSON, Frank Weston **
American (1862–1951)
Old Tom, 1926   (83.3.3)
Etching, 15 1/2 x 10 1/4 in. (39.4 x
 26 cm) (comp.)
Gift of the Estate of Florence
 Rossbach

Two Crows, 1920   (83.3.4)
Etching with drypoint and roulette,
 2 1/2 x 3 1/4 in. (6.4 x 8.3 cm)
 (comp.)
Gift of the Estate of Florence
 Rossbach

BENTON, Thomas Hart
American (1889–1975)
Spring Tryout   (00.229)
Lithograph, 10 11/16 x 14 11/16 in.
 (27.2 x 37.3 cm)
Gift of Mrs. Irene Gayas Jungwirth
Gift of Mr. and Mrs. Philip Pinsof

BEN-ZION
American (1897–   )
Moses, 1954   (00.168)
Etching and aquatint, 22 3/8 x 17 7/8
 in. (56.8 x 45.5 cm)
Gift of Mr. and Mrs. Philip Pinsof

BERCHEM, Nicholaes
Dutch (1620–1683)
Shepherd and the Resting Flock*
 (83.32.9)
Engraving, 10 1/4 x 8 1/8 in. (26 x
 20.6 cm) (sight)
Gift of Dr. and Mrs. Sidney M. Boxer

**BERNIER, Charles-Théodore,
 Attributed to**
Belgian (active late 19th–early 20th
 century)
Cour de ferme (Farmhouse Yard)
 (00.8)
Etching, 8 5/8 x 10 1/8 in. (21.9 x
 25.7 cm) (comp.)
Anonymous Gift

BERTAUX, Jacques, Attributed to
French (active 1793–1802)
*Untitled (Napoleon Reviewing the
 Army (?))*   (00.267.1)
Engraving, 5 1/4 x 8 1/8 in. (13.3 x
 20.6 cm)
Anonymous Gift

*Untitled (Napoleon Reviewing the
 Army (?))*   (00.267.2)
Engraving, 4 3/4 x 8 3/16 in. (12.1 x
 20.8 cm)
Anonymous Gift

BERTERHAM, Jan Baptist
Flemish (late 17th–early 18th century)
*Philippe François, Prince de
 Rubempré*   (00.283)
Engraving, 9 1/16 x 6 1/2 in. (23 x
 16.5 cm)
Anonymous Gift

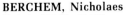

Shepherd and the Resting Flock, Nicholaes Berchem, engraving

Four Equal Colors, Max Bill, serigraph

Illustration for the Book of Job (no. 19), William Blake, engraving

Farmer Dentist   (83.3.7)
Etching with drypoint, 10 1/2 x 15 5/8
    in. (26.8 x 39.7 cm) (comp.)
Gift of the Estate of Florence
    Rossbach

Gaston the Chef, 1931   (83.3.5)
Lithograph, 10 x 14 1/4 in. (25.4 x
    36.2 cm) (comp.)
Gift of the Estate of Florence
    Rossbach

BO, Lars
Danish, (1924-   )
Untitled   (00.163)
Etching and aquatint, 11 1/4 x
    29 15/16 in. (28.6 x 76 cm)
Anonymous Gift

Untitled (Two Gondolas)   (00.164)
Etching, 19 5/8 x 25 3/4 in. (49.9 x
    65.4 cm)
Anonymous Gift

Portrait of a Lady with a Hat, Carl Bohnen,
charcoal on paperboard

BILL, Max
Swiss (1908-   )
Four Equal Colors, 1974*   (81.38.16)
Serigraph, 20 1/4 x 24 3/4 in. (76.8 x
    62.9 cm)
Gift of Mrs. Ann Steinberg

BIRD, Charles
English (n.d.)
Bristol Cathedral   (00.406)
Etching, 18 5/8 x 25 3/4 in. (47.3 x
    65.4 cm) (sight)
Anonymous Gift

BLAKE, William
English (1757-1827)
*Illustration for the Book of Job (no.
    19)* *   (64.31)
Engraving, 7 1/2 x 5 3/4 in. (19.1 x
    14.6 cm)
Gift of Mrs. George E. Whalen

BLAMPIED, Edmund **
English (1886-1966)
A Baker and a Woman   (83.3.6)
Etching, 11 x 8 1/4 in. (27.9 x 21 cm)
    (comp.)
Gift of the Estate of Florence
    Rossbach

BOHNEN, Carl
German (early 20th century)
Portrait of a Lady with a Hat, 1916*
(81.15.1)
Charcoal on paperboard, 23 1/2 x 17
    in. (59.7 x 43.2 cm) (sight)
Gift of Mr. and Mrs. Marvin L.
    Fishman

176

BOLOGNA, Giovanni da, Attributed to
Italian (16th century)
Study of Three Figures (83.29.14)
Pen and ink with wash, 6 9/16 x 4 3/4
in. (16.7 x 12.1 cm)
Gift of Mr. Paul P. Lipton

BOLSWERT, Boetius-Adams
Dutch (1580-1633)
Terrorists of the Spanish War*
(83.32.7)
Engraving, 8 1/2 x 11 1/8 in. (21.6 x
28.3 cm) (sight)
Gift of Dr. and Mrs. Sidney M. Boxer

BONFILS, Robert
French (1886-1972)
La Terrasse (The Terrace) (00.50)
Etching, 12 5/8 x 12 5/8 in. (32.1 x
32.1 cm)
Gift of Mr. and Mrs. Philip Pinsof

BOUCHOT, François, Attributed to
French (1800-1842)
*Voltaire à la Bastille composant la
Henriade (Voltaire in the Bastille
Writing the Henriade)* (00.118)
Engraving, 21 3/4 x 16 1/4 in. (55.3 x
41.3 cm)
Anonymous Gift

BOUDIN, Eugène **
French (1824-1898)
City Street Scene (82.10.2)
Watercolor, 4 x 7 3/8 in. (10.2 x 18.7
cm)
Anonymous Gift

Women in Gowns (82.10.1)
Watercolor, 4 x 7 3/8 in. (10.2 x
18.7 cm)
Anonymous Gift

BRADLEY, Dorothy
American (1920-   )
Iron Market (82.19.4)
Watercolor, 10 x 14 in. (25.4 x 35.6 cm)
Gift of Mr. Frederick D. Gore

Pierre's Garden (82.19.5)
Watercolor, 10 x 14 in. (25.4 x 35.6 cm)
Gift of Mr. Frederick D. Gore

BREWER, Henry Charles
English (1866-1943)
Doorway at Rheims (00.178)
Engraving, 29 13/16 x 21 13/16 in.
(75.7 x 55.4 cm)
Gift of Mr. Ray H. Wolf

View of Seville, Spain (00.127)
Engraving, 16 3/4 x 22 5/8 in. (42.6 x
57.5 cm)
Gift of Mr. Ray H. Wolf

Terrorists of the Spanish War, Boetius-Adams Bolswert, engraving

BREWER, James Alphège
English (late 19th-early 20th century)
Ratisbon (Regensburg Cathedral)
(00.496)
Etching, 25 1/2 x 19 1/2 in. (64.8 x
49.5 cm) (comp.)
Anonymous Gift

*Rheims Cathedral from the
Southwest* (00.488)
Etching, 20 x 23 7/8 in. (50.8 x 60.6
cm) (comp.)
Gift of Mr. Ray H. Wolf

West Front of Burgos Cathedral
(00.128)
Engraving, 22 7/8 x 17 3/4 in.
(58.1 x 45.1 cm)
Gift of Mr. Ray H. Wolf

*York Minster (The Great East
Window)*, 1921 (00.131)
Engraving, 20 3/4 x 12 3/4 in.
(52.7 x 32.4 cm)
Gift of Mr. Ray H. Wolf

BRIL, Paul
Flemish (1554-1626)
Untitled (Landscape) (00.56)
Engraving, 7 3/4 x 10 7/8 in.
(19.7 x 27.6 cm)
Anonymous Gift

BROUET, Auguste **
French (1872-1941)
Après la danse (After the Dance)
(00.13)
Roulette engraving, 12 3/4 x 15 in.
(32.4 x 38.1 cm)
Gift of Mr. and Mrs. Philip Pinsof

Le Cirque Pinder (The Pinder Circus)
(83.3.11)
Etching, 8 x 14 1/4 in. (20.3 x 36.2 cm)
Gift of the Estate of Florence
Rossbach

*L'Epluchage des pommes de terre
(Peeling Potatoes)* (83.3.9)
Etching, 6 3/4 x 6 1/2 in. (17.2 x
16.5 cm) (comp.)
Gift of the Estate of Florence
Rossbach

L'Habilleuse (The Dresser)
(83.3.10)
Roulette engraving, 6 3/4 x 8 1/2 in.
(17.2 x 21.6 cm) (comp.)
Gift of the Estate of Florence
Rossbach

La Relève (The Relief) (83.3.8)
Etching, 5 1/2 x 8 3/4 in. (14 x
22.2 cm) (comp.)
Gift of the Estate of Florence
Rossbach

177

BROUGH, Richard
American (1920–   )
Picnic, Muscle Shoals, Alabama
   (00.472)
Watercolor, 10 3/4 x 21 1/2 in.
   (42.6 x 54.8 cm) (sight)
Gift of the Ford Motor Company

BROWN, Butler
American (20th century)
Summer   (79.25)
Lithograph, 11 1/4 x 21 in. (28.6 x
   53.3 cm) (comp.)
Gift of Mr. E. C. Koerper/Marquette
   University Engineering Student
   Art Loan Fund

BURGER, Johannes
Swiss (b. 1829)
Violante   (00.290)
Engraving after Palma Vecchio,
   12 1/8 x 8 3/4 in. (30.8 x 22.2 cm)
Anonymous Gift

BYRD, Gibson
American (1923–   )
Four Innocents Assembled
   (82.19.3)
Conté crayon, 20 x 26 in. (50.8 x
   66 cm)
Gift of Mr. Frederick D. Gore

CAMERON, David Young
English (1865–1945)
Old St. Etienne   (79.14.1)
Etching, 9 5/8 x 17 3/8 in. (24.5 x
   44.1 cm)
Gift of Mrs. Douglass Van Dyke

CASSIRER, Paul
(Publisher)
German
*Kriegszeit. Künstlerflugblätter
   (Wartime. Artists' Pamphlets),*
   August 1914–March 1916 **
   (81.15.3.1–.57)
Series of fifty-seven offset litho-
   graphs on newsprint, 19 x 12 3/4
   in. (48.3 x 32.3 cm), each
Gift of Mr. and Mrs. Marvin L.
   Fishman

CASTELLANOS, Julio,
   Attributed to
Mexican (1905–1947)
Age and Youth   (00.109)
Lithograph, 16 5/8 x 12 7/8 in.
   (42.2 x 32.7 cm)
Gift of Mr. and Mrs. Philip Pinsof

CASTRO, (?)
Nationality Unknown (20th century)
Untitled (Woman Spinning Thread)
   (00.102)
Lithograph, 15 x 17 in. (38.1 x
   43.2 cm)
Anonymous Gift

CAULFIELD, Patrick
English (1936–   )
Big Sausage, 1978   (81.38.21.2)
Serigraph, 35 3/8 x 29 1/4 in.
   (89.9 x 74.3 cm)
Gift of Mr. Al Simon

Cigar, 1978   (82.23.4.2)
Serigraph, 22 5/8 x 23 7/8 in.
   (57.5 x 60.6 cm)
Gift of Mr. James Michael Posner

Sausage, 1978   (81.38.21.1)
Serigraph, 29 3/8 x 36 in. (74.6 x
   91.4 cm)
Gift of Mr. Al Simon

Three Sausages, 1978   (81.38.21.3)
Serigraph, 29 3/8 x 36 in. (74.6 x
   91.4 cm)
Gift of Mr. Al Simon

CHADWICK, Lynn
English (1914–   )
Two Sitting Figures on Stripes I,
   1972   (80.24.14.1)
Lithograph, 22 x 30 in. (55.9 x
   76.2 cm)
Gift of Mr. Thomas M. Lewyn

Two Sitting Figures on Stripes II,
   1972   (80.24.14.2)
Lithograph, 21 7/8 x 30 in. (55.6 x
   76.2 cm)
Gift of Mr. Thomas M. Lewyn

CHAGALL, Marc *
Russian (1887–   )
The Bible Series, 1957   (80.7.1–.105)
Suite of 105 hand-colored etchings,
   24 x 18 in. (61 x 45.7 cm), each
Gift of Mr. and Mrs. Patrick
   Haggerty

*The Blessing of Ephraim and
   Manasseh,* from the Bible Series,
   1957   (77.5)
Hand-colored etching, 24 x 18 in.
   (61 x 45.7 cm)
Gift of Mr. and Mrs. Raymond F.
   Newman

CHAMBARS, Thomas
English (1724–1789)
Claude la Fevre and Mr. John Hayls,
   1750   (00.285)
Engraving after Hoskins, 11 7/16 x
   9 in. (29.1 x 22.9 cm)
Anonymous Gift

CHARLOT, Jean
French (1898–1978)
Hawaiian Swimmer, 1972   (00.344)
Lithograph, 8 7/16 x 10 7/8 in. (21.4 x
   27.6 cm)
Anonymous Gift

CHEREAU, Jacques
French (1688–1776)
*Vestiges de plusieurs beaux
   monuments de l'ancienne Rome
   (Vestiges of Several Fine Monu-
   ments of Ancient Rome)*
   (80.20.11)
Hand-colored etching, 10 1/2 x 15 1/4
   in. (26.7 x 38.7 cm) (comp.)
Gift of Mr. Paul P. Lipton

CHRISTIE, John
Nationality Unknown (20th century)
Red Bird Portfolio, 1979
   (81.38.15.1–.12)
Set of twelve serigraphs with letter-
   press, c. 15 x 22 in. (38.1 x 55.9 cm),
   each
Gift of Mr. Stanley Myer

CLAUSEN, George *
English (1852–1944)
The Great Hammer, from the series,
   Britain's Efforts and Ideals in
   the Great War, 1917   (00.132)
Lithograph, 15 1/4 x 20 in. (38.7 x
   50.8 cm)
Gift of Mr. and Mrs. Philip Pinsof

Making Guns: Lifting an Inner Tube,
   from the series, Britain's Efforts
   and Ideals in the Great War, 1917
   (00.133)
Lithograph, 20 1/8 x 15 3/8 in.
   (51.1 x 39.1 cm)
Gift of Mr. and Mrs. Philip Pinsof

The Mill, from the series, Britain's
   Efforts and Ideals in the Great War,
   1917   (00.183)
Lithograph, 20 1/16 x 15 1/4 in.
   (51 x 38.7 cm)
Gift of Mr. and Mrs. Philip Pinsof

COFFEY, Brian and Stanley
William Hayter
Irish (20th century); English
(1901–)
The Death of Hector, 1979
(80.24.5.1-.15)
Set of fifteen engravings, 15 x 11 in.
(38.1 x 27.9 cm), each
Gift of Dr. Simon Levin

COHEN, Bernard
English (1933–)
Series of Images for J, 1976
(81.38.19.1-.6)
Set of six serigraphs, 18 x 36 1/4 in.
(45.7 x 92.1 cm), each
Gift of Mr. Al Simon

Untitled, 1965 (81.38.17)
Lithograph, 22 1/4 x 30 in. (56.5 x
76.2 cm)
Gift of Mr. Saul Steinberg

COLESCOTT, Warrington
American (1921–)
Trip to Rome, 1967 (82.16)
Ink and collage, 22 x 30 1/4 in.
(55.9 x 76.8 cm)
Gift of Mr. Jack M. Horner

COLLINS, W.
American (?)/English (?) (n.d.)
Rustic Civility (00.359)
Engraving, 10 9/16 x 14 1/2 in. (26.8
x 36.8 cm)
Anonymous Gift

COLT, John
American (1925–)
Night Garden, 1969 (82.19.1)
Pastel, 19 x 24 3/4 in. (48.3 x 62.9 cm)
Gift of Mr. Frederick D. Gore

Yellow Lights, 1977 (82.19.2)
Pastel, 18 3/4 x 25 in. (47.6 x 63.5 cm)
Gift of Mr. Frederick D. Gore

COORNHERT, Dirk Volkertsz.
Dutch (1518/22-1607)
Lot Leaving Sodom, 1545*
(83.32.5)
Engraving after Marten van
Heemskerck, 9 1/2 x 7 3/4 in.
(24.1 x 19.7 cm) (sight)
Gift of Dr. and Mrs. Sidney M. Boxer

COTTET, René, Attributed to
French (1902–)
Fireworks (80.17.47)
Engraving with remarque, 18 1/4 x
13 1/8 in. (46.4 x 33.3 cm) (comp.)
Gift of Mr. Paul P. Lipton

Lot Leaving Sodom, Dirk Volkertsz. Coornhert, engraving

COURIEN LITHO CO., Buffalo,
New York
American
*The Beautiful, Graceful, Arenic
Queen, M'lle Elena the Charming
Principal Bareback Equestrienne*
(00.320)
Offset lithograph, 24 1/2 x 16 3/4 in.
(62.2 x 42.6 cm)
Anonymous Gift

COUSINS, Henry
English (d. 1864)
The Right Honorable Lord Abinger,
1837 (00.122)
Mezzotint and etching, 19 3/4 x
15 1/2 in. (50.2 x 39.4 cm)
Gift of Mrs. Joseph D. Patton

COUY, Jean
French (1910–)
Dans un parc (In a Park)
(80.17.26)
Etching, 15 1/2 x 11 3/4 in. (39.4 x
29.9 cm) (comp.)
Gift of Mr. Paul P. Lipton

*La Reine des forains (The Queen
of the Carnival)* (80.17.28)
Etching, 13 3/4 x 9 3/4 in. (34.9 x
24.8 cm) (comp.)
Gift of Mr. Paul P. Lipton

Soleil Couchant (Setting Sun)
(80.17.27)
Etching, 11 5/8 x 15 1/2 in. (29.5 x
39.4 cm) (comp.)
Gift of Mr. Paul P. Lipton

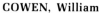
A Wood Scene, in Wentworth Park, York, from the series, Trees of England, William Cowen, India ink

Philip Melanchthon, Lucas Cranach the Younger, woodblock print

COWEN, William
English (1779–1860)
Trees of England, 1848*
   (00.135.1-.12)
Set of twelve India ink drawings, c.
   14 1/2 x 21 in. (36.8 x 53.3 cm), each
Gift of Mr. and Mrs. Philip Pinsof

CRANACH, Lucas, the Younger
German (1515–1586)
Philip Melanchthon, 1561*
   (83.32.2)
Woodblock print, 16 3/4 x 12 1/4 in.
   (42.6 x 31.1 cm)
Gift of Dr. and Mrs. Sidney M. Boxer

**CURRIER, Nathaniel and James
   Merritt Ives ** **
American (1813–1888); American
   (1824–1895)
The Soldier's Grave, 1862
   (82.7.10)
Hand-colored lithograph, 13 7/8 x 10
   in. (35.2 x 25.4 cm)
Gift of Dr. Kenneth Maier

D'ARCANGELO, Allan
American (1932–   )
Works from the Watertower Series,
   1973   (81.38.5.1-.5)
Set of five serigraphs, c. 33 1/8 x
   26 1/8 in. (84.1 x 66.4 cm), each
Gift of Mrs. Ann Steinberg

**DAUMIER, Honoré ** **
French (1808–1879)
*Works from Les Représentans
   Représentés (The Representatives
   Represented) series*
   (00.301.1-.12; .14-.23)
Set of twenty-two lithographs, c.
   14 3/8 x 9 3/4 in. (36.5 x 24.8 cm),
   each
Gift of Mr. and Mrs. Philip Pinsof

DAVID, Jacques Louis
French (1748-1825)
Portrait of Charles Pierre Pecoul
(76.29)
Oil on paper, 14 x 11 in. (35.6 x 27.9 cm)
Gift of Mr. and Mrs. Philip Pinsof

DEBAINES, H. (A.?) Brunet
Nationality Unknown (n.d.)
Bolton Abbey   (00.76)
Engraving, 14 1/4 x 10 1/2 in. (36.2 x 26.7 cm)
Anonymous Gift

Easley Abbey   (00.71)
Engraving, 10 1/2 x 14 1/8 in. (26.7 x 35.9 cm)
Anonymous Gift

DELVAILLE, Caro
French (?) (n.d.)
Nursing   (80.17.38)
Lithograph, 21 3/4 x 17 in. (55.3 x 43.2 cm) (comp.)
Gift of Mr. Paul P. Lipton

DeMARTELLY, John S.
American (1903-1980)
Give Us This Day   (83.6)
Lithograph, 15 7/8 x 18 1/2 in. (40.3 x 47 cm)
Gift of Dr. and Mrs. Adrian M. Dupuis

DePISIS, Filippo
Italian (1896-1956)
Study of Two Nudes, 1956
(80.25.22)
Conté crayon, 9 3/4 x 16 in. (24.8 x 40.6 cm) (sight)
Gift of Mr. Joseph P. Antonow

DIETRICY, Christian Wilhelm Ernst
German (1712-1774)
Untitled (Landscape with Stream), 1744   (00.35)
Etching, 6 1/2 x 8 5/8 in. (16.5 x 21.9 cm);
Anonymous Gift

Untitled (Landscape)   (00.246)
Engraving, 3 3/8 x 5 7/16 in. (8.6 x 13.8 cm)
Anonymous Gift

DISERTORI, Benvenuto **
Italian (1887-1967)
La Fortuna ed Apollo (Fortune and Apollo), 1928   (00.136)
Engraving and etching, 14 1/2 x 13 in. (36.8 x 33 cm)
Anonymous Gift

Il Piede della dea Giunone (The Foot of the Goddess Juno), 1919
(60.64)
Engraving and etching, 17 3/8 x 13 3/4 in. (44.1 x 34.9 cm)
Anonymous Gift

WALT DISNEY STUDIOS
American (20th century)
Bashful from Snow White
(83.3.12)
Acrylic on celluloid with veneer, 5 1/2 x 5 1/4 in. (14 x 13.3 cm) (comp.)
Gift of the Estate of Florence Rossbach

DOO, George T.
English (1800-1886)
The Earl of Eldon, 1828   (00.121)
Engraving after Sir Thomas Lawrence, 22 7/8 x 17 1/8 in. (58.1 x 43.5 cm)
Gift of Mrs. Joseph D. Patton

DORAZIO, Piero
Italian (1927-   )
Madrigale, 1979   (83.27.9)
Aquatint and etching, 20 x 27 1/2 in. (50.8 x 69.9 cm)
Gift of Mr. and Mrs. Ray Smith, Jr.

DOYLE, John
American (1940-   )
Drummer from the Cowboy Suite, 1974   (81.37)
Lithograph, 39 1/2 x 20 1/4 in. (100.3 x 51.4 cm) (comp.)
Gift of Mr. John Noble

The Great Human Race Series, 1983
(83.42.1-.10)
From the Builders Portfolio
Set of ten lithographs; dimensions vary
Gift of Mr. and Mrs. David J. Tolan

DÜRER, Albrecht **
German (1471-1528)
Book of Revelation Series

Four Horsemen   (56.2)
Woodcut, 15 1/2 x 11 in. (39.4 x 27.9 cm)
Gift of Mrs. Otto H. Falk

St. John Before God and the Elders   (56.9)
Woodcut, 15 1/2 x 11 7/8 in. (39.4 x 30.2 cm)
Gift of Mrs. Otto H. Falk

St. Michael Fighting the Dragon
(56.7)
Woodcut, 15 1/2 x 11 in. (39.4 x 28 cm)
Gift of Mrs. Otto H. Falk

Worship of the Lamb, 1510
(56.1)
Woodcut, 11 7/16 x 8 3/16 in. (29.1 x 20.8 cm)
Gift of Mrs. Otto H. Falk

Life of the Virgin Series

Assumption and Coronation of the Virgin   (56.10)
Woodcut, 11 1/2 x 8 1/8 in. (29.2 x 20.6 cm)
Gift of Mrs. Otto H. Falk

Flight into Egypt   (56.3)
Woodcut, 11 3/4 x 8 1/4 in. (29.9 x 21 cm)
Gift of Mrs. Otto H. Falk

Glorification of the Virgin
(56.6)
Woodcut, 11 9/16 x 8 1/4 in. (29.4 x 21 cm)
Gift of Mrs. Otto H. Falk

The Nativity   (56.8)
Woodcut, 10 3/4 x 8 1/8 in. (27.3 x 20.6 cm)
Gift of Mrs. Otto H. Falk

Melencolia
Engraving, 9 1/2 x 7 1/4 in. (24.1 x 18.4 cm)
Gift of Mrs. Otto H. Falk

St. Jerome in His Study, 1514
(64.3)
Engraving, 9 3/4 x 7 1/2 in. (24.8 x 19.1 cm)
Gift of Dr. and Mrs. John Pick

Virgin and Child Crowned by Two Angels, 1518   (56.4)
Engraving, 5 11/16 x 3 7/8 in. (14.4 x 9.8 cm)
Gift of Mrs. Otto H. Falk

DYCK, Anton van, Attributed to
Flemish (1599-1641)
*Portrait of Sir Kenelm Digby**
(76.31)
Graphite and crayon, 8 3/4 x 6 15/16 in. (22.2 x 17.6 cm)
Gift of Mr. and Mrs. Philip Pinsof

Portrait of Sir Kenelm Digby, Attributed to Anton van Dyck, graphite and crayon

ECHEUREN, Roberto Antonio Sebastian Matta (called Matta)
Chilean (1911-   )
Composition   (83.27.5)
Aquatint and etching, 14 3/4 x 19 1/2 in. (37.5 x 49.5 cm) (comp.)
Gift of Mr. and Mrs. Ray Smith, Jr.

EDWARDS, William Camden
English (1777-1855)
William Smith, Esquire, M.P. (00.353)
Engraving, 16 7/16 x 12 in. (41.8 x 30.5 cm)
Gift of Mrs. Joseph D. Patton

EHRENBERG, (?)
German (n.d.)
Untitled (Church Interior) (00.59)
Etching, 11 1/2 x 14 3/4 in. (29.2 x 37.5 cm)
Anonymous Gift

ELLIS, TRISTRAM J.
English (b. 1844)
Father and Mother Christmas on the Ice (00.268.4)
Engraving, 6 1/16 x 8 1/2 in. (15.4 x 21.6 cm)
Anonymous Gift

The Lancers: Ladies Chain (00.268.1)
Engraving, 6 1/16 x 8 1/2 in. (15.4 x 21.6 cm)
Anonymous Gift

Preparing for Action (00.268.3)
Engraving, 6 1/16 x 8 1/2 in. (15.4 x 21.6 cm)
Anonymous Gift

Thread the Needle (00.268.2)
Engraving, 6 1/16 x 8 1/2 in. (15.4 x 21.6 cm)
Anonymous Gift

ERSHI, Jiang
Chinese (1910-   )
Landscape (77.6)
Brush and ink on paperboard, 29 1/4 x 17 1/4 in. (74.3 x 43.8 cm) (sight)
Gift of Mr. and Mrs. Raymond F. Newman

ESCOBEDO, Jesús
Mexican (1917-   )
Man's Shadow, 1939 (00.165)
Lithograph, 23 5/8 x 17 15/16 in. (60 x 45.6 cm)
Gift of Mr. and Mrs. Philip Pinsof

FAINI, Umberto
Italian (1933-   )
Aria di Neve (Snow in the Air), 1979 (80.32.2)
Serigraph, 27 1/2 x 19 5/8 in. (69.9 x 49.9 cm)
Gift of Mr. E. C. Koerper/Marquette University Engineering Student Art Loan Fund

Nevica! (It's Snowing!), 1979 (80.32.1)
Serigraph, 27 9/16 x 19 5/8 in. (70 x 49.9 cm)
Gift of Mr. E. C. Koerper/Marquette University Engineering Student Art Loan Fund

FARREN, Robert
English (b. 1832)
Castle Street, 1880 (00.322)
Etching, 5 7/16 x 3 7/8 in. (13.8 x 9.8 cm)
Anonymous Gift

Chesterton Church, 1880 (00.189)
Etching, 11 x 16 in. (27.9 x 40.6 cm)
Anonymous Gift

Church of the Holy Sepulchre (Round Church), 1880 (00.188)
Engraving, 15 7/8 x 11 3/16 in. (40.3 x 28.4 cm)
Anonymous Gift

Manor House Ditton, 1881 (00.190)
Etching, 3 1/16 x 5 7/8 in. (7.8 x 14.9 cm)
Anonymous Gift

St. Mary the Less, 1880 (00.193)
Engraving, 16 x 11 1/8 in. (40.6 x 28.3 cm)
Anonymous Gift

Trumptington Church, 1880 (00.192)
Etching, 10 7/8 x 15 13/16 in. (27.6 x 40.2 cm)
Anonymous Gift

FEDER, Ben, Attributed to
American (1923-   )
Portrait of a Man (80.17.45)
Etching, 11 x 9 1/8 in. (27.9 x 23.2 cm) (comp.)
Gift of Mr. Paul P. Lipton

Old Clothes Dealer, Cairo, Stephen James Ferris, etching

FERRIS, Stephen James
American (1835-1915)
*Old Clothes Dealer, Cairo** (00.61)
Etching after J. L. Gérôme, 12 1/8 x 8 7/8 in. (30.8 x 22.5 cm)
Anonymous Gift

Untitled, 1879 (00.77)
Etching with roulette, 12 1/8 x 8 7/8 in. (30.8 x 22.5 cm)
Anonymous Gift

FILDES, Sir Samuel Luke
English (1844-1927)
Young Girl   (83.27.8)
Varnished etching, 20 1/2 x 12 3/4 in. (52.1 x 32.4 cm) (sight)
Gift of Mr. and Mrs. Ray Smith, Jr.

FINLAY, Ian Hamilton
English (1925-   )
Taschenbuch der Panzer (82.23.7.2)
Book, 9 15/16 x 11 13/16 in. (25.2 x 30.8 cm)
Gift of Mr. Bruce Koepfgen

FITTLER, J.
English (1758-1835)
Lord Kenyon, 1789   (00.119)
Engraving after J. Opie, 19 1/2 x 14 1/4 in. (49.5 x 36.2 cm)
Gift of Mrs. Joseph D. Patton

FITTON, Hedley
English (b. 1859)
Chichester Cross, 1926   (00.126)
Engraving, 21 1/2 x 17 1/2 in. (54.6 x 44.5 cm)
Gift of Mr. Ray H. Wolf

The Monument   (83.3.16)
Etching, 17 1/4 x 11 3/4 in. (43.8 x 29.9 cm) (comp.)
Gift of the Estate of Florence Rossbach

Old Bridge Dumfried   (83.3.13)
Etching, 13 x 9 in. (33 x 22.9 cm) (comp.)
Gift of the Estate of Florence Rossbach

St. Andrew's Castle in the Kingdom of Fife   (83.3.15)
Etching, 12 3/4 x 12 in. (32.4 x 30.5 cm) (comp.)
Gift of the Estate of Florence Rossbach

St. John Street, Canongate, 1926 (80.6)
Etching, 13 3/8 x 9 5/16 in. (34 x 23.7 cm) (sight)
Gift of Mrs. Eric C. Stern

St. John Street, Canongate, Edinburgh   (83.3.14)
Etching, 9 1/4 x 13 1/4 in. (23.5 x 33.7 cm) (comp.)
Gift of the Estate of Florence Rossbach

FLACK, Audrey **
American (1931-   )
Esperanza, or Macarena of Miracles, 1973   (80.29)
Lithograph, 34 x 24 in. (86.4 x 61 cm)
Gift of Mr. Michael H. Lord

FRINK, Elisabeth
English (1930-   )
Horse's Head, 1970   (81.38.29)
Lithograph, 15 1/8 x 23 in. (38.4 x 58.4 cm)
Gift of Mr. Al Simon

Lynx, 1970   (82.23.5.2)
Lithograph, 20 1/4 x 25 3/4 in. (51.4 x 65.4 cm)
Gift of Mr. Lloyd Hurst

GALLE, Cornelius and Theodor Galle
Flemish (1576-1650); Flemish (1571-1633)
Portrait of F. Matthaeus Basci (83.43.12)
Engraving, 6 x 4 1/4 in. (15.2 x 10.8 cm)
Gift of Mr. and Mrs. Marvin L. Fishman

GALLE, Philipp
Dutch (1537-1612)
Portrait of Professor D. Carolus Musitanus   (00.287)
Engraving, 8 9/16 x 6 1/4 in. (21.8 x 15.9 cm)
Anonymous Gift

GALLE, Theodor
Flemish (1571-1633)
Portraits of the Madonna (83.43.6.1&.2)
Engravings, 7 3/4 x 6 in. (19.7 x 15.2 cm), each
Gift of Mr. and Mrs. Marvin L. Fishman

GARCIA-BUSTOS, Arturo
Mexican (1926-   )
Untitled   (00.110)
Lithograph, 14 5/8 x 17 in. (37.2 x 43.2 cm)
Anonymous Gift

GAUERMANN, Jakob, Attributed to
German (1773-1843)
Untitled (Landscape)   (00.247)
Etching, 7 3/16 x 5 3/16 in. (18.3 x 13.5 cm)
Anonymous Gift

Untitled (Landscape Scenes) (00.249)
Etching, 7 3/16 x 5 3/16 in. (18.3 x 13.5 cm)
Anonymous Gift

GENOVÉS, Juan
Spanish (1930-   )
Afterwards, Now, and Before, from the Silensi, Silencio Series, 1971 (81.38.4.2)
Etching, 19 3/4 x 25 7/8 in. (50.2 x 65.8 cm)
Gift of Mrs. Ann Steinberg

Broken Man, from the El Lugar y El Tiempo Series, 1971 (80.24.29)
Etching, 19 3/4 x 26 in. (50.2 x 66 cm)
Gift of Mr. Robert Layton

Double Page, 1970   (81.38.4.4)
Etching, 19 3/4 x 26 in. (50.2 x 66 cm)
Gift of Mrs. Ann Steinberg

Order to Move Aside, 1970 (81.38.4.3)
Etching, 19 13/16 x 26 in. (50.2 x 66 cm)
Gift of Mr. Edward J. Safdie

Time and Place, from the El Lugar y El Tiempo Series, 1971 (81.38.4.1)
Etching, 19 13/16 x 26 in. (50.2 x 66 cm)
Gift of Mr. Edward J. Safdie

GEORGE, Herbert
English (b. 1863)
Canterbury Cathedral   (00.191)
Etching, 19 7/8 x 14 3/4 in. (50.5 x 37.5 cm)
Gift of Mr. Ray H. Wolf

St. Peter's, Rome   (00.187)
Engraving, 26 5/8 x 19 in. (67.6 x 48.3 cm)
Gift of Mr. Ray H. Wolf

GESSERT, Earl
American (1918-   )
Dancers Three   (55.5)
Watercolor, 24 x 18 1/2 in. (61 x 47 cm) (sight)
Gift of Milwaukee Equipment Company

GEYFEN, F.
Nationality Unknown (n.d.)
Portrait of Jacobus Groeneveld
    (83.43.7)
Engraving, 10 x 7 3/8 in. (25.4 x 18.7
    cm)
Gift of Mr. and Mrs. Marvin L.
    Fishman

GIELE, Ferdinand, Attributed to
Belgian (1867-1929)
Louvain Court   (00.10)
Etching, 11 1/4 x 8 in. (28.6 x 20.3 cm)
    (comp.)
Anonymous Gift

GOERG, Edouard-Joseph
French (1893-1969)
*Dans la main sept étoiles, de la
    bouche une épée à double file sort
    aérée (Seven Stars in the Hand,
    Emerging from the Mouth an
    Ethereal Sword in Double File),*
    1945   (80.17.7)
Lithograph, 13 1/2 x 9 3/4 in. (34.3 x
    24.8 cm) (comp.)
Gift of Mr. Paul P. Lipton

Forest Scene   (80.17.44)
Etching, 11 5/8 x 8 1/8 in. (29.5 x 20.6
    cm) (comp.)
Gift of Mr. Paul P. Lipton

GOFFEY, Harry, Attributed to
English (b. 1871)
Church Interior   (00.502)
Etching, 12 5/8 x 8 3/4 in. (32.1 x 22.2
    cm) (comp.)
Gift of Mr. Ray H. Wolf

*Christ, from Christ, St. Paul, and the
Twelve Apostles,* Hendrik Goltzius, engraving.

The Three Crosses, Hendrik Goltzius, engraving

**GOLTZIUS, Hendrik ** **
Dutch (1558-1617)
*Christ, St. Paul, and the Twelve
    Apostles,* 1589*   (83.32.14.1-.14)
Set of fourteen engravings, 5 3/4 x
    4 in. (14.6 x 10.2 cm) (comp.) each
Gift of Dr. and Mrs. Sidney M. Boxer

Mucius Scaevola, from the Warrior
    Series   (83.32.3)
Engraving, 22 1/4 x 17 1/2 in. (56.5 x
    44.5 cm)
Gift of Dr. and Mrs. Sidney M. Boxer

184

The Three Crosses, * c. 1600   (83.32.15)
Engraving, 7 3/4 x 5 in. (19.7 x 12.7
  cm) (sight)
Gift of Dr. and Mrs. Sidney M. Boxer

Titus Manlius Torquatus, from the
  Warrior Series   (83.32.4)
Engraving, 20 1/4 x 15 in. (51.4 x
  38.1 cm)
Gift of Dr. and Mrs. Sidney M. Boxer

GOODNOUGH, Robert
American (1917-   )
From One, Two, Three A-L, 1968
  (81.38.7)
Serigraph, 22 x 30 in. (55.9 x 76.2 cm)
Gift of Mrs. Ann Steinberg

Tea   (80.3.1)
Green ink, 6 1/4 x 9 1/4 in. (15.9 x
  23.5 cm) (sight)
Gift of Mr. Joseph P. Antonow

GORSE, André
French (active mid-late 19th century)
Vue générale des eaux chaudes
  (Panorma of the Hot Springs)
  (80.20.16)
Hand-colored lithograph, 9 5/8 x
  12 1/4 in. (24.5 x 31.1 cm)
Gift of Mr. Paul P. Lipton

GOTTLIEB, Adolph
American (1903-1974)
Black and Grey, 1967   (81.38.2.6)
Serigraph, 24 x 18 in. (61 x 45.7 cm)
Gift of Mr. Saul Steinberg

Black Field, 1972   (81.38.2.1)
Serigraph, 36 1/8 x 27 5/8 in. (91.8 x
  70.2 cm)
Gift of Mr. Saul Steinberg

Blue Night, 1970   (81.38.2.2)
Serigraph, 39 3/8 x 27 1/8 in. (100 x
  68.9 cm)
Gift of Mr. Saul Steinberg

Figure Eight, 1967   (81.38.2.5)
Serigraph, 18 x 24 in. (45.7 x 61 cm)
Gift of Mr. Saul Steinberg

Germination I, 1972*   (81.38.2.3)
Serigraph, 36 x 27 1/2 in. (91.4 x
  69.9 cm)
Gift of Mr. Saul Steinberg

Pink Ground, 1972   (81.38.2.4)
Serigraph, 36 1/8 x 27 1/2 in. (91.8 x
  69.9 cm)
Gift of Mr. Saul Steinberg

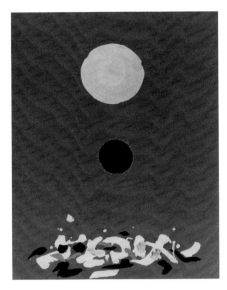

Germination I, Adolph Gottlieb, serigraph

GOTZ, F.
German (mid 18th-early 19th
  century)
Untitled (Figure Studies), 1790
  (00.223)
Ink and wash, 13 7/8 x 9 1/8 in. (35.2
  x 23.2 cm)
Gift of Mr. and Mrs. Philip Pinsof

GRIMM, Simon
German (mid 17th-early 18th
  century)
Untitled (Harbor Scene), 1669
  (00.276)
Engraving, 5 5/8 x 8 in. (14.3 x 20.3
  cm)
Anonymous Gift

GROMME, Owen Justus
American (1896-   )
Marshland Elegy-Aldo Leopold,
  1978   (83.28)
Photographic serigraph, 29 1/2 x
  22 1/2 in. (74.9 x 57.2 cm)
Gift of Dr. and Mrs. Charles W. Miller

*Salute to Dawn, Whooping Cranes
  at Wood Buffalo National Park,*
  1974   (81.6)
Photographic serigraph, 25 1/2 x
  32 1/2 in. (64.8 x 82.6 cm)
Gift of Dr. and Mrs. Charles W. Miller

GROOM, Emily
American (1876-1975)
Atitlan Lake   (59.7)
Watercolor on paper, 19 1/8 x 25 3/8
  in. (48.6 x 64.5 cm) (sight)
Anonymous Gift

GROSZ, George
German (1893-1959)
*Sturmwolken über Cape Cod (Storm
  Clouds over Cape Cod),* 1949
  (82.11.1)
Lithograph, 12 7/8 x 16 1/8 in. (32.7 x
  41 cm)
Gift of Mr. and Mrs. Marvin L.
  Fishman

GUCHT, Michiel von der,
  Attributed to
Flemish (1660-1725)
Edoardi Coke   (00.341)
Engraving, 8 9/16 x 6 in. (21.8 x 15.2
  cm)
Anonymous Gift

GUIBERT, François, Attributed to
French (active late 18th century)
Gaucher de Chastillon   (00.293)
Engraving after Simon Vouet, 10 1/4
  x 8 1/8 in. (26 x 20.6 cm)
Anonymous Gift

HADDAD, Farid
Lebanese (1945-   )
Untitled, 1978   (81.21.1)
Graphite, pastel, and dry pigment,
  25 1/2 x 40 in. (64.8 x 101.6 cm)
Gift of Mr. Michael H. Lord

Untitled, Farid Haddad, graphite, pastel
and dry pigment

Untitled, 1978*   (82.21.2)
Graphite, pastel, and dry pigment,
  25 1/2 x 40 in. (64.8 x 101.6 cm)
Gift of Mr. Michael H. Lord

HAELWEGH, Adriaen
Dutch (b. 1637)
Francis of Etruria   (00.26)
Engraving, 14 1/2 x 10 5/8 in. (36.8 x
  27 cm)
Anonymous Gift

HAGNE, Louis
Belgian (1806-1885)
Brewers Corporation Room, Antwerp
(00.500)
Hand-colored lithograph, 10 1/2 x
14 3/4 in. (26.7 x 37.5 cm) (sight)
Gift of Mr. and Mrs. James W.
Bergstrom

HAIG, Axel Herman
Swedish (1835-1921)
Canterbury Cathedral, 1912
(00.185)
Engraving, 25 5/16 x 20 7/8 in.
(66.8 x 53 cm)
Gift of Mr. Ray H. Wolf

Interior of St. Mark's, 1911
(00.194)
Etching, 23 13/16 x 28 3/4 in. (60.5 x
73 cm)
Gift of Mr. Ray H. Wolf

Limburg on the Lake, 1886
(00.195)
Engraving, 40 x 30 in. (101.6 x 76.2
cm)
Gift of Mr. Ray H. Wolf

Ponte S. Pietro, Verona, 1879
(00.116)
Etching, 10 1/4 x 14 in. (26 x 35.6 cm)
Anonymous Gift

Toledo (Cathedral Interior)
(00.497)
Etching, 28 1/2 x 19 5/8 in. (72.4 x
49.9 cm) (comp.)
Gift of Mr. Ray H. Wolf

View of the College Magdalene,
1886   (00.207)
Engraving, 29 3/4 x 20 7/8 in. (75.6
x 53 cm)
Gift of Mr. Ray H. Wolf

HAJDU, Etienne
Hungarian/French (1907-   )
Untitled, c. 1960   (80.25.14-.16)
Set of three cellocuts, 18 1/2 x 28 1/2
in. (47 x 72.4 cm), each
Gift of Mr. Joseph P. Antonow

HALL, Henry Bryan
Amercian (19th century)
John Marshall, 1877   (00.123)
Engraving after Henry Inman,
22 3/4 x 18 in. (57.8 x 45.7 cm)
Anonymous Gift

HALL, John
English (1739-1797)
The Right, Honorable Isaac Barre,
1787   (00.349)
Engraving, 13 3/8 x 9 3/8 in. (34 x
23.8 cm)
Gift of Mrs. Joseph D. Patton

HAMAGUCHI, Yôzô
Japanese (1909-   )
Untitled (Asparagus and Lemon)
(00.227)
Mezzotint, 19 5/8 x 29 5/16 in. (49.9 x
74.5 cm)
Gift of Mr. and Mrs. Philip Pinsof

**HAMMOND, Paul and Patrick
    Hughes**
Nationality Unknown (20th century);
English (1939-   )
Upon the Pun, 1978/1979
(81.38.36.10)
Book and set of six aquatints, 8 3/4 x
5 5/8 x 3/4 in. (22.2 x 14.3 x 1.9 cm)
Gift of Mr. Steven D. Sohackie and
Mrs. Bernice Sohackie

HARING, Keith
American (1958-   )
Untitled, 1983*   (83.12.1)
Marker ink on foam core, 40 1/4 x
60 1/2 in. (102.2 x 153.7 cm)
Gift of the artist

Untitled, 1983   (83.12.2)
Autographed book, 9 x 9 3/4 x 1/2 in.
(22.9 x 24.8 x 1.3 cm)
Gift of the artist

HEATH, William
English (1795-1840)
*Cambrio-Let or Shelter Versus
    Pelter*   (83.45.2)
Hand-colored engraving (?), 9 1/4 x
13 1/2 in. (23.5 x 34.3 cm) (comp.)
Gift of Dr. Kenneth Maier

HEEMSKERCK, Marten van **
Dutch (1498-1574)
Episodes from the Story of Esther,
1563   (67.5.1.1-.8)
Series of eight engravings, 10 5/8 x
13 7/8 in. (27 x 35.2 cm), each
Gift of Mr. and Mrs. Philip Pinsof

HENRIET, Israël
French (1590-1661)
*Livre de diverses perspectives et
paysages faits sur le naturel....
(Book of Various Views and Land-
scapes, Done Out of Doors....)*,
1651   (00.270)
Engraving, 5 3/4 x 10 1/16 in. (14.6
x 25.6 cm)
Anonymous Gift

HEPWORTH, Barbara
English (1903-1975)
*Opposing Forms**   (80.24.16.1)
Serigraph, 30 1/2 x 22 13/16 in.
(77.5 x 57.9 cm)
Gift of Mr. Thomas M. Lewyn

Untitled, Keith Haring, marker on foam core

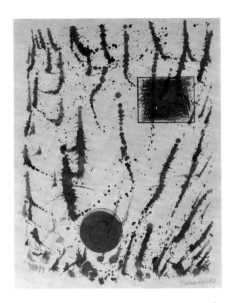

Opposing Forms, Barbara Hepworth, serigraph.

HERMAN, Josef
English (1911-   )
On the Way Home, 1975
(82.23.4.1)
Lithograph, 19 7/8 x 24 15/16 in.
(50.5 x 63.3 cm)
Gift of Mr. James Michael Posner

HERON, Patrick
English (1920-   )
January, 1973   (82.23.1.1-.3)
Set of three serigraphs, 27 5/8 x
35 3/4 in. (70.2 x 90.8 cm)
Gift of Mr. and Mrs. Ben Wunsch and
gift of Mr. Hamilton Richardson

Small Red January 1973:2, 1973
(82.23.1.3)
Serigraph, 19 7/8 x 23 in. (50.5 x
58.4 cm)
Gift of Mr. and Mrs. Ben Wunsch

HIROSHIGE, Andô
Japanese (1797-1858)
Figures in a Landscape   (83.14.9)
Woodcut, 9 5/8 x 15 in. (24.5 x 38.1
cm)
Gift of Mr. Samuel Gansheroff

Scene of Edo   (77.7)
Woodcut, 13 11/16 x 9 1/16 in.
(34.8 x 23 cm) (sight)
Gift of Mr. and Mrs. Raymond F.
Newman

Young Woman Holding an Umbrella
(83.14.4)
Woodcut, 15 3/8 x 10 1/4 in. (39.1 x
26 cm)
Gift of Mr. Samuel Gansheroff

HIRSCH, Joseph
American (1910-1981)
Lunch Hour   (83.43.1)
Lithograph, 11 x 14 1/8 in. (27.9 x
35.9 cm)
Gift of Mr. and Mrs. Marvin L.
Fishman

HOCH, Johann Jakob
German (1750-1829)
Holy Day Prayers, 1799   (76.28)
Watercolor, 18 1/4 x 15 5/16 in. (46.4
x 38.9 cm) (comp.)
Gift of Mr. and Mrs. Philip Pinsof

Jew Praying in the Synagogue, 1799
(76.27)
Watercolor, 23 1/4 x 19 7/8 in. (59.1 x
50.5 cm)
Gift of Mr. and Mrs. Philip Pinsof

HOFMANN, Douglas
American (1945-   )
Night, 1979   (79.23.1)
Graphite, 13 1/2 x 11 in. (34.3 x
27.9 cm)
Gift of Mr. E. C. Koerper/Marquette
University Engineering Student
Art Loan Fund

HOGARTH, William
English (1697-1764)
Analysis of Beauty, Plate I
(00.153)
Engraving, published 1798, 16 1/2 x
21 9/16 in. (41.9 x 54.8 cm)
Anonymous Gift

Analysis of Beauty, Plate II
(00.154)
Engraving, published 1798, 16 1/2 x
21 1/2 in. (41.9 x 54.6 cm)
Anonymous Gift

*And as He Reasoned of Righteous-
ness, Temperance, and Judgment
to Come, Felix Trembled*
(00.149)
Engraving, published 1799, 16 1/2 x
21 1/4 in. (41.9 x 54 cm)
Anonymous Gift

The Battle of the Pictures   (00.212)
Engraving, 9 x 9 11/16 in. (22.9 x
24.6 cm)
Anonymous Gift

The Beggar's Opera   (00.159)
Engraving, 10 5/8 x 12 7/8 in. (27 x
32.7 cm)
Gift of Mr. and Mrs. Philip Pinsof

The Bruiser   (00.217)
Engraving, published 1800, 18 9/16
x 15 9/16 in. (47.2 x 39.5 cm)
Anonymous Gift

Burning the Rumps at Temple Barr
(00.148)
Engraving, published 1801, 13 5/8 x
21 5/8 in. (34.6 x 54.9 cm)
Gift of Mr. and Mrs. Leslie S. Pinsof

Canvassing for Votes   (00.150)
Engraving, 16 3/4 x 21 3/4 in. (42.6 x
55.3 cm)
Anonymous Gift

The Company of Undertakers
(00.161)
Engraving, 12 9/16 x 9 1/2 in.
(31.9 x 24.1 cm)
Gift of Mr. and Mrs. Philip Pinsof

A Country Inn Yard   (00.158)
Engraving, published 1800, 10 1/2 x
15 1/8 in. (26.7 x 38.4 cm)
Gift of Mr. and Mrs. Philip Pinsof

Cruelty in Perfection   (00.139)
Engraving, published 1799, 19 1/2 x
15 7/8 in. (49.5 x 40.3 cm)
Anonymous Gift

*An Emblematic Print on the South
Sea*   (00.231)
Engraving, published 1800, 11 3/4 x
15 1/2 in. (29.9 x 39.4 cm)
Gift of Mr. and Mrs. Philip Pinsof

England   (00.142)
Engraving, published 1799, 15 1/2 x
18 7/8 in. (39.4 x 47.9 cm)
Anonymous Gift

First Stage of Cruelty   (00.141)
Engraving, published 1799, 19 3/8 x
16 1/4 in. (49.2 x 41.3 cm)
Anonymous Gift

*The Five Orders of Perriwigs as They
Were Worn at the Late Coronation
Measured Architectonically*
(00.230)
Engraving, published 1800, 15 5/8 x
10 1/4 in. (39.7 x 26 cm)
Gift of Mr. and Mrs. Philip Pinsof

France   (00.143)
Engraving, published 1798, 15 1/2 x
18 1/2 in. (39.4 x 47 cm)
Anonymous Gift

*Hudibras Encounters the
    Skimmington*   (00.147)
Engraving, published 1802, 13 3/8
    x 21 3/8 in. (34 x 54.3 cm)
Gift of Mr. and Mrs. Leslie S. Pinsof

John Wilkes, Esq.   (00.241)
Engraving, published 1800, 15 9/16
    x 10 1/8 in. (39.5 x 25.7 cm)
Gift of Mr. and Mrs. Philip Pinsof

Midnight Modern Conversation
    (00.209)
Engraving, published 1798, 16 1/4 x
    21 3/8 in. (41.3 x 54.3 cm)
Anonymous Gift

Moses and the Pharaoh's Daughter
    (00.151)
Engraving, published 1801, 16 3/4 x
    21 1/2 in. (42.6 x 54.6 cm)
Anonymous Gift

O the Roast Beef of Old England
    (00.144)
Engraving, published 1797, 16 3/8 x
    21 3/8 in. (41.6 x 54.3 cm)
Anonymous Gift

Pit Ticket   (00.137)
Engraving, published 1796, 15 7/8 x
    18 1/4 in. (40.3 x 46.4 cm)
Anonymous Gift

The Polling   (00.152)
Engraving, published 1801, 16 7/8 x
    21 15/16 in. (42.9 x 55.7 cm)
Anonymous Gift

The Reward of Cruelty   (00.138)
Engraving, published 1799, 18 7/8 x
    15 3/8 in. (48 x 39.1 cm)
Anonymous Gift

*Sancho at the Feast Starved by His
    Physician*   (00.146)
Engraving, published 1802, 13 1/2 x
    15 5/8 in. (34.3 x 39.7 cm)
Gift of Mr. and Mrs. Leslie S. Pinsof

Second Stage of Cruelty   (00.140)
Engraving, published 1799, 19 1/4 x
    16 in. (48.9 x 40.6 cm)
Anonymous Gift

Simon Lord Lovat   (00.156)
Engraving, published 1800, 19 x
    13 15/16 in. (48.3 x 35.4 cm)
Anonymous Gift

Sleeping Congregation   (00.160)
Engraving, 11 9/16 x 8 1/2 in. (29.4 x
    21.6 cm)
Gift of Mr. and Mrs. Philip Pinsof

3 Caricaturas, 4 Characters, William Hogarth, engraving

Tail Piece/The Bathos   (00.145)
Engraving, published 1798, 16 x
    18 5/8 in. (40.6 x 47.3 cm)
Anonymous Gift

3 Caricaturas, 4 Characters*
    (00.162)
Engraving, published 1802, 12 1/2 x
    9 5/8 in. (31.8 x 24.5 cm)
Gift of Mr. and Mrs. Philip Pinsof

The Times   (00.157)
Engraving, 10 1/2 x 14 15/16 in.
    (26.7 x 37.9 cm)
Gift of Mr. and Mrs. Philip Pinsof

HOKUSAI, Katsushika
Japanese (1760-1849)
Fisherman with Lines   (83.14.5)
Woodcut, 10 7/8 x 15 3/4 in. (27.6 x
    40 cm)
Gift of Mr. Samuel Gansheroff

Untitled   (00.263)
Woodcut, 7 1/8 x 4 7/8 in. (18.1 x
    12.4 cm)
Anonymous Gift

**HOKUSAI, Katsushika,
    Attributed to**
(Japanese (1760-1849)
Street Scene   (00.316)
Ink and wash, 10 5/16 x 14 15/16 in.
    (26.2 x 37.9 cm) (sight)
Anonymous Gift

Untitled   (00.235)
Woodcut, 11 1/4 x 4 11/16 in.
  (28.6 x 11.9 cm)
Anonymous Gift

HOLLAR, Wenzel
Czechoslovakian (1607-1677)
*Divers Prospects in and about
  Tangier, 1669*   (00.277)
Etching, 5 1/4 x 8 9/16 in. (13.3 x
  21.8 cm)
Anonymous Gift

HOLLAR, Wenzel, Attributed to
Czechoslovakian (1607-1677)
Tootehill Fields, 1669   (00.279)
Engraving, 3 15/16 x 6 15/16 in.
  (10 x 17.6 cm)
Anonymous Gift

HONE, Horace
English (1756-1825)
Ganden (?) Architect   (00.350)
Engraving, 17 1/8 x 11 7/8 in.
  (43.5 x 30.2 cm)
Gift of Mrs. Joseph D. Patton

HOUBRAKEN, Jacobus
Dutch (1698-1780)
John, Duke of Lauderdale, 1740
  (00.23)
Etching and engraving after Peter
  Lely, 17 3/4 x 11 1/2 in. (45.1 x
  29.2 cm)
Gift of Mrs. Joseph D. Patton

*Portrait of Henrik, Heer van
  Brederode*   (83.43.3)
Engraving, 10 1/2 x 7 15/16 in. (26.7
  x 20.2 cm)
Gift of Mr. and Mrs. Marvin L.
  Fishman

*Portrait of Mr. Romein DeHooghe,
  1733*   (83.43.4)
Engraving after H. Bos, 9 x 7 1/8 in.
  (22.9 x 18.1 cm)
Gift of Mr. and Mrs. Marvin L.
  Fishman

HOWARTH, Albany E.
English (b. 1872)
Burgos Cathedral   (00.181)
Engraving, 37 x 27 1/4 in. (94 x
  69.2 cm)
Gift of Mr. Ray H. Wolf

Chancel, Ely Cathedral   (00.67)
Etching, 19 3/4 x 10 1/2 in. (50.2 x
  26.7 cm) (comp.)
Gift of Mr. Ray H. Wolf

Chancel, Ely Cathedral   (79.15.1)
Etching, 19 3/4 x 10 5/8 in. (50.2 x
  27 cm) (comp.)
Gift of Mr. and Mrs. Hugo Gorski

Facade of Rheims, 1914   (00.182)
Engraving, 36 1/4 x 25 7/8 in. (92.1
  x 65.9 cm)
Gift of Mr. Ray H. Wolf

Five Sisters York   (79.15.2)
Etching, 19 1/2 x 10 3/4 in. (49.5 x
  27.3 cm) (comp.)
Gift of Mr. and Mrs. Hugo Gorski

Winchester Cathedral   (00.495)
Etching, 24 1/4 x 16 3/8 in. (61.6 x
  41.6 cm) (comp.)
Gift of Mr. Ray H. Wolf

HOYLAND, John
English (1934-   )
Yellow and Pink, from the New York
  Suite, 1971   (82.23.5.1)
Serigraph, 28 x 40 3/4 in. (71.1 x
  103.5 cm)
Gift of Mr. Lloyd Hurst

HRATCHYA
French (1939-   )
Art Expo New York   (80.33)
Embossed etching, 26 7/8 x 19 5/8
  in. (68.3 x 49.9 cm)
Gift of Mr. E. C. Koerper/Marquette
  University Engineering Student
  Art Loan Fund

HUGGINS, Wilfrid
English (1873-   )
St. Paul's   (00.66)
Etching, 23 1/2 x 18 in. (59.7 x 45.7
  cm)
Gift of Mr. Ray H. Wolf

HUGHES, Patrick
English, (1939-   )
*The Domestic Life of the Rainbow
  Portfolio, 1979*   (81.38.36.1-.9)
Set of nine serigraphs, 5 1/4 x 9 in.
  (13.3 x 22.9 cm), each
Gift of Mr. Steven D. Sohackie and
  Mrs. Bernice Sohackie

Moon Room, 1980   (81.38.22.2)
Aquatint, 35 7/8 x 29 3/8 in. (91.1 x
  74.6 cm)
Gift of Mr. Steven D. Sohackie and
  Mrs. Bernice Sohackie

Simsonapiss, 1980   (81.38.22.1)
Aquatint, 35 3/4 x 29 1/2 in. (90.8 x
  74.9 cm)
Gift of Mr. Steven D. Sohackie and
  Mrs. Bernice Sohackie

HUGO, Valentine
French (1890-1968)
Woman   (80.17.40)
Drypoint, 9 1/4 x 7 in. (23.5 x 17.8
  cm) (comp.)
Gift of Mr. Paul P. Lipton

IRVING, Washington
American (1783-1859)
*Autograph Letter and Image of the
  Author, 1837*   (80.25.6a&b)
  a. pen and ink, 9 1/2 x 7 1/2 in.
    (24.1 x 19.1 cm) (sight)
  b: etching, 8 3/4 x 6 1/4 in. (22.3 x
    16 cm) (sight)
Gift of Mr. Joseph P. Antonow

JACQUE, Charles Emile
French (1813-1894)
Le Lameau (The Hamlet)   (82.7.14)
Etching, 5 3/4 x 9 in. (14.6 x 22.9 cm)
  (sight)
Gift of Dr. Kenneth Maier

JOHNSON, Cecile Ryden
American (20th century)
Front Street, Hamilton, Bermuda
  (00.473)
Watercolor, 16 1/2 x 22 7/8 in.
  (41.9 x 58.1 cm) (sight)
Gift of Ford Motor Company

KAISER, Charles James
American (1939-   )
*Chapel Dedicated to Joan of Arc,
  1966*   (66.7)
Watercolor, 24 3/8 x 17 3/4 in. (61.9 x
  45.1 cm) (sight)
Gift of the artist

Medieval Font, 1966   (66.6)
Watercolor, graphite, and highlighting, 20 3/4 x 21 5/8 in. (52.7 x
  54.9 cm) (sight)
Gift of the artist

KATSUKAWA, Shunshô
Japanese (1726-1792)
*Two Women with Picture**
  (00.308)
Woodcut, 23 7/8 x 4 1/2 in. (60.6 x
  11.4 cm) (sight)
Anonymous Gift

Untitled (Two Women)   (00.225)
Woodcut, 24 7/8 x 4 9/16 in. (63.2 x
  11.6 cm)
Anonymous Gift

KIDNER, Michael
Nationality Unknown (20th century)
Elastic Membrane, 1979
  (80.24.1.1-.11)
Set of eleven etchings and litho-
  graphs with book, 17 3/4 x 14 x
  2 1/2 in. (45.1 x 35.6 x 6.4 cm)
Gift of Mr. Joseph M. McNasby

Two Women with Picture,
Shunshô Katsukawa, woodcut

KIHAN, B.
German (17th century)
M. Georg Paulus Jenisch,
  Evangelischer Prediger (M. Georg
  Paulus Jenisch, Protestant
  Minister), 1684   (00.286)
Engraving, 7 1/2 x 10 7/8 in. (19.1 x
  27.6 cm)
Anonymous Gift

KIKUGAWA, Eisen
Japanese (1790-1848)
A Woman   (00.317)
Woodcut, 13 13/16 x 9 1/8 in. (35.1 x
  23.2 cm) (sight)
Anonymous Gift

KILIAN, Wolfgang
German (1581-1662)
Untitled (Portrait of a Man)
  (00.292)
Engraving, 7 3/16 x 4 15/16 in. (18.3
  x 12.5 cm)
Anonymous Gift

KING, Ronald
American (20th century)
Anthony and Cleopatra, 1979
  (80.24.6.1-.11)
Set of eleven serigraphs, 15 1/4 x
  11 1/4 in. (38.7 x 28.6 cm), each
Gift of Mr. Dean Stephens

KLASS, (?)
German (n.d.)
Untitled (Landscape with Figures)
  (00.250)
Etching, 3 1/8 x 4 in. (7.9 x 10.2 cm)
Anonymous Gift

KLEINHOLZ, Frank
American (1901-   )
Studies for Children at Play
  (59.11.1-.3)
Charcoal on paperboard
  .1: 79 1/2 x 60 3/4 in. (201.9 x
    154.3 cm)
  .2: 75 1/2 x 25 5/8 in. (191.8 x
    65.1 cm)
  .3: 74 1/4 x 25 1/4 in. (188.6 x
    64.1 cm)
Gift of Mr. Joseph P. Antonow

KLEMM, Walter
German (1883-1957)
Robinson Crusoe Series, 1919
  (00.300.1-.10)
Set of ten lithographs, c. 12 x 10 in.
  (30.5 x 25.4 cm), each
Anonymous Gift

KOBELL, Ferdinand
German (1740-1799)
Untitled (Landscape), 1781
  (00.248)
Etching, 4 1/2 x 6 5/8 in. (11.4 x
  16.8 cm)
Anonymous Gift

Untitled (Landscape)   (00.280)
Etching, 3 3/8 x 5 3/8 in. (8.6 x 13.7
  cm)
Anonymous Gift

KOHLSHEIN, Joseph
German (1841-1915)
Untitled (Portrait of a Man), 1860
  (00.343)
Engraving, 6 3/8 x 4 5/8 in. (16.2 x
  11.8 cm)
Anonymous Gift

KOHLSTEDT, Dale
American (1949-   )
Tourmaline   (79.5)
Lithograph, 25 x 37 3/4 in. (63.5 x
  95.9 cm)
Gift of Mr. E. C. Koerper/Marquette
  University Engineering Student
  Art Loan Fund

KOKOSCHKA, Oskar
Austrian/English (1886-1980)
In Memory of the Children of Vienna
  Who Will Die of Hunger This Year,
  1946*   (81.25.3)
Lithograph, 24 1/4 x 19 1/4 in. (61.6
  x 48.9 cm) (comp.)
Gift of Mr. and Mrs. Ray Smith, Jr.

King Lear, 1963   (80.24.4.1-.32)
Set of thirty-two lithographs, 18 x
  14 3/4 in. (45.7 x 37.5 cm), each
Gift of Mr. R. B. Kitaj

Manhattan Series, 1967
  (80.24.23.1-.5)
Set of five lithographs, 29 3/4 x
  35 in. (75.6 x 88.9 cm), each
Gift of Mr. R. B. Kitaj

Persian War, 1969   (80.24.24)
Lithograph, 22 x 17 13/16 in. (55.9 x
  45.2 cm)
Gift of Mr. R. B. Kitaj

Portrait of a Woman   (80.24.25)
Lithograph, 30 1/4 x 22 1/2 in. (76.8
  x 57.2 cm)
Gift of Mr. R. B. Kitaj

In Memory of the Children of Vienna Who Will Die of Hunger This Year, 1946, Oskar Kokoschka, lithograph

KORIUSAI, Isoda
Japanese (active 1750–1800)
At Sweet Cake Store Nomuraya
(00.306)
Woodcut, 25 3/4 x 4 7/16 in. (65.4 x
11.3 cm) (sight)
Anonymous Gift

The Game   (00.305)
Woodcut, 27 7/16 x 4 3/8 in. (69.7 x
11.1 cm) (sight)
Anonymous Gift

KRASNER, Lee
American (1911–   )
Untitled, from the Primary Series
(80.24.26)
Lithograph, 22 3/4 x 30 1/8 in. (57.8
x 76.5 cm)
Gift of Mr. Ira Howard Levy

KRETZSCHMAR, Bernhard
German (b. 1889)
Head of a Man, 1924   (00.12)
Drypoint, 16 1/8 x 12 1/4 in. (41 x
31.1 cm)
Anonymous Gift

A Woman, Yasou Kuniyoshi, woodcut

KUNIYOSHI, Yasuo
Japanese (1893–1953)
*A Woman**   (00.309)
Woodcut, 13 1/2 x 9 3/16 in. (34.3 x
23.3 cm) (sight)
Anonymous Gift

KYOKO, Harunobu
Japanese (n.d.)
Hana Awase (A Woman)   (00.318)
Woodcut, 14 3/8 x 9 5/8 in. (36.5 x
24.5 cm) (sight)
Anonymous Gift

LACHAISE, Gaston **
French (1882–1935)
Reclining Nude Seen from the Front
(80.3.3.2)
Graphite on envelope, 3 5/8 x 6 1/4
in. (9.2 x 15.9 cm) (sight)
Gift of Mr. Joseph P. Antonow

Recling Nude Seen from the Front
(80.3.3.2)
Graphite on envelope, 3 3/8 x 6 1/4
in. (8.6 x 15.9 cm) (sight)
Gift of Mr. Joseph P. Antonow

*Two Reclining Nudes Seen from
    Behind*   (80.3.3.3)
Graphite on envelope, 3 7/8 x 6 3/4
in. (9.8 x 17.2 cm) (sight)
Gift of Mr. Joseph P. Antonow

LAFITTE, Louis (?)
French (1770–1828)
Untitled (Battle Scene)   (00.266.3)
Etching, 3 13/16 x 5 1/2 in. (9.7 x
14 cm)
Anonymous Gift

Untitled (Battle Scene)   (00.266.4)
Etching, 3 7/8 x 5 5/8 in. (9.8 x
14.3 cm)
Anonymous Gift

LA GRIVE, Jean de, After
French (1689–1757)
Collection of Maps of Paris, 1754
(84.10.1–.11)
Set of eleven etchings; dimensions
vary
Gift of Mrs. Mary M. Carmichael

**LALANNE, Maxime, Attributed
    to**
French (1827–1886)
Weymouth Bay   (00.75)
Etching, 10 3/8 x 14 in. (26.4 x 35.6
cm)
Anonymous Gift

LANDSEER, Sir Edwin Henry
English (1802–1873)
*Return of the Hunters in Ancient
    Times**   (83.32.13)
Engraving, 15 1/2 x 18 3/8 in. (39.4
x 46.7 cm) (comp.)
Gift of Dr. and Mrs. Sidney M. Boxer

LAURENT, Charrier
French (19th century)
Le grand frère (The Big Brother),
1881   (80.17.48)
Charcoal and pastel, 15 1/2 x 10 1/4
in. (39.4 x 26 cm) (comp.)
Gift of Mr. Paul P. Lipton

LEBENSON, R.
Nationality Unknown (20th century)
Doorway on Dekalb, 1967   (00.11)
Etching, 13 3/8 x 12 in. (34 x 30.5 cm)
(comp.)
Anonymous Gift

LEDESMA, J. F.
Nationality Unknown (20th century)
*Mueran los traidores fachistas
    (Death to the Fascist Traitors)*
(00.113)
Linoleum engraving, 6 3/4 x 10 5/8
in. (17.2 x 27 cm)
Gift of Mr. and Mrs. Philip Pinsof

Return of the Hunters in Ancient Times, Sir Edwin Henry Landseer, engraving

Un Soir (An Evening)   (80.17.29)
Drypoint on vellum, 5 3/8 x 11 3/8 in.
  (13.7 x 28.9 cm) (comp.)
Gift of Mr. Paul P. Lipton

Le Tub (The Tub)   (80.17.31)
Drypoint, 8 1/8 x 5 5/8 in. (20.6 x
  14.3 cm) (comp.)
Gift of Mr. Paul P. Lipton

LEIGHTON, Frederic **
English (1830–1896)
Head of Venus   (00.239)
Charcoal, 13 5/8 x 10 1/2 in. (34.6 x
  26.7 cm)
Gift of Mr. and Mrs. Philip Pinsof

LEONI, Ottavio
Italian (1542–1612)
Portrait of Simon Vouet, 1625
  (83.43.9)
Etching, 5 3/4 x 4 1/2 in. (14.6 x
  11.4 cm)
Gift of Mr. and Mrs. Marvin L.
  Fishman

LEPÈRE, Auguste
French (1849–1918)
*Paris sous la neige, vu du haut de
St. Gervais (Paris Covered with
Snow, View from the Top of St.
Gervais)** *   (83.3.17)
Wood engraving, 12 x 17 1/2 in. (30.5
  x 44.5 cm) (comp.)
Gift of the Estate of Florence
  Rossbach

LEE-HANKEY, William
English (1869–1952)
L'Enfant satisfait (Sated Infant)
  (00.57)
Drypoint, 12 1/8 x 9 3/4 in. (30.8 x
  24.8 cm)
Anonymous Gift

LEGGE, Willow
Nationality Unknown (20th century)
An African Folktale, 1979
  (80.24.7.1-.9)
Set of nine embossed serigraphs, 15
  x 11 in. (38.1 x 27.9 cm), each
Gift of Mr. Jay Fleming

LEGRAND, Louis
French (1863–1951)
Full Seated Nude   (80.17.32)
Drypoint, 8 x 6 3/8 in. (20.3 x 16.2
  cm) (comp.)
Gift of Mr. Paul P. Lipton

Head Studies, 1884   (80.17.30)
Drypoint on vellum, 8 3/4 x 5 3/4 in.
  (22.2 x 14.6 cm) (comp.)
Gift of Mr. Paul P. Lipton

Paris sous la neige, vu du haut de St. Gervais (Paris Covered with Snow, View from the Top of St. Gervais, Auguste Lepère, wood engraving

Le Point du jour (The Break of Day)
(83.3.18)
Wood engraving, 4 1/2 x 5 in. (11.4 x
12.7 cm) (comp.)
Gift of the Estate of Florence
Rossbach

LESSER-URY
German (1861-1931)
Street Scene   (83.9.2)
Etching, 23 5/8 x 17 3/16 in. (60 x
43.7 cm)
Gift of Mr. and Mrs. Marvin L.
Fishman

LEVINE, Les
Canadian (1935-   )
Culture Hero, 1970   (81.38.38)
Lithograph, 22 5/8 x 17 1/2 in. (57.5
x 44.5 cm)
Gift of Mr. Edwin E. Jedeikin

LIM, Kim
Thai/English (1936-   )
Ladder-Series I, 1972   (81.38.26)
Etching, 23 5/8 x 23 1/16 in. (60 x
58.6 cm)
Gift of Mr. Al Simon

Untitled, 1972   (81.38.30)
Aquatint, 24 1/2 x 23 1/4 in. (62.2 x
59.1 cm)
Gift of Mr. Al Simon

Back View of a Man, from the Shoot Series,
Richard Lindner, serigraph

LINDNER, Richard
German/American (1901-1978)
The Shoot Series, 1971*
(80.24.22.1-.5)
Set of five serigraphs, 40 1/2 x 29 1/4
in. (102.9 x 74.3 cm), each
Gift of Mr. George Friedman and
Ms. Diane Love

LIPTON, Seymour
American (1903-   )
Study for Sculpture I, 1969
(80.24.18.1-.3)
Set of three lithographs, 25 5/8 x
19 7/8 in. (65.1 x 50.5 cm), each
Gift of Dr. Frank J. Hildner

LOETHAL (?), Albert
Nationality Unknown (n.d.)
*Bruges: La tour des halles (Bruges:
The Tower of the Marketplace)*
(00.523)
Lithograph, 19 1/2 x 11 1/2 in. (49.5
x 29.2 cm) (comp.)
Gift of Mr. and Mrs. Clifford A.
Randall

LOEWY, Raymond
American (1893-   )
Locomotive   (79.23.2)
Lithograph, 13 1/2 x 25 in. (34.3 x
63.5 cm) (comp.)
Gift of Mr. E. C. Koerper/Marquette
University Engineering Student
Art Loan Fund

Venus, Alexis Loir, engraving

LOIR, Alexis
French (1640-1713)
Venus*   (83.32.8)
Engraving, 8 1/4 x 11 in. (21 x 27.9
cm) (sight)
Gift of Dr. and Mrs. Sidney M. Boxer

**LONGFELLOW, Henry
  Wadsworth**
American (1807-1882)
*Autograph Letter and Image of the
Poet*   (80.25.5a&b)
  a: Pen and ink, 6 3/4 x 4 1/2 in.
  (17.2 x 11.4 cm.) (sight)
  b: Etching, 7 1/2 x 5 1/2 in. (19.1 x
  14 cm) (sight)
Gift of Mr. Joseph P. Antonow

LORRAIN, Claude
French (1600-1682)
Meeting Place of the Brigands, c. 1650
(83.32.12)
Engraving, 5 x 7 5/8 in. (12.7 x 19.4
cm) (sight)
Gift of Dr. and Mrs. Sidney M. Boxer

LOWELL, James Russell
American (1819-1891)
*Autograph Letter and Image of the
Poet, 1890*   (80.25.7a&b)
  a: Pen and ink, 6 1/2 x 4 1/2 in.
  (16.5 x 11.4 cm) (sight)
  b: Etching, 3 3/4 x 2 1/2 in. (9.5 x
  6.4 cm) (sight)
Gift of Mr. Joseph P. Antonow

Untitled (Figure of a Man), Mino Maccari,
woodblock print

MACCARI, Mino
Italian (1898-   )
Untitled (Figure of a Man)*
(80.3.5)
Woodblock print, 10 1/4 x 7 in. (26 x
17.8 cm)
Gift of Mr. Joseph P. Antonow

193

*Untitled (Two Nude Women on
    Couch)*   (80.3.6)
Woodblock print, 9 5/8 x 12 in. (24.5
    x 30.5 cm)
Gift of Mr. Joseph P. Antonow

Untitled (Faces)   (80.3.7)
Etching, 10 x 13 1/8 in. (25.4 x 33.3
    cm)
Gift of Mr. Joseph P. Antonow

Untitled (Man Hanging)   (80.3.8)
Woodblock print, 8 5/8 x 6 5/8 in.
    (21.9 x 16.8 cm) (sight)
Gift of Mr. Joseph P. Antonow

*Untitled (Nude Female Figure
    Holding Head of Man)*
    (80.25.21)
Woodblock print, 8 5/8 x 6 1/2 in.
    (21.9 x 16.5 cm) (sight)
Gift of Mr. Joseph P. Antonow

MacLAUGHLAN, Donald Shaw
American (1876-1938)
The Ghetto, Venice   (00.69)
Etching printed in brown ink, 11 1/8
    x 9 in. (28.3 x 22.9 cm)
Anonymous Gift

Untitled (Portrait of a Man), Edouard
Manet, engraving

MANET, Edouard
French (1832-1883)
Untitled (Portrait of a Man), 1865*
    (00.215)
Engraving, 12 3/4 x 8 11/16 in. (32.4
    x 22.1 cm)
Anonymous Gift

MANNA, (Anlino ?)
Italian (20th century)
Untitled   (00.104)
Hand-colored engraving, 9 7/8 x 8 in.
    (25.1 x 20.3 cm)
Anonymous Gift

MARCA-RELLI, Conrad
American (1913-   )
Litt-1-73, 1973   (81.38.34)
Lithograph, 32 1/16 x 25 7/8 in. (81.4
    x 65.7 cm)
Gift of Mr. Thorne Barnes Donnelley

Untitled, from the Summer Suite,
    1970   (81.38.3.1&.2)
Mixed media
    .1: 26 1/16 x 19 3/4 in. (66.2 x 50.2
        cm)
    .2: 20 1/16 x 25 3/4 in. (51 x 65.4
        cm)
Gift of Mr. Edward J. Safdie

MARCHESI, Agostino
Italian (1810-1867)
Portrait of Antonio Allegri
    (00.54)
Engraving after Antonio Allegri,
    19 3/8 x 15 in. (49.2 x 38.1 cm)
Anonymous Gift

MARTIN, Kenneth
English (1905-   )
Rotation-Frankfurt III, 1977
    (81.38.27)
Serigraph, 29 1/8 x 29 1/8 in. (74 x
    74 cm)
Gift of Mr. Al Simon

MATHAM, Theodor Dirck
Dutch (1606-1676)
*Doctor & Professor in Academia
    Lovaniensi . . .*   (00.288)
Engraving after J. Backer, 10 1/2 x
    6 3/4 in. (26.7 x 17.2 cm)
Anonymous Gift

**MAVROMICHALI, Chryssa
    Vardea (called Chryssa)**
American (1933-   )
Chinatown Portfolio
    (82.23.6.1-.11)
Set of eleven serigraphs, 38 1/4 x
    31 1/4 in. (97.2 x 79.4 cm), each
Gift of Mr. Robert Layton

MAY, William Holmes
English (1839-1920)
The Avenue, Haddon Hall, 1883
    (00.74)
Etching, 10 3/4 x 15 in. (27.3 x 38.1
    cm)
Anonymous Gift

McBEY, James
English (1883-1959)
Jewish Quarter, Tetuan, 1912
    (00.51)
Etching, 8 1/2 x 10 1/2 in. (21.6 x
    26.7 cm)
Anonymous Gift

McCOMB, Leonard
English (20th century)
Energy Is Eternal Delight, 1979
    (81.38.14.3)
Letterpress, 25 x 19 in. (63.5 x 48.3
    cm)
Gift of Mr. Edward J. Safdie

Blossoms and Flowers Portfolio, 1979
    (81.38.14.1-.8)
Set of eight lithographs, c. 25 x 19 in.
    (63.5 x 48.3 cm), each
Gift of Mr. Edward J. Safdie

McCRADY, John
American (1911-   )
Steamboat Round the Bend
    (00.208)
Lithograph, 11 15/16 x 16 in. (30.3 x
    40.6 cm)
Gift of Mrs. Irene Gayas Jungwirth

McLAUGHLIN, William
American (?) (late 19th-early 20th
    century)
Mill   (00.130)
Etching, 13 3/4 x 20 in. (34.9 x 50.8
    cm)
Gift of Mr. and Mrs. Philip Pinsof

Mill Town   (00.129)
Etching, 13 3/4 x 20 in. (34.9 x 50.8
    cm)
Gift of Mr. and Mrs. Philip Pinsof

MEISSONIER, Jean-Louis-Ernest
French (1815-1891)
*Untitled (Sketches of Heads)**
    (80.3.4)
Pen and ink, 8 1/4 x 6 3/16 in. (21 x
    15.7 cm) (sight)
Gift of Mr. Joseph P. Antonow

MELLING, (?)
French (late 19th-early 20th century)
*Chateau de Lagarde, Canton de
    Mirefroix*, c. 1840   (80.20.10)
Aquatint, 14 1/4 x 19 5/8 in. (36.2 x
    49.9 cm)
Gift of Mr. Paul P. Lipton

Untitled (Sketches of Heads), Jean-Louis-Ernest Meissonier, pen and ink

MENDEZ, Leopoldo
Mexican (1902–   )
Untitled (Mexican Peasants)
   (00.103)
Lithograph, 17 5/8 x 15 1/8 in. (44.8
   x 38.4 cm)
Anonymous Gift

MERTON, Thomas
American (1915–1968)
The North American Ride, 1964
   (65.16)
Ink wash, 13 1/8 x 10 in. (33.3 x 25.4
   cm)
Gift of Dr. and Mrs. John Pick

**MEYER, Thomas and John
   Furnival**
American (1947–   ); English
   (1933–   )
Blind Date, 1979   (80.24.8.1-.21)
Set of twenty-one embossed etchings,
   11 x 11 in. (27.9 x 27.9 cm), each
Gift of Dr. Gary M. Tearston

MILLAIS, Sir John Everett
English (1829–1896)
Untitled (Mother and Child)
   (00.177)
Conté crayon, 12 1/8 x 18 in. (30.8 x
   45.7 cm)
Anonymous Gift

*Ubu, roi aux Baléares (Ubu, King of
Baléares),* Joan Miró, lithograph

MIRÓ, Joan
Spanish (1893–1983)
*Ubu, roi aux Baléares (Ubu, King of
   the Baléares)*,* 1971   (77.8)
Lithograph, 19 7/8 x 25 3/4 in. (50.6
   x 65.4 cm)
Gift of Mrs. W. W. Busby

MOITTE, Jean Baptiste Philibert
French (19th century)
*Vue de la porte S. Denis (View of the
   Arch of St. Denis),* c. 1840
   (80.17.36)
Hand-colored engraving, 6 x 8 7/8
   in. (15.2 x 22.5 cm) (comp.)
Gift of Mr. Paul P. Lipton

*Vue de la porte S. Martin (View of the
   Arch of St. Martin)*   (80.17.37)
Hand-colored engraving, 6 x 8 7/8 in.
   (15.2 x 22.5 cm) (comp.)
Gift of Mr. Paul P. Lipton

MONK, William, Attributed to
English (1863–1937)
Cathedral (St. Patrick's ?)
   (00.486)
Etching, 20 1/4 x 25 1/2 in. (51.3 x
   64.8 cm) (comp.)
Gift of Mr. Ray H. Wolf

MONRO, Nicholas
English (1936–   )
Gazelles, 1973   (81.38.20)
Serigraph, 27 5/16 x 40 1/2 in (69.4 x
   102.8 cm)
Gift of Mr. Al Simon

MOORE, Henry
English (1898–   )
Henry Moore Catalogue, 1976
   (81.38.11.2)
Offset with handmade paper cover,
   8 7/8 x 6 3/4 in. (22.5 x 17.2 cm)
Gift of Ms. Susan Bondy

High Wire Walkers, 1926
   (81.38.11.3)
Etching, 14 1/2 x 11 5/8 in. (36.9 x
   29.5 cm)
Gift of Ms. Susan Bondy

Sketch Book, 1926   (81.38.11.1)
Collograph, 8 13/16 x 6 3/4 in. (22.4 x
   17.2 cm)
Gift of Ms. Susan Bondy

MOORE, Marianne Craig
American (1887–1972)
In Distrust of Merits   (80.25.8a&b)
Autograph manuscript in pen and
   ink, 9 1/2 x 5 3/4 in. (24.1 x 14.6
   cm), each panel
Gift of Mr. Joseph P. Antonow

MORA, Francisco
Mexican (1922–   )
Untitled (Workers Going to Church)
   (00.100)
Woodcut, 6 3/4 x 10 1/2 in. (17.2 x
   26.7 cm)
Gift of Mr. and Mrs. Philip Pinsof

Untitled (A Miner)   (00.108)
Lithograph, 17 5/8 x 15 1/4 in. (44.8
   x 38.7 cm)
Anonymous Gift

**MORTIMER, John Hamilton,
   Attributed to**
English (1741–1779)
Tragedy, 1778   (00.272)
Etching, 11 5/8 x 7 5/16 in. (29.5 x
   18.6 cm)
Anonymous Gift

Untitled, Robert Motherwell, serigraph

MOTHERWELL, Robert
American (1915-   )
Untitled, 1972*   (80.24.28.1-.5)
Set of five serigraphs, 41 1/8 x 28 1/8
   in. (104.5 x 71.4 cm), each
Gift of Mr. Sy Hyman

Untitled, 1972   (81.38.8.1-.5)
Set of five serigraphs, 28 1/4 x 41 1/8
   in. (71.8 x 104.5 cm), each
Gift of Mrs. Ann Steinberg

Untitled, 1982   (81.38.9)
Serigraph, 28 1/4 x 40 7/8 in. (71.8 x
   104 cm)
Gift of Mr. Edward J. Safdie

MUHS, Frederick
American (1919-1961)
Burgos Cathedral   (68.2)
Watercolor on crescent board, 40 1/8
   x 29 7/8 in. (101.9 x 75.9 cm)
Gift of Mrs. Myra Peache

Haloed Woman   (62.10)
Casein on paperboard, 29 1/2 x
   39 1/4 in. (74.9 x 99.7 cm) (sight)
Gift of Mr. Karl Priebe

MUNCH, Edvard
Norwegian (1863-1944)
*Omegas Augen (The Eyes of Omega)**
Lithograph, 25 5/8 x 18 7/8 in. (65.1
   x 47.9 cm)
On extended loan from Mr. and Mrs.
   Edward H. Meldman

MYERS, Jerome
American (1867-1940)
Untitled (Woman and Children)
   (00.58)
Engraving, 15 7/8 x 13 1/4 in. (40.3 x
   33.7 cm)
Anonymous Gift

NAKAGAWA, Hachirô
Japanese (1877-1922)
Mt. Fuji   (83.3.19)
Watercolor, 12 3/4 x 19 1/2 in. (32.4
   x 49.5 cm) (comp.)
Gift of the Estate of Florence
   Rossbach

NASON, Thomas Willoughby
American (1899-1971)
Untitled (House and Trees)
   (00.252)
Wood engraving, 8 5/8 x 7 in. (21.9 x
   17.8 cm)
Anonymous Gift

NESBITT, Lowell
American (1933-   )
Boots, 1974   (81.38.10)
Aquatint, 29 13/16 x 41 7/8 in. (75.7 x
   106.4 cm)
Gift of Mr. Edward J. Safdie

NEUMANCY, F.
Nationality Unknown (n.d.)
Untitled (Cathedral Interior)
   (00.402)
Etching, 23 1/2 x 19 5/8 in. (59.7 x
   49.9 cm)
Anonymous Gift

NEW, George
American (c. 1894-1963)
*Marquette University Buildings
   Series*   (00.358; 00.454; 00.519;
   53.3-.14)
Set of forty-two etchings; dimensions
   vary
Gift of the artist

NIELSON, John A.
American (1882?-1954)
Père Jacques Marquette, S.J.
   (37.1)
Pastel, 27 3/4 x 21 1/2 in. (70.5 x
54.6 cm) (sight)
Gift of the Marquette University
   Alumni, 1937

NISHIMURA, Shiganaga
Japanese (1695/1716-1756)
Buncho   (00.310)
Woodcut, 5 1/2 x 17 5/8 in. (14 x 44.8
   cm) (sight)
Gift of Mr. and Mrs. Philip Pinsof

NIXON, Job
English (1891-1938)
Rome, The Spanish Steps   (00.49)
Engraving, 11 1/8 x 18 1/4 in. (28.3 x
   46.4 cm)
Anonymous Gift

NUGENT, (?)
Nationality Unknown (n.d.)
Horton Haynes, Esquire   (00.352)
Engraving, 8 1/2 x 6 1/4 in. (21.6 x
   15.9 cm)
Gift of Mrs. Joseph D. Patton

OCAMPO, Isidro
Mexican (1910/12-   )
Sleeping, 1940   (00.111)
Lithograph, 16 7/8 x 24 in. (42.9 x 61
   cm)
Gift of Mr. and Mrs. Philip Pinsof

Untitled   (00.167)
Lithograph, 17 x 15 1/8 in. (43.2 x
   38.4 cm)
Anonymous Gift

OPPENHEIMER, Max
German (1895-1954)
Hungarian Farmhouse   (83.26.2)
Etching, 6 3/4 x 8 1/2 in. (17.2 x 21.6
   cm) (comp.)
Gift of Mr. and Mrs. Marvin L.
   Fishman

ORLIK, Emil
Czechoslovakian (1870-1932)
Am Felde (By the Field)   (83.9.3)
Etching, 6 1/2 x 8 1/16 in. (16.5 x
   20.5 cm)
Gift of Mr. and Mrs. Marvin L.
   Fishman

Kurzweil (Fun)   (83.9.6)
Etching, 5 5/8 x 4 7/8 in. (14.3 x
   12.4 cm)
Gift of Mr. and Mrs. Marvin L
   Fishman

Landschaft (Landscape)   (83.9.4)
Etching, 5 5/8 x 8 7/8 in. (14.3 x 22.5
   cm)
Gift of Mr. and Mrs. Marvin L.
   Fishman

Würfler (Dice Players)   (83.9.5)
Etching, 4 3/4 x 6 15/16 in. (12.1 x
   17.6 cm)
Gift of Mr. and Mrs. Marvin L.
   Fishman

ORLOWSKI, Hans Otto
German (b. 1894)
Untitled   (00.115)
Linoleum engraving, 12 3/8 x 9 5/16
   in (31.4 x 23.7 cm)
Anonymous Gift

OROZCO, José Clemente
Mexican (1883-1949)
Distrust, 1945   (00.46.8)
Lithograph, 15 1/2 x 21 3/4 in. (39.4
   x 55.3 cm)
Gift of Mr. and Mrs. Philip Pinsof

Entwined, 1945   (00.46.9)
Lithograph, 15 1/2 x 21 3/4 in. (39.4 x 55.3 cm)
Gift of Mr. and Mrs. Philip Pinsof

Figures, 1945   (00.46.3)
Lithograph, 15 1/2 x 21 3/4 in. (39.4 x 55.3 cm)
Gift of Mr. and Mrs. Philip Pinsof

Hate, 1945   (00.46.7)
Lithograph, 15 1/2 x 21 3/4 in. (39.4 x 55.3 cm)
Gift of Mr. and Mrs. Philip Pinsof

King, 1945   (00.46.4)
Lithograph, 15 1/2 x 21 3/4 in. (39.4 x 55.3 cm)
Gift of Mr. and Mrs. Philip Pinsof

Man at War, 1945   (00.46.2)
Lithograph, 15 1/2 x 21 3/4 in. (39.4 x 55.3 cm)
Gift of Mr. and Mrs. Philip Pinsof

Man's Future, 1945   (00.46.5)
Lithograph, 15 1/2 x 21 3/4 in. (39.4 x 55.3 cm)
Gift of Mr. and Mrs. Philip Pinsof

Men, 1945   (00.46.1)
Lithograph, 15 1/2 x 21 3/4 in. (39.4 x 55.3 cm)
Gift of Mr. and Mrs. Philip Pinsof

Torso-Legs-Hands, 1945   (00.46.6)
Lithograph, 15 1/2 x 21 3/4 in. (39.4 x 55.3 cm)
Gift of Mr. and Mrs. Philip Pinsof

OVENDEN, Graham S.
English, (1943-   )
The Lolita Series, 1974   (81.38.25.1-.12)
Set of twelve aquatints, 26 x 26 in. (66 x 66 cm), each
Gift of Mr. Al Simon

Margie Doll, 1971   (81.38.31)
Serigraph, 31 1/8 x 22 13/16 in. (79.1 x 57.9 cm)
Gift of Mr. Al Simon

You Ought To Be Ashamed, from the Alice in Wonderland Series, 1970   (82.23.2.1)
Serigraph, 25 3/4 x 20 in. (65.4 x 50.8 cm)
Gift of Mr. Edwin E. Jedeikin

Wake Up, Alice Dear, from the Alice in Wonderland Series, 1970   (82.23.2.2)
Serigraph, 25 3/4 x 20 in. (65.4 x 50.8 cm)
Gift of Mr. Edwin E. Jedeikin

PALACIOS, J.
Spanish (n.d.)
The Bullfight Suite, c. 1900   (00.47.1-.4)
Set of four lithographs, 15 x 21 1/8 in. (38.1 x 53.7 cm), each
Anonymous Gift

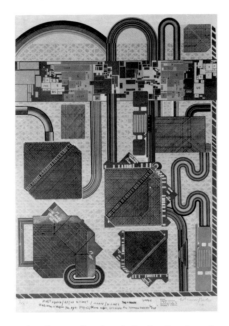

Turkis the Musik, Eduardo Paolozzi, serigraph.

PAOLOZZI, Eduardo
Scottish (1924-   )
The Conditional Probability Machine, 1970   (81.38.1.1-.32)
Set of thirty-two photogravure prints, 23 1/2 x 15 1/2 in. (59.7 x 39.4 cm), each
Gift of Ms. Susan Bondy

General Dynamic F.U.N. (Volume A) Volume II, of Moonstrips Empire News, 1970   (81.38.37.1-.55)
Set of fifty-five serigraphs and lithographs, 15 x 10 in. (38.1 x 25.4 cm) (comp.)
Gift of Mr. Steven D. Sohackie and Mrs. Bernice Sohackie

Turkis the Musik, 1974*   (81.38.18)
Serigraph, 38 1/2 x 28 1/2 in. (97.8 x 72.4 cm)
Gift of Mr. Robert E. Green

Joseph and Potiphar's Wife, Bartolomeo Passarotti, engraving and etching

PASSAROTTI, Bartolomeo
Italian (1529-1592)
Joseph and Potiphar's Wife, 1570*   (83.32.11)
Engraving and etching, 6 1/4 x 15 1/4 in. (15.9 x 38.7 cm) (sight)
Gift of Dr. and Mrs. Sidney M. Boxer

PAUL, John Dean
English (1795-1852)
Symptoms of a Skurry in Pewy County   (00.323)
Lithograph, 15 1/4 x 27 1/2 in. (38.7 x 69.9 cm)
Anonymous Gift

PAYNE, George T.
English (19th century)
The Right Honorable Lord Lyndhurst, 1841   (00.120)
Engraving after H. W. Pickersgill, 20 1/8 x 16 in. (51.1 x 40.6 cm)
Gift of Mrs. Joseph D. Patton

PEEL, Michael
Nationality Unknown (20th century)
The Camera Never Lies, 1979   (80.24.9.1-.26)
Offset lithographs with photographs, 12 x 9 1/4 in. (30.5 x 23.5 cm)
Gift of Mr. Frank Lipcius

PEPPER, Beverly
American (1924-   )
Blue and Black Frame, 1968   (81.38.33)
Colored paper, 19 1/4 x 28 in. (48.9 x 71.1 cm)
Gift of Mr. Edwin E. Jedeikin

PHILIPPE, David
Dutch (17th century)
*Arrival of English Noblewoman in
Amsterdam* (00.298)
Engraving, 11 13/16 x 15 1/2 in.
(30 x 39.4 cm)
Anonymous Gift

PHILIPPE, Jean Marc
French (1939-)
Chateau Cantemerle (80.20.13)
Hand-colored lithograph, 10 3/4 x
15 1/2 in. (27.3 x 39.4 cm)
Gift of Mr. Paul P. Lipton

Le vieux boucau (The Old Harbor)
(80.20.12)
Lithograph, 7 3/4 x 11 in. (19.7 x
27.9 cm)
Gift of Mr. Paul P. Lipton

PHILLIPS, Tom
English (1937-)
A Humument, 1980 (82.23.7.1)
Book, 7 1/8 x 5 1/4 x 1 1/2 in.
(18.1 x 13.3 x 3.8 cm)
Gift of Mr. Bruce Koepfgen

The New National Theatre Is Yours,
1977 (80.24.10)
Serigraph, 35 1/2 x 23 5/8 in. (90.2 x
60 cm)
Gift of Mr. and Mrs. Ben Wunsch

Six Pieces Op. X., 1968 (82.23.5.3)
Serigraph, 30 x 22 in. (76.2 x 55.9 cm)
Gift of Mr. Lloyd Hurst

PICART, Bernard
French (1673-1733)
Untitled, 1726 (83.43.14 S)
Etching, 15 1/2 x 11 in. (39.4 x 27.9
cm)
Gift of Mr. and Mrs. Marvin L.
Fishman

PICASSO, Pablo
Spanish (1881-1973)
*Danseurs espagnols (Spanish
Dancers)* (79.2)
Pen and ink wash, 9 1/8 x 12 5/8 in.
(23.2 x 32.1 cm)
Gift of Mr. Joseph P. Antonow

L'Atelier (The Studio), 1927*
(81.31)
Etching, 13 3/4 x 15 5/8 in. (34.9 x
39.7 cm) (comp.)
Gift of Mr. Jack M. Horner

PINET, Charles F.
French (1867-1932)
*Intérieur du béguinage de Bruges
(Interior of the Beguinage of
Bruges)* (00.504)
Etching, 15 3/4 x 20 1/4 in. (40 x 51.4
cm) (comp.)
Gift of Mr. Ray H. Wolf

PIPER, John
English (1903-)
Untitled (80.24.21.1-.6)
Set of six serigraphs; dimensions
vary
Gift of Mr. Samuel E. Hunter

PIRANESI, Giovanni Battista
Italian (1720-1778)
*Veduta degli avanzi delle fabbriche
del secondo piano delle terme di
Tito (The Baths of Trajan)*
(83.37.2)
Engraving, 19 1/4 x 27 3/4 in. (48.9 x
70.5 cm) (comp.)
Gift of Mr. and Mrs. Marvin L.
Fishman

*Veduta delle cascatelle a Tivoli
(Small Waterfall)* (83.37.1)
Engraving, 18 1/2 x 27 1/2 in. (47 x
69.9 cm) (comp.)
Gift of Mr. and Mrs. Marvin L.
Fishman

PLÜNNEKE, Wilhelm
German (1894-1954)
The Fair, 1919 (00.171)
Lithograph, 20 5/16 x 14 1/2 in. (51.6
x 36.8 cm)
Gift of Mr. and Mrs. Philip Pinsof

*Untitled (Landscape with Fence and
Horses)*, 1919 (00.172)
Lithograph, 20 1/4 x 14 1/2 in. (51.4
x 36.8 cm)
Gift of Mr. and Mrs. Philip Pinsof

POEHLMANN, Joanna
American (1932-)
Collection of Drawings
(83.49.9-.14)
Graphite and watercolor; dimensions
vary
Gift of Mr. Frederick D. Gore

L'Atelier (The Studio), Pablo Picasso, etching

POMODORO, Arnaldo
Italian (1926-   )
Rotante, 1968   (81.38.6)
Serigraph, 19 15/16 x 28 1/16 in.
  (50.6 x 71.3 cm)
Gift of Mrs. Ann Steinberg

POSKA, Roland
Scottish/American (1938-   )
Untitled   (83.9.1)
Hand-made paper, 16 1/4 x 10 1/4 in.
  (41.3 x 26 cm)
Gift of Mr. and Mrs. Marvin L.
  Fishman

POUND, D. J.
English (19th century)
Mrs. Stirling   (00.356)
Engraving after a photograph by
  John and Charles Watkins, 9 1/4 x
  7 7/16 in. (23.5 x 18.9 cm)
Anonymous Gift

*Thomas Wilson, Esquire, Chevalier
  de Lordrede Lime*   (00.357)
Engraving, 15 11/16 x 11 1/16 in.
  (39.9 x 28.1 cm)
Anonymous Gift

*Untitled (Portrait of a Man Seated
  at a Table)*   (00.355)
Engraving, 9 13/16 x 8 1/16 in. (24.9
  x 20.5 cm)
Anonymous Gift

POZZATTI, Rudy
American (1925-   )
Cosmorama, 1976   (80.16)
Lithograph, 29 1/4 x 25 in. (74.3 x
  63.5 cm)
Gift of Mr. and Mrs. John Ahlhauser

PRIEBE, Karl
American (1914-1976)
Collection of Works in Casein
  (83.49.4-.7; 83.49.15)
Dimensions vary
Gift of Mr. Frederick D. Gore

*Collection of Watercolors, Drawings,
  Paintings, Personal Papers, and
  Correspondence**   (00.369;
  78.9.9-.16; 82.15.1-.107)
Dimensions vary
Gift of Mr. Emil Priebe

Late Afternoon Arrangement, 1950
  (55.23)
Casein on paperboard, 19 1/2 x
  27 1/2 in. (49.5 x 69.9 cm)
Gift of Gimbel Brothers

Bird on Rock, Karl Priebe, casein on paper

Portrait of Charles Seebree, 1940
  (79.17)
Casein on mat board, 24 1/8 x 20 1/8
  in. (61.3 x 51.1 cm)
Gift of Mr. Victor J. Williams

Portrait of Mrs. Anna D. Braun, 1947
  (82.6)
Casein, 21 x 16 7/8 in. (53.3 x 42.9 cm)
Gift of Mr. Ralph Resenhoeft

Robin, 1975   (00.491)
Watercolor, 10 1/4 x 13 1/8 in. (26 x
  33.3 cm) (sight)
Gift of the artist

A Robin on a Rock, 1956   (76.63)
Casein on paperboard, 14 1/2 x 9 1/4
  in. (36.8 x 23.5 cm)
Gift of Mr. and Mrs. Raymond F.
  Newman

Shorebird, 1960   (83.8)
Casein on paperboard, 13 1/2 x
  19 1/4 in. (34.3 x 48.9 cm)
Gift of Mr. Ralph Resenhoeft

Woman   (74.1)
Casein on paperboard, 10 x 8 in. (25.4
  x 20.3 cm)
Gift of Dr. and Mrs. John Pick

The Woodpecker Tree, 1958
  (00.408)
Casein, 23 1/2 x 17 3/8 in. (59.7 x
  44.1 cm) (sight)
Gift of Dr. and Mrs. John Pick

PRIMAVESI, Johann Georg
German (1776-1855)
Untitled (Fisherman), 1801
  (00.251)
Etching, 4 15/16 x 6 13/16 in. (12.5 x
  17.3 cm)
Anonymous Gift

Untitled (Landscape with House)
  (00.282)
Etching after J. Ruysdael, 8 3/4 x
  10 7/16 in. (22.2 x 26.5 cm)
Anonymous Gift

**PRISSE D'ARENNES, Archille
  Emile Théodore and Eugene
  Leroux**
French (1830-1879); French (b. 1833)
Indian Pottery Kilns, c. 1880
  (80.17.42)
Lithograph, 10 1/4 x 14 1/4 in. (26 x
  36.2 cm)
Gift of Mr. Paul P. Lipton

PROCKTOR, Patrick
English/Irish (1936-   )
The Rime of the Ancient Mariner
  (80.24.12.1-.12)
Set of twelve etchings, 25 5/8 x 19 5/8
  in. (65.1 x 49.9 cm)
Gift of Mr. James W. Harpel

PUGH, Edward
English (d. 1813)
The Cambrian Shakespeare
  (00.348)
Engraving, 15 1/4 x 11 1/4 in. (38.7 x
  28.6 cm)
Anonymous Gift

RAFFET, Denis Auguste Marie
French (1804-1860)
*École de jeunes filles tatares (School
  of the Young Girls of Tatary)*,
  1841   (80.20.15)
Lithograph, 12 x 14 3/4 in. (30.5 x
  37.5 cm)
Gift of Mr. Paul P. Lipton

RANDOLPH, V.
American (20th century)
St. Patrick's, New York   (00.179)
Etching, 30 13/16 x 22 9/16 in. (78.3
  x 57.3 cm)
Gift of Mr. Ray H. Wolf

**RASSENFOSSE, André Louis
  Armand**
Belgian (1862-1934)
*L'Amateur d'estampes (The Print
  Enthusiast)*   (00.63)
Drypoint, 17 5/8 x 12 1/2 in. (44.8 x
  31.8 cm)
Gift of Mr. Oscar M. Pinsof

Femme nue couchée (Reclining Nude), Pierre Auguste Renoir, etching

RAUSCHER, Charles
German (b. 1841)
The Visit, 1875   (00.70)
Engraving after Franz von
    Defregger, 14 1/4 x 10 1/4 in. (36.2
    x 26 cm)
Anonymous Gift

RENOIR, Pierre Auguste
French (1841–1919)
*Femme ne couchée (Reclining
    Nude)*   (00.211)
Etching, 9 x 10 3/8 in. (22.9 x 26.4 cm)
Gift of Mr. and Mrs. Philip Pinsof

RIEGE, Rudolf
German (1892–   )
Faust Suite   (00.303.1-.16)
Set of sixteen woodcuts; dimensions
    vary
Gift of Mr. Oscar M. Pinsof and Mr.
    and Mrs. Philip Pinsof

RIGAUD, Jacques, After
Collection of Views of Paris
    (84.10.12-.26)
Set of fifteen etchings; dimensions
    vary
Gift of Mrs. Mary M. Carmichael

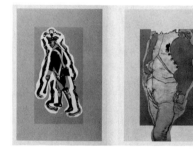

Cover, from the Boston Massacre Series,
Larry Rivers, serigraph

RIVERS, Larry
American (1923–   )
Boston Harbor, from the Boston
    Massacre Series, 1970   (80.24.17)
Serigraph, 19 5/16 x 27 9/16 in. (49.1
    x 70 cm)
Gift of Mr. Thomas Lewyn

Cover, from the Boston Massacre
    Series, 1970*   (80.24.13)
Serigraph, 19 1/4 x 28 1/4 in. (48.9 x
    71.8 cm)
Gift of Mr. Thomas Lewyn

Victims, 1970   (81.38.32)
Serigraph, 19 1/8 x 27 3/4 in. (48.6 x
    70.5 cm)
Gift of Mr. Robert Brooks

RIZZI, James
American (1950–   )
Sunset, 1979   (79.24)
Relief etching with acrylic, marker
    ink, and foam core, 6 x 4 in. (15.2 x
    10.2 cm) (comp.)
Gift of Mr. E. C. Koerper/Marquette
    University Engineering Student
    Art Loan Fund

ROPS, Felicien
Belgian (1833–1898)
*L'oliviera de Monaco (Monaco Olive
    Gatherer),* 1876   (80.17.46)
Drypoint, 14 x 9 1/4 in. (35.6 x 23.5
    cm) (comp.)
Gift of Mr. Paul P. Lipton

**ROTH, Dieter and Emmett
Williams**
German (1930–   ); Nationality
    Unknown (20th century)
*Hansjorg Mayer Collection of Seven
    Books*   (80.24.2.1-.7)
Letterpress with drawings, 9 x 6 3/4
    in. (22.9 x 17.2 cm)
Gift of Mr. William A. Graham IV

ROTH, Dieter
German (1930–   )
The Trophies Portfolio, 1978
    (81.38.12.1-.12)
Set of twelve offset prints;
    dimensions vary
Gift of Mr. Edward J. Safdie

ROTHENSTEIN, Michael
English (1908–   )
The Song of Songs Portfolio, 1979
    (80.24.20.1-.18)
Set of eighteen serigraphs with letter-
    press, 20 7/8 x 14 3/8 in. (53 x 36.5
    cm), each
Gift of Mr. Jerome J. Zeller

ROUAULT, Georges *
French (1871–1958)
Baie des Trespassés, Vollard, 1939
    (83.27.6)
Aquatint and etching, 24 1/8 x 17 3/4
    in. (61.3 x 45.1 cm) (comp.)
Gift of Mr. and Mrs. Ray Smith, Jr.

Miserere, 1948   (58.1.1-.58)
Series of fifty-eight prints in aqua-
    tint, drypoint and etching;
    dimensions vary
Gift of Mr. Leonard J. Scheller

*Nous devons mourir; nous et tout ce
    qui est notre (We Must Die and All
    That Is Ours),* from the Miserere
    Series, 1948   (81.25.2)
Aquatint, drypoint and etching, 20 x
    14 1/4 in. (50.8 x 36.2 cm)
Gift of Mr. and Mrs. Ray Smith, Jr.

Vierge aux sept glaives (Virgin of the Seven Swords), from the Miserere Series, 1948 (81.25.1)
Aquatint, drypoint and etching, 22 1/4 x 16 in. (56.5 x 40.6 cm)
Gift of Mr. and Mrs. Ray Smith, Jr.

ROWLANDSON, Thomas, Attributed to
English (1756-1827)
The Cook (00.220.1)
Ink wash and crayon, 8 1/2 x 6 5/8 in. (21.6 x 16.8 cm)
Anonymous Gift

A Lover and His Lass (80.25.19)
Watercolor, 7 3/4 x 6 1/2 in. (19.7 x 16.5 cm) (sight)
Gift of Mr. Joseph P. Antonow

Madonna and Child with St. John (00.220.2)
Crayon and wash, 8 1/2 x 6 5/8 in. (21.6 x 16.8 cm)
Anonymous Gift

Scene in Tavern Wine Cellar, 1784 (80.25.20)
Watercolor, 7 3/4 x 11 1/4 in. (19.7 x 28.6 cm) (sight)
Gift of Mr. Joseph P. Antonow

Venus (80.3.2)
Pen and ink wash, 7 3/8 x 4 1/2 in. (18.7 x 11.4 cm)
Gift of Mr. Joseph P. Antonow

RUBENS, Peter Paul *
Flemish (1577-1640)
Marcus Brutus, 1638 (00.224)
Engraving, 11 1/2 x 7 7/8 in. (29.2 x 20 cm)
Gift of Mrs. Joseph D. Patton

M. Tullius Cicero, 1638 (00.234)
Engraving, 14 7/16 x 9 15/16 in. (36.7 x 25.2 cm)
Gift of Mrs. Joseph D. Patton

RUBIN, Frank
American (20th century)
Untitled (00.254)
Etching, 6 1/8 x 4 3/8 in. (15.6 x 11.1 cm)
Anonymous Gift

SADELER, Egidius and Marcus Sadeler
Flemish (1570-1629); Flemish (b. 1614)
Untitled (Tavern in Landscape) (00.62)
Engraving, 9 x 11 1/4 in. (22.9 x 28.6 cm)
Anonymous Gift

Adam and Eve, Jan Saenredam, engraving

SAENREDAM, Jan
Dutch (1565-1607)
*Adam and Eve**, c. 1602 . (83.32.6)
Engraving, 12 7/8 x 8 5/8 in. (32.7 x 21.9 cm) (sight)
Gift of Dr. and Mrs. Sidney M. Boxer

SALANTOS, Louis
American? (20th century)
Crucifixion, 1949 (55.3)
Woodcut, 26 3/4 x 18 3/4 in. (68 x 47.6 cm)
Anonymous Gift

SAMPLE, Paul Starrett *
American (1896-1974)
Whistle Stop, c. 1940 (83.3.20)
Watercolor, 14 x 21 in. (35.6 x 53.3 cm) (comp.)
Gift of the Estate of Florence Rossbach

SAMUEL, Herbert
Nationality Unknown (20th century)
Untitled (Portrait of a Man) (00.134)
Brown conté crayon, 12 1/2 x 11 3/8 in. (31.8 x 28.9 cm)
Anonymous Gift

SCANLAN, Robert Richard, Attributed to
Irish (active 1832-1876)
The Right, Honorable Sir Robert Peel (00.346)
Engraving, 12 7/8 x 10 15/16 in. (32.7 x 27.8 cm)
Gift of Mrs. Joseph D. Patton

SCHENK, Pieter
Dutch (19th century)
Portrait of Adrianus van Costrum (83.43.10)
Engraving, 7 1/2 x 5 7/16 in. (19.1 x 13.8 cm)
Gift of Mr. and Mrs. Marvin L. Fishman

SCOTT, William
English (1913-)
From Odeon Suite I, 1966 (80.24.11)
Lithograph, 24 7/8 x 30 1/4 in. (63.2 x 76.8 cm)
Gift of Mr. Avram Dorman

SCRIVEN, Edward
English (1775-1841)
The Right, Honorable Sir Edward Burtenshaw Sugden (00.347)
Engraving, 18 9/16 x 13 1/2 in. (47.2 x 34.3 cm)
Gift of Mrs. Joseph D. Patton

SEVERINI, Gino
Italian (1883-1966)
*Jester Playing Guitar** (80.25.9)
Pen and ink, 15 7/8 x 12 1/2 in. (40.3 x 31.8 cm)
Gift of Mr. Joseph P. Antonow

SEYDELMANN, Crescentius Josephus Jacob
German (1750-1829)
Portrait of a Youth (76.30)
Sepia wash, 16 5/8 x 13 7/8 in. (42.2 x 35.2 cm) (comp.)
Gift of Mr. and Mrs. Philip Pinsof

SHARLAND, E.
English (n.d.)
Winchester Cathedral (00.278)
Embossed etching, 14 15/16 x 7 3/4 in. (37.9 x 19.7 cm)
Gift of Mr. Ray H. Wolf

SHEPHERD, Thomas Hosmer
English (active 1817-1840)
Temple Bar from the Strand, 1829
  (83.45.1)
Hand-colored engraving, 5 1/2 x 5 in.
  (14 x 12.7 cm) (comp.)
Gift of Dr. Kenneth Maier

SIEVIER, Robert William
English (1794-1865)
Lord Ellenborough, 1815   (00.244)
Engraving after Sir Thomas
  Lawrence, 20 9/16 x 15 1/4 in. (52.2
  x 38.7 cm)
Gift of Mrs. Joseph D. Patton

SIGRIST, Franz, Attributed to
Austrian (1727-1803)
Ruth and Boaz   (00.27)
Engraving, 11 7/8 x 8 in. (30.2 x
  20.3 cm)
Anonymous Gift

SIMON, T. Frantisek
French (1877-1942)
*L'Abside de Notre Dame de Paris
  (The Apse of Notre Dame of Paris)*,
  1911   (83.45.3)
Etching, 11 x 14 in. (28 x 35.6 cm)
  (comp.)
Gift of Dr. Kenneth Maier

SINTENIS, Renée
German (1888-1965)
Untitled (The Fox)   (00.169)
Etching, 13 3/8 x 9 3/4 in. (34 x
  24.8 cm)
Anonymous Gift

SMITH, John Thomas
English (1766-1833)
*On Merrow Common, Surrey, the
  Residence of Dame Battey, Aged
  102*, 1797   (00.274)
Engraving, 7 15/16 x 6 5/16 in. (20.2
  x 16 cm)
Anonymous Gift

SMITH, L. S.
English (?) (19th century)
St. Paul, 1845   (00.32)
Ink and wash, 11 1/2 x 4 5/8 in.
  (29.2 x 11.8 cm)
Gift of Mr. and Mrs. Philip Pinsof

SMITH, Richard
English (1931-   )
Folded Paperclip I, 1975   (81.38.28)
Lithograph, 28 x 28 in. (71.1 x 71.1
  cm)
Gift of Mr. Al Simon

A Mauve, 1971   (80.24.27)
Serigraph, vacuum formed in relief,
  23 5/8 x 19 5/8 in. (60 x 49.9 cm)
Gift of Dr. Marvin A. Sachner

SŌTATSU, Nonomura
Japanese (1688-1703)
The Nengo of Genroku I   (83.14.6)
Woodcut, 11 3/8 x 15 5/8 in. (28.9 x
  39.7 cm)
Gift of Mr. Samuel Gansheroff

The Nengo of Genroku II
  (83.14.7)
Woodcut, 11 1/4 x 15 3/8 in. (28.6 x
  39.1 cm)
Gift of Mr. Samuel Gansheroff

SPICUZZA, Francesco J.
Italian/American (1883-1962)
Untitled (Portrait of Christ?), 1910
  (00.360)
Lithograph, 13 7/8 x 10 7/8 in. (35.2 x
  27.6 cm)
Anonymous Gift

Wood Scene   (81.19.2)
Pastel, 19 13/16 x 25 7/16 in. (50.3 x
  64.6 cm) (sight)
Gift of Mr. Edward J. O'Keefe

**STADLER, Joseph C., Thomas
Rowlandson, and Auguste
Pugin**
German (active 1780-1812); English
  (1756-1827); French (1762/69-1832)
Court of Chancery, 1808   (80.17.6)
Hand-colored engraving, 7 5/8 x
  10 1/8 in. (19.4 x 25.7 cm) (comp.)
Gift of Mr. Paul P. Lipton

STAMOS, Theodore
American (1922-   )
The Infinity Field Series, 1971-72
  (81.38.23.1-.4)
Set of four serigraphs, dimensions
  vary
Gift of Mr. Emanuel Azenberg

STANTON, John
American (1829-1911)
Portrait Series   (00.256-.259)
Set of four engravings; dimensions
  vary
Anonymous Gift

STERN, Lucia
American (1900-   )
*Collection of Works in Mixed Media,
  Watercolor, Colored Marker, and
  Pen and Ink*   (79.11; 79.29.1-.12)
Dimensions vary
Gift of the artist

Pair of Works in Mixed Media
  (00.483; 79.23.4)
Dimensions vary
Gift of Mr. E. C. Koerper/Marquette
  University Engineering Student
  Art Loan Fund

STERNER, Albert
American (1863-1946)
Untitled (Worker and Shovel)
  (00.125)
Lithograph, 17 3/4 x 13 3/8 in. (45.1
  x 34 cm)
Anonymous Gift

**STORM VAN S'GRAVEN-
SANDE, Carel Nicolaas**
Dutch (1841-1924)
Harbor at Hamburg   (81.15.2)
Lithograph, 22 1/2 x 28 in. (57.2 x
  71.1 cm)
Gift of Mr. and Mrs. Marvin L.
  Fishman

STRANG, William
English (1859-1921)
The Beggar   (00.72)
Etching, 15 1/8 x 10 7/8 in. (38.4 x
  27.6 cm)
Anonymous Gift

Justice   (00.273)
Etching, 7 15/16 x 7 in. (20.2 x 17.8
  cm)
Gift of Mr. and Mrs. Philip Pinsof

*Time**   (00.48)
Engraving with etching, 8 7/8 x
  14 1/8 in. (22.5 x 35.9 cm)
Gift of Mr. and Mrs. Philip Pinsof

**STROBRIDGE LITHO CO.,
Cincinnati and New York**
American (late 19th-early 20th
  century)
*The Barnum & Bailey Greatest Show
  on Earth*, 1900   (77.4)
Offset lithograph, 26 5/8 x 17 in.
  (67.6 x 43.2 cm) (comp.)
Gift of Mr. and Mrs. Raymond F.
  Newman

Time, William Strang, engraving with etching

Cleopatra with Women Presenting Marc Anthony's Gift, Giovanni Battista Tiepolo, etching

SUYDERHOFF, Jonas
Dutch (1613-1686)
Portrait of Van Bloemaerts, 1659
(83.43.2)
Engraving after Jan VerSpronck,
16 5/8 x 11 1/2 in. (42.2 x 29.2 cm)
Gift of Mr. and Mrs. Marvin L.
Fishman

SWANEVELDT, Herman van
Dutch (1600-1655)
St. Adriano in Via Flaminia
(82.7.13)
Etching, 4 1/2 x 7 1/8 in. (11.4 x 18.1
cm)
Gift of Dr. Kenneth Maier

**SWEBACH, Jacques François
Joseph, Attributed to**
French (1769-1823)
Untitled (Battle Scene)   (00.266.1)
Etching, 4 x 5 3/8 in. (10.2 x 13.7 cm)
Anonymous Gift

Untitled (Battle Scene)   (00.266.2)
Etching, 4 1/4 x 5 9/16 in. (10.8 x
14.1 cm)
Anonymous Gift

TESTA, Angelo
American (20th century)
Study, 1958   (61.22)
Watercolor and marker, 30 x 23 3/4
in. (76.2 x 60.3 cm)
Gift of Mr. Harry G. Sundheim, Jr.

THOMAS, Percy
English (1846/47-1922)
Dean Stanley, 1881   (00.79)
Etching, 15 1/8 x 10 7/8 in. (38.4 x
27.6 cm)
Anonymous Gift

TIEPOLO, Giovanni Battista
Italian (1696-1770)
*Cleopatra with Women Presenting
Marc Anthony's Gift**   (83.32.1)
Etching, 16 3/8 x 14 3/8 in. (41.6 x
36.5 cm)
Gift of Dr. and Mrs. Sidney M. Boxer

TORII, Kiyonaga
Japanese (1752-1815)
Lovers Under an Umbrella
(00.307)
Woodcut, 27 7/8 x 4 1/2 in. (70.8 x
11.4 cm) (sight)
Anonymous Gift

**TRAUTSCHOLD, Karl Friedrich
Wilhelm**
German (1815-1877)
Portrait of Eliza Cook   (00.354)
Engraving, 16 x 11 3/16 in. (40.6 x
28.3 cm)
Anonymous Gift

TUNICLIFFE, Charles Frederick
English (1901-   )
The New Calf   (00.52)
Etching, 10 3/8 x 16 3/4 in. (26.4 x
42.6 cm)
Gift of Mr. and Mrs. Leslie S. Pinsof

TURNER, Don La Viere
American (1929-   )
Draped Figure, 1959   (80.17.15)
Linoleum engraving, 29 1/2 x 11 5/8 in.
(74.9 x 29.5 cm) (comp.)
Gift of Mr. Paul P. Lipton

UNGER, W.
Nationality Unknown (n.d.)
Untitled (Landscape)   (00.304)
Hand-colored etching, 14 1/4 x 17 1/2
in. (36.2 x 44.5 cm)
Anonymous Gift

UNKNOWN ARTIST
Nationality Unknown (19th century)
Battle Scene   (00.219)
Ink and wash, 11 15/16 x 8 in. (30.3 x
20.3 cm)
Gift of Mr. and Mrs. Philip Pinsof

203

UNKNOWN ARTIST
Bust Portrait of Ianus Lutma
 (83.43.13)
Etching, 12 3/16 x 8 1/2 in. (31 x
 21.6 cm)
Gift of Mr. and Mrs. Marvin L.
 Fishman

UNKNOWN ARTIST
Nationality Unknown (19th century)
Conversion of St. Paul, 1875 (?)
 (00.218)
Ink and wash, 7 3/8 x 12 3/4 in. (18.7
 x 32.4 cm)
Gift of Mr. and Mrs. Philip Pinsof

UNKNOWN ARTIST
French (20th century)
*Les Désastres de la guerre (The
 Disasters of War)* (80.20.14)
Hand-colored lithograph, 12 5/8 x
 17 1/2 in. (32.1 x 44.5 cm)
Gift of Mr. Paul P. Lipton

UNKNOWN ARTIST
Japanese (19th–20th century)
Night Scene with Three Cranes
 (83.14.2)
Woodcut, 17 3/4 x 11 3/4 in. (45.1 x
 29.9 cm)
Gift of Mr. Samuel Gansheroff

UNKNOWN ARTIST **
British (19th century)
No Escape! My God! (00.377)
Graphite, 10 x 6 5/8 in. (25.4 x 16.8
 cm) (sight)
Gift of Mr. and Mrs. Philip Pinsof

UNKNOWN ARTIST
Dutch (18th century)
*Nobles Relaxing at an Outdoor
 Tavern* (00.297)
Ink and wash, 9 1/8 x 12 7/8 in. (23.2
 x 32.7 cm)
Gift of Mr. and Mrs. Philip Pinsof

UNKNOWN ARTIST
Italian (16th century ?)
Untitled (Monk Praying) (00.173)
Ink and wash, 16 1/8 x 11 1/2 in. (41 x
 29.2 cm)
Gift of Mr. and Mrs. Philip Pinsof

UNKNOWN ARTIST (JH)
French (mid-late 18th century)
Untitled (Mill Scene), 1776
 (73.1)
Gouache, 4 3/8 x 4 1/4 in. (11.1 x 10.8
 cm)
Gift of Mr. and Mrs. James W.
 Bergstrom

Untitled (Mill Scene), 1776
 (73.3)
Gouache, 4 1/4 x 4 3/8 in. (10.8 x 11.1
 cm)
Gift of Mr. and Mrs. James W.
 Bergstrom

UNKNOWN ARTIST (CJV)
French (mid-late 18th century)
Untitled (Fishing Scene), 1755
 (73.2)
Gouache, 5 1/8 x 5 1/8 in. (13 x 13 cm)
Gift of Mr. and Mrs. James W.
 Bergstrom

Untitled (Harbor Scene), 1755
 (73.4)
Gouache, 5 1/8 x 5 1/8 in. (13 x 13 cm)
Gift of Mr. and Mrs. James W.
 Bergstrom

UNKNOWN ARTIST
Untitled (83.43.5)
Engraving, 8 1/2 x 6 1/2 in. (21.6 x
 16.5 cm)
Gift of Mr. and Mrs. Marvin L.
 Fishman

UNKNOWN ARTIST
Untitled (Reclining Woman)
 (83.51)
Lithograph, 9 1/2 x 12 3/4 in. (24.1 x
 32.4 cm)
Gift of Mr. and Mrs. Marvin L.
 Fishman

URBAN, Albert
Dutch, (1909–1959)
Brown Horseman (00.180)
Lithograph, after Honoré Daumier, 26
 x 36 in. (66 x 91.4 cm)
Anonymous Gift

UTAGAWA KUNIMASA
Japanese (1773–1810)
Two Warriors (84.8.1)
Woodcut, 14 1/2 x 9 1/2 in. (36.2 x
 24.2 cm)
Gift of Mr. Samuel Gansheroff

UTAGAWA KUNISADA
Japanese (1786–1864)
The Actor Ichikawa (00.312)
Woodcut, 9 x 6 3/8 in. (22.9 x 16.2 cm)
 (sight)
Anonymous Gift

Actor in the Fifty Three Wars
 (00.311)
Woodcut, 9 x 6 5/8 in. (22.9 x 16.8 cm)
 (sight)
Anonymous Gift

Young Lady Selecting Her Costume
 (83.14.10.1–.3)
Woodcut, 14 x 9 1/2 in. (35.6 x 24.1 cm)
Gift of Mr. Samuel Gansheroff

UTAGAWA KUNIYOSHI
Japanese (1797–1861)
Two Samurai with Swords
 (83.14.8)
Woodcut, 14 3/8 x 9 1/2 in. (36.5 x 24.1
 cm)
Gift of Mr. Samuel Gansheroff

Woman with Branch (84.8.2)
Woodcut, 14 1/8 x 9 3/4 in. (35.8 x
 24.8 cm)
Gift of Mr. Samuel Gansheroff

**UTAGAWA KUNIYOSHI,
 Attributed to**
Japanese (1797–1861)
Standing Warrior (83.14.12)
Woodcut, 14 7/8 x 10 in. (37.8 x 25.4
 cm)
Gift of Mr. Samuel Gansheroff

UTAGAWA TOYOHIRO
Japanese (1773–1828)
Pages from Storybook Inugashira
 (00.16.1–.5)
Set of five woodcuts; dimensions vary
Anonymous Gift

UTAGAWA TOYOKUNI
Japanese (1777–1835)
The Actor (00.236)
Woodcut, 13 7/8 x 9 1/8 in. (35.2 x
 23.2 cm)
Anonymous Gift

Two Actors (00.315)
Woodcut, 13 13/16 x 9 5/8 in. (35.1 x
 24.5 cm) (sight)
Anonymous Gift

Letter Being Delivered to Young Lady
 (83.14.1.2)
Woodcut, 13 3/4 x 9 5/8 in. (34.9 x 24.5
 cm)
Gift of Mr. Samuel Gansheroff

Night Figural Scene (83.14.1.1)
Woodcut, 13 7/8 x 9 1/2 in. (35.2 x
 24.1 cm)
Gift of Mr. Samuel Gansheroff

Woman with Napkin in Mouth
 (83.14.3)
Woodcut, 14 7/16 x 10 1/8 in. (36.7 x
 25.7 cm)
Gift of Mr. Samuel Gansheroff

UTAGAWA TOYOKUNI and Kiyomitsu Torii
Japanese (1769-1825); Japanese (1735-1785)
Scenes of Priests　(00.21)
Brush and ink, 9 1/4 x 13 3/4 in. (23.5 x 34.9 cm)
Anonymous Gift

VANDERBILT, Gloria
American (1924-　　)
Amour　(82.5)
Mixed media collage, 26 1/2 x 22 1/2 in. (67.3 x 57.2 cm)
Gift of Mr. and Mrs. John Ogden in memory of Nancy Kieckhefer Hogue

VAN NORTH(?), H.
American (late 19th-early 20th century)
Spires of Trinity Church and Broadway　(00.65)
Aquatint, 19 3/4 x 12 3/4 in. (50.2 x 32.4 cm)
Gift of Mr. Ray H. Wolf

The Emperor Greeting Soldiers, Agostino Veneziano, engraving

VENEZIANO, Agostino (Musi)
Italian (1480-1540)
The Emperor Greeting Soldiers, 1525*　(83.32.10)
Engraving, 15 5/8 x 10 1/4 in. (39.7 x 26 cm) (sight)
Gift of Dr. and Mrs. Sidney M. Boxer

VERTUE, George
English (1684-1756)
Edward IV King of England and France, Lord of Ireland　(00.25)
Engraving and etching after an unidentified fifteenth-century painting, 11 7/8 x 8 1/8 in. (30.2 x 20.6 cm)
Gift of Mrs. Joseph D. Patton

Matthaus Henry, V.D.M.　(00.242)
Engraving, 10 13/16 x 6 3/8 in. (27.5 x 16.2 cm)
Gift of Mrs. Joseph D. Patton

Portrait of the Honorable Robert Boyle 1739/1740　(00.29)
Etching after J. Kersseboom, 16 1/8 x 10 1/4 in. (41 x 26 cm)
Gift of Mrs. Joseph D. Patton

Sr. Matthew Hale Rt. Lord Chief Justice of His Majesty's Court of King's Bench, 1735　(00.20)
Engraving after Michael Wright, 13 1/4 x 8 5/8 in. (33.7 x 21.9 cm)
Gift of Mrs. Joseph D. Patton

VINKELES, Reinier
Dutch (1741-1816)
Joh. Jac. Serrurier, 1769　(00.24)
Engraving and etching after Pieter Frederik de la Croix, 14 1/2 x 10 1/2 in. (36.8 x 26.7 cm)
Anonymous Gift

VLAMINCK, Maurice de
French (1876-1958)
*L'Oise à Chapauval (The Oise at Chapauval)**　(00.210)
Lithograph, 21 1/8 x 25 3/4 in. (53.7 x 65.4 cm)
Gift of Mr. and Mrs. Philip Pinsof

VON NEUMANN, Robert
American (1888-1976)
Collection of Etchings, Lithographs, Wood Engravings, and a Watercolor　(81.26.1-.6)
Dimensions vary
Gift of Mr. Frederick D. Gore

Collection of Lithographs, Wood Engravings, and Engravings　(81.17.1-.26)
Dimensions vary
Gift of Dr. Richard A. Berk

L'Oise à Chapauval (The Oise at Chapauval), Maurice de Vlaminck, lithograph

WALCOT, William
English (1874-1943)
Koni Irubo   (00.33)
Etching, 10 5/8 x 14 1/4 in. (27 x
    36.2 cm)
Gift of Mr. Ray H. Wolf

WARHOL, Andy
American (1930-   )
Marilyn, 1967   (83.27.7)
Serigraph, 35 3/4 x 36 in. (90.8 x 91.4
    cm)
Gift of Mr. and Mrs. Ray Smith, Jr.

WEYROTTER, Franz Edmund
Austrian (1730-1771)
Untitled (Farm Scene)   (00.262)
Etching, 4 1/4 x 7 11/16 in. (10.8 x
    19.5 cm)
Anonymous Gift

Untitled (Harbor Scene)   (00.264)
Engraving, 8 1/8 x 3 5/8 in. (20.6 x
    9.2 cm)
Anonymous Gift

WICAR, Jean-Baptiste Joseph
French (1762-1834)
*Toilette de Venus/Pierre gravée
    antique*   (83.10.2.1&.2)
Engraving after School of Rubens,
    .1: 8 1/8 x 6 1/2 in. (20.6 x 16.5 cm)
        (comp.)
    .2: 4 3/4 x 6 1/2 in. (12.1 x 16.5 cm)
        (comp.)
Gift of Dr. Kenneth Maier

WILDE, John
American (1919-   )
Self-Portrait   (82.19.6)
Graphite, 13 1/4 x 9 1/4 in. (33.7 x
    23.5 cm) (comp.)
Gift of Mr. Frederick D. Gore

WILLETTE, Adolphe
French (1857-1926)
Seven Deadly Sins, 1916
    (80.17.19-.25)
Set of seven lithographs with
    remarques; dimensions vary
Gift of Mr. Paul P. Lipton

WILLIAM, V.
American (?) (late 19th century)
*Untitled (Landscape with Felled
    Tree), 1880*   (00.19)
Etching, 11 1/8 x 7 7/16 in. (28.3 x 18.9
    cm)
Anonymous Gift

WILLIAMS, Emmett
American (1925-   )
Coptic Optics Portfolio, 1979
    (81.38.13.1-.13)
Set of thirteen offset prints, 13 3/4 x
    19 3/4 in. (34.9 x 50.2 cm), each
Gift of Mr. Robert Steinberg, Mr. Saul
    Steinberg, and Mrs. Ann Steinberg

WILSON, Richard *
English (1713(?)-1782)
Twelve Original Views of Italy Series
    (00.296.1-.11)
Set of eleven engravings; dimensions
    vary
Anonymous Gift

WORTHINGTON, William Henry
English (1790-1839)
Portrait of John Block, 1835
    (00.351)
Engraving, 11 7/16 x 9 in. (29.1 x
    22.9 cm)
Gift of Mrs. Joseph D. Patton

WRIGHT, Frank Lloyd *
American (1869-1957)
*Plans for the Leesburg Floating
    Gardens, Leesburg, Florida, 1952*
    (78.4.1-.4)
Set of four colored pencil and ink
    drawings on tracing paper; dimen-
    sions vary
Gift of Mr. and Mrs. Kirby Raab

YOKOO, Tadanori
Japanese (1936-   )
Collection of Prints, 1968-1982
    (82.8.1-.15)
Set of fifteen photographic serigraphs;
    dimensions vary
Gift of the artist

ZALCE, Alfredo
Mexican (1908-   )
*Untitled (Figures Controlling Human
    Puppets)*   (00.99)
Woodcut, 6 3/4 x 10 5/8 in. (17.2 x
    27 cm)
Gift of Mr. and Mrs. Philip Pinsof

ZORN, Anders Leonard, Attributed to
Swedish (1860-1920)
Mona, 1911   (79.14.3)
Engraving, 12 3/4 x 16 1/8 in. (32.4 x
    41 cm)
Gift of Mrs. Douglass Van Dyke

PHOTOGRAPHS

FARBER, Edward R.
American (1914–1982)
Communist Picket-Bund Rally,
Milwaukee, Wisconsin, 1941
(83.37.3)
Photograph, 24 x 19 3/8 in. (61 x 49.2
cm) (sight)
Gift of Mr. and Mrs. Marvin L.
Fishman

MARTENS, Frédéric (?)
German (1809–1875)
Temple de Vesta a Rome   (80.17.3)
Daguerreotype, 5 3/4 x 7 7/8 in. (14.6 x
20 cm) (comp.)
Gift of Mr. Paul P. Lipton

MORGAN, Barbara **
American (1900–   )
Barbara Morgan Dance Photographs,
1935–1944   (78.1.1-.10)
Portfolio of ten photographs,
published 1977; dimensions vary
Gift of Mr. and Mrs. John Ogden

City Sound, 1972/1980   (83.2.7)
Photomontage, 20 x 16 in. (50.8 x 40.6
cm)
Gift of Mr. Douglas Morgan

Collection of Vintage Photographs,
1935–1944: Set of 270 photographs;
dimensions vary. On extended loan
from an anonymous donor.

Corn Leaf Rhythm, 1945/1980
(83.2.13)
Photograph, 20 x 16 in. (50.8 x 40.6 cm)
Gift of Mr. Douglas Morgan

Doris Humphrey-With My Red Fires
(Matriarch Swirl), 1938/1980
(83.2.2)
Photograph, 16 x 20 in. (40.6 x 50.8 cm)
Gift of Mr. Douglas Morgan

Emanation, 1940/1980   (83.1.3)
Photograph, 20 x 16 in. (50.8 x 40.6 cm)
Gift of Mr. Lloyd Morgan

Fossil in Formation, 1965/1980*
(83.1.6)
Photomontage, 16 x 20 in. (40.6 x 50.8
cm)
Gift of Mr. Lloyd Morgan

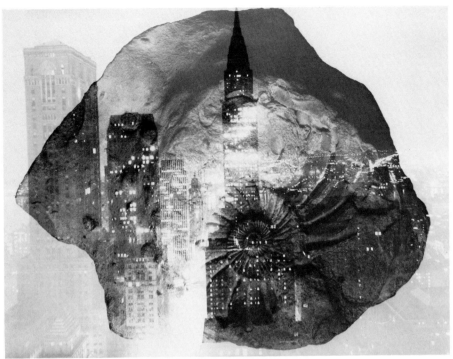

Fossil in Formation, Barbara Morgan, photomontage

Hearst over the People, 1939/1980
(83.1.15)
Photomontage, 16 x 20 in. (40.6 x 50.8
cm)
Gift of Mr. Lloyd Morgan

José Limón-Chaconne, 1944/1980
(83.1.9)
Photograph, 20 x 16 in. (50.8 x 40.6 cm)
Gift of Mr. Lloyd Morgan

José Limón-Cowboy Song,
1938/1980   (83.1.12)
Photomontage, 20 x 16 in. (50.8 x 40.6
cm)
Gift of Mr. Lloyd Morgan

Leaping in the Blender, 1965/1980
(83.2.6)
Photomontage, 20 x 16 in. (50.8 x 40.6
cm)
Gift of Mr. Douglas Morgan

Le Corbusier in New York,
1946/1980   (83.2.5)
Photograph, 20 x 16 in. (50.8 x 40.6 cm)
Gift of Mr. Douglas Morgan

Macy's Window, 1939/1980
(83.1.2)
Photomontage, 16 x 20 in. (40.6 x 50.8
cm)
Gift of Mr. Lloyd Morgan

Martha Graham-American Document
(Solo-Hawkins), 1940/1980
(83.2.12)
Photograph, 16 x 20 in. (40.6 x 50.8 cm)
Gift of Mr. Douglas Morgan

Martha Graham-American Document
(Trio), 1938/1980   (83.2.9)
Photograph, 16 x 20 in. (40.6 x 50.8
cm)
Gift of Mr. Douglas Morgan

Martha Graham-American Document
(Trio-Maslow, Flier, Mazia),
1938/1980   (83.1.5)
Photograph, 20 x 16 in. (50.8 x 40.6
cm)
Gift of Mr. Lloyd Morgan

Martha Graham-Celebration (Trio),
1937/1980   (83.1.7)
Photograph, 20 x 16 in. (50.8 x 40.6 cm)
Gift of Mr. Lloyd Morgan

Martha Graham-El Penitente
(Hawkins-El Flagellante),
1940/1980   (83.1.4)
Photograph, 20 x 16 in. (50.8 x 40.6 cm)
Gift of Mr. Lloyd Morgan

Martha Graham-Lamentation,
1935/1980   (83.1.14)
Photomontage, 20 x 16 in. (50.8 x 40.6
cm)
Gift of Mr. Lloyd Morgan

Protest, Barbara Morgan, photograph

Martha Graham-Lamentation,
  1935/1980   (83.2.4)
Photograph, 16 x 20 in. (40.6 x 50.8 cm)
Gift of Mr. Douglas Morgan

*Martha Graham-Letter to the World
  (Swirl)*, 1940/1980   (83.1.8)
Photograph, 16 x 20 in. (40.6 x 50.8 cm)
Gift of Mr. Lloyd Morgan

Martha Graham-Primitive Mysteries,
  1935/1980   (83.1.13)
Photograph, 16 x 20 in. (40.6 x 50.8 cm)
Gift of Mr. Lloyd Morgan

*Martha Graham-Primitive Mysteries
  (Group)*, 1935/1980   (83.2.1)
Photograph, 16 x 20 in. (40.6 x 50.8 cm)
Gift of Mr. Douglas Morgan

Merce Cunningham-Root of Unfocus,
  1944/1979   (83.2.11)
Photomontage, 16 x 20 in. (40.6 x 50.8
  cm)
Gift of Mr. Douglas Morgan

Pregnant, 1945/1980   (83.2.8)
Photograph, 20 x 16 in. (50.8 x 40.6 cm)
Gift of Mr. Douglas Morgan

Protest, 1940/1970/1980*   (83.2.10)
Photograph, 20 x 16 in. (50.8 x 40.6 cm)
Gift of Mr. Douglas Morgan

Pure Energy and Neurotic Man,
  1945/1980   (83.1.10)
Photomontage, 20 x 16 in. (50.8 x 40.6
  cm)
Gift of Mr. Lloyd Morgan

Spring on Madison Square,
  1938/1980*   (83.1.1)
Photomontage, 16 x 20 in. (40.6 x 50.8
  cm)
Gift of Mr. Lloyd Morgan

Third Avenue El, 1936/1980
  (83.2.14)
Photomontage, 20 x 16 in. (50.8 x 40.6
  cm)
Gift of Mr. Douglas Morgan

Valerie Bettis-Desperate Heart (A),
  1944/1980   (83.1.11)
Photograph, 20 x 16 in. (50.8 x 40.6 cm)
Gift of Mr. Lloyd Morgan

Valerie Bettis-Desperate Heart (B),
  1944/1980   (83.2.3)
Photograph, 20 x 16 in. (50.8 x 40.6 cm)
Gift of Mr. Douglas Morgan

STEINER, Ralph
American (1904-   )
Vanderbilt Garage, 1924/1981
  (84.3)
Photograph, 4 x 5 1/16 in. (10.2 x
  12.9 cm)
Gift of the artist

UNKNOWN ARTIST
The Alhambra, Granada, Spain
  (80.5)
Hand-colored photograph, 17 1/2 x
  22 3/4 in. (44.5 x 57.8 cm) (sight)
Gift of Mrs. Eric C. Stern

Spring on Madison Square, Barbara Morgan, photomontage

SCULPTURE

AMERICAN ARTS BRONZE CO.
American (late 19th–early 20th
century)
Lioness (65.19.3)
Bronze, after a sculpture by Barye,
16 x 23 x 8 1/2 in. (40.6 x 58.4 x
21.6 cm)
Gift of Mrs. Fred A. Miller

CHALON, Louis
French (b. 1866)
The Emergence of Spring* (63.8)
Bronze, 29 x 17 x 14 in. (73.7 x 43.2 x
35.6 cm)
Gift of Mr. Julius C. Theilacker

CIPRIUNY (CIPRIUNI ?), T.
Nationality Unknown (late 19th–early
20th century)
The Lovers (56.14)
Marble, 22 x 15 x 10 in. (55.9 x 38.1 x
25.4 cm)
Gift of Mr. Vincent J. Lucareli

DELAIGUE, Victor-Constantine **
French (active early 20th century)
Dante in the Inferno (64.2)
Bronze and ivory, 30 x 15 x 17 1/2 in.
(76.2 x 38.1 x 44.5 cm)
Anonymous Gift

DENNETEAU, Felix B.
French (20th century)
Bust of Louise Lemp Pabst
(77.11S)
Marble, 19 1/2 x 17 1/2 x 10 3/4 in.
(49.5 x 44.5 x 27.3 cm)
Gift of Mr. and Mrs. John Ogden

FABERGÉ, Peter Carl
Russian (1846–1920)
Cossack Figure (81.27.2)
Silver, 4 3/4 x 8 7/8 x 5 1/4 in.
(12.1 x 22.5 x 13.3 cm)
Gift of Dr. Kenneth Maier

FARRELLI, R. (F.?) W.
Nationality Unknown (20th century)
Aux Champs (00.375)
Bronze, 27 x 15 x 9 in. (68.6 x 38.1 x
22.9 cm)
Anonymous Gift

FESSLER, Sr. Mary Thomasita
American (1912–   )
The Holy Family (70.15)
Terra-cotta and bronze, 18 1/4 x 5 1/4
x 3 3/4 in. (46.4 x 13.3 x 9.5 cm)
Gift of Mr. Eliot G. Fitch

The Emergence of Spring, Louis Chalon, bronze

*Unless the Lord Builds the City You
Labor in Vain Who Built It* (67.7)
Wire and plaster of paris on walnut,
49 1/2 x 95 3/4 in. (125.7 x 243.2 cm)
Gift of Mr. Richard J. Panlener in
memory of his wife, Gertrude

HARRISON, Carol
American (20th century)
Horse (83.27.1)
Bronze and copper, 13 x 26 x 9 in. (33 x
66 x 22.9 cm)
Gift of Mr. and Mrs. Ray Smith, Jr.

JUNGWIRTH, Leonard D.
American (1903–1964)
Jesus Scourged (70.2)
Terra-cotta, 25 x 10 x 10 1/2 in. (63.5 x
25.4 x 26.7 cm)
Gift of Mrs. Irene Gayas Jungwirth

KNEALE, Collan B.
American (1934–   )
Seed Pod (83.27.2)
Bronze, 37 x 18 x 15 in. (94 x 45.7 x
38.1 cm)
Gift of Mr. and Mrs. Ray Smith, Jr.

LEHMBRUCK, Wilhelm *
German (1881-1919)
Geneigter Frauenkopf (called Head of a Kneeling Woman), 1911 (64.15)
Bronze, 16 1/2 x 16 x 9 in. (41.9 x 40.6 x 22.9 cm)
Gift of Mr. Joseph P. Antonow

LEMOYNE, Paul
French (1784-1873)
The Lion Tamer (62.2)
Bronze, 23 x 29 1/4 x 14 1/2 in. (58.4 x 74.3 x 36.8 cm)
Gift of Mr. Julius C. Theilacker

LEO, Brian
American (20th century)
Landscape (64.29)
Bronze, 6 1/2 x 19 1/4 x 12 1/2 in. (16.5 x 48.9 x 31.8 cm)
Gift of the Ford Foundation

FERDINANDO MARINELLI FOUNDRY, Florence, Italy
Pietà, 1945* (64.28)
Bronze, after the sculpture by Michelangelo, 66 x 62 x 32 in. (167.6 x 157.5 x 81.3 cm)
Gift of Boston Store

MILDENAU, Karl V.
Austrian (20th century)
Stag and Two Does (65.13)
Bronze, 25 1/4 x 30 3/4 x 9 3/4 in. (64.1 x 78.1 x 24.8 cm)
Gift of Mrs. Fred A. Miller

MIRALDA, Antoni
Spanish (1942-)
Marching Soldiers (80.25.29)
Plastic toy soldiers on Plexiglas, motorized, 29 3/4 x 24 x 18 in. (75.6 x 61 x 45.7 cm)
Gift of Mr. Joseph P. Antonow

MONTORNY, E.
American (late 19th-early 20th century)
Joan of Arc (66.12)
Marble, 14 1/2 x 15 x 7 in. (36.8 x 38.1 x 17.8 cm)
Gift of Mr. Vincent J. Lucareli

NOLENSKEW, Nilge
Nationality Unknown (20th century)
Seated Child (64.22)
Bronze, 12 5/8 x 4 1/4 x 6 1/4 in. (32.1 x 10.8 x 15.9 cm)
Gift of Mr. Joseph P. Antonow

Pietà, After the sculpture by Michelangelo, Ferdinando Marinelli Foundry, bronze

SOTO, Jésus Raphael
Venezuelan (1923-1950)
Jai alai Series, 1969 (80.24.15.1-.9)
Set of nine works in wood, metal sheeting, and polymer; dimensions vary
Gift of Mr. Thomas M. Lewyn

SPECK, Paul, After *
Swiss (1896-1966)
Death Mask of James Joyce (77.10)
Bronze, 12 x 7 x 6 1/2 in. (30.5 x 17.8 x 16.5 cm)
Gift of Mr. and Mrs. Paul J. Polansky

STEYER, Peter *
Czechoslovakian (1927-)
Porträt Amir (Portrait of Amir), 1955 (80.25.1)
Bronze, 16 1/2 x 9 1/2 x 9 1/2 in. (41.9 x 24.1 x 24.1 cm)
Gift of Mr. Joseph P. Antonow

SUNDERLAND, Nita Kathleen
American (1927-)
Solitary Figure (81.1)
Stainless steel, 17 x 4 1/4 x 10 in. (43.2 x 10.8 x 25.4 cm)
Gift of Dr. V. Michael Miller

UNKNOWN ARTIST
Italian (c. 1685-1725)
Corpus of Christ (66.1)
Wood, 48 x 14 x 12 in. (121.9 x 35.6 x 30.5 cm)
Gift of Mr. and Mrs. Carl W. Moebius, Jr.

UNKNOWN ARTIST
Indian (n.d.)
Birth of Siva Sadyojata (82.18.8)
Slate, 7 1/4 x 11 1/2 x 3 1/2 in. (18.4 x 29.2 x 8.9 cm)
Gift of Mr. Joseph P. Antonow

Head of an Angel, Italian, Seventeenth-Eighteenth Century, wood

UNKNOWN ARTIST
Burmese (19th century ?)
Court Dancer   (71.2)
Iron, 51 3/4 x 13 x 5 in. (131.5 x 33 x
   12.7 cm)
Gift of Dr. and Mrs. Ben Z. Rappaport

UNKNOWN ARTIST
European (16th century ?)
Figure of a Saint   (81.13)
Limewood, 11 1/2 x 5 x 3 in. (29.2 x
   12.7 x 7.6 cm)
Gift of Mr. Joseph P. Antonow

UNKNOWN ARTIST
French (17th century)
Figure of a Woman.   (80.19.4)
Wood, 26 x 7 x 5 1/4 in. (66 x 17.8 x
   13.3 cm)
Gift of Dr. Kenneth Maier

UNKNOWN ARTIST
Italian (17th–18th century)
Head of an Angel *   (78.3)
Wood, 12 3/4 x 23 3/4 x 6 in. (32.4 x
   60.3 x 15.2 cm)
Gift of Mrs. Charles P. Vogel

UNKNOWN ARTIST
Nationality Unknown (19th century)
*Madonna**   (63.3)
Carrara marble, 19 3/4 x 18 1/2 x 6 in.
   (50.2 x 47 x 15.2 cm)
Gift of Mr. and Mrs. Donald B. Abert
   in memory of Harry J. Grant

UNKNOWN ARTIST
German (?) (late 17th–early 18th
   century ?)
*Madonna and Child**   (82.9)
Limewood with pigment, 26 x 15 x 10
   in. (66 x 38.1 x 25.4 cm)
Gift of Mr. Philip J. Petersen

UNKNOWN ARTIST
Madonna and Child   (83.7)
Marble, 19 5/8 x 13 1/4 x 1 1/2 in.
   (49.9 x 33.7 x 3.8 cm)
Gift of Mrs. Ralph N. Harkness in
   memory of Mr. Francis D. Frost

UNKNOWN ARTIST
Nationality Unknown (19th century)
Oriental Deity   (59.16)
Teakwood, 43 1/4 x 20 x 16 1/2 in.
   (109.9 x 50.8 x 41.9 cm)
Gift of Mr. and Mrs. Morris Zolin

UNKNOWN ARTIST
Italian (c. 1685–1725)
Pair of Saints   (66.2&3)
Wood, 32 x 20 x 12 in. (81.3 x 50.8 x
   30.5 cm), each
Gift of Mr. and Mrs. Carl W.
   Moebius, Jr.

UNKNOWN ARTIST
European (19th century)
*Portrait of a Renaissance Noble-
   woman*   (84.9.2)
Marble relief, 24 1/8 x 18 1/2 x 3 1/4
   in. (61.3 x 47 x 8.3 cm)
Gift of Mr. and Mrs. Donald B. Abert

UNKNOWN ARTIST
Nationality Unknown (19th century)
Reclining Cossack Figure   (83.10.1)
Bronze, 4 x 6 1/2 x 5 in. (10.2 x 16.5 x
   12.7 cm)
Gift of Dr. Kenneth Maier

UNKNOWN ARTIST
Egyptian, Ptolemaic Period (?)
   (c. 322–30 B.C.)
Recumbent Ram   (82.18.7)
White alabaster, 8 x 10 1/4 x 5 in. (20.3
   x 26 x 12.7 cm)
Gift of Mr. Joseph P. Antonow

UNKNOWN ARTIST
German (18th century)
St. Paul   (80.23.2)
Wood, 9 1/2 x 5 1/4 x 2 3/4 in. (24.1 x
   13.3 x 7 cm)
Gift of Dr. and Mrs. Paul A. Duden-
   hoefer in memory of Clarence and
   Bernardine Dudenhoefer

St. Peter   (80.23.1)
Wood, 9 1/2 x 3 3/4 x 3 in. (24.1 x 9.5 x
   7.6 cm)
Gift of Dr. and Mrs. Paul A. Duden-
   hoefer in memory of Clarence and
   Bernardine Dudenhoefer

UNKNOWN ARTIST
French (17th–18th century)
Ten Apostles   (55.15)
Oak, 12 1/2 x 10 1/2 in. (31.8 x
   26.7 cm)
Gift of Mr. and Mrs. Charles Zadok

UNKNOWN ARTIST
Nationality Unknown (n.d.)
Three Graces   (50.2)
Marble, 38 1/2 x 26 x 14 in. (97.8 x 66 x
   35.6 cm)
Anonymous Gift

211

UNKNOWN ARTIST
Spanish (?) (17th century)
Untitled (Figure of a Man) (67.6)
Wood with pigment, 31 3/4 x 17 1/2
    x 11 in. (80.7 x 44.4 x 28 cm)
Gift of Mr. Joseph P. Antonow

VIVIANO (VIVIANI ?), G. **
Italian (19th century)
Rebecca at the Well (79.19)
Marble, 43 x 14 1/2 x 12 in. (109.2 x
    36.8 x 30.5 cm)
Gift of Miss Frances F. Gumina in
    memory of Sam and Concetta
    Gumina

WYNNE, David
English (1926–   )
The Beatles* (82.4.2.1-.4)
Bronze,
    .1: 7 3/4 x 5 5/8 x 3 in. (19.7 x 14.3 x
        7.6 cm)
    .2: 8 1/4 x 3 5/8 x 2 5/8 in. (21 x 9.2 x
        6.7 cm)
    .3: 5 5/8 x 5 5/8 x 5 1/4 in. (14.3 x
        14.3 x 13.3 cm)
    .4: 8 1/4 x 4 1/2 x 5 1/4 in. (21 x 11.4
        x 13.3 cm)
Gift of Mrs. Lloyd H. Pettit

The Beatles, David Wynne, bronze

Madonna and Child, German (?), Late Seventeenth-Early Eighteenth Century (?),
limewood with pigment

212

Puppet Figure of an Ancient Woman, Malian, Bamana Tribe, wood and trade cloth (?)

Hereafter dates in parentheses following nationality represent the approximate date of the item listed. When a specific artist is named, however, the dates given are those of the artist.

ANTIPHONALS AND ILLUMINATED MANUSCRIPTS

CHURCH OF ST. JAMES, Ecija, Spain
Spanish (16th century ?)
Antiphonal   (70.9)
Ink on vellum with leather-bound cover, 26 1/2 x 20 1/4 x 4 in. (67.3 x 51.4 x 10.2 cm)
Gift of Mr. and Mrs. Carl W. Moebius, Jr.

MONASTERY OF BURGOS LAS HUELGAS, Spain
Spanish (16th century ?)
Set of Twelve Antiphonals (51.4.1-.12)
Ink on vellum; dimensions vary
Gift of Colonel Howard M. Greene

THE SPANISH FORGER, Attributed to
Spanish (20th century)
Illuminated Manuscript   (61.15)
Ink on vellum, 20 7/8 x 15 1/8 in. (53 x 38.4 cm)
Gift of Mr. and Mrs. Richard B. Flagg

Illuminated Manuscript   (79.21)
Gold leaf and ink on vellum, 21 1/2 x 17 1/2 in. (54.6 x 44.5 cm)
Gift of Miss Eva K. Ford

UNKNOWN ARTIST
Collection of Illuminated Manuscripts (64.23; 72.9.-.19)
Ink on vellum with tempera and gold leaf; dimensions vary
Gift of Dr. and Mrs. John Pick

Illuminated Manuscript   (68.7)
Ink on vellum, 26 x 17 in. (66 x 43.2 cm)
Gift of the Association of Marquette University Women

CERAMICS, CHINA, AND PORCELAIN

CERAMICS

ROBBIA, Andrea della, Attributed to the School of
Italian (1435-1525)
Dante Alighieri (68.1)
Terra-cotta, glazed, 15 1/4 x 15 1/4 in.
(38.7 x 38.7 cm) (sight)
Gift of Mr. and Mrs. Carl W.
Moebius, Jr.

ROBBIA, Andrea della, Follower of
Italian (1435-1525)
Madonna and Child with Angels **
(49.1)
Terra-cotta, glazed, 43 x 23 1/8 in.
(109.2 x 58.7 cm)
Gift of Boston Store

Amphora, Roman, terra-cotta

UNKNOWN ARTISTS
*Amphora** (57.5)
Roman (c. 300 B.C.)
Terra-cotta, 23 1/4 x 12 1/2 in. d. (59.1
x 31.8 cm d.)
Gift of Mr. Stanley Slotkin

Frieze Fragment (83.36.4)
Grecian (c. 320 B.C.)
Terra-cotta, 7 1/2 x 4 5/8 x 1 5/8 in.
(19.1 x 11.8 x 4.1 cm)
Gift of Mr. Joseph P. Antonow

Urn (71.6)
Israeli (c. 930-500 B.C. ?)
Terra-cotta, 8 3/4 x 4 3/4 in. d. (22.2 x
12.1 cm d.)
Gift of Mr. Albert B. Adelman

Covered Urn, Wedgwood. basalt ceramic stoneware

WEDGWOOD
English
Covered Urn. 1800-1825*
(80.18.1 a&b)
Basalt ceramic stoneware, 12 3/4 x
7 1/4 in. d. (32.4 x 18.4 cm d.)
Gift of Mr. and Mrs. Ernest F. Rice, Jr.

WHIELDON, Thomas
English (c. 1755-1760)
Platter (84.4.1)
Ceramic, 1 1/4 x 17 1/4 x 14 in. (3.2 x
43.8 x 35.6 cm)
Gift of Dr. Kenneth Maier

Teapot (84.4.2a&b)
Ceramic,
pot: 4 1/4 x 8 1/4 x 5 in. (10.8 x 21 x
12.7 cm)
lid: 1 1/8 x 2 3/4 in. (2.9 x 7 cm)
Gift of Dr. Kenneth Maier

CHINA

CAULDON
English (late 19th-early 20th century)
Collection of Dinnerware (51.3)
China; dimensions vary
Gift of Mrs. John E. Schroeder

ROCKINGHAM
English (1765-1843)
*Collection of Dinnerware and Serving
Dishes* (80.19.3.1-.23)
Bone china; dimensions vary
Gift of Dr. Kenneth Maier

ROYAL BAVARIAN, Limoges and Minton
German; French; English (late 19th-
early 20th century)
Collection of Dinnerware
Bone china and porcelain; dimensions
vary
Gift of Mr. and Mrs. Clifford A.
Randall

SPODE
English (1754-1827)
Oblong Dish (82.7.5)
China, 2 x 11 1/4 x 11 1/8 in. (5.1 x
28.6 x 28.3 cm)
Gift of Dr. Kenneth Maier

UNKNOWN ARTIST
English (19th century)
Dessert Plate (78.6.3)
China, 1 x 7 7/8 in. d. (2.5 x 20 cm d.)
Gift of Mr. and Mrs. Ernest F. Rice, Jr.

WEDGWOOD
English (18th century)
Insignia Plate (82.7.2)
China, 10 3/4 in. d. (27.3 cm d.)
Gift of Dr. Kenneth Maier

PORCELAIN

BELLANGER, F. (Francis ?)
French (late 19th century)
Pair of Vases (62.5&.6)
Porcelain with ormolu stand, 25 1/2 x
  13 x 7 in. (64.8 x 33 x 17.8 cm), each
Gift of Mrs. Martin Fladoes

BOEHM, Edward
American (20th century)
Pontif Statuette (00.400)
Porcelain, 7 7/8 x 5 1/4 x 3 1/2 in. (20 x
  13.3 x 8.9 cm)
Anonymous Gift

CAPODIMONTE
Italian (late 19th–early 20th century)
Pair of Classical Female Figurines,
  1821 (73.15.1&.2)
Porcelain,
  .1: 9 x 4 x 2 3/4 in. (22.9 x 10.2 x 7
    cm)
  .2: 8 x 3 1/8 x 3 1/4 in. (20.3 x 7.9 x
    8.3 cm)
Gift of Mr. and Mrs. Waldemar
  Kopmeier

Pair of Urn Covers (65.18.13.1&.2)
Porcelain, 4 x 3 3/4 x 3 3/4 in. (10.2 x
  9.5 x 9.5 cm), each
Gift of Mrs. Jetta Muntain Smith in
  memory of her son, Aurel Muntain

Three Cherubs with Flowers
  (65.9.1.2)
Porcelain, 13 3/4 x 11 x 7 1/2 in. (34.9
  x 27.9 x 19.1 cm)
Gift of Dr. William L. Herner

CAPODIMONTE, designed by L.
  Badessi
Italian (late 19th–early 20th century)
Three Cherubs with Flowers
  (65.9.1.1)
Porcelain, 12 1/8 x 10 5/16 x 6 1/4 in.
  (30.8 x 26.2 x 15.9 cm)
Gift of Dr. William L. Herner

CHELSEA
English (early 19th century)
Pair of Figurines (82.7.3.1&.2)
Porcelain,
  .1: 9 x 4 3/4 x 4 1/4 in. (22.9 x 12.1 x
    10.8 cm)
  .2: 8 1/2 x 5 1/2 x 5 in. (21.6 x 14 x
    12.7 cm)
Gift of Dr. Kenneth Maier

Pair of Pastille Burners, Chelsea-Derby, porcelain

CHELSEA, designed by Hans Sloan
English (18th century)
Plate (83.5)
Porcelain, 1 x 8 3/8 in. d. (2.5 x 21.3
  cm d.)
Gift of Dr. Kenneth Maier

CHELSEA-DERBY
English (c. 1790)
*Pair of Pastille Burners**
  (80.27.1.1&.2)
Porcelain, 4 x 5 in. d. (10.2 x 12.7 cm
  d.), each
Gift of Dr. Kenneth Maier

DERBY
English (c. 1810)
Soup Bowl (78.6.5)
Porcelain, 1 9/16 x 8 1/2 in. d. (4 x
  21.6 cm d.)
Gift of Mr. and Mrs. Ernest F. Rice, Jr.

DOULTON
English (19th century)
Centerpiece Bowl (00.439)
Porcelain, 8 x 14 3/4 in. d. (20.3 x 37.5
  cm d.)
Anonymous Gift

DRESDEN, painted by McKiesel
German (late 19th–early 20th century)
Portrait of Clementine (00.383)
Porcelain, 1 1/8 x 9 1/2 in. d. (2.7 x
  24.1 cm d.)
Anonymous Gift

T. FURNIVAL & SONS
English (19th century)
Punch Bowl (73.14)
Porcelain, 10 5/8 x 19 1/2 x 19 1/2 in.
  (27 x 49.5 x 49.5 cm)
Gift of the Marquette Women's League

HAVILAND AND CO.
French (late 19th–early 20th century)
Set of Twelve Two-Handled Soup
  Cups with Saucers
  (00.389.1–.12a&b)
Porcelain,
  cups: 2 1/4 x 5 3/8 x 4 1/4 in. (5.7 x
    13.7 x 10.8 cm), each
  saucers: 3/4 x 5 1/2 in. d. (1.9 x 14
    cm d.), each
Anonymous Gift

MEISSEN
German (late 19th–early 20th century)
Fan Vase (81.30.3)
Porcelain, 6 1/2 x 10 1/2 x 6 in. (16.5 x
  26.1 x 15.2 cm)
Gift of Mr. and Mrs. John Odgen in
  memory of Mr. and Mrs. Walter
  Harnischfeger

MEISSEN
German (20th century)
Figurine Group (81.30.1)
Porcelain, 10 x 13 3/4 x 6 1/2 in. (25.4
  x 34.9 x 16.5 cm)
Gift of Mr. and Mrs. John Ogden in
  memory of Mr. and Mrs. Walter
  Harnischfeger

MEISSEN
German (c. 1860–1916)
Four Figures with Donkey (66.17)
Porcelain, 8 1/2 x 8 1/2 x 5 1/2 in.
  (21.6 x 21.6 x 14 cm)
Gift of Mrs. Linda C. Gilbert

MEISSEN
German (c. 1750–1760)
Pair of Deep Dishes (83.11.1&.2)
Porcelain, 1 1/2 x 9 3/4 in. d. (3.8 x
  24.8 cm d.), each
Gift of Dr. Kenneth Maier

Pair of Cornucopias, Old Paris Group, porcelain

MEISSEN
German (c. 1750)
Set of Three Soup Bowls
   (83.45.5.1-.3)
Porcelain, 1 1/2 x 9 5/8 in. d. (3.8 x
   24.5 cm d.), each
Gift of Dr. Kenneth Maier

MEISSEN
German (18th century)
Three Cherubs   (81.39.3)
Porcelain, 10 1/2 x 6 x 7 in. (26.7 x 15.2
   x 17.8 cm)
Gift of Dr. Kenneth Maier

MEISSEN (?)
German (late 19th-early 20th century)
*Set of Nine Armorial Plates with
   Pierced Borders*   (83.46.1.1-.9)
Porcelain, 1 1/2 x 8 1/4 in. d. (3.8 x 21
   cm d.), each
Gift of Mr. and Mrs. Robert L. Pagel, Sr.

**MEISSEN, CAULDON, VILLEROY
   AND BOCH, WEDGWOOD, and
   HAVILAND AND CO.**
German; English; French (late 19th-
   early 20th century)
*Collection of Dinnerware and
   Accessories*
Porcelain; dimensions vary
Gift of the Estate of Mr. C. Frederic
   (Todd) Wehr

OLD PARIS GROUP
French (early 19th century)
Pair of Cache Pots   (81.39.1.1&.2)
Porcelain, 6 1/2 x 8 in. d. (16.5 x 20.3
   cm d.), each
Gift of Dr. Kenneth Maier

OLD PARIS GROUP
French (c. 1810)
*Pair of Cornucopias**
   (80.19.1.1&.2)
Porcelain, 11 x 10 x 7 1/2 in. (27.9 x
   25.4 x 19.1 cm), each
Gift of Dr. Kenneth Maier

OLD PARIS GROUP
French (early 19th century)
Pair of Vases   (81.39.2.1&.2)
Porcelain, 14 x 9 1/2 x 6 3/4 in. (35.6 x
   24.1 x 17.2 cm), each
Gift of Dr. Kenneth Maier

POWELL, BISHOP AND STONIER
English
Covered Dessert Tureen with Stand,
   1882   (80.18.2a-d)
Creamware,
   cover: 2 1/2 x 6 1/2 x 4 in. (6.4 x 16.5
      x 10.2 cm)
   tureen: 3 1/4 x 8 1/4 x 5 in. (8.3 x 21
      x 12.7 cm)
Gift of Mr. and Mrs. Ernest F. Rice, Jr.

ROYAL WORCESTER
English (late 19th century)
Cylindrical Jar with Cover
   (83.46.5a&b)
Porcelain,
   jar: 2 3/4 x 3 in. d. (7 x 7.6 cm d.)
   cover: 1/2 x 3 1/4 in. d. (1.3 x 8.3
      cm d.)
Gift of Mr. and Mrs. Robert L.
   Pagel, Sr.

ROYAL WORCESTER
English (c. 1886–1888)
Pair of Plates   (78.6.1&.2)
Porcelain, 1 1/8 x 10 1/2 in. d. (2.9 x
   26.7 cm d.), each
Gift of Mr. and Mrs. Ernest F. Rice, Jr.

SALOPIAN (Caughley)
English (c. 1775–1799)
Oblong Dish   (82.7.4)
Porcelain, 1 3/4 x 10 1/2 x 6 7/8 in.
   (4.5 x 26.7 x 17.5 cm)
Gift of Dr. Kenneth Maier

SÈVRES
French (c. 1780)
Bowl   (79.28.3)
Porcelain after a painting by Teniers,
   2 7/8 x 10 7/8 x 8 3/8 in. (7.3 x 27.6 x
   21.3 cm)
Formerly of the collection of the Duke
   of Kent; gift of Dr. Kenneth Maier
   to the University

Bowl   (79.28.4)
Porcelain after a painting by Teniers,
   2 1/8 x 11 1/8 x 9 in. (5.4 x 28.3 x
   22.9 cm)
Formerly of the collection of the Duke
   of Kent; Gift of Dr. Kenneth Maier
   to the University

*Bowl with Cover**   (79.28.6a&b)
Porcelain, 4 3/4 x 5 1/2 x 4 3/4 in. (12.1
   x 14 x 12.1 cm)
Formerly of the collection of the Duke
   of Kent; Gift of Dr. Kenneth Maier
   to the University

Bowl with Handles   (79.28.7)
Porcelain, 4 5/8 x 9 x 7 3/8 in. (11.8 x
   22.9 x 18.7 cm)
Formerly of the collection of the Duke
   of Kent; Gift of Dr. Kenneth Maier
   to the University

Gravy Boat   (79.28.2)
Porcelain, 2 3/4 x 9 3/8 x 5 3/4 in. (7 x
   23.8 x 14.6 cm)
Formerly of the collection of the Duke
   of Kent; Gift of Dr. Kenneth Maier
   to the University

Pair of Oval Dishes with Fitted Urns
   (79.28.1.1&.2)
Porcelain, 3 3/8 x 11 7/8 x 6 7/8 in. (8.6
   x 30.2 x 17.5 cm), each
Formerly of the collection of the Duke
   of Kent; Gift of Dr. Kenneth Maier
   to the University

Bowl with Cover, Sèvres, porcelain

Set of Ten Plates   (79.28.1.1-.10)
Porcelain, 1 1/8 x 9 5/8 in. d. (2.9 x
    24.5 cm d.), each
Formerly of the collection of the Duke
    of Kent; Gift of Dr. Kenneth Maier
    to the University

SÈVRES
French (18th century)
Pair of Tazzas with Pedestals
    (80.19.5.1&.2)
Porcelain, 1 1/2 x 8 3/4 in. d. (3.8 x
    22.2 cm d.), each
Gift of Dr. Kenneth Maier

Saucer   (83.33.3)
Porcelain, 7/8 x 4 3/16 in. d. (2.2 x 10.6
    cm d.)
Gift of Dr. Kenneth Maier

**SÈVRES, designed by Adolphe-
Jean Baptiste Callot**
French (b. 1830)
Fruit Bowl   (60.21)
Porcelain, with gilt bronze, 7 1/8 x
    16 3/4 x 14 1/2 in. (18.1 x 42.6 x
    36.8 cm)
Gift of Mr. Bauer F. Bullinger

SÈVRES, decorated by Gerard
French (18th century)
Set of Seven Plates   (80.19.6.1-.7)
Porcelain, 1 x 9 1/2 in. d. (2.5 x 24.1
    cm d.), each
Gift of Dr. Kenneth Maier

SPODE
English (c. 1810)
Pair of Baskets with Stands
    (83.33.1.1-.4)
Porcelain,
    .1&.2: 3 1/2 x 10 1/2 x 5 3/4 in. (8.9
        x 26.7 x 14.6 cm)
    .3&.4: 3/4 x 9 5/8 x 7 7/8 in. (1.9 x
        24.5 x 20 cm)
Gift of Dr. Kenneth Maier

STAFFORDSHIRE GROUP
English (early 19th century)
Mug   (82.7.7)
Porcelain, 5 1/8 x 5 x 3 3/4 in. (13 x
    12.7 x 9.5 cm)
Gift of Dr. Kenneth Maier

UNKNOWN ARTISTS
Basket   (83.15.1)
English (c. 1790)
Porcelain, 5 3/4 x 9 1/2 x 7 1/2 in. (14.6
    x 24.1 x 19.1 cm)
Gift of Mr. Ralph Resenhoeft

Basket   (84.4.6)
Nationality Unknown (c. 1765-1770)
Porcelain, 2 3/8 x 7 3/8 in. d. (6 x 18.7
    cm d.)
Gift of Dr. Kenneth Maier

Bowl   (79.28.5)
French (?) (18th century)
Porcelain, 2 1/2 x 4 3/8 in. d. (16.4 x
    11.1 cm d.)
Gift of Dr. Kenneth Maier

Bowl   (84.4.8)
English (1780)
Porcelain with gold gilt trim, 1 3/8 x
    7 1/8 in. d. (3.5 x 18.1 cm d.)
Gift of Dr. Kenneth Maier

Dish   (78.6.10)
English (c. 1820)
Porcelain, 1 1/4 x 5 7/8 in. d. (3.2 x
    14.8 cm d.)
Gift of Mr. and Mrs. Ernest F. Rice,
    Jr.

Gravy Boat/Creamer   (82.7.11)
Nationality Unknown (c. 1770)
Porcelain, 2 3/4 x 6 3/4 x 3 1/2 in.
    (7 x 17.2 x 8.9 cm)
Gift of Dr. Kenneth Maier

Mantel Clock, 1817   (81.30.2)
German (19th century)
Porcelain, 10 x 5 1/2 x 2 3/4 in. (25.4 x
    14 x 7 cm)
Gift of Mr. and Mrs. John Ogden in
    memory of Mr. and Mrs. Walter
    Harnischfeger

Pitcher   (83.45.4)
English (c. 1810)
Creamware, 7 3/4 x 8 1/4 x 5 in. (19.7
    x 21 x 12.7 cm)
Gift of Dr. Kenneth Maier

Set of Seven Dessert Plates
    (83.46.2.1-.7)
French (?) (late 19th-early 20th
    century)
Porcelain, 1 x 8 3/4 in. d. (2.5 x 22.2
    cm d.), each
Gift of Mr. and Mrs. Robert L.
    Pagel, Sr.

VIENNA
Austrian (c. 1870-1880)
Portrait Cup and Saucer
    (83.33.2a&b)
Porcelain,
    cup: 2 3/4 x 3 3/8 x 2 1/2 in. (7 x 8.6
        x 6.4 cm)
    saucer: 3/4 x 4 7/8 in. d. (1.9 x 12.4
        cm d.)
Gift of Dr. Kenneth Maier

WEDGWOOD
English (late 19th-early 20th
    century)
Collection of Portrait Medallions
    (70.4.1-.9)
Porcelain; dimensions vary
Gift of Mr. and Mrs. Philip Pinsof

**WEDGWOOD, designed by Daisy
Makeig-Jones**
English (1881-1945)
Bowl   (80.18.5)
Faience with Butterfly luster, 2 x
    3 3/4 in. d. (5.1 x 9.5 cm d.)
Gift of Mr. and Mrs. Ernest F.
    Rice, Jr.

Bowl (80.18.6)
Faience with Fairyland luster, 1 1/8
x 2 1/4 in. d. (2.9 x 5.7 cm d.)
Gift of Mr. and Mrs. Ernest F.
Rice, Jr.

Bowl (80.18.7)
Faience with Fairyland luster, 1 3/4
x 3 in. d. (4.5 x 7.6 cm d.)
Gift of Mr. and Mrs. Ernest F.
Rice, Jr.

Bowl (80.18.8)
Faience with Fairyland luster, 1 1/2
x 2 1/4 in. d. (3.8 x 5.7 cm d.)
Gift of Mr. and Mrs. Ernest F.
Rice, Jr.

Octagonal Bowl (80.18.4)
Faience with Fairyland luster, 1 3/4
x 2 5/8 in. d. (4.5 x 6.7 cm d.)
Gift of Mr. and Mrs. Ernest F.
Rice, Jr.

Octagonal Bowl (80.18.9)
Faience with Fairyland luster, 2 3/4
x 4 7/8 in. d. (7 x 12.4 cm d.)
Gift of Mr. and Mrs. Ernest F.
Rice, Jr.

Three-Handled Mug (80.18.3)
Faience with Fairyland luster, 2 1/8
x 3 1/4 in. d. (5.4 x 8.3 cm d.)
Gift of Mr. and Mrs. Ernest F.
Rice, Jr.

Vase (81.2)
Faience with Fairyland luster, 12 x
6 1/2 in. d. (30.5 x 16.5 cm d.)
Gift of Mr. and Mrs. Ernest F.
Rice, Jr.

WORCESTER
English (c. 1770)
Basket (84.4.4)
Porcelain, 3 1/4 x 7 x 6 1/4 in. (8.3 x
17.8 x 15.9 cm)
Gift of Dr. Kenneth Maier

WORCESTER
English (c. 1770)
Bowl (81.22.3)
Porcelain, 2 1/8 x 5 7/8 in. d. (5.4 x
14.9 cm d.)
Gift of Mr. and Mrs. Ernest F.
Rice, Jr.

WORCESTER
English (20th century)
Bowl (81.22.7)
Porcelain, 2 1/2 x 6 1/16 in. d. (6.4 x
15.4 cm d.)
Gift of Mr. and Mrs. Ernest F.
Rice, Jr.

WORCESTER
English (c. 1760)
Butter Tub with Lid (84.4.7a&b)
Porcelain,
    lid: 2 x 4 5/8 x 3 3/4 in. (5.1 x 11.8 x
        9.5 cm)
    tub: 1 5/8 x 5 1/8 x 3 1/4 in. (4.1 x
        13 x 8.3 cm)
Gift of Dr. Kenneth Maier

WORCESTER
English (c. 1810)
Coffee Cup (78.6.7)
Porcelain, 2 3/8 x 4 1/4 x 3 5/16 in.
(6 x 10.8 x 8.4 cm)
Gift of Mr. and Mrs. Ernest F.
Rice, Jr.

WORCESTER
English (c. 1780)
Dish (81.22.2)
Porcelain, 3/4 x 6 1/2 in. d. (1.9 x 16.5
cm d.)
Gift of Mr. and Mrs. Ernest F.
Rice, Jr.

WORCESTER
English (c. 1760)
Plate (80.2)
Porcelain, 1 x 9 3/8 in. d. (2.5 x 24
cm)
Gift of Dr. Kenneth Maier

WORCESTER
English (c. 1760)
Platter (84.4.5)
Porcelain, 1 x 9 3/8 in. d. (2.5 x 24 cm)
Gift of Dr. Kenneth Maier

WORCESTER
English (c. 1810)
Saucer (78.6.8)
Porcelain, 1 1/8 x 5 5/16 in. d. (2.9 x
13.5 cm d.)
Gift of Mr. and Mrs. Ernest F.
Rice, Jr.

WORCESTER
English (c. 1765)
Saucer (81.22.6)
Porcelain, 1 1/4 x 5 1/8 in. d. (3.2 x 13
cm d.)
Gift of Mr. and Mrs. Ernest F.
Rice, Jr.

WORCESTER
English (late 18th century)
Tea Bowl and Saucer
    (81.22.5a&b)
Porcelain,
    bowl: 2 x 3 1/4 in. d. (5.1 x 8.3
        cm d.)
    saucer: 1 x 5 1/2 in. d. (2.5 x 14
        cm d.)
Gift of Mr. and Mrs. Ernest F.
Rice, Jr.

WORCESTER
English (c. 1765–1770)
Tea Caddy (81.22.4)
Porcelain, 5 x 3 in. d. (12.7 x 7.6
cm d.)
Gift of Mr. and Mrs. Ernest F.
Rice, Jr.

WORCESTER
English (c. 1760)
Teacup (82.7.6)
Porcelain, 1 5/8 x 3 1/2 x 2 3/4 in.
(4.1 x 8.9 x 7 cm)
Gift of Dr. Kenneth Maier

WORCESTER
English (c. 1760)
Teacup and Saucer (80.9a&b)
Porcelain,
    cup: 1 3/4 x 2 15/16 in. d. (4.5 x
        7.5 cm d.)
    saucer: 1 x 4 3/4 in. d. (2.5 x 12.1
        cm d.)
Gift of Dr. Kenneth Maier

WORCESTER
English (c. 1830)
Teapot (82.7.1a&b)
Porcelain,
    teapot: 6 1/8 x 11 x 5 1/4 in. (15.6 x
        27.9 x 13.3 cm)
    lid: 2 1/2 x 4 1/2 in. d. (6.4 x 11.4
        cm d.)
Gift of Dr. Kenneth Maier

**WORCESTER, designed by Dr.
Wall**
English (c. 1770)
Pair of Plates (84.4.3.1&.2)
Porcelain, 1 1/4 x 7 1/2 in. d. (3.2 x
19.1 cm d.), each
Gift of Dr. Kenneth Maier

FURNITURE

UNKNOWN ARTISTS

Bureau   (81.14)
American (19th century)
Cherry, 49 1/2 x 38 1/2 x 21 3/4 in.
  (125.7 x 98.4 x 55.3 cm)
Gift of Dr. Kenneth Maier

Case Clock   (81.32.1)
French (1715–1723)
Oak inlaid with marquetry with
  enamel and ormolu, 96 x 19 1/2 x 8
  in. (243.8 x 49.5 x 20.3 cm)
Gift of Dr. and Mrs. E. Esch Davies

Chair   (62.14)
Walnut (?) with caning and
  embroidery, 48 3/4 x 19 1/2 x 20
  in. (123.8 x 49.5 x 50.8 cm)
Gift of Mrs. Norman J. Kopmeier

Collection of Furniture
  (56.15.1&2; 00.501.1-.6; 00.506)
Including tables, side chairs, bookcase, and sideboard
Gift of Mrs. Carl A. Forster

Collection of Furniture   (58.27)
Including dining table, refectory
  table, card table, chairs, and
  accessories
Gift of Mr. George L. N. Meyer

Collection of Furniture   (79.26)
Including tables, chairs, loveseat,
  rugs, sofa, and accessories
European and American (late 19th–
  early 20th century)
Gift of Mr. and Mrs. E. Esch Davies

*Collection of Furniture and
  Accessories*   (84.9.1, 84.9.5.1&.2,
  84.9.6, 84.9.7.1&.2)
Including a pair of chairs, settee, pair
  of candelabra, and coffer
Oak, tapestry and wood, brass and
  inlaid walnut; dimensions vary
Gift of Mr. and Mrs. Donald B. Abert

Empire Sofa   (81.4)
American (c. 1830)
Rosewood and black walnut with
  green velvet upholstery, 36 7/8 x
  90 x 25 3/4 in. (93.7 x 228.6 x 65.4
  cm)
Gift of Dr. Kenneth Maier

Écritoire (Writing Desk)   (65.18.9)
French (19th century)
Rosewood, 52 x 36 1/2 x 16 1/2 in.
  (132 x 92.7 x 41.9 cm)
Gift of Mrs. Jetta Muntain Smith in
  memory of her son, Aurel Muntain

Mantelpiece   (79.8)
American (20th century)
Mahogany with mirrored glass,
  38 1/4 x 74 7/8 x 10 7/8 in. (97.2 x
  190.2 x 27.6 cm)
Gift of Dr. Kenneth Maier

Pair of Chairs   (60.22.1&.2)
American (late 19th–early 20th
  century)
Mahogany,
  .1: 40 x 24 x 25 1/2 in. (101.6 x 61 x
    64.8 cm)
  .2: 39 3/4 x 26 x 27 in. (101 x 66 x
    68.6 cm)
Gift of Dr. Joseph P. McMahon

Pair of Loveseats   (60.20.1.1&.2)
French (19th century)
Walnut with petit point, 36 1/2 x
  43 1/2 x 24 in. (92.7 x 110.5 x 61 cm),
  each
Gift of Mr. and Mrs. Joseph F. Heil

Secretary*   (81.12)
German (c. 1740–1760)
Walnut veneer with marquetry, 80 x
  50 x 26 in. (203.2 x 127 x 66 cm)
Gift of Mrs. Victoria S. Higgins in
  memory of Richard Calvin Roll

Sofa   (72.22.1)
French (late 19th–early 20th century)
Needlepoint and walnut, 40 1/4 x 75
  x 31 in. (102.2 x 190.5 x 78.7 cm)
Gift of Mr. and Mrs. Waldemar
  Kopmeier

Table Lamp   (65.18.11)
American (?) (late 19th–early 20th
  century)
Gilt bronze with enameled porcelain,
  33 1/4 x 16 3/8 in. d. (84.5 x 41.6
  cm d.)
Gift of Mrs. Jetta Muntain Smith in
  memory of her son, Aurel Muntain

*Secretary, German, Eighteenth Century,
walnut veneer with marquetry*

William IV Table   (79.7)
English (19th century)
Inlaid mahogany with inset leather,
  28 x 54 3/8 x 25 1/4 in. (71.1 x 138.1
  x 64.1 cm)
Gift of Dr. Kenneth Maier

GLASSWARE, ENAMELS, AND MOSAICS

GLASSWARE

T. G. HAWKES AND CO.
American (20th century)
Box with Cover   (83.46.4a&b)
Crystal, sterling silver and enamel,
  lid: 1 3/4 x 6 x 3 3/4 in. (4.5 x 15.2
    x 9.5 cm)
  box: 2 3/8 x 5 13/16 x 3 5/8 in. (6 x
    14.8 x 9.2 cm)
Gift of Mr. and Mrs. Robert L.
  Pagel, Sr.

LALIQUE, René
French (1860-1945)
The Crucifixion   (81.24)
Glass, 12 5/8 x 6 9/16 x 1 1/2 in. (32.1
  x 16.7 x 3.8 cm)
Gift of Mr. and Mrs. Robert L.
  Pagel, Sr.

Cup and Saucer   (83.46.3a&b)
Crystal with blue etched leaf and
  arcade pattern,
  cup: 1 7/8 x 4 3/4 x 4 in. (4.8 x 12.1
    x 10.2 cm)
  saucer: 1/2 x 7 1/8 in. d. (1.3 x 18.1
    cm d.)
Gift of Mr. and Mrs. Robert L.
  Pagel, Sr.

Vase   (83.46.8)
Glass with oval convex panels and
  standing female motifs, 10 3/4 x
  7 1/2 in. d. (27.3 x 19.1 cm d.)
Gift of Mr. and Mrs. Robert L.
  Pagel, Sr.

LEJEUNE, Louis Aimé (?)
French (1884-1969)
Hummingbird and Blossom
  (81.5a&b)
Glass, 16 x 5 1/2 x 5 1/2 in. (40.6 x 14
  x 14 cm)
Gift of Mrs. Marie Kerwin

UNKNOWN ARTISTS
Collection of Glassware   (60.14)
Including red wine, white wine, and
  sherry glasses
Bohemian (19th and 20th centuries)
Dimensions vary
Gift of Mrs. Gustave Blatz

*Collection of Hinged Boxes and
  Vases*   (81.30.4-.8)
Bohemian (19th and 20th centuries)
Glass; dimensions vary
Gift of Mr. and Mrs. John Ogden in
  memory of Mr. and Mrs. Walter
  Harnischfeger

Pair of Vases   (83.46.6.1&.2)
Nationality Unknown (20th century)
Glass, 9 3/8 x 5 1/2 in. d. (23.8 x 14
  cm d.)
Gift of Mr. and Mrs. Robert L.
  Pagel, Sr.

Pokal   (62.9a&b)
Belgian (c. 1880-1890)
Glass,
  pedestal: 16 3/4 x 8 in. d. (42.6 x
    20.3 cm d.)
  lid: 8 x 6 1/2 in. d. (20.3 x 16.5 cm d.)
Gift of Mrs. Karl Ratzsch, Sr.

Vase   (82.7.8)
American (20th century)
Glass, 4 1/4 x 4 in. d. (10.8 x 10.2
  cm d.)
Gift of Dr. Kenneth Maier

ENAMELS AND MOSAICS

LEWANDOWSKI, Edmund D.
American (1914-   )
Father Brooks Mural   (57.1)
Tesserae mosaic, 7 ft. 4 1/2 in. x
  16 ft. 6 in. (2.3 x 4.9 m)
Gift of Gimbel Brothers

UNKNOWN ARTISTS
American? (20th century)
Allotropic Forms   (66.22)
Mosaic with enamel on copper, 30 ft.
  x 7 ft. 6 in. (9.1 x 2.3 m)
Gift of Mr. Willard Feldman

Portrait of a Saint   (79.27.2)
Russian (late 19th-early 20th
  century)
Enamel, 1 3/8 x 1 1/16 in. (3.5 x
  2.7 cm)
Gift of Dr. and Mrs. John Pick

Roman Colosseum   (65.18.12)
Italian (19th century)
Mosaic, 10 x 12 1/2 in. (25.4 x 31.8 cm)
Gift of Mrs. Jetta Muntain Smith in
  memory of her son, Aurel Muntain

IVORY

UNKNOWN ARTISTS

Bishop of St. Denis   (76.1)
French (19th century)
Ivory, 11 1/4 x 3 3/8 x 2 5/8 in. (28.6 x
  8.6 x 6.7 cm)
Gift of Mrs. Charles P. Vogel

Christ as Child   (63.12)
Spanish (18th-19th century)
Ivory, 5 3/8 x 2 1/2 x 1 5/8 in. (13.7 x
  6.4 x 4.1 cm)
Gift of Mr. Norbert J. Beihoff

Christ Enthroned   (65.12)
German (17th century)
Ivory and wood, 5 1/8 x 1 3/4 in. d.
  (13 x 4.5 cm d.)
Gift of Mr. and Mrs. Richard B. Flagg

Crucifixion   (50.1a&b)
German (1858)
Ivory,
  base: 16 3/4 x 11 x 7 1/2 in. (42.6 x
    27.9 x 19.1 cm)
  crucifix: 23 1/8 x 8 7/8 x 2 1/4 in.
    (58.7 x 22.5 x 5.7 cm)
Gift of Mr. Abraham D. Braun

Libation Cup**   (63.11)
Flemish (19th century?)
Ivory, 7 1/16 x 1 3/4 in. d. (18.1 x 4.5
  cm d.)
Gift of Mr. Norbert J. Beihoff

Madonna and Child**   (63.15)
Goan (early 19th century)
Ivory, 20 1/2 x 4 1/2 x 4 in. (52.1 x
  11.4 x 10.2 cm)
Gift of Mr. Norbert J. Beihoff

Mary Magdalene**   (63.14)
Spanish/Portuguese (18th-19th
  century)
Ivory, 7 7/8 x 2 3/8 x 2 in. (20 x
  6 x 5.1 cm)
Gift of Mr. Norbert J. Beihoff

Mitred Bishop   (68.4)
Nationality Unknown (20th century)
Ivory, 7 1/2 x 4 1/4 x 2 in. (19.1 x 10.8
  x 5.1 cm)
Gift of Miss Jean Messmer

Monk** (63.16)
Spanish (17th century)
Ivory, 19 7/8 x 5 3/4 x 4 in. (50.5 x
  14.6 x 10.2 cm)
Gift of Mr. Norbert J. Beihoff

Primitive Heads (79.22.1&.2)
Nationality Unknown (20th century)
Ivory,
  .1: 13 5/8 x 3 1/2 x 2 1/4 in. (34.6 x
    8.9 x 5.7 cm)
  .2: 16 1/8 x 5 1/4 x 3 1/2 in. (41 x
    13.3 x 8.9 cm)
Gift of Mr. and Mrs. Harry G. John

*Pair of Scenes from the Third
  Crusade* (60.9&.10)
French (19th century)
Ivory, 5 7/8 x 11 3/4 x 1 1/2 in. (14.9
  x 29.2 x 3.8 cm), each
Gift of Mr. Norbert J. Beihoff

*St. Anthony of Padua and Christ
  Child*** (63.13)
Italian (18th century)
Ivory, 5 x 1 1/2 x 1 1/8 in. (12.7 x 3.8
  x 2.9 cm)
Gift of Mr. Norbert J. Beihoff

St. Sebastian** (63.9)
French (19th century)
Ivory, 6 1/4 x 1 5/8 x 1 3/8 in. (15.9 x
  4.1 x 3.5 cm)
Gift of Mr. Norbert J. Beihoff

Seated Moon Sprite** (63.10)
French (mid-19th century)
Ivory, 17 1/16 x 8 x 6 1/4 in. (43.3 x
  20.3 x 15.9 cm)
Gift of Mr. Norbert J. Beihoff

Tankard (62.3)
German (c. 1820)
Ivory, 22 1/2 x 12 1/8 x 8 1/2 in. (57.2
  x 30.8 x 21.6 cm)
Gift of Mrs. Julius C. Theilacker

METALS

BARBEDIENNE, Ferdinand
French (1810-1892)
Pair of Cylindrical Footed Goblets
  (83.46.7.1&.2)
Bronze, 6 3/16 x 3 3/16 in. d. (15.7 x
  8.1 cm d.), each
Gift of Mr. and Mrs. Robert L.
  Pagel, Sr.

Urn, Ferdinand Barbedienne, bronze and
marble

Pair of Urns* (79.6.1a&b & .2a&b)
Bronze and marble,
  lids: 3 1/2 x 5 1/8 x 5 1/8 in. (8.9 x
    13 x 13 cm), each
  urns: 15 1/2 x 9 1/4 x 8 1/2 in. (39.4
    x 23.5 x 21.6 cm), each
Gift of Dr. Kenneth Maier

BERGE, Edward
American (1876-1924)
Ingrid with Swan (83.3.22a&b)
Bronze, 9 1/4 x 8 1/4 x 8 1/4 in. (23.5
  x 21 x 21 cm)
Gift of the Estate of Florence
  Rossbach

FAURE DE BROUSSÉ, Vincent-
Désiré
French (19th century)
Pair of Figurines: One Repetition
  (63.5.1&2)
Enameled bronze with marble, 12 x
  5 1/2 x 4 in. (30.5 x 14 x 10.2 cm)
Gift of Mr. and Mrs. Clifford A.
  Randall

MONNAIE (MINT) of Paris
French (20th century)
Commemorative Medal (68.5)
Bronze, 7 3/4 x 7 3/4 in. (19.7 x
  19.7 cm)
Gift of Mr. and Mrs. Jean-Louis
  Mandereau

PABST, Louise Lemp
American (1910-1977)
Bust of Edwin Pabst (77.12)
Bronze, 5 x 5 x 1 in. (12.7 x 12.7 x
  2.5 cm)
Gift of Mr. and Mrs. John Ogden

PRAXMAYER, Anna
Polish (1979)
Portrait of Pope John Paul II
  (81.10)
Bronze, 8 3/4 x 8 x 1 3/4 in. (22.2 x
  20.3 x 4.5 cm)
Gift of Mrs. Beth J. McKenty

THOMIRE, Pierre Philippe
French (1751-1843)
Pair of Candelabra (64.8.1&.2)
Bronze, 33 x 13 1/2 in. d. (83.3 x 34.3
  cm d.), each
Gift of Mrs. Erna A. Moebius

UNKNOWN ARTISTS
French (14th century?)
Chapel Bell (64.36)
Iron and wood, 24 x 21 x 14 in. (61 x
  53.3 x 35.6 cm)
Gift of Mr. and Mrs. Marc B. Rojtman

Crucifix (00.475)
Italian (17th century?)
Bronze, 20 x 12 x 1 1/2 in. (50.8 x
  30.5 x 3.8 cm)
Gift of Mr. and Mrs. Marc B. Rojtman

Cruficix (64.5)
Italian (16th century)
Rock crystal and bronze, 23 1/4 x
  9 1/8 x 6 1/4 in. (59.1 x 23.2 x
  15.9 cm)
Gift of Mr. and Mrs. Richard B. Flagg

Ink Reservoir (55.13)
Italian (19th century)
Bronze, 3 x 5 in. d. (7.6 x 12.7 cm d.)
Gift of Mr. and Mrs. Charles Zadok

Ink Reservoir (55.14)
Italian (19th century)
Bronze, 4 1/8 x 5 1/2 in. d. (10.5 x 14
  cm d.)
Gift of Mr. and Mrs. Charles Zadok

Madonna and Child (55.8)
Flemish (late 18th-early 19th
  century)
Bronze, 12 3/4 x 6 in. d (32.4 x 15.2
  cm d.)
Gift of Mr. and Mrs. Richard B. Flagg

Pair of Candelabra (73.10.1&.2)
Nationality Unknown (c. 1810)
Wrought iron, 50 1/2 x 21 1/4 in. d.
  (128.3 x 54 cm d.), each
Gift of Mr. and Mrs. James W.
  Bergstrom

Pair of Candelabra (80.19.2.1&.2)
French (late 19th century)
Bronze ormolu, 19 7/8 x 7 in. d. (50.5
  x 17.8 cm d.), each
Gift of Dr. Kenneth Maier

Pair of Oil Lamps (55.12.1&.2)
Italian (19th century)
Bronze, 9 x 6 1/8 in. d. (22.9 x 15.6
  cm d.), each
Gift of Mr. and Mrs. Charles Zadok

Pair of Torch Stands (63.26.1&.2)
Spanish (19th century)
Wrought iron, 58 x 24 in. d. (147.3
  x 61 cm d.), each
Gift of Mr. and Mrs. Donald B. Abert

Planter (80.27.2a&b)
French (c. 1880)
Bronze ormolu, 5 1/2 x 18 1/2 x 12 in.
  (14 x 47 x 30.5 cm)
Gift of Dr. Kenneth Maier

PRECIOUS METALS AND STONES

FABERGÉ, Peter Carl
Russian (1846–1920)
Letter Opener and Pencil Holder
  (81.27.1)
Gold, red jasper, and cabochon
  sapphire, 15 3/8 in. long (39.1 cm
  long)
Gift of Dr. Kenneth Maier

FABERGÉ STUDIOS
Russian (1846–1920)
Purse (82.7.9)
Sterling silver and silver mesh, 7 x 9
  in. (17.8 x 22.9 cm)
Gift of Dr. Kenneth Maier

FRANKLIN MINT
American (1972–1975)
*Set of Thirty-Eight Presidential
  Plates* (81.29.1-.38)
Sterling silver and gold, 3/4 x 8 x 8
  in. (2 x 20.3 x 20.3 cm), each
Gift of Dr. and Mrs. Robert S. Pavlic

GORHAM COMPANY
German (1902)
*Christening Set used by Alice
  Roosevelt Longworth on the
  occasion of the launching cere-
  monies of Kaiser Wilhelm II's yacht,
  "The Meteor", New York, 1902*
  (81.34.1.1-.3)
Sterling silver, wood, glass, and
  brass; dimensions vary
Gift of Ms. Joanna Sturm

NAPPIN AND WEBB, LTD.
English (late 19th–early 20th
  century)
Teakettle with Stand
  (83.36.15a&b)
Silver plate,
  teakettle: 13 x 11 1/2 x 7 in. (33 x
    29.2 x 17.8 cm)
  stand: 5 1/2 x 8 1/4 x 7 in. (14 x 21
    x 17.8 cm)
Gift of Mr. Joseph P. Antonow

SHREVE & CO.
American (20th century)
Centerpiece Bowl (81.39.4)
Sterling silver, 20 in. d. (50.8 cm d.)
Gift of Dr. Kenneth Maier

Pope John XXIII, Renato Signorini, gold-plated sterling silver with precious stones

SIGNORINI, Renato
Italian (1902–1966)
*Pope John XXIII** (79.1)
Gold-plated sterling silver with
  precious stones, 10 3/8 x 10 3/8 x
  5/8 in. (26.4 x 26.4 x 1.6 cm)
Gift of Mr. and Mrs. James A.
  Schelble

SMITH, SISSONS and CO.
English (c. 1848)
*Tilting Kettle** (61.11)
Sheffield silver plate, 13 1/2 x 10 x
  7 1/2 in. (34.3 x 25.4 x 19 cm)
Gift of Mr. Oscar M. Pinsof

UNKNOWN ARTISTS
Chalice (55.16)
German (19th century)
Silver gilt, 8 1/2 x 6 1/16 in. d. (21.6 x
  15.4 cm d.)
Gift of Mr. and Mrs. Charles Zadok

*Chalice with Inlaid Portraits of
  Saints* (55.11)
French (19th century)
Silver gilt and copper, 8 1/4 x 5 3/4
  in. d. (21 x 14.6 cm d.)
Anonymous Gift

*Domestic Shrine with Scene of the
  Marriage of St. Catherine**
  (63.17)
Italian (16th century)
Oil on lapis lazuli with marble and
  semiprecious stones, 20 1/4 x
  12 3/8 x 3 1/2 in. (51.4 x 31.4 x
  8.9 cm)
Gift of Mr. and Mrs. Richard B. Flagg

Dress Dagger   (83.36.11a&b)
Turkish (19th century ?)
Silver repoussé,
  sheath: 10 1/2 x 7/8 x 1 1/8 in.
    (26.7 x 2.2 x 2.9 cm)
  dagger: 13 1/8 x 7/8 x 3/4 in. (33.2
    x 2.2 x 1.9 cm)
Gift of Mr. Joseph P. Antonow

St. George Slaying the Dragon
  (79.27.1)
Russian (19th century)
Silver, 2 7/8 x 2 1/8 x 1/4 in. (7.3 x
  5.4 x .6 cm)
Gift of Dr. and Mrs. John Pick

Scene of Desert Oasis   (69.5)
Nationality Unknown (19th century)
Sterling silver, 35 x 25 x 14 in. (88.9
  x 63.5 x 38.6 cm)
Gift of Mr. Julius C. Theilacker

Wrist Guard (Bazu Band)
  (83.36.12)
Turkish (late 19th-early 20th
  century)
Silver with beading and pierced
  bosses, 4 5/16 x 3 x 3 in. (11 x 7.6 x
  7.6 cm)
Gift of Mr. Joseph P. Antonow

Tilting Kettle, Smith, Sissons and Co., silver

TEXTILES

APPLIQUÉ, EMBROIDERY, AND NEEDLEPOINT

RIPBERGER, Clara
American (?) (late 19th century)
Sistine Madonna, 1897   (63.21)
Embroidery after a painting by
    Raphael, 102 1/2 x 75 1/4 in.
    (206.4 x 191.1 cm)
Gift of Mr. and Mrs. William A. Jahn
    in memory of Amalie Luedke Jahn

UNKNOWN ARTISTS
Altarpiece Panel   (80.4.7)
English (late 19th century)
Embroidery, 24 1/2 x 23 3/4 in. (62.2
    x 60.3 cm)
Gift of Dr. Kenneth Maier

Betrothal Banquet Scene   (62.8)
French (late 19th century)
Embroidery and petit point, 58 1/2 x
    77 1/4 in. (148.6 x 196.2 cm)
Gift of Mr. Peter Kunz

Chapel Banner   (00.434)
European (16th century)
Appliqué on velvet, 36 x 24 in. (91.4 x
    61 cm)
Gift of Mr. and Mrs. Marc B. Rojtman

Collection of Vestments   (71.1)
French (19th century)
Embroidery on silk and velvet;
    dimensions vary
Gift of Miss Avrina Pugh

Five-Paneled Screen   (00.453)
Appliquéd velvet and brocade, 58 3/8
    x 100 x 1 in. (135.6 x 254 x 2.5 cm)
Gift of Mr. and Mrs. Donald B. Abert
    in memory of Mr. Harry J. Grant

Floral Spray   (80.4.1)
English (early 19th century)
Embroidery on satin, 12 1/4 x
    9 7/16 in. (31.1 x 24 cm)
Gift of Dr. Kenneth Maier

Floral Spray with Border   (80.4.4)
English (late 18th–early 19th
    century)
Embroidery on satin, 16 3/8 x 15 1/8
    in. (41.6 x 38.4 cm)
Gift of Dr. Kenneth Maier

The Hunt   (63.2)
French (late 19th century)
Embroidery and needlepoint, 30 x
    53 3/4 in. (76.2 x 136.5 cm)
Gift of Mr. and Mrs. Donald B. Abert
    in memory of Mr. Harry J. Grant

Portrait of Jenny Packharnis
    (80.4.3)
English (late 18th–early 19th
    century)
Crewelwork on satin, 11 7/8 x
    9 15/16 in. (30.2 x 25.2 cm)
Gift of Dr. Kenneth Maier

*Still Life with Flowers in Basket**
    (80.4.2)
English (early 19th century)
Embroidery on satin, 10 5/8 x 8 5/8
    in. (27 x 22 cm)
Gift of Dr. Kenneth Maier

Woman with Basket   (80.4.5)
English (early 19th century)
Embroidery on satin, 11 3/16 x 9 5/8
    in. (28.4 x 24.5 cm)
Gift of Dr. Kenneth Maier

Young Lovers with Animals
    (81.27.3)
English (early 19th century)
Embroidery, 9 x 10 1/4 in. (22.9 x 26
    cm)
Gift of Dr. Kenneth Maier

Still Life with Flowers in Basket, English, Early Nineteenth Century,
embroidery on satin

225.

TAPESTRIES

AUBUSSON
French (18th century)
Pastoral Scene　(59.8)
Tapestry, 8 ft. 2 in. x 8 ft. 2 in. (2.5 x 2.5 m)
Gift of Mr. and Mrs. Edwin A. Gallun, Jr.

GOBELINS WORKSHOP
French (18th century)
Foliate Woodland Scene　(00.5)
Tapestry, 13 ft. 6 in. x 10 ft. 6 in. (4.1 x 3.2 m)
Gift of Miss Marion C. Wagner, Mrs. Jane W. Kranick, Mr. F. E. Wagner, and Mr. Robert S. Wagner

KLEISER, Lorentz
American (20th century)
Joan of Arc in Floral Landscape　(70.10)
Tapestry, 48 x 60 1/2 in. (122 x 153.7 cm)
Gift of Mr. and Mrs. Marc B. Rojtman

LEYNIERES FAMILY
Flemish (17th–18th century)
Rustic Scene　(60.13)
Tapestry, 10 ft. 10 in. x 6 ft. 10 in. (3.3 x 2.1 m)
Gift of Mrs. John C. Pritzlaff

MORTLAKE FACTORY
English (c. 1711)
Verdure Forest Scene　(60.12)
Tapestry, 8 ft. 6 in. x 10 ft. 6 in. (2.9 x 3.2 m)
Gift of Mr. Ray H. Wolf

UNKNOWN ARTISTS
Flight of Fancy　(65.19.1)
Tapestry, 74 x 58 1/4 in. (188 x 148 cm)
Gift of Mrs. Fred A. Miller

Garden Scene with Royal Lady and Attendants　(65.19.2)
Tapestry, 5 ft. 7 in. x 7 ft. 10 in. (1.7 x 2.4 m)
Gift of Mrs. Fred A. Miller

Royal Windsor　(00.7)
Tapestry, 9 ft. 6 in. x 4 ft. 9 1/2 in. (2.9 x 1.5 m)
Gift of Mr. Philip Fina

Seven Men　(56.12)
Tapestry, 11 ft. 10 in. x 6 ft. 6 in. (3.6 x 2 m)
Gift of Mr. Philip Fina

The Triumph of Alexander the Great, Flemish, Early-mid Seventeenth Century, tapestry

Sheepherder and Farm Scene (00.422)
Tapestry, 129 x 88 in. (327.7 x 223.5 cm)
Anonymous Gift

*The Triumph of Alexander the Great** (74.2)
Flemish (early-mid 17th century)
Tapestry, 106 x 177 in. (269.2 x 449.6 cm)
Gift of Mr. and Mrs. Omar Bittman

Woodland Scene　(56.11)
Tapestry, 10 ft. 1 in. x 8 ft. 7 in. (3.1 x 2.6 m)
Gift of Mrs. Carl A. Forster

TRIBAL ARTS

AFRICAN, PRE-COLUMBIAN, AND NATIVE AMERICAN

CRUZ SAAVEDRA, Juan de la
Colombian (c. 1964)
Untitled (72.2)
Mandrake root, 40 1/2 x 22 x 16 in.
(102.9 x 55.9 x 40.6 cm)
Gift of Mr. and Mrs. Joseph M.
Baisch

UNKNOWN ARTISTS
*Ancestral Figure of a Tabwa Male**
(83.23.4)
Zairian
Wood, 22 x 6 in. d. (55.9 x 15.2 cm d.)
Gift of Mr. and Mrs. Philip Pinsof

Ancestor Headdress (83.47.8)
Nigerian, Yoruba Tribe, Egungun
Style
Wood with pigment, 27 x 9 1/2 x
11 1/2 in. (68.6 x 24.1 x 29.2 cm)
Gift of Mr. Avery Z. Eliscu

Animal Dance Mask (83.47.6)
Malian, Koré Society (?)
Wood, 23 1/4 x 10 x 7 in. (59.1 x 25.4
x 17.8 cm)
Gift of Mr. Avery Z. Eliscu

Bovine Dance Mask (83.47.7)
West Guinea Coast, Bijoga Tribe
Wood with animal horns and glass,
8 1/2 x 25 1/4 x 11 1/2 in. (21.6 x
64.1 x 29.2 cm)
Gift of Mr. Avery Z. Eliscu

Bovine Dance Mask (83.47.11)
West Guinea Coast, Bijoga Tribe
Wood with animal horns, glass, and
rope, 9 x 26 1/4 x 14 in. (22.9 x 66.7
x 35.6 cm)
Gift of Mr. Avery Z. Eliscu

*Bush-Cow Ceremonial Headdress
with Tassels* (83.39.3)
Cameroon
Basketry and cloth, 17 3/4 x 11 1/2 x
5 in. (45.1 x 29.2 x 12.7 cm)
Gift of Meryl Hollis Pinsof

Ancestral Figure of a Tabwa Male, Zairian,
wood

*Ceremonial Dress Kris with Carved
Finial* (83.36.13a&b S)
Malayan
Wood, iron, and semiprecious stones,
knife: 24 1/4 x 4 1/4 x 2 in. (61.6 x
10.8 x 5.1 cm)
sheath: 21 x 7 1/4 x 1 in. (53.3 x
18.4 x 2.5 cm)
Gift of Mr. Joseph P. Antonow

Ceremonial Face Mask (83.36.7)
Cameroon (?), Elkoi Tribe
Wood, 9 1/2 x 7 1/4 x 3 1/2 in. (24.1 x
18.4 x 8.9 cm)
Gift of Mr. Joseph P. Antonow

*Ceremonial Shama's Staff with
Carved Finial* (83.36.10a-c)
Zairian, Beba Lulua Tribe
Wood, 55 x 4 5/8 in. d. (139.7 x 11.8
cm d.)
Gift of Mr. Joseph P. Antonow

*Chief's Stool** (83.36.8)
Zairian or Cameroon, Tikar Area,
Batshioko Tribe
Wood, 13 x 15 3/8 x 15 1/8 in. (33 x
39.1 x 38.4 cm)
Gift of Mr. Joseph P. Antonow

Crawling Child Figure (83.36.3)
Pre-Columbian, Olmec Culture,
LaVenta Area
Terra-cotta, glazed, 4 x 3 3/4 x 5 in.
(10.2 x 9.5 x 12.7 cm)
Gift of Mr. Joseph P. Antonow

Dance Headdress (83.47.9)
Malian, Tyi-Wara Society,
Bamana Tribe
Wood, 18 7/8 x 3 1/8 x 3 7/16 in. (48
x 7.9 x 8.7 cm)
Gift of Mr. Avery Z. Eliscu

Feathered Headdress (83.39.2)
Cameroon, Bamoun Society
Basketry, feathers, and colored
thread, 25 x 10 1/2 x 7 1/2 in. (63.5
x 26.7 x 19.1 cm) (in compacted
state)
Gift of Meryl Hollis Pinsof

*Female Figure with Ear and Hair
Ornaments* (83.36.2)
Peruvian, Chimo Style
Silver, 4 1/4 x 1 7/8 x 1 5/8 in. (10.8
x 4.8 x 4.1 cm)
Gift of Mr. Joseph P. Antonow

Group of Burial Beads
(83.36.1-.40)
Pre-Columbian, Musica Style
Terra-cotta; dimensions vary
Gift of Mr. Joseph P. Antonow

Half Fetish Figure (83.47.12)
Congolese
Wood, 6 x 3 1/4 x 3 3/8 in. (15.2 x 8.3
x 8.6 cm)
Gift of Mr. Avery Z. Eliscu

Heddle Pulley with Cord (83.20.2)
Ivory Coast, Guro Tribe
Wood, 8 1/2 x 2 7/8 x 2 3/8 in. (21.6
x 7.3 x 6 cm)
Gift of Dr. William M. Pinsof

Ijo Headpiece (84.1)
Nigerian, Niger River Delta
Wood with pigment, 21 1/2 x 49 x
12 in. (54.6 x 124.5 x 30.5 cm)
Gift of Mr. Avery Z. Eliscu

Mask (83.20.1)
Ivory Coast, Baule Tribe
Wood with pigment, 18 x 9 1/2 x 6 1/4
in. (45.7 x 24.1 x 15.9 cm)
Gift of Dr. William M. Pinsof

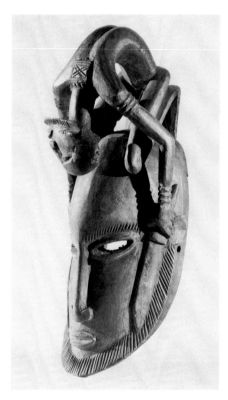

Chief's Stool, Zairian or Cameroon, Tikar Area, Batshioko Tribe, wood

Ritual Mask, Malian, Marka Type, wood

Maternity Idol/Dance Wand
  (83.22.5)
Zairian, Luba Style
Wood with cowrie shells, 28 1/2 x
  6 1/4 x 16 1/2 in. (72.4 x 15.9 x
  41.9 cm)
Gift of Mr. Oscar M. Pinsof

N'tomo Ritual Mask   (83.22.1)
Malian, Marka Tribe
Wood, brass, and aluminum, 19 1/2 x
  7 1/2 x 5 1/4 in. (49.5 x 19.1 x 13.3
  cm)
Gift of Mr. Oscar M. Pinsof

Pair of Ritual Masks
  (83.23.1.1&.2)
Malian, Marka type
Wood with patterned metal and red
  cloth,
  .1: 21 x 6 7/8 x 6 in. (53.3 x 17.5 x
    15.2 cm)
  .2: 19 x 6 1/4 x 4 3/4 in. (48.3 x 15.9
    x 12.1 cm)
Gift of Mr. and Mrs. Philip Pinsof

Puppet Figure of an Ancient Woman
  (84.26)
Malian, Bamana Tribe*
Wood and trade cloth (?), 44 x 12 x
  12 in. (112 x 30 x 30 cm)
Gift of Mr. Julian Ettelson

Ritual Figure   (83.23.5)
Malian, Bamana Tribe
Wood, 18 x 4 5/8 x 4 3/8 in. (45.7 x
  11.8 x 11.1 cm)
Gift of Mr. and Mrs. Philip Pinsof

Ritual Mask   (83.21)
Liberian, Poro Society, Don Tribe
Wood with pigment, 13 x 9 x 5 in. (33
  x 22.9 x 12.7 cm)
Gift of Mr. and Mrs. Leslie S. Pinsof

Ritual Mask   (83.22.2)
Malian
Wood, 17 3/4 x 7 1/4 x 7 1/4 in. (45.1 x
  18.4 x 18.4 cm)
Gift of Mr. Oscar M. Pinsof

Ritual Mask*   (83.22.3)
Malian, Marka type
Wood with brass and red cloth, 18 1/2
  x 6 1/4 x 4 in. (47 x 15.9 x 10.2 cm)
Gift of Mr. Oscar M. Pinsof

Ritual Mask   (83.23.2)
Malian, Tshokwe style
Wood, 16 7/8 x 8 1/4 x 4 1/4 in. (42.9 x
  21 x 10.8 cm)
Gift of Mr. and Mrs. Philip Pinsof

Ritual Mask   (83.23.3)
Malian, Koré Society
Wood with pigment, 16 1/4 x 6 1/4 x
  6 in. (41.3 x 15.9 x 15.2 cm)
Gift of Mr. and Mrs. Philip Pinsof

Set of Fifteen Hairpins
  (83.47.1.1-.15)
Congolese, Mangbetu Tribe
Brass; dimensions vary
Gift of Mr. Avery Z. Eliscu

Set of Two Parfleches   (83.39.1&.2)
Sioux Tribe (?), North American
  Plains
Vegetable dye on leather hide,
  .1: 23 1/2 x 11 1/2 x 2 3/4 in. (59.7
    x 29.2 x 7 cm)
  .2: 23 1/2 x 11 1/2 x 2 1/2 in. (59.7
    x 29.2 x 6.4 cm)
Gift of Meryl Hollis Pinsof

Sogoni Koun Headpiece*   (83.22.4)
Malian, Tyi-Wara Society, Bamana
  Tribe
Wood with copper, bronze, antelope
  hair and cowrie shells, 32 7/8 x
  12 x 3 1/4 in. (83.5 x 30.5 x 8.3 cm)
Gift of Mr. Oscar M. Pinsof

Standing Female Figure*   (83.47.3)
Nigerian, Yoruba Tribe
Wood, 34 1/2 x 11 1/2 x 7 in. (87.6 x
  29.2 x 17.8 cm)
Gift of Mr. Avery Z. Eliscu

228

Sogoni Koun Headpiece, Malian, Tyi-Wara Society, Bamana Tribe, wood with copper, bronze, antelope hair and cowrie shells

Standing Female Figure, Nigerian, Yoruba Tribe, wood

Standing Female Figure   (83.47.4)
Malian, Bamana Tribe
Wood with beads, 11 3/4 x 2 1/2 x 3 in.
    (29.9 x 6.4 x 7.6 cm)
Gift of Mr. Avery Z. Eliscu

Standing Female Figure   (83.47.5)
Nigerian, Northern Ibo Tribe
Wood, 19 3/4 x 4 1/2 x 4 in. (50.2 x
    11.4 x 10.2 cm)
Gift of Mr. Avery Z. Eliscu

Standing Figure   (83.47.10)
Nigerian, Waja Tribe
Wood, 30 1/2 x 3 1/2 x 3 1/4 in. (77.5
    x 8.9 x 8.3 cm)
Gift of Mr. Avery Z. Eliscu

ASIAN

SATSUMA, In the Style of
Japanese (mid-19th century)
Oriental Urn*   (00.378)
Ceramic with raised gold filigree,
    38 5/8 x 16 in. d. (98.2 x 41 cm d.)
Anonymous Gift

UNKNOWN ARTISTS
Bowl   (66.18.1)
Chinese, Ming Dynasty (1363-1644)
Cloisonné on copper, 4 3/8 x 8 15/16
    in. d. (11.1 x 22.7 cm d.)
Gift of Mr. and Mrs. Philip Pinsof

Bowl   (76.6)
Chinese, Ch'ien-lung Period
    (1736-1795)
Jade, 1 3/4 x 4 x 4 in. (4.5 x 10.2 x
    10.2 cm)
Gift of Mr. and Mrs. Philip Pinsof

Bowl   (76.8)
Chinese, Kuang-hsü Period (1875-
    1908)
Porcelain, 3 5/8 x 8 7/8 in. d. (9.2 x
    22.5 cm d.)
Gift of Mr. and Mrs. Philip Pinsof

Bowl   (76.9)
Chinese, Ch'ien-lung Period (1736-
    1795)
Jade, 1 3/4 x 4 x 4 in. (4.5 x 10.2 x
    10.2 cm)
Gift of Mr. and Mrs. Philip Pinsof

Bowl   (76.10)
Chinese (early 18th century)
Porcelain, 4 1/4 x 5 3/4 in. d. (10.8 x
    14.6 cm d.)
Gift of Mr. and Mrs. Philip Pinsof

Bowl   (76.13.1)
Chinese, Ch'ien-lung Period (1736-
    1795)
Porcelain, 2 13/16 x 5 5/8 in. d. (7.1 x
    14.3 cm d.)
Gift of Mr. and Mrs. Philip Pinsof

Bowl   (76.21)
Chinese, Ch'ien-lung Period (1736-
    1795)
Jade, 2 x 7 x 7 in. (5.1 x 17.8 x 17.8 cm)
Gift of Mr. and Mrs. Philip Pinsof

Bowl   (82.7.12)
Chinese (18th century)
Porcelain, 1 3/4 x 5 1/4 in. d. (4.5 x
    13.3 cm d.)
Gift of Dr. Kenneth Maier

Oriental Urn, Satsuma Style, ceramic with raised gold filigree

Buddha (81.11.1)
Chinese (18th century)
Gouache on rice paper, 63 x 34 in.
   (160 x 86.4 cm)
Gift of Dr. Kenneth Maier

*Chinese Princess Carrying
   Chrysanthemums* (64.13)
Chinese (late 19th-early 20th century)
Ivory, 25 x 5 3/8 x 4 1/4 in. (63.5 x
   13.7 x 10.8 cm)
Gift of Mr. Arthur Rubloff

*Chinese Princess Carrying Prunus
   Blossom Branch* (64.12)
Chinese (late 19th-early 20th
   century)
Ivory, 25 3/4 x 5 1/4 x 4 1/8 in. (65.4
   x 13.3 x 10.5 cm)
Gift of Mr. Arthur Rubloff

*Chinese Princess Holding Magnolia
   Branch* (64.11)
Chinese (late 19th-early 20th
   century)
Ivory, 25 3/4 x 5 1/4 x 4 1/8 in. (65.4
   x 13.3 x 10.5 cm)
Gift of Mr. Arthur Rubloff

Figure of Chinese Royalty
   (80.11.3)
Chinese (late 19th-early 20th
   century)
Ivory with tea staining, 12 1/8 x
   3 1/4 x 3 in. (30.8 x 8.3 x 7.6 cm)
Gift of Mr. and Mrs. Bernard Soref

Four-Tiered Box (00.390a-e)
Japanese (19th century)
Lacquered wood, 5 x 3 3/4 x 2 in.
   (12.7 x 9.5 x 5.1 cm)
Gift of Mr. and Mrs. Philip Pinsof

Gift Box (76.55a&b)
Japanese (late 19th century)
Lacquered wood, 3 x 8 1/2 x 8 3/8
   in. (7.6 x 21.6 x 21.3 cm)
Gift of Mr. Oscar M. Pinsof

Imari Plate (64.35.49)
Japanese (late 19th-early 20th
   century)
Porcelain, 1 3/4 x 11 3/8 in. d. (4.5 x
   28.9 cm d.)
Gift of Mr. C. Frederic (Todd) Wehr

Incense Box (76.53a&b)
Japanese (mid-18th century)
Lacquered wood, 3 1/4 x 4 7/8 x
   4 7/8 in. (8.3 x 12.4 x 12.4 cm)
Gift of Mr. Oscar M. Pinsof

Incense Jar (76.52)
Japanese (late 18th century)
Porcelain, 5 7/8 x 4 1/4 x 2 5/8 in.
   (14.9 x 10.8 x 6.7 cm)
Gift of Mr. Oscar M. Pinsof

Ladle (76.23)
Chinese, Wan-li Period (1573-1619)
Porcelain, 8 9/16 x 3 1/4 x 4 in. (21.8
   x 8.3 x 10.2 cm)
Gift of Mr. and Mrs. Philip Pinsof

Lady with Fan and Flowers (64.9)
Chinese (late 19th-early 20th
   century)
Ivory, 20 1/8 x 7 1/4 x 3 1/2 in. (51.1
   x 18.4 x 8.9 cm)
Gift of Mr. Arthur Rubloff

Letter Box (76.56a&b)
Japanese (late 18th century)
Lacquered wood, 1 1/4 x 4 3/8 x 1 1/4
   in. (3.2 x 11.1 x 3.2 cm)
Gift of Mr. Oscar M. Pinsof

Octagonal Plate (78.6.9)
Chinese (1840-1850)
Porcelain, 1 1/8 x 8 7/8 in. d. (2.9 x
   22.5 cm d.)
Gift of Mr. and Mrs. Ernest F.
   Rice, Jr.

Oval Deep Dish (78.6.4)
Chinese (c. 1790)
Porcelain, 2 1/2 x 12 1/2 in. d. (6.4 x
   31.8 cm d.)
Gift of Mr. and Mrs. Ernest F.
   Rice, Jr.

Pair of Bowls (76.12.1&.2)
Japanese (18th century)
Porcelain, 2 x 5 1/4 in. d. (5.1 x 13.3
   cm d.), each
Gift of Mr. and Mrs. Philip Pinsof

Pair of Covered Jars (81.3.2.1&.2)
Chinese (19th century)
Porcelain with wooden covers,
   jars: 11 x 6 1/2 in. d. (27.9 x 16.5
      cm d.), each
   lids: 3 1/2 x 5 3/4 in. d. (8.9 x 14.6
      cm d.), each
Gift of Mrs. Douglass Van Dyke

Pair of Eggshell Bowls (76.5.1&.2)
Chinese, Yung-lo Period (1402-1424)
Porcelain, 1 5/8 x 5 1/8 in. d. (4.1 x
   13 cm d.), each
Gift of Mr. and Mrs. Philip Pinsof

*Pair of Gift Dishes** (76.59.1&.2)
Japanese (late 18th century)
Lacquered wood, 8 3/8 x 8 7/8 in. d.
   (21.3 x 22.5 cm d.), each
Gift of Mr. Oscar M. Pinsof

Pair of Imperial Eggshell Wine Cups
   (76.7.1&.2)
Chinese, Yung-chêng Period (1723-
   1735)
Porcelain, 1 1/2 x 2 3/8 in. d. (3.8 x
   6 cm d.), each
Gift of Mr. and Mrs. Philip Pinsof

Pair of Plates (83.15.2.1&.2)
Chinese (c. 1723-1735)
Porcelain, 7/8 x 8 7/8 in. d. (2.2 x
   22.5 cm d.), each
Gift of Mr. Ralph Resenhoeft

Pair of Spinach Bowls
   (80.10.2.1&.2)
Chinese (17th century)
Porcelain, 2 3/8 x 4 3/4 in. d. (6 x
   12.1 cm d.), each
Gift of Dr. Kenneth Maier

Pair of Urns (81.3.1.1&.2)
Chinese (late 19th-early 20th
   century)
Porcelain, 14 1/8 x 8 1/2 in. d. (39.5 x
   21.6 cm d.), each
Gift of Mrs. Douglass Van Dyke

Pair of Gift Dishes, Japanese, Late Eighteenth Century, lacquer on wood

*Pair of Water Buffaloes**
  (76.20.1&.2)
Chinese, Ch'ien-lung Period (1736-
  1795)
Porcelain,
  .1: 5 1/4 x 8 5/8 x 4 in. (13.3 x 21.9
    x 10.2 cm)
  .2: 5 1/4 x 8 x 5 in. (13.4 x 20.3 x
    12.7 cm)
Gift of Mr. and Mrs. Philip Pinsof

Plate   (76.11)
Japanese, Edo Period (1615-1868)
Ceramic, 1 1/8 x 8 1/4 in. d. (2.9 x
  21 cm d.)
Gift of Mr. and Mrs. Philip Pinsof

Plate   (80.14)
Persian (late 19th-early 20th
  century)
Porcelain, 2 1/2 x 18 3/4 in. d. (6.4 x
  47.6 cm d.)
Gift of Mrs. Ray M. Schweiger

Plate   (81.22.1)
Chinese, Ch'ien-lung Period (c. 1740)
Porcelain, 1 1/4 x 8 5/8 in. d. (3.2 x
  21.9 cm d.)
Gift of Mr. and Mrs. Ernest F.
  Rice, Jr.

Portrait of a Chinese Princess
  (83.4)
Chinese (late 18th-early 19th
  century)
Gouache on silk, 56 1/8 x 32 1/8 in.
  (142.6 x 81.6 cm) (sight)
Gift of Dr. Selma Jeanne Cohen

Screen   (79.18)
Japanese (late 17th century)
Watercolor and gouache with
  brocade,
  left side: 67 1/4 x 36 1/2 in. (170.8
    x 92.7 cm)
  right side: 67 3/8 x 36 5/8 in. (171.1
    x 93 cm)
Gift of Dr. Kenneth Maier

Scroll Box   (76.58a&b)
Japanese (late 18th century)
Lacquered wood, 3 x 9 3/4 x 3 1/4 in.
  (7.6 x 24.8 x 8.3 cm)
Gift of Mr. Oscar M. Pinsof

*Set of Three Graduated Shallow
  Footed Bowls*   (76.57.1-.3)
Japanese (early 19th century)
Lacquered wood,
  .1: 1 1/2 x 4 3/8 x 4 3/8 in. (3.8 x
    11.1 x 11.1 cm)
  .2: 1 3/4 x 4 3/4 x 4 3/4 in. (4.5 x
    12.1 x 12.1 cm)
  .3: 1 1/4 x 3 3/4 x 3 3/4 in. (3.2 x
    9.5 x 9.5 cm)
Gift of Mr. Oscar M. Pinsof

Statuette Vase   (83.36.5)
Chinese (late 19th-early 20th
  century)
Soapstone, 6 1/4 x 10 1/2 x 2 1/2 in.
  (15.9 x 26.7 x 6.4 cm)
Gift of Mr. Joseph P. Antonow

Table   (66.20.2)
Chinese (late 19th-early 20th
  century)
Lacquered wood with inlaid mother-
  of-pearl, 6 x 22 x 13 1/2 in. (15.2
  x 55.9 x 34.3 cm)
Gift of Mr. and Mrs. Philip Pinsof

Table   (66.20.1)
Chinese (late 19th-early 20th
  century)
Lacquered wood with inlaid mother-
  of-pearl, 5 3/8 x 17 7/8 x 11 1/4 in.
  (13.7 x 45.4 x 28.6 cm)
Gift of Mr. and Mrs. Philip Pinsof

Tea Bowl   (78.6.6)
Chinese, Ch'ien-lung Period (c. 1792)
Porcelain, 2 x 3 5/8 in. d. (5.1 x 9.2
  cm d.)
Gift of Mr. and Mrs. Ernest F.
  Rice, Jr.

Pair of Water Buffaloes, Chinese, Ch'ien-lung Period, 1736-1795,
porcelain

231

Tea Bowl and Saucer
  (81.22.8a&b)
Chinese, Ch'ien-lung Period (c. 1785)
Porcelain, 2 x 3 3/8 in. d. (5.1 x 8.6
  cm d.)
Gift of Mr. and Mrs. Ernest F.
  Rice, Jr.

Temple Valence   (79.4)
Chinese (late 19th century)
Pine with gold leaf, 13 1/4 x 176 in.
  (34.3 x 447 cm)
Gift of Dr. Kenneth Maier

Thang-ka   (83.3.21)
Tibetan (18th century)
Gouache on linen, 20 x 12 1/4 in.
  (50.8 x 31.1 cm)
Gift of the Estate of Florence
  Rossbach

Thang-ka: Green Tara (Doljang)
  (65.2)
Tibetan (late 18th century)
Gouache on linen bordered with
  brocade, 46 x 26 1/4 in. (116.8 x
  66.7 cm)
Gift of Mr. George P. Bickford

Thang-ka: Mandala of
  Bhaisajyaguru (Manla), Buddha of
  Medicine   (65.3)
Tibetan (late 17th-early 18th
  century)
Gouache on linen bordered with
  brocade, 42 3/4 x 23 3/8 in. (108.6
  x 59.4 cm)
Gift of Mr. George P. Bickford

Thang-ka; Mandala of
  Guhyasamaja   (65.4)
Nepalese (17th century)
Gouache on linen bordered with
  brocade, 48 1/2 x 25 1/2 in. (123.2
  x 64.8 cm)
Gift of Mr. George P. Bickford

Thang-ka: Sakyamuni Buddha-The
  Thirty-five Confession Buddhas
  (65.6)
Tibetan (18th century)
Gouache on linen bordered with
  brocade, 48 3/4 x 29 1/2 in. (123.8
  x 74.9 cm)
Gift of Mr. George P. Bickford

Thang-ka: Vajrasattua (Dorje
  Sempa) and Assemblage   (65.5)
Nepalese (late 17th-early 18th
  century)
Gouache on linen bordered with
  brocade, 46 1/4 x 28 1/4 in. (117.5
  x 71.8 cm)
Gift of Mr. George P. Bickford

Tusk Vase   (64.10)
Chinese (late 19th-early 20th
  century)
Ivory, 24 x 8 x 5 in. (61 x 20.3 x
  12.7 cm)
Gift of Mr. Arthur Rubloff

Tusk Vase with Cover   (64.34a&b)
Chinese (late 19th-early 20th
  century)
Ivory,
  vase: 16 5/8 x 6 1/2 x 4 1/2 in.
    (42.2 x 16.5 x 11.4 cm)
  cover: 6 3/8 x 4 3/8 x 3 3/4 in. (16.2
    x 11.1 x 9.5 cm)
Gift of Mr. Arthur Rubloff

Untitled (Scene of Elder Giving
  Dictation)   (81.11.2)
Chinese (18th century)
Watercolor on silk, 40 1/2 x 20 1/2 in.
  (102.9 x 52.1 cm)
Gift of Dr. Kenneth Maier

Vase   (76.15)
Chinese, K'ang'hsi Period (1622-
  1722)
Porcelain, 4 3/4 x 2 3/4 in. d. (12.1 x
  7 cm d.)
Gift of Mr. and Mrs. Philip Pinsof

Water Pot   (76.54a&b)
Japanese (early 18th century)
Ceramic, 4 1/2 x 6 1/2 x 3 1/2 in.
  (10.8 x 16.5 x 8.9 cm)
Gift of Mr. Oscar M. Pinsof

Writing Box   (76.51)
Japanese (19th century)
Lacquered wood, 12 1/2 x 9 1/2 x 6
  in. (31.8 x 24.1 x 15.2 cm)
Gift of Mr. Oscar M. Pinsof

ARTIST INDEX

DONORS TO THE COLLECTION
Past and Present

Anonymous
Mr. and Mrs. Donald B. Abert
Mr. Albert B. Adelman
Mr. and Mrs. John Ahlhauser
Mr. John Ahrens
Mr. and Mrs. Ray J. Aiken
Mrs. Mortimer P. Allen
American Association of University
    Women
Georgiana Angelo and Family
Mr. Joseph P. Antonow
Dr. Bernard Appel
Mr. Alexander Archipenko
Mr. Henry Arthur
Association of Marquette University
    Women
Mr. Emanuel Azenberg
Dr. and Mrs. Alfred Bader
Mr. and Mrs. Joseph M. Baisch
Mr. Norbert J. Beihoff
Estate of Gertrude Bergstrom
Mr. and Mrs. James W. Bergstrom
Dr. Richard A. Berk
Mr. George P. Bickford
Dr. Edwin P. Bickler
Mr. and Mrs. Omar Bittman
Miss Mary Black
Mrs. Gustave Blatz
Boegner Foundation
Ms. Susan Bondy
Boston Store
Dr. and Mrs. Sidney M. Boxer
Brandt, Inc.
Mr. Abraham D. Braun
Mr. Guido P. Brink
Mr. Robert Brooks
Mr. Bauer F. Bullinger
Mrs. W. W. Busby
Dr. Mary Alice Cannon
Mrs. Mary M. Carmichael
Mr. O. W. Carpenter
Mrs. Michael J. Cleary
Dr. Selma Jeanne Cohen
Mrs. Bernard I. Connolly
Dr. and Mrs. John E. Cordes
Mrs. Colet Coughlin
Mr. Robert M. Coughlin
Mrs. William E. Cramer
Mrs. Frederick Crawford
Mrs. Bertha Cudgwirth
Mrs. V. B. Cuttone
Mr. Gardiner Dalton
Dr. and Mrs. E. Esch Davies
Mr. I. A. Dinerstein
Mr. Ralph Dodge
Mr. Thorne Barnes Donnelley
Mrs. Roy W. Doolittle
Mr. Avram Dorman
Dr. and Mrs. Paul A. Dudenhoefer

Dr. and Mrs. Adrian M. Dupuis
Mr. Henry Edmiston
Mr. Avery Z. Eliscu
Mr. Julian Ettelson
Mrs. Otto H. Falk
Mr. Daniel Farber
Mrs. Edmond A. Faulkner
Mr. Willard Feldman
Mrs. J. D. Ferguson
Mr. and Mrs. Frank F. Filut
Mr. Philip Fina
Mr. and Mrs. Marvin L. Fishman
Mr. Eliot G. Fitch
Mrs. Martin Fladoes
Mr. and Mrs. Richard B. Flagg
Mr. Jay Fleming
Miss Eva K. Ford
Ford Foundation
Ford Motor Company
Mrs. Carl A. Forster
Franklin Forum
Mr. Paul A. Frederick
Frederick & Company, Inc.
Mr. George Friedman
Mr. and Mrs. Edwin A. Gallun, Jr.
Mr. Samuel Gansheroff
Mr. Fred V. Gardner
Mrs. Linda C. Gilbert
Gimbel Brothers
Rabbi Sidney Goldstein
Mr. John Golembiewski and Family
Mr. Frederick D. Gore
Mr. and Mrs. Hugo Gorski
Mr. William A. Graham IV
Mr. Robert E. Green
Colonel Howard M. Greene
Mr. and Mrs. Eckhart G. Grohmann
Grohmann Industries
Dr. John M. Gules
Miss Frances F. Gumina
Mr. and Mrs. Allen Guttenberg
Mr. and Mrs. Patrick Haggerty
Dr. and Mrs. Joseph E. Halloin
Mr. Keith Haring
Mrs. Ralph N. Harkness
Mr. James W. Harpel
Mr. and Mrs. Ira Haupt
Mrs. William P. Hayes
Mr. and Mrs. David M. Hecht
Mr. and Mrs. Joseph F. Heil, Sr.
Mr. and Mrs. James R. Heller
Estate of Dr. John Heraty
Dr. William L. Herner
Mrs. Victoria S. Higgins
Dr. Frank J. Hildner
Mr. Joseph F. Hlavacek
Miss Catherine M. Hormuth
Mr. Jack M. Horner

Mr. Samuel E. Hunter
Mr. Lloyd Hurst
Mr. Sy Hyman
Mr. and Mrs. William A. Jahn
Mr. Edwin E. Jedeikin
Mr. and Mrs. Harry G. John
Mr. and Mrs. Elmer A. Johnson
Mrs. Irene Gayas Jungwirth
Miss Marie Jussen
Mr. Charles James Kaiser
Mr. and Mrs. Igor Kamlukin
Mr. Fred Kaneshiro
Dr. Stanley Kaplan
Dr. and Mrs. Richard F. C. Kegel
Rev. William Kelley, S.J.
Mr. James W. Kern
Mrs. Marie Kerwin
Mrs. Elsie D. Kipp
Mr. R. B. Kitaj
Mr. Wolfgang Klein
Mrs. Frank Kleinholz
Mr. Ralph G. Klieforth
Mr. Bruce Koepfgen
Mr. E. C. Koerper
Mrs. Norman J. Kopmeier
Mr. and Mrs. Waldemar Kopmeier
Mrs. Jane W. Kranick
Mr. and Mrs. Richard L. Kronzer
Mr. Peter Kunz
Rev. Stanislaus L. Lalumière, S.J.
Mr. William M. Lamers, Sr.
Mr. Robert Layton
Dr. Samuel Sheldon Leavitt
Dr. Simon Levin
Mr. Ira Howard Levy
Mr. Thomas M. Lewyn
Mr. Frank Lipcius
Mr. Paul P. Lipton
Mr. J. Victor Loewi
Mr. Michael H. Lord
Ms. Diane Love
Mr. Vincent J. Lucareli
Mr. Reuben T. Lueloff
Dr. Kenneth Maier
Mr. Louis E. Madden
Mrs. Adolph I. Mandelker
Mr. and Mrs. Jean-Louis Mandereau
Dr. and Mrs. William Markowitz
Marquette University Alumni, 1931
Marquette University Alumni, 1937
Marquette University Athletic
    Department
Marquette University College of
    Nursing Alumni, 1983
Marquette University Dental School
    and Faculty
Marquette University Engineering
    Student Art Loan Fund
Marquette University Faculty Staff

Marquette University Law School
Marquette University Law School
    Alumni, 1929
Marquette University Law School
    Alumni, 1942
Marquette University Law School
    Alumni, 1963
Marquette University Women's
    Student Club
Marquette Women's League
Mr. Leo Carl Massopust
Dr. Yacoub L. Massuda
Dr. and Mrs. Louis Maxey
Dr. and Mrs. Michael F. McCanles
Mr. and Mrs. Charles B. McCanna
Mrs. Beth J. McKenty
Dr. Joseph P. McMahon
Mr. William A. McMillen
Mr. Joseph M. McNasby
Mr. and Mrs. Donald T. McNeill
Mr. Louis L. Meldman
Miss Jean Messmer
Mr. George L. N. Meyer, Sr.
Oscar Meyer Foundation
Dr. and Mrs. Francis J. Millen
Miller Brewing Company
Dr. and Mrs. Charles W. Miller
Mrs. Fred A. Miller
Dr. V. Michael Miller
Friends of Lt. William Millman
Milwaukee Equipment Company
Milwaukee Fraternal Order of Eagles
Milwaukee Public Museum
Mr. and Mrs. Carl W. Moebius, Jr.
Mrs. Erna Moebius
Mr. Frank R. Moebius
Mr. Howard E. Moebius
Mr. Kenneth D. Moebius
Mr. and Mrs. John F. Monroe
Mr. Douglas Morgan
Mr. Lloyd Morgan
Mr. Stanley Myer
Dr. George E. New
Mr. and Mrs. Raymond F. Newman
Mr. John M. H. Nichols
Mr. John Noble
Mr. and Mrs. John Ogden
Mrs. Joseph C. O'Hearn
Mr. Edward J. O'Keefe
Miss Alice Olwell
Mr. and Mrs. Robert L. Pagel, Sr.
Mr. Richard J. Panlener
Mrs. Joseph D. Patton
Dr. and Mrs. Robert S. Pavlic
Mrs. Myra Peache
Mr. and Mrs. John Pekrul
Mr. A.G. Pelikan, M.A., F.R.S.A.
Mr. Philip J. Peterson
Mrs. Lloyd H. Pettit
Dr. and Mrs. John Pick
Mr. and Mrs. Leslie S. Pinsof
Meryl Hollis Pinsof
Mr. Oscar M. Pinsof
Mr. and Mrs. Philip Pinsof
Dr. William M. Pinsof

Mrs. Herbert Polacheck
Mr. and Mrs. Paul J. Polansky
Mr. James Michael Posner
Mr. Stephen Elliot Posner
Mrs. Geraldine Powers
Mr. Emil Priebe
Mr. Karl Priebe
Mrs. John C. Pritzlaff
Miss Avrina Pugh
Mrs. George Raab
Mr. and Mrs. Kirby Raab
Dr. Miguel Valverde Ramis
Mr. and Mrs. Clifford A. Randall
Dr. and Mrs. Ben Z. Rappaport
Mrs. Karl Ratzsch, Sr.
Mr. Ralph Resenhoeft
Mr. and Mrs. Ernest F. Rice, Jr.
Mr. Hamilton Richardson
Miss Dorothy Riedl
Mr. and Mrs. Marc B. Rojtman
Rojtman Foundation
Mr. and Mrs. Michael Rosenbaum
Mr. Pierce Rosenberg
Mr. and Mrs. Joel H. Rosenthal
Mrs. Will Ross
Estate of Florence Rossbach
Mrs. William B. Rubin
Mr. Arthur Rubloff
Mr. and Mrs. John A. Russell
Dr. Marvin A. Sachner
Mr. Edward J. Safdie
Dr. and Mrs. Sando S. Sakaguchi
Mr. Charles Schaaf
Dr. and Mrs. James A. Schelble
Mr. Leonard J. Scheller
Dr. Alfred O. Schmidt
Conrad Schmitt Studios, Inc.
Estate of Chris Schroeder
Mr. and Mrs. John E. Schroeder
Schroeder Hotels, Inc.
Mr. Walter Schroeder
Estate of Walter Schroeder
Mr. John H. Schunk
Mrs. Ray M. Schweiger
Mr. and Mrs. Peter G. Scotese
Mrs. Arthur M. Sells
Mr. Frank J. Sensenbrenner
Sigma Tau Delta
Mr. Al Simon
Mr. Stanley Slotkin
Mr. Roman S. Smal-Stocki
Mr. Amos K. Smith
Mrs. Jetta Muntain Smith
Mr. and Mrs. Matthew N. Smith
Mr. and Mrs. Ray Smith, Jr.
Mr. Steven D. Sohackie and
    Mrs. Bernice Sohackie
Mr. David M. Solinger
Mr. and Mrs. Bernard Soref
Spaeth Foundation
Mr. James J. Staak
Mrs. Peter M. Stanka
Mrs. Ann Steinberg
Mr. Robert Steinberg
Mr. Saul Steinberg

Mr. Ralph Steiner
Mr. Dean Stephens
Mrs. Eric C. Stern
Mr. and Mrs. Loren B. Stone
Mrs. Barbara Stratman
Mr. and Mrs. Norman A. Straub
Dr. and Mrs. Gerhard D. Straus
Mr. and Mrs. George H. Struthers
Ms. Joanna Sturm
Mr. Harry G. Sundheim, Jr.
Mrs. Alice L. Tallmadge
Dr. Gary M. Tearston
Dr. John Tcheng
Mr. and Mrs. Richard R. Teschner
Mr. Julius C. Theilacker
Mr. and Mrs. Peter G. Theis
Mr. and Mrs. David J. Tolan
Estate of Claire Hoff Toole
Miss Paula Uihlein
Mr. and Mrs. Fred D. Usinger
Dr. and Mrs. George E. Vander Beke
Mrs. Douglass Van Dyke
Mrs. Charles P. Vogel
René von Schleinitz Foundation
Mr. F. E. Wagner
Miss Marion C. Wagner
Mr. Robert S. Wagner
Dr. Kenneth J. Waliszewski
Mr. C. Frederick (Todd) Wehr
Mrs. George E. Whalen
Mr. and Mrs. Malcolm K. Whyte
Mr. Victor J. Williams
Mr. Ray H. Wolf
Women's Club of Wisconsin
Mr. and Mrs. Ben Wunsch
Mr. Tadanori Yokoo
Mr. and Mrs. Charles Zadok
Mr. Jerome J. Zeller
Mr. and Mrs. Morris Zolin

EXTENDED LOANS
AND PROMISED GIFTS

Anonymous
Mr. and Mrs. Marvin L. Fishman
Mr. and Mrs. Edward H. Meldman
Mr. and Mrs. E. James Quirk
Estate of Maurice Sterne
Ms. Joanna Sturm

MARQUETTE UNIVERSITY

University Officials

Reverend John P. Raynor, S.J., President
Quentin L. Quade, Executive Vice President
Edward D. Simmons, Vice President for Academic Affairs
Reverend Richard A. McGarrity, S.J., Associate Vice
 President for Academic Affairs